Professions of Taste

Professions of Taste

Henry James, British Aestheticism, and Commodity Culture

Jonathan Freedman

Stanford University Press Stanford, California

Stanford University Press
Stanford, California
©1990 by the Board of Trustees
of the Leland Stanford Junior University
Printed in the United States of America

Original printing 1990

Last figure below indicates year of this printing:
02 01 00 99 98 97 96 95 94 93

CIP data appear at the end of the book

Acknowledgments

There are too many figures standing behind this book (and withstanding the eccentricities of its author) to acknowledge fully; the names I list below are both individually important and representative of a wealth of others. From my undergraduate days at Northwestern University, I need to thank especially Leonard Barkan and T. W. Heyck—inspiring teachers, and good friends. From my time in graduate school, I want to indicate my debt to Christopher Baswell, Kimberly Benston, Dana Brand, John Burt, Sheila Fisher, Debra Fried, Elissa Greenwald, Christopher Kendrick, Joseph Loewenstein, Richard Millington, Adela Pinch, John Rieder, Ed Schiffer, and David Wippmann, LLD.: I learned far more from them than I knew at the time, and am still learning how much I am in their debt. I need also to acknowledge the moral support and intellectual stimulation afforded by my students at Yale—particularly Amy Adams, Bernardine Connolley, Monica Feinberg, Dan Hack, Jim Shapiro, Blake Vermeule, and Sarah Zimmerman—and at the Bread Loaf School of English—especially Louise Burnham, Janet Gray, Kate Greenebaum, George Johnson, Emma Lipton (who gave me a possible title for this book by referring to a "hard, James-like phlegm"), and Anne Marshall.

This is also the place to acknowledge both the friendship and solidarity offered by Yale friends and colleagues now elsewhere—Hugh Baxter, David Kaufmann, Clare Kinney, Alan Liu, Anita Sokolsky, Patricia Spacks, Stephen Tifft—and those in New Haven—Jill Campbell, Harriet Chessman, Kevin Dunn, Langdon Hammer, Margaret Homans, Victor Luftig, Gordon Turnbull, Lynn Wardley, Susanne Wofford, and Mark Wollaeger. To my fellow editors on the *Yale Journal of Criticism*—Celeste Brusati, Lars Engle, Anne Fabian, Christopher Miller, Sheila Murnaghan, and Sara Suleri—go special thanks.

And special gratitude needs to be expressed as well to a number of people who have read and commented on portions of this manuscript: Anne Badger, Martha Banta, Lawrence Buell, Mary Cregan, Paul Fry, Kirsten Gruesz, R. W. B. Lewis, Jim Maddox, Gary Saul Morson, Anita Sokolsky, Roger Stein, William Stowe, Sara Suleri, Eric Sundquist, and Bryan Wolf have all made helpful marks and noises that have found their inadequate reflections and echoes on these pages. Charles Feidelson directed the dissertation that grew and grew into the present project; he needs to be thanked for his patience and faith. Richard Brodhead has offered advice, inspiration, aid, and comfort above and beyond any possible call of duty.

I had the help of Lucile Bruce and Amelia Zurcher in producing much of this manuscript; special thanks need to go to the indefatigable Laurie Edelstein, who squandered too much of her time and talent in fact- and quote-checking. I would like to thank the American Philosophical Association, the Yale College Morse Fellowship, and the Griswold Fund for providing crucial support for travel and research. Some of the material in Chapter 2 appeared in *In Pursuit of Beauty*, a volume connected with an exhibit on American aestheticism at the Metropolitan Museum of Art. I am grateful to the Metropolitan, and in particular to Alice Cooney Freylinghuysen and Catherine Hoover Voorsanger, for welcoming me to the project and allowing me to reprint this material here. Julia Johnson Zafferano has been the very model of a copyeditor: at once rigorous and patient, she survived this author with both her authority and her sense of humor intact. Helen Tarter breaks the mold of acquisitions editor; her comments and advice have made this a much richer book than it would have been without her, and her faith in the project sustained me in moments of doom, gloom, and professional panic. Needless to say, none of the above bear any responsibility for the inadequacies and deformities of the present project, which rests with me alone.

I want particularly to thank Anne Badger for bearing with me during the composition of this tome—from its inception to its conclusion. And I must thank above all my family—Ralph, Lila, Mark, Kate, and the Weli-monster—for teaching me all about love.

J.F.

Contents

Abbreviations   ix

Introduction   xi

1. Aestheticism: The Embrace of Contraries   1
2. British Aestheticism and American Culture   79
3. James, Pater, and the Discovery of Aestheticism   133
4. James, Wilde, and the Incorporation of Aestheticism   167
5. The Decadent Henry James: British Aestheticism and the
   Major Phase   202

   Notes   261
   Works Cited   281
   Index   293

Fourteen pages of illustrations follow page 132

Abbreviations

The abbreviations following each author below are used throughout the text and notes to refer to these editions.

James, Henry

LC 1 *Henry James: Literary Criticism.* Vol. 1: *Essays on Literature; American Writers; English Writers.* New York: Library of America, 1984.

LC 2 *Henry James: Literary Criticism.* Vol. 2: *French Writers; Other European Writers; The Prefaces to the New York Edition.* New York: Library of America, 1984.

Letters *Henry James: Letters.* 4 vols. Ed. Leon Edel. Cambridge, Mass.: Harvard University Press / Belknap Press, 1974–84.

NY *Novels and Tales of Henry James.* 26 vols. The New York Edition. New York: Charles Scribner's Sons, 1907–9.

PL *The Portrait of a Lady.* In William Stafford, ed., *Henry James: Novels, 1881–1886.* New York: Library of America, 1985.

RH *Roderick Hudson.* In William Stafford, ed., *Henry James: Novels, 1871–1880.* New York: Library of America, 1983.

TM *The Tragic Muse.* Harmondsworth, Engl.: Penguin, 1978.

Pater, Walter

WP *The Works of Walter Pater.* 8 vols. London: Macmillan, 1900–1.

Rossetti, Dante Gabriel

DGR *The Collected Works of Dante Gabriel Rossetti.* 2 vols. Ed. William Michael Rossetti. London: Ellis and Elvey, 1890.

Ruskin, John

JR *The Works of John Ruskin.* 39 vols. Ed. E. T. Cook and Alexander Wedderburn. London: George Allen, 1903–12.

Swinburne, Algernon Charles

ACS *The Complete Works of Algernon Charles Swinburne.* 20 vols. Ed.

Sir Edmund Gosse and Thomas James Wise. London: William
Heinemann, 1925–27.

Wilde, Oscar

Artist *The Artist as Critic: Critical Writings of Oscar Wilde*. Ed. Richard
Ellmann. New York: Random House, 1968.

DG *The Picture of Dorian Gray*. Ed. Isobel Murray. London: Oxford
University Press, 1974.

Works *The Works of Oscar Wilde*. 15 vols. New York: Lamb Publishing,
1909.

Introduction

It is not without some trepidation that I have set out to trace the complex interaction of Henry James and the tradition of British aestheticism, and to place this interaction in the context of something called "commodity culture." For each aspect of this double enterprise is itself doubly problematic. On the one hand, the first endeavor—the delineation of yet another context through which the shape of James's career might more fully be traced and the scope of his achievement more accurately assessed—might appear superfluous, or irrelevant, or both. It might seem superfluous because over the past twenty years the James industry has diligently mined just about every other contextual lode. James's "Hawthorne aspect"; his responses to Balzac, Flaubert, Arnold, Browning, Chekhov, Ibsen; his reworkings of transcendentalism, popular fiction, and melodrama; his anticipations of phenomenological philosophy or postmodern metafiction—all these have been treated so thoroughly that simply to claim that there exists another, hitherto unacknowledged, contextual lens through which James's "true" dimensions might finally be brought into full focus borders on the ludicrous.[1] Further, this undertaking might seem somewhat irrelevant because that same period has witnessed the burgeoning of a remarkable skepticism about the notion of "context" itself, whether understood as an exclusively literary terrain or more powerfully as one in which "literary" texts are positioned in homologous relation to larger ideological configurations or discursive formations. Here especially a simple discussion of James's relation to the tradition of British aestheticism might appear less compelling than an account of his vexed and agonistic relation to literary tradition itself or his equally problematic relation to the exigencies of social power.

My second enterprise—the placement of James and British aestheticism in the larger framework of "commodity culture"—might seem equally fraught. First, the concept of commodity culture itself, although undoubtedly a valuable tool for historians and literary critics alike, is not without its theoretical difficulties. To put a very complex matter simply, this concept might be seen as presupposing a relation between "culture" and "the commodity"—or more generally between what marxist critics would call formations on the level of the super-structure and those on what they would refer to as the economic base —which is far more simple than one is, after the last twenty years of theoretical worrying about just this very issue, allowed to be.[2] And even if one does accept the notion of "commodity culture" on a theoreti-cal basis, its application to the texts at hand still proves problematic. For the aesthetes and Henry James both consciously set themselves in opposition to the market economy, and particularly to the com-modification of art and literature wrought by such an economy; both, however, participated in as they critiqued this process, largely through what we might want to call the concomitant commodification of the ar-tistic vocation, the professionalization of literary and artistic practice —or what I call below the rise of aesthetic professionalism. To raise the question of the relation of these figures to such a culture is thus also, a fortiori, to raise the question of the possibilities and problematics of cultural critique itself.

These qualifications are important, and I will have much to say in response to them in the chapters that follow, largely along the lines of suggesting that it is with respect to *all* of these issues that an in-quiry into Henry James and the British stem of the aestheticist project may prove to be of crucial importance. "British aestheticism," in other words, might most profitably be viewed not simply as a literary or ar-tistic tendency or movement, but rather as an intricately articulated arena in which new definitions of the aesthetic and its relation to the social were negotiated and renegotiated; and James's own perfor-mance within that arena must similarly be seen in its full—and fully problematic—complexity. The end result of this encounter, as I want to suggest more fully here before arguing for it in the following chap-ters, is thus not one with exclusively literary or artistic ramifications, although these ramifications are quite significant, particularly to our understanding of the rise and self-definition of literary modernism. For the fruits of that encounter entered into the engorging but in-creasingly articulated fin de siècle literary and artistic marketplace in such a way as not merely to confirm the ubiquity of commodity cul-ture, but also so as to accomplish the commodification of "culture" itself—to help create a sphere of autonomous high culture that could be accessed not only through the exercise of innate taste or even at the end of a rigorous education, but also, and more directly, through the acquisition of goods whose possession would confirm the high cultural status of their consumers. It is a further irony, and one I shall muse over somewhat below, that some of the most crucial of these goods turned out to be artifacts that critiqued commodity culture itself.

Before I turn to these many tasks in my book proper, however, let me sketch some of the lines of inquiry I shall be following there by describing three rationales that lie behind my endeavor and by placing those rationales in a larger historical frame. Merely for the sake of efficiency, let me group these concerns under three problematic terms: "Henry James," "British aestheticism," and "and."

To begin with the first: I wish to signal the skeptical reader that there does indeed exist a significant and unexplored tradition in which both the writings and the career trajectory of Henry James might more fully be understood, and that placing James in this context might not only offer a new angle on James's texts but would also address a problem that has remained at the center of James criticism from (at least) the 1920's to the present day: the question of James's own "aestheticism." The shifting configurations of critical discourse have inflected that issue differently for different critics of different periods, to be sure; but for a substantial body of Jamesians from that time to our own, Henry James has been consistently treated as an aesthete *tout court*—an "impassioned geometer . . . some arachnid of art," in Van Wyck Brooks's marvelous phrase—and thus for an equally substantial group, was to be defended from the "taint" of aestheticism at all costs.[3] Indeed, it might be said without too much exaggeration that the entire course of James criticism from the time of Van Wyck Brooks and Vernon Parrington has consisted of a series of arguments over their vision of Henry James as a second Gilbert Osmond: an effete aesthete expatriate whose works are marred by his withdrawal from the soil of social reality (an exclusively American terrain) into the consoling never-never land of art (the country of the mauve as well as the blue); a figure of fastidious reserve and mandarin hauteur whose proclamation of his own status as Master masked and mystified his own severe will to power.

Despite all the transformations of critical approach or idiom that the last 65 years have witnessed, this strain in the discourse of anti-Jacobitism has proved astonishingly stable, down even to patterns of figuration. Here is Brooks: "Magnificent pretensions, petty performances!—the fruits of an irresponsible imagination, of a deranged sense of values, of a mind working in the void, uncorrected by any clear consciousness of human cause and effect" (134). Here is Parrington:

Life, with him, was largely a matter of nerves. In this world of sprawling energy, it was impossible to barricade himself against the intrusion of the unpleasant. His organism was too sensitive, his discriminations too fine, to subject them to the vulgarities of the Gilded Age, and he fled from it all. . . . And so, like Whistler, he sought other lands, there to refine a meticulous technique, and draw out ever thinner the substance of his art.[4]

Here is Maxwell Geismar, writing some 40 years later: "And perhaps never in the history of humane letters had a novelist done so much with so little content as Henry James himself: the Dark Prince of the American leisure class, the self-made orphan of international culture, the romantic historian of the *ancien régime*, the European inheritor, the absolute esthete, the prime autocrat of contemporary (and contrived) art."[5] And here is Michael Gilmore, writing twenty years after that: "The unbreakable link between the gazing [Jamesian] artist and the commodifying dilettante is their aloofness from the doings of their fellow beings."[6]

Moreover, these explicit identifications of Henry James with the figure of the aesthete have been supplemented by implicit ones that circulate throughout some of the most significant works of James criticism—particularly, needless to say, the more skeptical or revisionary works of that tradition. I have already alluded to the example of R. P. Blackmur, whose fascinatingly volatile response to James centered itself on the simultaneity of James's quests for the delineation of a sphere of aesthetic transcendence and for the exercise of his own artistic will to power—precisely the dire conflation suggested, as we shall see, in the tradition of British aestheticism itself and the source of the alternately fascinated and horrified response of its contemporaries to that tradition. This identification has more recently been extended into the question of James's aesthetic engagement (or lack thereof) with his ambient social sphere. To cite the most powerful examples: writing out of the "Western Marxist" and the Foucauldian traditions, respectively, Carolyn Porter and Mark Seltzer have both recently argued that James's spectacular admixture of aesthetic detachment and will to social power are fused in—but mystified by—James's valorizing of art. And, whether understood as the archetypal modernist author/God or as the very embodiment of Foucauldian power/knowledge, Henry James is for Porter and Seltzer, as he was for Brooks and Parrington, best approached as a second Gilbert Osmond: a figure who in

Porter's analysis combines the detached, reifying gaze of the aesthete with the willful if disavowed exercise of manipulative power; one who, in Seltzer's, exemplifies in his conflation of the aesthete's ostentatious disinterestedness with an unrelieved aggressivity the "two-tiered" or "double discourse of art and power"—or, in words that seem a virtual summary of Osmond's self-presentation, "on one level, an aesthetic resistance to the exercises of power, on another, a discreet reinscription of strategies of control [that] act as a relay of mechanisms of social control."[7]

The persistence of this habit of thought in the criticism of the past 50 years has had two effects, both of which this book is intended to address and, largely, to counter. On the one hand, it has led to a tactical effacement of the significant and long-lived interrelation of Henry James and the tradition of British aestheticism itself—an effacement largely accomplished by the critics who managed the "James revival" of the 1940's and 1950's. This suppression was startlingly effective. In criticism of the 1910's and 1920's, comparisons between James and aesthetes were fairly common, and not necessarily negative. In 1917, for example, Stuart Sherman concluded an essay entitled "The Aesthetic Idealism of Henry James" with the blunt assertion that "James's works throb with the fine passion from the beginning to the end—just as Pater's do. . . . He is not an historian of manners; he is a trenchant idealistic critic of life from the aesthetic point of view." Sherman's essay also contains an extensive comparison between James and Walter Pater that has remained unmatched by any subsequent critic for either thoroughness or accuracy:

James is like Pater in his aversion from the world, his dedication to art, his celibacy, his personal decorum and dignity, his high aesthetic seriousness, his Epicurean relish in receiving and reporting the multiplicity and intensity of his impressions, and in the exacting closeness of his style. . . . On the whole, there is no better side light on James's "philosophy" than Pater's Conclusion to the *Studies in the Renaissance* and his *Plato and Platonism*; no better statement of his general literary ideals than Pater's essay on Style; no more interesting "parallel" to his later novels than *Marius the Epicurean* and *Imaginary Portraits*.[8]

But for revivalists or (to adopt Geismar's trope) the Jacobites of the 1940's and 1950's, such a line of inquiry had to be avoided, because to explore it would be to move onto the ground of James's detractors, to focus explicitly on those elements of James's character and art that the anti-Jacobites had attacked, and to focus not only on his expatriation or his dedication to an idealized form of art, or even on the voyeuristic dimension of his techniques of "point of view," but also on James's homoeroticism, an unspoken subject that clearly underlies the language of effeteness and effeminacy that anti-Jacobites persistently used to describe James's putative aestheticism, and for which the term "aesthete" long served as a virtual synonym. I suspect that it was largely to exonerate James from this implication that James criticism of this classic and influential period devoted so little of its time to accounting for James's rich and subtle response to the aestheticist tradition and so much to ringing defenses of his moralism, his realism, and his Americanism. Whatever its motives, I am sure that one effect of this move was a perpetuation of the same silence by the generation trained by F. O. Matthiessen, Quentin Anderson, Marius Bewley et al. —a silence made all the more remarkable by the fact that, as I have suggested above, this later generation took as one of its central tasks the placing of James in just about every possible literary or intellectual context *except* that of aestheticism. This book, then, is at least in part an effort to set the record straight, to restore to critical attention a significant and neglected issue in James scholarship—to do, in other words, what Jamesians have gone about doing for the past 40 years, only a little more thoroughly.

But I will also need to do more. I want to respond here to the effects of the other side of the question of Henry James's "aestheticism," to the implications of that line of critical analysis which extends, under different guises, from the socially conscious modernism of Brooks and Parrington—a line we can trace fairly directly into the denunciations of Geismar and Phillip Rahv, more indirectly into the subtler studies of Blackmur and Laurence Holland, and thence (particularly from the latter) into the recent efflorescence of marxist and "new historicist" readings.[9] The persistent positioning (witting or unwitting) of James as aesthete by these critics has led, by an opposite path, to the same problem created by their antagonists: in defining James as an aesthete in the most negative sense of the word, the anti-Jacobites, too, have blocked from critical view the full intricacy and importance of the interplay between James and the tradition of British aestheticism.

Perhaps the best way of sketching this problem would be to point to a remarkable phenomenon in such criticism: the ways that the anti-Jacobite responses to James the aesthete reenact with uncanny precision James's own responses to aestheticism itself. Again, this habit of thought begins early. Thus—as we shall see in more detail in the pages that follow—it is precisely what Brooks calls the "magnificent pretensions and petty performances" of James's fiction, the gap between aesthetic aspiration and artistic achievement, that so disturbed James in the aesthete, particularly as it seemed to be represented to him by that aesthete of aesthetes, Oscar Wilde. It is exactly what Parrington called the "thinness" of James's art that James himself critiqued in the high aesthetic movement of the 1880's and early 1890's, as when, for example, he complained that the problem with the aesthetic movement was that it was not "esthetic enough." It is specifically as what Geismar calls the "Dark Prince of the American leisure class" that James anatomized such figures as Gilbert Osmond (who imagines himself as being just that) or, mutatis mutandis, his two dark princesses Milly Theale and Maggie Verver. And finally and most important, it is specifically in order to raise the question of the relation between "seeing" and "being" and between "art" and "power" that the aesthete recurs as such a powerful and problematic figure in James's fiction, from *Roderick Hudson*, the first novel James deemed admissible to his self-created canon, the New York edition, to the last one so included, *The Golden Bowl*. James, we might say, stands to his critics as the aesthetic movement stood to James, and his responses to the phenomenon of aestheticism—alternately critical and celebratory, antagonistic and obsessed, and finally deeply, powerfully assimilative—might serve as the best gloss on theirs to him.

What I am claiming here might seem something of a truism: Henry James was always already there before the Jamesians; the very terms of their critique were themselves first established and are inevitably anticipated by the object they set out to comprehend. But the phenomenon I am pointing to—the uncanny reenactment of James's responses to aestheticism by the critical portrayal of James as aesthete—is of more than theoretical interest. It may also be seen as symptomatic of a larger and more significant phenomenon: a persistent misreading by Jamesians of the tradition of British aestheticism itself, a misreading that—or so I shall be arguing—was largely crafted for these critics by none other than Henry James himself. These critics are, in other words, at their most Jamesian when they reproach James for being an aesthete, for in doing so they reinscribe in their critical effort the very oppositions and assumptions that mark James's own response to aestheticism—oppositions and assumptions that, as I shall argue more fully in the following pages, helped Henry James transform the volatile and unstable example of aestheticism in England into that more austere form of aestheticism we call modernism.

Here, then, I must move from my first rationale for this project to my second. For, I want to claim, to understand James's responses to

aestheticism and to grasp his powerful role in its subsequent remodeling, we need a suppler, more capacious, and more historically precise
understanding of that phenomenon—of aestheticism in its general
manifestations, to be sure, but more important, of that specific historical inflection in which James encountered aestheticism: aestheticism as
it flourished in late-nineteenth-century England and as it was disseminated with extraordinary rapidity and received with extraordinary
enthusiasm throughout late-nineteenth- and early-twentieth-century
America. Indeed, when gauged against the remarkably varied and
complicated forms that aestheticist art and ideology took in both England and America, both Jacobite and anti-Jacobite understandings
of aestheticism seem remarkably reductive. Both tend to view aestheticism as the exposition and enactment of a doctrine of "art for
art's sake," whether embedded in certain artworks or as performed in
flamboyantly dandiacal behavior; this is the vision that informs Geismar's identification of James as an "absolute aesthete," for example,
or Anderson's defense of his moralism in "the very decade of art for
art." But, as critics of the past 30 years or so have shown in abundant
detail, this view does not represent the full extent of British aestheticism—and hence misrepresents as well Henry James's relation to that
phenomenon.

   In the first place, it understates the fascinating volatility of aestheticist art and artifacts, works that far transcend in their intricacy and
ambitiousness the relatively simple doctrine of "art for art" or even
its more sophisticated variants (Morse Peckham's identification of aestheticism as "Stylism," for example, which has immediate but misleading relevance to the example of James).[10] Indeed, I shall suggest at
greater length below that one crucial reason British aestheticism was
not more fully appreciated for most of the twentieth century was that
its representational practices failed to comport themselves to the aesthetic agendas of high modernism—agendas that, to recur to my other
topic, Henry James had much to do with shaping. It is, I shall be arguing, only when they came to be approached through the perspective
we might broadly label "postmodern" that their full range, depth, and
audaciousness comes into view; indeed, as I shall be suggesting, these
works are frequently so audacious as to call the complacent periodiza-
tion implied by the term "postmodernism" itself into question.

   Second, the relatively simple notion of aestheticism deployed by
Jamesians ignores what seems to me the most significant aspect of
the aestheticist project in both England and America—and the most
important way of understanding Henry James's intervention in that

project. For what I find most significant about the entire range of Anglo-American aestheticism—and a feature that distinguishes it from the concurrent aestheticism in France or the fin de siècle German aestheticism of Hugo von Hoffmannsthal and Stefan George—is its complete but complex entanglement with the development of a cultural apparatus at once thoroughly professionalized and wholly commodified. The former point seems the more unexpected, but it is in fact the simpler of the two to make. The "aesthetic movement" itself may represent in part the formation of an avant-garde beachhead on the resistant shores of London or Boston, but it also represents a process by which the newly emergent sphere of the "aesthetic"—a sphere hitherto defined for the Anglo-American audience by the likes of German idealist philosophers and romantic poets—got put into social play as a startlingly successful form of professionalism. For what is the aesthete but the consummate professional: the possessor of a "monopoly of knowledge" about the provenance and extent of this mysterious entity, "the aesthetic"—the man (and sometimes the woman) who responds to the demands of a rapidly professionalizing world by forging a career for himself out of the imparting of knowledge about this new "field" to an awed and appreciative public? That the notion of the aesthete as professional strikes us as anomalous may actually be the surest sign of its success. For like all true professionals, the aesthete claims that the purity of his vocation—in this case, the disinterestedness of his dedication to the ideal realm of art—places him beyond the demands of grubbier occupations, lesser trades. It is this claim in particular that allows the aesthete to ply his own trade with the greatest of efficiency, for it guarantees the self-authenticating authority of his own expertise (the aesthete is the person, after all, who validates the aesthete's taste) and hence grants him a virtual monopoly over his chosen field.

My second assertion—that the aesthete both enacts and represents the commodification of art—may seem equally simple, but it is one that ultimately poses greater historical and theoretical problems. On the face of it, such a claim seems all too obvious. By so hyperbolically locating the source of his pleasure in the reified form of the detached, autonomous aesthetic artifact and by seeking to cut that object off from any end or use other than sheer sensual enjoyment, the aesthete would seem to reproduce directly in the sphere of aesthetic appreciation the purely sensory engagement with a world of commodities that marxist critics—particularly those influenced by the "Frankfurt school"—have argued defines experience in a mature, consumption-oriented capi-

talist economy. Students of commodification have not failed to seize
upon the aesthete as an example of precisely this process—as we have
seen, for example, in Gilmore's description of James as a "commodifying dilettante." Or, to cite a more theoretically elaborated case, we
could instance Theodor Adorno; for in Adorno's *Aesthetic Theory*, it is
precisely in aestheticism, and specifically in aestheticism's art-for-art
phase, that the commodification of art in a market economy becomes
clearest. While all art in a commodified world is what Adorno calls an
"absolute commodity"—that is, "social products which have discarded
the illusion of being-for-society, an illusion tenaciously retained by all
other commodities"—it is nevertheless the case that when art takes full
advantage of its "absolute" status and proclaims its autonomy outright,
it submits fully to the reification it otherwise resists.[11] "The ideological
essence of *l'art pour l'art* lies not in the emphatic antithesis it posits between art and empirical life, but in the abstract and facile character of
this antithesis. . . . Art of this kind brackets the world of commodities,
denying its existence. In so doing its products become commodities
themselves. They are condemned to being kitsch because latent in
them there is the commodity form" (336–37). And, taking this line
of argument further, Adorno suggests that aesthetes of the order of
Wilde, Gabriele d'Annunzio, and Maurice Maeterlinck are ultimately
to be seen as "precursors of the culture industry" because "the growth
of subjective differentiation and the intensification and expansion of
aesthetic stimuli" that their work performed accompanied and mimicked "the shift to market-oriented cultural production. Attuning art
to ephemeral individual responses meant allying it with reification. As
art became more and more similar to physical subjectivity, it moved
more and more away from objectivity, ingratiating itself with the public. To that extent, the code-word of *l'art pour l'art* is the opposite of
what it claims to be" (339).

   Adorno's critique is as problematic as it is important, and I shall soon
say a word about its theoretical difficulties—difficulties that, as we shall
see, are distinctly Jamesian in flavor. First, however, I need to observe
that the recognition of the aesthete as arch-commodifier is not one that
is limited to twentieth-century cultural criticism. Indeed, it is in these
very terms that the aesthete was perceived by his contemporaries, who
launched a series of satirical jibes at the "aesthetic movement" throughout the later years of the nineteenth century for performing precisely
this conflation of the realms of art and commerce. The classic example
of these jibes is the satirical cartoons of George Du Maurier, in which
the aesthete is positioned as a commodity fetishist par excellence: one

who avidly, at times even lasciviously, devotes himself to the appreciation of obscure works of art, to the collection of fine pieces of china, and to the cultivation of himself as artwork in order to advance his social standing and, frequently, to gain a fortune. This is also, as I shall show in more detail, precisely the structure of thought and cluster of associations that underlie James's heavily satirical portrayal of the aesthete in the 1880's and early 1890's, most notoriously, of course, that of *The Portrait of a Lady*.

It is with this historical recognition that problems begin to proliferate with the aestheticism-as-commodification line of analysis. For it is important to note that the critique of the aesthete launched by Du Maurier and mimed by James is somewhat mystified, both about the nature and status of the aesthete and about its own. It is mystified about the aesthete because its criticism of that figure for his perverse devotion to the project of commodification under the guise of "art for art" postulates, as the enabling condition of its critique, a sphere of aesthetic transcendence that stands above and beyond other forms of social process. To criticize the aesthete for fetishizing art as a "mere commodity" is to posit that art is not a commodity, or is able to be more than "just" a commodity; and to do this is to participate in the very tendency of thought for which the aesthete is so vigorously rebuked by his indignant critic. Indeed, we might say that the critique of aestheticism chides the aesthete precisely in order to advance a surpassing aestheticism of its own; what the aesthete is being criticized for is not his successful aestheticism but rather an inadequate one, an insufficient devotion to the purity and perfection of the realm of art—a realm to which the critic is able to pay allegiance negatively, implicitly, through the mechanism of critique.

Du Maurier and James's experience thus suggests that there frequently exists an unusually compelling affinity between the critic of aestheticism and the aesthete himself, a link that, we might speculate, it is also the very purpose of the project of critique itself to evade or obfuscate. This suspicion may be heightened by the fact that Du Maurier and James themselves participated in not only the thought structure, but also the very activities for which they so vigorously castigated the aesthete. They, like the "commodifying dilettante" they condemned, were thoroughly implicated in the mass marketing of aesthetic artifacts—Du Maurier as popular cartoonist and as author of one of the earliest and most enduringly successful bestsellers, *Trilby* (significantly, a mass-market romance of Left Bank aestheticism); James as earnest suitor of the new literary market whose initial success (with *Daisy Miller* and then, to a lesser extent, with *Portrait*) but subsequent rejection by that market nevertheless ultimately enabled him to make a niche for himself within it as the elite modern novelist, the Master of the new Art of Fiction.[12]

These ironies suggest the precise nature of the problems with the analysis of aestheticism under the sign of commodification. To put it a bit reductively, the aestheticism-as-consummation-of-commodity-fetishism line implies, but cannot resolve, the problem of either its own potential aestheticism or its own potential commodification (or both). This is true not just of Du Maurier and James but of later critics of aestheticism as well. For all his grim wit and boundlessly ironic self-knowledge, for example, Adorno falls into the former error no less powerfully than do Du Maurier and James; Adorno's denunciations of aestheticism's expression of the essence of the commodity form conceals the essentially aestheticist agenda of his own theoretical project, which is to position an autonomous aesthetic sphere, however fragmentary, deformed, or "mutilated" it may be, in a critical role vis-à-vis social exigencies—to position such a sphere, in fact, as the *only* means of accessing critical knowledge in an administered, reified world, even if such knowledge can properly be only a negative one. And the experience of the actual aesthetes Adorno cites as examples of the nexus between aestheticism and the "culture industry" exemplifies the latter error. What marks Wilde's avid and undeniably brilliant course of self-promotion as a—as *the*—aestheticist critic of the crudities and deformations of industrial society, after all, but its own recognition of the inevitable commodification of cultural critique itself?

It is precisely its ability to raise questions like these without proposing any resolution to them that makes British aestheticism itself so difficult either to define or to assess, either under the sign of commodification or, for that matter, under virtually any heading at all. Aestheticism in England bore the same irresolute relation to the issue of commodification and professionalization as it did to that of "art for art's sake": it took up and explored those new social realities, turning them to its full advantage on the one hand but remaining skeptically outside or beyond them on the other. It thereby volatilized these social facts: at once reflecting them and critiquing them, aestheticism served to put its own professionalization and commodification in perpetual—and perpetually irresolute—play. It is this fundamental and destabilizing irresolution, I would suggest, that caused aestheticism's deeply unsettling effect on its contemporaries—and, as I shall suggest later, on ourselves as well. Also—not to anticipate my argument too far—it

is with respect to precisely these kinds of volatilities that Henry James's
response to the aestheticist project proved to be so crucial, for the artists and the public struggling to come to terms with aestheticism's challenge and, ultimately, for us as well. For what he undertook to do was
to smooth its volatilities out by *re-aestheticizing them*—by bringing them
under firm and final control by invoking the authority of art. It is this
deeply powerful move—one that was at once anticipated and resisted
by aestheticism itself—that helped accomplish the full commodification of high art under the sign of institutionalized bohemianism, of
perpetual—and perpetually popular—avant-gardism.

But before I turn to this aspect of my argument—before I turn
to the full unfolding of the notion of "and"—I need to note in even
greater detail the specific manifestation of aestheticism James encountered and responded to: its endlessly metamorphosing American variant. For the American response to British aestheticism poses far more
clearly than did its British counterpart the issues of the commodification and professionalization of the newly defined aesthetic sphere. It
is a remarkable—and remarkably rarely discussed—historical datum
that the influence of British aestheticism was felt early and powerfully in America, but not where we might expect it, in the sphere of
high art or even that of social criticism, both of which were dominated
by the twinned (and mutually reinforcing) doctrines of Emersonian
transcendentalism and Ruskinian moralism largely as articulated by
such established and magisterial cultural authorities as Charles Eliot
Norton. Instead, it was directly in the marketplace—in the vending
of "aesthetic" domestic goods and in the development of advertising
strategies for them—that the terminology, topoi, and thought structures of British aestheticism were first given their American expression. Aestheticism in America was from the first, in other words, fully
integrated into the nascent "culture industry" and the culture of consumption it organized, incited, and controlled; it was only twenty
or thirty years thereafter that the established American intelligentsia
gave up their initially scornful, moralistic response to aestheticism and
began, however ambivalently, to grant it literary and artistic respectability.

Here especially, the American reception of British aestheticism was
marked by social conflict. In finally coming to terms with the example
of aestheticism, the ensconced literary tastemakers—liberal ministers, conservative journalists, and established high-culture intellectuals
alike—were also attempting to maintain their hegemony in the increasingly conflict-torn sphere of high culture. It was precisely over the

question of aestheticism that their power in that sphere was being actively contested by the new, rising professional and managerial elites; for these new elites sought to assert their own cultural authority by privileging the newer, more fashionable modes of British art and literature that their elders—and rivals—consistently condemned. They sought to validate their newly won status by buying new aesthetic goods, by decorating their houses in the new "aesthetic" styles, by supporting the new "little" or "dinky" aesthetic magazines—by invoking as their own, in other words, the example of British aestheticism in order to breach the walls of the cultural establishment and make themselves fully at home there. The reception of aestheticism in America thus rapidly became the center of a struggle for cultural power, with each side battling with the other by attempting to admit it to their own particular canon. But given the particular terms under which that struggle was waged—terms that carefully circumscribed the moral and aesthetic freedom of even the most revolutionary artists and critics—these maneuvers also sheared aestheticism of its critical power and sexual subversiveness. The established elites and their challengers struggled with each other to invoke aestheticism but also, at the same time, to tame it.

Both of these phenomena—the commodification of aestheticism from "below," the normalization of aestheticism from "above"—make the official entrance of aestheticism onto the American cultural scene in the 1890's interestingly problematic. For they suggest that self-proclaimed "American aesthetes" or decadents—such resolutely minor figures as the novelists James Huneker and Edgar Saltus or the poets George Cabot Lodge or Trumbull Stickney—were continuing a process begun 30 years before: a process by which a zone was defined in the rapidly enlarging cultural marketplace where artists and writers could connect with an expanding audience eager to purchase high-cultural artifacts and the prestige that went along with them. The chief cultural office of aestheticism in America, we might suggest, was its training of this segment of the enlarging and increasingly enthusiastic audience for "high culture" in patterns of expectation and response that a subsequent generation of writers and artists—the "modernists" —were able to call upon and take for granted. To be somewhat more specific, the function of aestheticism's early, premodernist intervention in American culture was to train the middle-class reading public to expect its writers and artists to be alienated, self-satisfied, and flamboyant; to expect their discourse to be hermetic, privatized, and self-referential; and, at the same time, to instruct these writers and artists to walk the delicate line between insulting and indulging the middle-class audience who patronized their work with increasing avidity.

It is in this process that Henry James performed a particularly vital role. For James reshaped the essential agendas of the British "aesthetic movement" into ones more easily assimilated into the particular needs of his own cultural moment. James took the stance of fastidious artistic dedication cultivated by the aesthete and detached it from what seemed to their contemporaries to be the aesthete's hedonism and artistic inefficiency; he remodeled the figure of the aesthete into that of the Jamesian high-art novelist—a figure, like the aesthete, of supple and ample consciousness ("one of those upon whom nothing is lost," as James says in *The Art of Fiction*, in words that paraphrase Pater and that were to be lifted, directly, by Wilde) but one who, unlike the aesthete, is capable of acts of sustained and disciplined creativity and dedicated professionalism. This process was wrought, as I shall be suggesting in the pages that follow, through a complicated process of narrative internalization and transformation—a process in which James echoed and altered significant aestheticist terminology, topoi, and plot devices in such a way as to cull out those he found assimilable to his own project from those subversive of (if only by conforming too explicitly to) its agenda. This process—initiated as early as *Roderick Hudson* and continued in various guises through quarrels with Pater and Wilde conducted in such texts as *The Ambassadors*, *The Tragic Muse*, and, especially, *The Wings of the Dove*—reaches both its moment of apotheosis and its moment of collapse in *The Golden Bowl*, a novel that may be read as the great work of aestheticist art that the aesthetic movement was never able to engender—and a work whose very taunting perfection and surpassing coldness suggests why the value of British aestheticism may well have inhered in its very inability to realize its own ambitions.

It is my claim that James's various, subtle, and shifting response to aestheticism not only shaped his own art but ultimately remodeled the expectations and understanding of the Anglo-American cultural elite as well—that he played a particularly crucial role in the remodeling of the uncanny, unstable, fascinatingly volatile and constantly critical discourse of aestheticism in England into the austere, hermetic, and resolutely self-satisfied discourse of high Anglo-American modernism. James's role in the stabilization or normalization of British aestheticism is part of the larger cultural pattern I have described above, it is true, but it is one that moves in precisely the opposite direction from the essentially moralizing or commodifying taming of aestheticism performed by austere Boston Brahmins or middle-class art patrons alike. For what James accomplished was both to complete and to supplant the aestheticist project by fully resolving its irresolute if playful problematics through the valorizing of his own imaginative processes and aesthetic performance. This move had both individual and institutional consequences. Through it, James was able to claim for himself the artistic sufficiency he saw the aesthetic movement as lacking; he was enabled to assert that he, rather than his problematic rivals Ruskin, Pater, and Wilde, was "esthetic enough." And by this move, James was also able to complete the professionalization of the high-culture artist that the aesthetic movement began but failed to accomplish; he was enabled to institutionalize himself in the competitive literary marketplace of Edwardian London as the great Master of the new Art of Fiction, and thus to create a career model for the writers and artists who were to follow in his wake. It is this strategy, for example, that was explicitly pursued by modernist successors like T. S. Eliot and Ezra Pound, who modeled themselves on James precisely in order to gain the same artistic status they saw their predecessor as achieving—and, simultaneously, it must be added, to efface their own powerful affinities with the aesthetes. But James's self-authorizing aestheticism and that of his own modernist successors had the effect (heightened through the efforts of the New Critical descendants of both in the academy) of blocking from critical view the possibilities that remain embedded within the aesthetic movement itself—possibilities that, when brought to the surface, put in critical perspective both James's stabilizing intervention and the subsequent construction of modernist ideology.

This, then, is what I mean to suggest by bringing together Henry James, British aestheticism, and commodity culture under the sign of "and": my "and" is the sign of mutually modifying interchange and is meant to suggest that all of my concerns shaped and were shaped by each other. James's encounter with British aestheticism significantly transformed both his own fiction and his understanding of his fictional vocation; but James's response to aestheticism had considerable impact on aestheticism itself, remaking or remodeling it in such a way as to prepare it for full entry into the cultural mainstream under the sign of modernism, negating its subversive play with a multitude of irresolute possibilities by—ironically enough—fulfilling its desire to achieve resolution through the valorizing of art. And this move, born equally of the commodification of art and the artistic career and the resistance to such commodification, helped accomplish the full delineation of a zone of "high culture," the creation of a separate niche amidst a complex market economy for the earnest production and avid consumption of austere, self-regarding, art.

Having unfolded my argument to the point of near closure, the unresolved example of my subject compels me to mention one final dimension of the notion of "and." The question of "and"—of the "relations [that] stop nowhere," as James, speaking at his most aestheticist, would say—does not cease ramifying with the explication of my title. For it has become in recent years a cliché of critical discourse that no wholly disinterested or objective analysis of a given literary or cultural phenomenon is possible, that the interests, desires, historical contingencies, and political necessities facing the critic shape the very terms of the analysis she or he performs. This is as true of the present enterprise as of any other. To write about the social performance of the Anglo-American aesthetic movement, the professionalization of the aesthetic, or the interrelation between the project of social critique and commodity culture is not only to confront these questions as they were posed at the turn of the nineteenth century, but also to face them as they have been formulated at our own fin de siècle moment. Specifically, it is to confront the problematic role that the privileging of art plays in the lives of those who ambivalently and indeed often rebelliously find themselves positioned to educate others in the lineaments of aesthetic knowledge and judgment—those "aesthetic professionals" we call literary academics.

This project takes on even greater urgency because those professionals are currently engaged in a thorough critique of what they see as their own lingering aestheticism. Whether launched from within the tradition of European discourse on the aesthetic—as is the case with Paul de Man, as Christopher Norris has recently argued with great cogency [13]—or from outside that tradition—as in the current analysis of the determination of aesthetic categories by exigencies of race, class, and gender—the academy is busily engaged in a critique of the privileging of the aesthetic itself, which it sees either as a mode of judgment that (in de Man's words) "has trespassed beyond its legitimate epistemological reach" or one that serves as a means of enforcing and reproducing structures of social domination by (in Pierre Bourdieu's terms) endowing certain privileged classes with excessive amounts of cultural capital.[14] From this angle, it might well appear that we are living at the end of the aesthetic era—the end, that is, of the era for which Anglo-American aestheticism provides the most fully articulated, if resolutely unacknowledged, expression: that era initiated with Kant and Schiller and carried forth through the various transformations of European Romantic thought from that day to our own in which an autonomous aesthetic realm was not only positioned as a separate "world elsewhere" or a distinct category of judgment, but also, if somewhat paradoxically, valorized as a socially redemptive sphere of being.

Perhaps we are at the end of the era; certainly, this is one of the questions that this book wittingly or unwittingly finds itself musing over. To be sure, over the eight years I have spent writing it, a vast sea change has taken place in the Anglo-American academy's understanding of these issues, and my understanding of my own project has shifted along with it. Begun as a Bloomian influence study, transformed into a treatment of the relation between aestheticist discourse and the rise of literary modernism, this work has turned increasingly to the analysis of the social construction of the aesthetic itself. Rather than seeing my topic as circumscribed by aesthetic or literary categories, in other words, I have been led increasingly to historicize these very terms, to try to understand their origins and destiny in changing social definitions of the aesthetic and, ultimately, in the shifting patterns of the making and remaking of culture itself. And rather than idealizing, however tenuously or ironically, my own repertoire of terms, I have been led to understand their highly problematic role in the establishment and renewal of patterns of social power.

But for many reasons, I have not fully made the turn toward a wholly historicized vision, preferring instead to let my no-doubt-retrograde nostalgia for the literary coexist, however tensely, with the very analysis that would undo it. To a certain extent, this reticence is as much a product of my professional training and situation as it is of my personal inclination; but to a greater extent, it is fueled by a suspicion that the Anglo-American academy's recent demolition of the aesthetic as a category of analysis is no more definitive than the aestheticism it purports to reject or transcend. Indeed, I would suggest that the current social critique of the aesthetic is no less bound up in the dialectic of aestheticism itself than was the New Critical aesthetic idealism it would replace. Thus, for example, the student of aestheticism will recognize these kinds of arguments in not only the shocked and horrified responses of the retrograde Victorian literary establishment to the aesthetes but within aestheticism itself, in that mood of anti-aesthetic *ascesis* or ritual purgation to which even (especially) the most fervent aesthetes fell prey, often at their moment of greatest ecstasy. Moreover, as I have been trying to suggest here, the history of the Anglo-American response to aestheticism suggests that the critique of aestheticism from outside aestheticism frequently shares unexpected affinities with aestheticism itself—that this critique serves all too frequently as a way of advancing a surpassing aestheticism of its own. Far more even than Adorno, for example, whose privileging of the aesthetic sphere was at least openly acknowledged and fully thematized, the current critique of the social deficiencies of the aesthetic often reveals a surprisingly naive sense of what art can and cannot do. To say that the aesthetic as such is produced and determined by an oppressive social structure, that judgments of taste no less than any other social manifestation enforce the onerous realities of social domination, is still to participate in the aestheticist dream of art as providing the lineaments of a redeemed, transfigured world—if only in the repeated and vociferous expression of the disappointment when art is discovered not to do these things. Similarly, nothing could be more grimly true to aestheticism's vision of the socially redemptive power of art than the current understanding of high-cultural art as a prime mechanism of social control; for such a perception would seem to grant to art through the means of critique the very social power and ideological primacy that the aestheticist tradition so vigorously, and so unsuccessfully, sought to claim for it.

This is not to say that the aesthetic realm does or can exist as a separate, disinterested category of analysis or sphere of existence— that high-cultural aesthetic artifacts, no less than other products of human culture and desire, do not further mechanisms of social domination or serve an essential role in the production and maintenance of hegemonic ideologies. But it is to say that the consequences of this recognition are by no means clear: not only does this recognition undo itself through the perverse monotony of its own insistence, but it presumes, prematurely, to foreclose the unstable and frequently undecidable questions that the aestheticist tradition in England and America pose so insistently. For the aesthetes and their followers and critics, those questions revolved around the twinned issues of the professionalization and commodification of cultural life. To mix terminologies, aestheticism can ultimately be seen as a vast cultural reaction formation to these forces that simultaneously served to critique and to reinforce them: often reinforcing what it seemed most powerfully to critique, and critiquing most powerfully what it would seem to reinforce. For us, these problems are not entirely different and may be said to center on later, more advanced versions of these same phenomena, which we might label the professionalization of the critique of professionalism and the commodification of the critique of commodity culture. To describe these phenomena more explicitly is to pose them in the form of the question: to what extent does the social critique of "taste" participate in the very mechanisms of social domination it would disavow? How does ideology critique—and specifically, the critique of aesthetic ideology—institutionalize itself in the very lineaments of the cultural formations it would allegedly deconstruct? And, perhaps most problematically of all, how does one—how do *we*—negotiate our way through our culture's tendency to subvert our purported subversiveness by professionalizing it, thereby generating a space for the proper care, feeding, and *control* of the ostensibly "counterhegemonic"?

I pose these questions as genuine ones, because, like so many of the issues posed by the writers I have chosen to discuss, they can never be fully answered. Indeed, it is only in the act of writing this introduction that I have become fully aware of their shadowy but nevertheless powerful presence in my text—as, of course, is necessarily the case with introductions, which, as it has also become banal to observe, are acts of retrospective revision for the writer as much as they are gestures of greeting to the reader. And so, as I conclude here, I do so in the knowledge that meditating on Henry James and British aestheticism has been the means by which I have been enabled to pose these questions to myself, and to pose them *as questions*—as issues that demand meditation, cogitation, and agitation, and that refuse to offer any certain answer or codified statement of belief. I hope that whatever else this work does for its readers—whatever they are able to glean from it about "Henry James," "British aestheticism," and "and"—it may have something of the same effect for them as well.

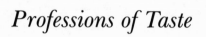

Professions of Taste

Chapter One

Aestheticism:
The Embrace of Contraries

Around 1880, Max Beerbohm wrote, "were [felt] the primordia of a great change. The aristocracy could not live by good breeding alone. The old delights seemed vapid, waxen. Something new was wanted. And thus came it that the spheres of fashion and of art met, thus began the great social renascence." The discovery of the "cult of Beauty" that had hitherto only inhabited Chelsea led to a "social vogue" for Art, the result of which was that "peacock feathers and sunflowers glittered in every room, the curio shops were ransacked for the furniture of Annish days, men and women, fired by the fervent words of the young Oscar, threw their mahogany into the streets. A few smart women even dressed themselves in suave draperies and unheard-of greens. Into whatever ballroom you went, you would surely find, among the women in tiaras and the fops and the distinguished foreigners, half a score of comely Ragamufins in velveteen, murmuring sonnets, posturing, waving their hands." [1]

Beerbohm's comic retrospective, published in the notorious *Yellow Book* at the height of the so-called "decadence," captures brilliantly our usual vision of British aestheticism: its witty tone acknowledging, indeed reveling, in its own artifice; its resolute inconsequentiality; its alliance between the worlds of high fashion and avant-garde art. It is a vision we recognize not only in Beerbohm's own pastiches and parodies, but also in Gilbert and Sullivan's marvelous operetta *Patience* or in George Du Maurier's famous *Punch* cartoons of the 1870's and early 1880's. And it is more crucially the vision we associate with the comic career and tragic fate of Oscar Wilde.

Yet at the same time, we are conscious of another form of British aestheticism: one that we associate with writers like John Ruskin, Dante Gabriel Rossetti, A. C. Swinburne, and Walter Pater—all of whom may be accused of many things, but not (frequent) frivolity. Whether

we label them "Pre-Raphaelites," "aesthetes," "decadents," or merely
avatars of the fin de siècle, these writers all represent a serious and
novel turn in English letters. All represent a moment in which the
enterprise we have since come to see as central to the tradition of
Anglo-American poetry and prose—the Romantic tradition—reaches
its moment of climax, or its moment of exhaustion, or both. All represent the turn within Victorian culture toward valorizing art in general
and visual art in particular as a means of provoking intense experience in a society that seems able to deaden the senses and the spirit
alike. All represent a protest against the sexual mores of Victorian
England, whether implicitly (as in the case of Ruskin's confused and
sorry sexual history, or Pater's subtle evocation of his deeply repressed
homosexuality) or explicitly (as in the case of Wilde, Swinburne, or
Rossetti's flamboyant sexual adventurism). All represent as well the
first instances of a social phenomenon we in the twentieth century
have come to know well: that of the alienated artist or critic, feeling
acutely a separation from the increasingly middle-class public that he
or she addresses (and from which he or she is likely to spring); desiring in consequence to shock, to offend, or to alter the conditions of
perception that characterize this audience, yet discovering thereby the
impossibility of doing so.

     What, we might therefore ask, is the relation between these two aes-
theticisms—between the aestheticism of fashion and frivolity and that
of austere or flamboyant Romantic fervor and social alienation? A few
observations spring to mind. Cynically, we might want to argue that
the link between social alienation and high fashion is hardly a surprising one. We have only to look at our own modes of high fashion—at,
for example, pre-washed designer jeans or neo-"punk" designer hair-
styles—to understand the astounding capacity of a consumer society to
incorporate and ultimately to profit from challenges to its own ethos.
Much of this was implicit in the social fate of British aestheticism:
Oscar Wilde was in many ways the first literary "celebrity," the first literary figure who consciously sought to make his career by publicizing
himself in and then writing for the new mass-circulation newspapers
and women's magazines of the 1880's and early 1890's; and the fact
that much of what Wilde argued for was directly opposed to the popularization of high culture that these journals effected was never felt
as a deficiency by either Wilde or those journals themselves. Similarly,
we might want to say, the very commodification of cultural values performed by the popular "aesthetic craze" of the 1870's and early 1880's
was mimicked by the privileging of art promulgated by Ruskin and

Pater. We might want to suggest that they objectify or reify intangible values in specific artworks, or, more subtly, in their privileging of the notion of a subtle, sensitive, and expansive response to those artworks, and thereby prepare the way for the marketing of those intangible values through the heightened sensual experience of commodities that characterizes a mature consumer society.

All this is true, I think, but it is also premature. There are ways, indeed important ways, in which British aestheticism prepares for the establishment of a consumer culture; but there are also ways in which it represents and anticipates a variety of different forms of opposition to such an ethos as well. There are ways, further, in which the means by which it does so—its own distinctive, unstable, and curious or exotic art and literature—tend to be ignored in the confusion of aestheticism as fashion with aestheticism as imaginative response. And, finally, there are ways in which the premature collapse of the one into the other serves to blunt the poignancy of aestheticism's fate and thereby prevents us from seeing how aestheticism's very failure prepares the way for Henry James's relative—if problematic—success. My goal here, accordingly, is briefly to delineate the particular aesthetic assumptions and social practices that we can identify with the tradition of British aestheticism, and to suggest the scope of its concerns and—finally unresolved—problematics. Indeed, my suggestion will be that irresolution and ultimately failure itself are written into the program of British aestheticism, but that this very failure, paradoxically enough, may serve to define the ultimate ground of its value.

The Discontents of Definition

"Aestheticism" is one of those terms in literary criticism that are impossible fully to define. Like other such terms—"baroque," for example, or "realism"—it can be used either to describe or to evaluate and, if the latter, either to praise or to damn, although, it should be admitted, usually to damn. And, when we turn to consider the application of this notoriously vague term to the literary situation of nineteenth-century England, matters become impossibly confused. Of whom, for example, do we speak when we refer to the "aesthetic movement"? Is Ruskin the central force behind aestheticism in England? Is Rossetti its truest practitioner? Or is Swinburne, or Pater, or Wilde? And what of its provenance? Is aestheticism merely a French import? It was, after all, Swinburne who brought that notorious French slogan, *l'art pour l'art*, into currency, as it was Pater and Wilde who brought the idea of *decadence* to the attention of both the literary and the general public; and hostile contemporaries and respectful successors alike have consistently identified the aesthetic movement with the entrance of Gallic forms of discourse about art, beauty, and morality onto the British stage.[2] Or does it signal the incorporation of the doctrines of German idealist philosophy into British criticism? Pater, we may remember, was kept on at Oxford despite the fervent opposition of Benjamin Jowett, because of his knowledge of Hegel; and one can clearly see the privileging of art as the resolution to otherwise insoluble philosophical problematics making its way from German idealist philosophy directly into Pater's work and thence into the mainstream of British criticism.[3] Or does aestheticism represent the last flourish of British Romanticism? After all, the link between Wordsworth and Keats (via Browning and Tennyson) and the Pre-Raphaelites or poets of the "decadence" is an obvious one.[4]

Questions like these, of course, are nearly insoluble, because they presuppose a single, unitary definition of a diverse, fractious, and ultimately disjunctive group of writers, artists, and critics. Nevertheless, the notion of an "aesthetic movement" is not without its utility. For one thing, that notion was one that Victorians within and without the so-called aesthetic movement used to describe it, or at least did so after 1881, when Sir Walter Hamilton published a pseudohistorical account of this current in British thought called *The Aesthetic Movement in England*. For another, it might impel us to look at the ways in which the members of that movement sought to define themselves, and particularly the ways they sought to use the notion of the "aesthetic" itself to provide such a definition.

No better example exists than Pater's famous essay *Aesthetic Poetry*, first published as part of his review of the works of William Morris in the august pages of the *Westminister Review* in 1868.[5] There, Pater argues that Morris's work represents a wholly new kind of poetry, one whose "atmosphere . . . belongs to no simple form of poetry, no actual form of life." Pater continues: "Greek poetry, medieval or modern poetry, projects above the realities of its time, a world in which the forms of things are transfigured. Of that transfigured world, this new poetry takes possession, and sublimates beyond it another still fainter and more spectral, which is literally an artificial or 'earthly paradise.' It is a finer ideal, extracted from what in relation to any actual world is already an ideal. Like some strange second flowering afterdate, it renews on a more delicate type the poetry of a past age, but must not be confounded with it." Needless to say, this definition is as significant for the way it defines as much as for what it defines. The passage balances delicately between metaphoric systems of the organic and the artificial and between the language of assertion and that of denial. Pater neatly collapses the "earthly" into the "artificial," for example, by the authorial fiat of a carefully placed "or," or, at best, by the paradoxical claim of literalness for that which is triumphantly figurative, the artificiality of Morris's *Earthly Paradise*. Similarly, "aesthetic poetry" is described in the language of alchemy, "sublimat[ing]" and "extract[ing]" elements from the real and artificial alike, but it is also described in natural language, in terms of "flowering." Further, this form of poetry seems languid, enervated, decadent, perverse; it is "fainter," "strange," an unnatural "second flowering." But this unnatural phenomenon is also praised as a form of renewal and rebirth.

And this rhetorical complexity has a striking effect. It shifts the reader's attention from the ostensible subject of praise to the mode of praise itself. The paragraph performs the virtue it claims for its subject, the human capacity to make complex distinctions and create unexpected syntheses that have been anticipated neither in the "actual world" nor in the artificial worlds of poetry and human thought. It thus illustrates an "ideal" that is "finer" in both senses of the word: the human act of "differentiation," of making minute distinctions, "in which," Pater writes in his essay *Style*, "all progress of mind consists" (WP, 5:5).

This passage from the Morris review suggests the ways in which the concept of aestheticism is appropriately derived from Pater's work. The values he upholds are fundamentally aesthetic, at least in the terms of the Kantian tradition. That is, following Kant, Pater conceives of the aesthetic as a separate realm of experience, removed from those of "the actual forms of life" or of most human judgments. The ways Pater communicates these values are also aesthetic, at least insofar as a post-Kantian critic would wish to identify the aesthetic as a fundamentally non- or transcognitive form of experience, one existing beyond the bounds of "mere" reason. Pater does not argue rationally for the values he perceives in Morris, nor does he describe them in clear, expository prose. Rather, he enacts these virtues in the delicate dualisms of his own language. "The aim of the true student of aesthetics," Pater writes in a famous passage from the Preface to *The Renaissance*, is "to define beauty, not in the most abstract, but in the most concrete terms possible"; here Pater achieves such concreteness by erasing the already shadowy line between aesthetic poetry and aesthetic criticism (WP, 1: vii–viii).

But the performative tendency of Pater's prose and its implicit assertion of its own aesthetic autonomy are not its most distinguishing features. After all, one might also talk about the performative capacities of John Donne's prose, or Sir Thomas Browne's, or William Hazlitt's, with equal authority; and one could easily look to Coleridge or Keats for British claims for the necessary removal of the aesthetic from other forms of knowledge or judgment. Rather, I would suggest that it is the ability to play with differing, even contradictory resolutions to a given problem that we may cite as the most distinguishing feature of this moment in Pater's work. "Aesthetic poetry" is defined by a series of "logical monstrosities" (the phrase is David Newsome's), a series of oxymorons wheeling vertiginously into each other, never finding union in a larger synthesis on the one hand, but never collapsing into an abyss of nonmeaning on the other.[6] The result is that Pater has his cake and eats it too. He is able to assert without asserting, to define without defining; his definition is able to hover suggestively on the threshold of logical discourse without crossing over a generic divide that Pater seems to fear.

And, I want to argue here, it is the ability, inclination, or even the desire to hold onto contradictory assertions without giving up either their contradictoriness or the wish somehow to unify them that I find most characteristic not only of Pater's work, but of aestheticism's imaginative labor as well. Again, this inclination is hardly unique; one can obviously find in the works of many writers assertions that contradict or qualify other such assertions expressed with equal fervor. But, I want to suggest, it is distinctive; the work of the aestheticists often reads like a mosaic composed of such contradictory moments carefully tessellated to produce an exquisite but ultimately enigmatic whole. Indeed, I would suggest that the defining quality of British aestheticism —the only way these various and distinctive writers and artists may be seen to share any characteristic at all—is the desire to embrace contradictions, indeed the desire to seek them out the better to play with the possibilities they afford.

I need to offer a few more examples here, both to validate my claim and sketch out its implications. Let me turn to texts that antedate and follow directly from Pater's: first, to a poem of A. C. Swinburne's, *Genesis*. In this lyric, Swinburne attempts with typical modesty to rewrite the Judeo-Christian creation myth, substituting for its anthropocentrism and logocentrism a wholly different primary principle. For in this poem, the search for the primal principle or originating structure that lies at the beginning of existence ends with the discovery of the "divine contraries of life":

> For if death were not, then should growth not be,
>   Change, nor the life of good nor evil things;
> Nor were there night at all nor light to see,
>   Nor water of sweet nor water of bitter springs. (ACS, 2: 182)[7]

To Swinburne, the primary contradiction that lies so enigmatically at the center of our experience, the coexistence of life and death, gives rise to a series of contraries that define its nature and limits: good and evil, night and light, sweetness and bitterness. Such contraries bear a necessary relation to each other; good means little without evil, light without dark, and sweetness without bitterness. But this intimate interdependence of the things that people prize and the things they distrust or fear is not some dim and dark horror to be mourned or abhorred; rather, it is a positive value, something to be praised, to be celebrated, even to be worshipped.

Oscar Wilde shares Swinburne's binary vision, and in a far different mode performs the same celebration of contradiction. For the basic structure of the art form for which Wilde is most justly celebrated, the epigram, depends on the same values that Swinburne praises explicitly. The wit of a Wildean epigram inheres in its ability to express conventional sentiments in the form of an antinomy, then to revise that opposition by reversing one crucial term:

London is full of women who trust their husbands. One can always recognize them. They look so thoroughly unhappy. (*Works*, 11: 58)

It is perfectly monstrous the way people go about nowadays saying things against one behind one's back, that are absolutely and entirely true. (*Works*, 11: 92)

As Wilde writes in another context, "The well-bred contradict other people. The wise contradict themselves" (*Artist*, p. 433).[8] Here wit, and perhaps wisdom as well, parody the self-contradictions of the "well-bred" the better to demonstrate the hypocrisy of their bifurcated morality. The wit (in every sense of the word) of the poet and reader alike inheres in their ability to understand and master the binary terms of their society and then to play with these terms in a spirit utterly frivolous and thus (to adopt one of Wilde's own terms) deeply earnest. But, as a result, his paradoxes must submit themselves to their own critical logic. Wilde critiques the limitations of such binary thought and bifurcated behavior from within, but also suggests their inevitability. The way to escape contradiction, he implies, is to contradict it, which is to say that he confesses his own inability to transcend the forms of his culture in the very means by which he satirizes them.

What I am suggesting here is that Swinburne and Pater and Wilde are joined by Rossetti and Morris and Arthur Symons and Ernest Dowson and a host of other figures by their characteristic expression of the inevitability of a bifurcated, fragmentary, and ultimately contradictory vision. Indeed, we might go so far as to say that aestheticism represents that moment in British literary history in which a group of writers and artists took to claiming that the things they valued—the life of the mind, for example, or art itself—called forth a compelling awareness of the value of their opposites—the life of the body, for example, or the virtues of sincerity and artlessness that Pater, Rossetti, and even Wilde all found themselves yearning after. Moreover, since such a multiplicity of desires is hardly a defining characteristic of this particular moment in literary history, what I want to assert here is that not only is an acceptance of the absolutely irreconcilable nature of human wishes built into British aestheticism, but so is the decision to explore the experience of irreconcilability. The aesthetes, wrote G. K. Chesterton in 1910, "not only tried to be in all ages at once (which is a very reasonable ambition, though not often realised), but they wanted to be on all sides at once; which is nonsense."[9]

Exactly: except that seeing this desire to "be on all sides at once" (or "lost on both sides," as Rossetti puts it) as a species of non-sense, we might want to look at it as a kind of other-sense, as a response to the disintegration of every possible form of synthesis or ground of belief that so conspicuously marks virtually all forms of high-cultural discourse in late Victorian England. The aestheticists, no less than many other anxious intellectuals of their time, felt the aftershocks of industrialism, social reform, class conflict, evolution, the Higher Criticism.[10] Their response, however, was not to return to Rome or Romish ways, to embrace the new positivist order, or—with the significant exception of Morris—to ally themselves directly with efforts at social transformation. Rather, the aestheticists responded to their predicament by expressing the desire or the will to find or forge another such synthesis even while articulating a severe skepticism over the value of any such potentially unifying force or vision. The result is a complicated vision, which seeks to explore the experience of fragmentation, loss, and disintegration without necessarily giving up the possibility of reuniting these shards. Aestheticism in England represents the embrace of hateful contraries, the exploration of cultural contradictions—but without abandoning the option of contradicting contradiction itself, without the loss of the nostalgia for a lost unity and the desire to project such a unity into the vision of a future consummation.

Or such at least is the theory. What I need to do now is to discuss the enactment of this broad imaginative habit or tendency in specific works dealing with specific issues. I want briefly to define aestheticism's practice by looking at the way the aestheticists expressed or embodied three central contradictions: the perception of time as flux and the quest for perfect moments that could arrest such flux; the perception of the self in solipsistic isolation and the yearning for consummation or, at least, contact, with another; and the desire to purify experience from contact with the material world and the rise of aestheticism as a form of high fashion within that world. Such an analysis, I will suggest, will serve to distinguish the aestheticists from their forebears, both in England and on the Continent, and to set the aestheticist endeavor in England in its proper literary and social setting.

Before I do so, however, there is one issue that needs to be discussed: the relation between aestheticism and two doctrines or assertions with which it is frequently confused—the doctrine of "art for art's sake" and that of the autonomy of the aesthetic. It is perhaps more urgent to speak to the first issue, since as it has been activated in literary criticism of the last 40 years, the complicated notion of art for art has come to be deployed as a reductive battering ram directed with particular force at the tradition of British aestheticism by critics of the right and the left alike. But such criticism ignores, for a number of reasons, the fact that when aestheticist writers like Swinburne or Pater deployed the slogan of "art for art," they did so as part of a larger argument or dialectic that is trivialized when compacted into so simple and rigid a notion. Swinburne imported the concept into English criticism, for example, in an 1866 monograph on William Blake; and in the monograph it is clear that his purpose in doing so is to claim a political role for art itself, to assert that, in a thoroughly utilitarian culture, even the seemingly apolitical, disinterested pursuit of art is necessarily oppositional in nature. Similarly, when Pater quotes the phrase at the end of the Conclusion to *The Renaissance*, he is making at best a limited and tentative claim—hedged around with qualification and uncertainty— for art as the experience most capable of supplying intense sensations for a perfect moment; Pater emphasizes the transience and ineffability of this moment as much as its possible perfection. "Art comes to you professing frankly to give nothing but the highest quality to your moments as they pass, and simply for those moments' sake," Pater writes

(WP, 1: 239). The value of art, then, lies not in its own static perfection, but rather in its "frank" participation in the transience of things, in the succession of discrete perceptual experiences that defines our experience.

It might be wise, then, to drop the term "aestheticism," and substitute another in its place—"late Romanticism," for example, or (as Morse Peckham suggests) "Stylism." I do not do so, however, for several reasons. Not only is it, as I have suggested above, the term by which Victorian culture understood this group of writers and poets, and by which they came to understand themselves, but, mutatis mutandis, it is the most accurate way of designating them. For if we view the word "aesthetic" not in the reductive sense of art for art's sake but in terms of its root meaning, the term proves perfectly assimilable with the definition I wish to employ. The word was originally used by Alexander Baumgarten (following Aristotle) to designate the perfection of the act of perception, particularly visual perception, wrought most frequently, but not exclusively, by a work of art; and it is in this sense, I think, that Pater, Rossetti, Swinburne, Wilde, et al. may be understood as fundamentally aesthetic in orientation. "The more I think of it I find this conclusion more impressed upon me," wrote Ruskin in a famous passage of *Modern Painters III*, "that the greatest thing a human soul ever does in this world is to *see* something, and tell what it *saw* in a plain way. Hundreds of people can talk for one who can think, but thousands can think for one who can see. To see clearly is poetry, prophecy, and religion,—all in one" (JR, 5: 333). And all of the major adherents of aestheticism would have assented to Ruskin's proposition. An aesthete, says Swinburne, is simply someone who sees. Pater defines the aesthete—and, by extension, the "aesthetic critic"— as one who is able to discriminate most finely among the multiplicity of impressions offered by experience of the phenomenal world. Rossetti, Millais, and the rest of the Pre-Raphaelites enact their assent by creating poetry and painting that depict the minute particulars of experience with excruciating fidelity. And vision of a different sort marks the scopophilic intensities of Wilde's work, most impressively, perhaps, in *The Picture of Dorian Gray*.

Aestheticism, I would suggest, represents primarily an angle of vision that aims at the purification of vision Ruskin sought but which increasingly discovers the impossibility of such preternatural clarity of sight; it privileges art not as an end in and of itself, but as a focusing or a sharpening of the contradictions one thereby faces and as the field in which these wildly differing images wrought by so partially a

purified vision are played out. Aestheticism therefore comes to prob-
lematize the very art it would seem to erect as the locus of value;
moreover, it problematizes that art by the same gesture with which it
valorizes it. Aestheticism as a broad-based literary, artistic, and cultural
phenomenon in late-nineteenth-century England therefore needs to
be detached from what one might call "aesthetic-ism"—from, that is,
a privileging of art as an ontological ground, an epistemological category ("art as a way of knowing"), or as a moral value. Detached, but
not disaffiliated; for as I shall argue more fully below, it is the generation that followed the aestheticists to cultural prominence in England
and America—the generation of self-styled "modernists"—that may
be most accurately described as forming an "aesthetic movement," that
most fully articulated an ideology that centered itself on the privileging of art as a locus of value and a guarantee of authority. The story
of the movement from the generation of the 1880's and 1890's, with
its intensely contradictory vision and hesitant privileging of a newly
demarcated aesthetic realm as that sphere in which the most crucial
issues of the moment could be played out most fully, and the generation of the 1920's and 1930's, with its mandarin self-assurance and
aesthetic certitudes, is the narrative this book has to tell; for, I shall
argue, it is through the fictional practice and career model provided
by Henry James that the movement from the one to the other was
wrought.

The question of the relation between aestheticism in England and
the philosophical doctrine of the autonomy of art is more complicated,
in part because the analysis of this issue has been performed with such
exemplary tact by Peter Bürger. In *Theory of the Avant Garde*, Bürger
complicates the traditional notion of both that doctrine and of aestheticism itself by grounding both in an analysis of the nature and
function of art in a bourgeois society. "The *autonomy of art* is a category of bourgeois society," Bürger writes. "It permits the description
of art's detachment from the context of practical life as a historical development. . . . [but] does not permit the understanding of its referent
as one that developed historically."[11] And aestheticism can be defined
as that moment in the unfolding of bourgeois art when this dynamic
is articulated explicitly. "Apartness from the praxis of life, which had
always been the condition that characterized the way art functioned in
bourgeois society . . . becomes [in aestheticism] its content" (48).

The relevance of Bürger's analysis to British aestheticism is indisputable, and has much influenced the account I offer below. Its suppleness, its ability to historicize autonomy theories and aestheticism alike

while still interrogating their transformation of "the relative dissocia-
tion of the work of art from the praxis of life in bourgeois society . . .
into the (erroneous) idea that the work of art is totally independent
of society" is admirable and important, as is its careful disentangling
of the "moment of truth" from the "untruth of the category, the ele-
ment of distortion that characterizes every ideology" (46). Yet perhaps
the greatest importance of Bürger's analysis lies in its unwitting reminder of the crucial difference between the aestheticist project in
England and its counterparts on the Continent—the forms of aestheticism that Bürger, like Arnold Hauser before him, takes as paradigmatic of aestheticism as a whole. For Bürger's critique of autonomy
theory, and indeed of the nature and role of art in a bourgeois society itself, unwittingly recapitulates one of the critical enterprises on
which British aestheticism—unlike its Continental counterparts—was
founded: the admixture of social and aesthetic criticism performed
by John Ruskin. The essence of Ruskin's imaginative effort in *Modern
Painters*, in *The Stones of Venice*, and indeed in all his voluminous and
massive writings on art, is precisely to trace the debased condition of
art and society alike in Ruskin's England to the detachment of art
from full participation in social experience. And while aestheticism in
England grew in such a way as to supplement or revise Ruskin and
Ruskinism, it never fully abandoned either his social commitment or
his understanding of the political obligations of the artist. Not only
William Morris, who moved directly from Ruskinism to socialism, but
also Dante Gabriel Rossetti and Algernon Charles Swinburne consistently affirmed radical political sympathies—leading, in the case of
the latter two men, to the writing of explicitly political poetry (to this
day ignored by critics) in support of European nationalist revolutions
and, more generally, to the writing of a poetry that offered a powerful, if ultimately fallible, critique of established social authorities of
all stripes. Even the most avowedly aestheticist of the British aesthetic
writers, Oscar Wilde, remained determinedly critical even as he made
his way through the salons and cenacles of British high society; as we
shall see, his satirical plays offer a powerful, immanent critique of the
social institutions of his moment, and his remarkable essay, *The Soul
of Man Under Socialism*, undertakes the project of uniting aestheticism
and socialism by arguing that the freedom the former preaches in the
purely "aesthetic" realm ought to be realized in the political realm as
well.

British aestheticism's understanding of itself was thus always already
political, and this fact complicates the application of Bürger's para-

digm to its analysis. Indeed, aestheticism in England seems closer in spirit and execution to Bürger's description of "the avant-garde manifestation" for which, in Bürger's analysis, aestheticism prepares, than it does to his description of aestheticism itself. "The European avant-garde movements can be defined as an attack on the status of art in bourgeois society," Bürger writes. "What is negated is not an earlier form of art (a style) but art as an institution that is unassociated with the life praxis of man. When the avant-gardistes demand that art become practical once again, they do not mean that the contents of works of art should be socially significant. . . . Rather, [their demand] directs itself to the way art functions in society, a process that does as much to determine the effect that works have as does the particular content" (49). It is this "demand" that aestheticism in England persistently and powerfully made—sometimes in flawed or distorted or self-annulling ways, it is true, but often in eloquent and undeniably prescient ones as well.

Aestheticism in England corresponds to Bürger's paradigm of avant-gardism in another, more grimly ironic, sense as well. For, as Bürger notes, the project of the European avant-garde was ironically realized by the very social institutions it set out to supplant. "During the time of the historical avant-garde movements," Bürger writes, "the attempt to do away with the distance between art and life still had all the pathos of historical progressiveness on its side. But in the meantime, the culture industry has brought about the false elimination of the distance between art and life, and this also allows one to recognize the contradictoriness of the avant-gardiste undertaking" (50). The "contradictoriness" confronted by the avant-garde project in Europe afflicted the unfolding of the aestheticist undertaking in England. As we shall see, from the beginning, the politically progressive ambitions of aestheticism were continually thwarted not by the hostility of the press or the public—although such hostility was an undeniable component of the public response to aestheticism, the aestheticists frequently seemed to gain rhetorical power from their opponents' mean-minded moralism—but rather by the eager adoption of its central tenets by the commercial press, by the advertising industry, and by the manufacturers and vendors of new "aesthetic" commodities. The reception of aestheticism in America was even more powerfully marked by this phenomenon; as we shall see in Chapter 2, the "aesthetic mania" or "craze" that accompanied the first American encounter with aestheticism metamorphosed into the advertising and marketing strategies that governed the transition from a culture organized around the incitement to continual and sober-minded production to one structured by the celebration of acts of avid and gleeful consumption.

The Rhetoric of Atemporality

To begin, then, with the problem of time: the Victorian age was, as Jerome Buckley has shown, massively dominated by a sense of temporal crisis.[12] The rapidity of technological progress, the dissemination of German theories of history, the rise of evolutionism, the decline of a conventional religious eschatology: all these factors created a widespread sense among writers, artists, and intellectuals that time ran on the grooved rails of change toward an uncetain end. The aestheticists, like their contemporaries, experienced time as a liner progression that leads inexorably to loss and death. For Pater, time bounds and limits all experience, even the most beautiful and intense: "To such a tremulous wisp constantly re-forming itself on the stream, to a single sharp impression, with a sense in it, a relic more or less fleeting, of such moments gone by, what is real in our life fines itself down" (WP, 1: 236). The "real" is here redefined as the experience of temporality itself, a perception that is inevitably linked to a sense of entropy and loss. What is "really real" for Pater, in other words, is not just the experience of time, but the sense of attenuation and exhaustion that it brings.

Rossetti also adopts this metaphor of time as a quick-eddying stream, and he, too, understands that such a vision leads to a heightened awareness of loss. In *The Stream's Secret*, a lover addresses a stream, demanding from it news of his beloved. "Shall Time not still endow / One hour with life, and I and she / Slake in one kiss the thirst of memory?" he asks, but the stream refuses to answer, except insofar as its ceaseless motion silently enacts the continual passage of time (DGR, 1: 95). Despite all his yearning for "Love's Hour" (l. 164), the speaker ends the poem knowing only that the loveless hours continue to pass, and becomes part of the ceaseless motion of the stream as his tears fall into it.

But there is another moment in the aestheticist response to time. For Pater, the response to time as loss leads to the moral and aesthetic reminder that "our one chance lies in expanding that interval, in getting as many pulsations as possible into the given time" (WP, 1: 238); the very medium that leads to a sense of transience and limitation also provokes us into valuable and meaningful experience—is, in fact, the only source of value and meaning available to us. Swinburne, like Pater, celebrates *The Triumph of Time* by understanding its resolute doubleness. On the one hand, time's destructive force is always near:

> Before our lives divide for ever
>   While time is with us and hands are free
> (Time, swift to fasten and swift to sever
>   Hand from hand, as we stand by the sea) (ACS, 1: 169, ll. 1–4)[13]

But Swinburne here alters the Pre-Raphaelite topos of the time-separated lovers by suggesting that time brought these lovers together in the first place. Time "sayeth and gainsayeth" (l. 148); all human continuities as well as all human disjunctures take part in the "triumph of time." Swinburne is also distinct from his colleagues in his refusal to adopt the rhetoric of temporal loss. Like Rossetti and Pater, he images time as a stream—"one loose thin pulseless tremulous vein, / Rapid and vivid and dumb as a dream" that "works downward, sick of the sun and the rain" (ll. 58–60). But, just as this stream makes its way into larger bodies of water, so Swinburne's sense of time as loss flows into a celebration of its power. His image for this power is, of course, the sea, which is eternal—it existed "from the first" and will exist "in the end"—but is also as fluid and mutable as is our experience of mortal time (l. 304). To become unified with this force is to die into a sensual afterlife and thereby to attain for oneself a measure of its extensive power:

> I shall sleep, and move with the moving ships,
>   Change as the winds change, veer in the tide;
> My lips will feast on the foam of thy lips,
>   I shall rise with thy rising, with thee subside. (ll. 273–76)

But, whether they encounter it with a sense of loss or with one of ecstatic or thanatotic identification, the rhetoric of aestheticism is also constructed in order to search for an escape from the remorseless sense of time as ceaseless flux. We have seen one such suggestion in Rossetti's hint that a perfect moment, "Love's Hour," might arrive that would give meaning to the lover's time as loss, and, as we have seen, this is Pater's desideratum as well. The Conclusion ends with the valorization of the passing moment for its own sake; such vividly experienced moments, Pater hopes, may give meaning to experience lived on the stream of time. But how can a perfect moment enter a world of temporal flux? Can this flux be arrested? Two different answers are characteristically offered by the aestheticists. Love and art, they frequently suggest, may allow one to discover the perfect moment —at least for a moment.

To Rossetti, as to his predecessor Robert Browning, the power of love allows the perfect moment to erupt in the midst of temporality. Love is "the last relay / And ultimate outpost of eternity," he writes in *The Dark Glass*, and, in many of the sonnets in *The House of Life*, Rossetti's lovers attempt to fortify this outpost (DGR, 1: 193, ll. 7–8). In *Silent Noon*, for example, two lovers enjoying a fête champêtre share a moment of silent communion at which they "clasp we to our hearts, for deathless dower / This close-companioned, inarticulate hour / When twofold silence was the song of love" (1: 86, ll. 12–13). At this moment, nature itself seems to slip out of time. "[T]he dragon-fly / Hangs like a blue thread loosened from the sky:—" suspended in space as this moment is suspended in time (ll. 9–10). All around them, the lovers discover "visible silence, still as the hour-glass" (l. 8). But, as that last line suggests, this moment is also terribly fragile. That it should be compared to an hourglass implies, as Blake might say, that even the earthly outposts of eternity are in love with the products of time. An hourglass, it is true, may stand still for a moment before it is reversed. But it still remains only a fallible, human measure of time, a metaphor for time's progression; time itself continues relentlessly, without pause or surcease.

This is how such timeless moments fare throughout the course of the sonnet cycle itself. The two sections of *The House of Life*, after all, are entitled "Youth and Change" and "Change and Fate"; change, it would seem, is the only constant uniting these fragments. By the end of the cycle, the possibility of the perfect moment has shifted from the present to the future. "Look in my face; my name is Might-have-been; / I am also called No-More, Too-Late, Farewell," cries the lover; "Mark me, how still I am" (1: 225, ll. 1–2, 9). This new stillness is a thanatotic version of the erotic stillness celebrated in *Silent Noon*. It is the stillness of paralysis, of immanent death. But, continues the lover,

> should there dart
> One moment through thy soul the soft surprise
> Of that winged Peace which lulls the breath of sighs,—
> Then shalt thou see me smile, and turn apart
> Thy visage to mine ambush at thy heart
> Sleepless with cold commemorative eyes. (ll. 9–14)

The perfect moment may, perhaps, return, and transform the enmity that divides these two into a new love. But the eyes of the lady suggest the difficulty of such a consummation. They coldly commemorate the failures, the hesitations, and the betrayals that continue to divide the lovers.

If this "high passion" fails to satisfy, perhaps another might prove more successful. Even in these love sonnets, we can see hints of such a possibility: Rossetti aligns artistic experience with love as a means of escaping time. In the stillness of *Silent Noon*, for example, the world seems to have become a beautiful icon, its very insects frozen into the amber of art. This suggestion is fleshed out most completely in the first sonnet of *The House of Life*, in which the very form of the sonnet is celebrated for its ability to embody the perfect moment:

> A Sonnet is a moment's monument,—
> Memorial from the Soul's eternity
> To one dead deathless hour. Look that it be,
> Whether for lustral rite or dire portent,
> Of its own arduous fulness reverent. (1: 176, ll. 1–5)

Art is thus another form of human memory, preserving the all too transient experiences of life in the "arduous fulness" of its form. It offers other consolations as well, the most notable of which being the promise of immortality. It is with this consolation that the sonnet concludes:

> A Sonnet is a coin; its face reveals
> The soul,—its converse, to what Power 'tis due:—
> Whether for tribute to the august appeals
> Of Life, or dower in Love's high retinue,
> It serve; or, 'mid the dark wharf's cavernous breath,
> In Charon's palm it pay the toll to Death. (ll. 9–14)

Pater also celebrates these functions of art. Marius, at one point of his intellectual development, discovers an artistic calling. He has absorbed the "pleasure of the ideal present, of the mystic now" celebrated by the Epicurean Arstippius, but

there would come, together with that precipitate sinking of things into the past, a desire, after all, to retain "what was so transitive." Could he but arrest, for others also, certain clauses of experience, as the imaginative memory presented them to himself! In those grand, hot summers, he would have imprisoned the very perfume of the flowers. To create, to live, perhaps, a little while beyond the alloted hours, if it were but in a fragment of perfect expression:— it was thus his longing defined itself for something to hold by amid the "perpetual flux." (WP, 2: 158–59)

Art for Marius seems to "arrest" the flow of time, to allow memory to hold onto what is so invariably lost in the "precipitate sinking of things into the past." But its appeal is still greater. It allows the self, subject to that flux, to achieve some measure of immortality and thus live beyond its "allotted hours."

It would thus seem that, as one critic has written, "only in art and song could the [Pre-Raphaelite] special moment be arrested."[14] But this idealizing account remains, I think, incomplete. Despite its ostensible identification with the valorization of art, in aestheticist writing, the powers of art to arrest time and achieve immortality are always qualified, limited, or ambiguous. Consider what it means for Marius to "arrest the flux." His wish to "imprison" the "perfume of flowers" may serve to replicate the experience of his senses, but it also seems to violate the essence of the sensation he seeks to replicate. The "perfume of flowers" is beautiful precisely because it cannot be imprisoned, valuable precisely because it accentuates the ephemerality and fragility of all sense experience. A similar implication is contained within Rossetti's sonnet on the sonnet. If a sonnet is indeed a "moment's monument," it can entomb as well as preserve. The terms in which Rossetti praises the sonnet underscore this ambiguity. The sonnet is compared to a tomb or to a coin: it may be a beautiful, perdurable object, but it also seems hard, obdurate, "dead" in its very "deathlessness." It may pay the toll to death by surviving its maker, but it pays another price as well: it becomes an epitaph marking the passage of the experiences it seeks to record.

Aestheticist art, then, faces a temporal dilemma. It wishes to affirm two incompatible values: on the one hand, it seeks to celebrate the most transitory and exquisite of experiences—experiences that are exquisite, in fact, precisely because they are transitory—but on the other, it seeks to use this very means of celebration to escape time itself. *Ars longa, vita brevis est,* but it is precisely the brevity of experiences that aestheticism finds of value. It is this double imperative that finds its fullest expression in the multiplicity of artistic forms aestheticism generates. Aestheticist art habitually seeks simultaneously to valorize temporality and timelessness, to compact both into the same aesthetic form or shape. We have seen one version of this in the form of *The House of Life,* in which the recession of the perfect moment is enacted as the sonnet cycle depicts the fate of change; most of the sonnets in the cycle conform to this pattern as well. And the most famous imaginative structure of aestheticism captures precisely this doubleness: Pater's enigmatic (and much puzzled over, as we shall see) description of "success in life" as "to burn always with [a] hard, gem-like flame" (WP, 1: 236). For Pater's flame is temporally ambiguous.

It represents either a perpetual flickering of consciousness over time or an arrest of consciousness at one lambent moment of its ceaseless metamorphoses. Pater wants both to affirm the mobility, the flickering-ness, of the "quickened, multiplied consciousness," and to hypostatize a moment at which it might be frozen into one perfect moment of perception or revelation. By compacting each into a single figure, he is allowed to have both, but forced to give credence to neither. Like the "duck-rabbit" of Gestalt psychologists, the "hard, gemlike flame" can be understood in two radically different ways from two wholly divergent perspectives.[15] For those who emphasize the power of time, Pater's trope presents an emblem of mutability; for those who search for perfect moments, it provides an icon of perfection and stasis. Like so many of the artworks described throughout *The Renaissance*, the figure is an interpretive conundrum, designed to elicit the very quickened, multiplied thought it celebrates.

Aestheticism's desire simultaneously to hold on to both temporal flux and timeless moments has a number of significant effects on both the manner and the matter of its art. Two such effects are of particular importance to our endeavor, for they would seem to provide potential moments at which these dual imperatives might be fused into a new unity. But, as I shall briefly try to show, even these attempts are not sustained for long: they, too, rapidly move toward an acceptance of dichotomy and irresolution.

The first such effect is aestheticism's tendency toward *ekphrasis*, its habit of creating verbal descriptions of visual works of art and of describing natural scenes as if they were such artworks. One thinks of Rossetti's *Sonnets for Pictures*, Pater's descriptions of artworks in *The Renaissance*, and Wilde's *The Picture of Dorian Gray* as examples of the former, and of Rossetti's *Silent Noon* and *Willowwood* and Pater's landscapes in *Marius the Epicurean* (where the Italian Campagna, for example, is described in terms of a Rosa landscape) as examples of the latter. This imaginative habit would seem to resolve aestheticism's double attitude toward time. These verbal fictions attempt to claim as their own the ability that the nineteenth century defined, after Lessing, as visual art's defining characteristic: its ability to freeze action, its existence in a state of perpetual—and silent—stasis.[16] Ekphrastic verbal fictions, it would seem, thus successfully achieve the kind of synthesis aestheticism yearns for. They seem to bring the perfect moment into a world of temporality, to create timeless icons in the very medium that seems bound most irrevocably to time.

But this desire for unity remains problematic. The works of ek-

phrastic art created by the aestheticist imagination often emphasize
the disjuncture between the temporal modes its audience assumed to
be appropriate to visual and verbal expression. Consider, for example,
this sonnet of Rossetti's, *For a Venetian Pastoral by Giorgione*, often
treated by critics as one of the best examples of Pre-Raphaelite ekphrastic poetry:

> Water, for anguish of the solstice:—nay,
>   But dip the vessel slowly,—nay, but lean
>   And hark how at its verge the wave sighs in
> Reluctant. Hush! beyond all depth away
> The heat lies silent at the break of day:
>   Now the hand trails upon the viol-string
>   That sobs, and the brown faces cease to sing,
> Sad with the whole of pleasure. Whither stray
> Her eyes now, from whose mouth the slim pipes creep
>   And leave it pouting, while the shadowed grass
>   Is cool against her naked side? Let be:—
> Say nothing now unto her lest she weep,
>   Nor name this ever. Be it as it was,—
>   Life touching lips with Immortality. (DGR, 1: 345)

Rossetti interprets Giorgione's *Fête Champêtre* as the representation of a
perfect moment, "sad with the whole of pleasure." The painting seems
poised at the still moment between pleasure and satiety, joy and melan-
cholia. The conceit of the poem, however, is that by speaking a single
word, by uttering "this" (whatever that might be), the peace achieved
by the figures in the painting would be disrupted. At this point, questions begin to pose themselves to the curious reader: Who does Rossetti
hush? The lady? The musicians? Himself? An unruly spectator of the
painting? Rossetti's silence begins to collapse the distance between the
figures in the painting and its observer. Other questions begin to press
upon us, and they too serve to bring the figures in the painting closer
to the audience. What is meant by "this"? Is it the name of a faithless lover, or the fact of his faithlessness? Is one of the musicians this
lover? Is that why the lady has turned her eyes away from them? By
eliciting such questions, Richard Stein suggests, Rossetti "transforms
the painting into a narrative, which is especially striking in view of the
artificial and static relationships on the canvas."[17]

In the sestet, however, the poet appears to think twice about the possibilities he himself has suggested. "Whither stray her eyes now?" he
asks, that last word suggesting that the woman stands on the threshold
of temporality. Poised at this equivocal moment, she seems ready to

enter fully the world the poet and his audience both inhabit—a world that the poem insists is one of time, loss, and death: for she will enter that world, will be given voice in it, only as she "weeps." Rossetti must, then, retreat rapidly from his own narrative; the impending anima-tion of these figures would destroy the very qualities he has turned to the painting to celebrate: perfection, stasis, "Immortality." In the last two lines, he reaffirms the necessary boundary between painting and audience, space and time, silence and language: "Let be," he urges; "be it as it was." But, even as this line pushes the painting back into its resolute spatiality, it suggests other—more disturbing—possibilities. By its complicated play with tense, it suggests that in some completely unexpected way, the painting has already come alive—"be it as it *was*" —and that it must somehow be soothed back into the atemporal per-fection it has just abandoned. By the poem's last line, temporal order is fully restored. The symmetrical purity of the line, its resolute abstrac-tion, and the poem's own subsequent end all close off any possibility of further "speech" by or "life" of the painting with absolute finality; if it speaks at all, it does so to "Immortality." We end where we began, in a world of time, loss, and language, gazing in appreciative wonder at the mute perfection of the silent artifact; and, the poem suggests, we return to that place with some relief.

The implications of this lyric are multiple, and difficult to assess. On the one hand, its major thrust seems to be to disempower the viewer of the painting and the reader of the poem alike; the separation of both from the world of perfect stasis that the figures in the painting enjoy is supplemented by the poem's implication that, if these figures were to enter into our own world, our last glimpse of transcendence would be destroyed. (Perhaps our "lips," too, touch "Immortality" as we speak or write about the painting; perhaps, Rossetti suggests, this is the only way they can do so.) It seems to disempower even more fully Rossetti himself, for it suggests that the only way he can respond to the paint-ing is to hush it into silence. But there is another side to this process. For the conceit of the poem may finally reflect an authorial conceit, the fiction that, were he to express the secrets of these characters, they would be brought into full and resonant life. In a stunning, if wholly implicit, double reversal, Rossetti suggests that his silence testifies all the more powerfully to the thaumaturgic powers of the word; it posi-tions him as a potential poetic Pygmalion, able to bring a being of pure sensuous form into resonant life through the power of his language. Or perhaps it would be more accurate to say that this silence allows him to indulge in the authorial fantasy that he might be another Prospero, another speech-giver who pays the greatest tribute to his own powers by abjuring them. For, with his cry "be it as it was," he performs a kind of negative fiat. By *withholding* the all-powerful word, he claims some share in the painting's creation or, at least, its preservation. In this way, Rossetti's Pre-Raphaelite expression of loss merges into an expression of his potential power—and a power that, again like Prospero's, exerts itself in the enchantment of others (even, in this case, wholly fictive others), whose silence and "stillness" are essential in order to gratify the most compelling needs of the poetic self.

I have lingered on this poem for two reasons. First, it demonstrates the utility of the aestheticists' rhetoric of doubleness. Rossetti, like Pater on aesthetic poetry or Wilde on contradiction, is profoundly *energized* by his ability to, at least figuratively, have things both ways; when he suggests that his stance of passive detachment toward the aesthetic artifact is merely a sign of his greater power over it, he rewrites the rhetoric of loss as a new idiom of empowerment. Second, the poem suggests some of the ways that aestheticism functioned in relation to the central literary *ideés reçus* or topoi of its own moment. The poem enters into the canonical nineteenth-century distinction between verbal and visual art in order to complicate that distinction—to undo and then to remake it in its own terms. This complicated reworking occurs throughout the poem: in its play between poem and painting, time and space, language and vision, plentitude and loss. It is perhaps most evident in the poem's play with gender; for codes of gender, W. J. T. Mitchell has convincingly argued, form one of the master divisions underlying the canonical nineteenth-century distinction between artistic modes or genres. To Lessing, Mitchell writes,

Paintings, like women, are ideally silent, beautiful creatures designed for the gratification of the eye, in contrast to the sublime eloquence proper to the manly art of poetry. Paintings are confined to the narrow sphere of external display of their bodies and of the space which they ornament, while poems are free to range over an infinite realm of potential action and expression, the domain of time, discourse, and history. (110)

Like most nineteenth-century ekphrastic poetry, Rossetti's poem accepts these distinctions, but, unlike many of its contemporaries, it does so in order to complicate them. Thus, fulfilling Mitchell's description of Lessing's hidden agenda with spectacular vividness, Giorgione's painting is symbolized by the woman it depicts; she and it are one most fully in being subjected to the poet's desire for visual gratification. But the painting and woman alike pose a threat to the male poet: they

both threaten to come alive, to speak in their own language, perhaps
even—given the extent of his panic here—to challenge his linguistic
powers. We can see the full dimensions of Rossetti's panic when we
also note that the domain of "time, discourse, and history" he inhabits is itself profoundly limiting; far from offering possibilities for the
"manly" gratifications of action and speech, the world the poet inhabits is defined as a realm of failed desire, loss, and death. Far from
affirming a vision of poetry in which the male poet asserts his power
over the silent, feminized art object, then, this poem projects a world
in which the poet is doubly castrated: once by the universe of loss he
actually inhabits, a second time by the threat that the artwork might
enter that world and deny him a consoling glimpse of transcendence.

The strategy that Rossetti adopts in response is equally cunning and
effective. He concedes his weaknesses, but seeks to make them into
the source of a new imaginative strength. As we have seen, abjuring
speech becomes reinterpreted as a form of power; a negative fiat—let
it be as it was—is proposed as a form of creation; and the thaumaturgic
powers of the word are celebrated by the refusal to speak the magi-
cal word that would undo the painting's perfection. What Rossetti has
thereby done is to complicate Lessing's terms with elegant precision.
He suggests that, just as visual art can threaten to violate generic laws
and enter the order of time and language, so too poetry can annex a
property of painting. In suggesting that poetry can exert its greatest
power not by the speaking of a word but rather by its silencing, Rossetti plots poetry's invasion of the territory previously occupied by art.
To put Rossetti's revisionary move another way, his poem works by de-
taching silence from the visual, spatial, female realm to which Lessing
confines it and placing it in the verbal, temporal, masculine order of
language. In this poem, silence itself becomes a signifier, aspired to by
the gestures of silencing that the poem performs and embedded in it
by its pauses, hesitations, and lacunae; this kind of language, the poem
suggests, is all the more powerful because of the respect it continues
to pay to the power of the word it abjures.

In this resolutely contradictory manner, the poem masters the image
—and the woman it signifies—that had threatened to master it; and
Rossetti remakes himself as a more fully masculinized poet—as a poet
better able to surmount the challenges to his art—by his very abjuring
of the verbal powers conventionally claimed by the male poet. The
implications of this move are multiple, and would take more space
than I have here to delineate fully. Let it merely be said here that Rossetti's intervention in the tradition of Lessing revises that tradition's

notions of language, visual art, and the gender appropriate to each
alike, shaking up the order with which they were linked to one another
and proposing a new way of bringing them together.

To note the full audacity of this poem's revisionary performance is
to be in a position to assess both the possibilities and the problematics
of aestheticism's resolutely double vision. On the one hand, it shows
for us how thoroughly the works of British aestheticism were able to
recompose the traditions they inhabited, to rearrange received experiential, aesthetic, and ideological structures into new, defamiliarizing,
and often excitingly innovative combinations. Indeed, by doing so,
these poems come to perform revisionary moves we are more familiar with in contemporary poetry than in the poetry of the nineteenth
or even the early twentieth century. The giddy play to which Rossetti subjects the tradition of *ekphrasis* is surely unrivaled, not only by
other Romantic and Victorian ekphrastic lyrics but also by those of
the Anglo-American modernists who took up the ekphrastic agenda
of Pre-Raphaelitism and made it their own; it is not until John Ashbery's *Self-Portrait in a Convex Mirror*, I think, that we find a poem in
English that matches Rossetti's in the complexity of its recasting of
the interrelation between poetry, art, and gender. But Rossetti's poem
reminds us that aestheticism's destabilizing doublenesses also have a
self-annulling quality, a limiting effect. The poem pays the price for
its triumph over visual forms by fetishizing *itself*, instancing its own
linguistic performance as the means by which the challenge of visual
art to the male poet is both posed and overcome. And, while this move
is not always the only outcome of aestheticism's double vision, the impulse to cite the work itself as the ground of its own value is one that
aestheticism made so often as to invite the reductive dismissals with
which it has been greeted from its day to our own.

I need to be clear at this point on the scope of my argument. While I
am suggesting that British aestheticism's play with contradictory possibilities is proleptic or anticipatory of postmodern literary practice, I
am not implying that it represents a kind of postmodernism *avant la
lettre*, or even that it represents a significant stylistic resource that funds
or activates postmodern practice. Rather, I would argue that, while
British aestheticism may represent a habit of thought and of writing
whose closest analogue in our tradition is postmodernism, aestheticism
—like postmodernism itself—nevertheless deserves to be treated on its
own terms, as a complex, resolutely experimental mode of imaginative
procedure that achieves certain gains and sustains certain losses. But,
as I have suggested below, my argument *is* more fully directed at lit-

erary history than such a disavowal might initially suggest. For British aestheticism bears a faint but nevertheless perceptible relation to post-modernism, one that is mediated by and best understood in relation to Anglo-American modernism's recasting of the themes, techniques, and topoi of aestheticism itself. For, as I have begun to suggest above and shall suggest more fully below, aestheticism's complicating play with contradictory possibilities was quite directly molded into the static austerities of Anglo-American high modernism; and, as I shall also argue more fully later, one of the ways in which this task was ac-complished was by the modernists' removal of aestheticism's tendency toward autotelism, toward presenting the work itself as the solution to its own imaginative problems, from its vertiginous and irresolute play with contradictory possibilities. Postmodern literary practice, then, may be seen as the recovery of possibilities explored by a tradition that modernism blocked from view; it may thus be most accurately identi-fied not as an advance or a poetic revolution (this, after all, is the myth that fuels modernist discourse, and one from which postmodernism itself is not entirely free, despite its ironic reworkings of that myth), but as a return to possibilities that Anglo-American modernism had previously sought unsuccessfully to efface.

I will have more to say on this subject at the end of this chapter. Here, I want to turn to one other time-obsessed tradition of discourse that aestheticism entered into and complicated fruitfully: the tradi-tion of Victorian historicism. One of the most remarkable features of aestheticist writing in England is its obsessive concern with history, ranging from Morris and Rossetti's medievalism to Pater's privileg-ing of the Renaissance to Swinburne's classical dramatic monologues and visionary reworkings of early Christian, late classical, and Norse mythologies.[18] But when aestheticism turns its attention to the rep-resentation of historical process, it perceives synchronicity as well as diachronicity—and works, in its habitual fashion to mold the two into a complicated and ultimately contradictory aesthetic whole.

Thus—to cite one particularly rich example—Walter Pater's *Marius the Epicurean* is and is not a "historical novel," as Avrom Fleishman and U. C. Knoepflmacher have both observed.[19] On the one hand, the novel attempts imaginatively to recreate the intellectual conditions of the late Roman empire. At this time, historical process itself became acutely manifest. Pater depicts an era of transition: one age is dying, another is powerless to be born. Marius lives, in fact, at the watershed of Western civilization itself. Behind him, impelling the flow of his sensations and ideas, stand Homer, Plato, Aristotle, Epicurus, Virgil, Cicero. Contemporaneous with him are Apuleius, Lucian, and Marcus Aurelius. In front of him stand Augustine and Aquinas; further ahead lie empiricism, the skepticism of Montaigne and Descartes, and modern science. At the same time, however, a powerful anti-historical current courses through the novel. Modern skepticism, Pater reminds us frequently, was anticipated by the Greek skeptical thought that appeared before it. Similarly, the Romans adopted Greek ideas in forming their own; so too, the Christians will adopt classical ideals in forming their own civilization. It seems at times that all of these historical phenomena collapse into each other. The effect created is one of spatiality: Pater describes the whole of Western civilization existing (as Eliot was to put it, in an essay not untouched by Pater's influence) in "a simultaneous order."[20] And, as Fleishman observes, the effect of these acts of historical conflation is to destroy the novel's seeming historicity, its creation of a vivid sense of historical reality: it loses "that temporal specificity and local complexity which is the hallmark of the novel."[21]

We must resist, however, the temptation to emphasize either the novel's spatiality or temporality. For the two are rendered, through the delicate modulations of Paterian prose, inseparable. Let me adduce as an example of their intertwining the following passage, in which Marius's friend, Flavian, muses on the Greek poets who preceded him:

Homer was always telling things after this manner. And one might think that there had been no effort in it: that here was but the almost mechanical transcript of a time, naturally, intrinsically, poetic, a time in which one could hardly have spoken at all without ideal effect, or the sailors pulled down their boat without making a picture in "the great style," against a sky charged with marvels. Must not the mere prose of an age, itself thus ideal, have counted for more than half of Homer's poetry? Or might the closer student discover even here, even in Homer, the really mediatorial function of the poet, as between the reader and the actual matter of his experience; the poet waiting, so to speak, in an age which had felt itself trite and commonplace enough, on his opportunity for the touch of "golden alchemy," or at least for the pleasantly lighted side of things themselves? . . . [But] would not a future generation, looking back upon [Flavian's own work] under the power of the enchanted-distance fallacy, find it ideal to view, in contrast with its own languor—the languor that for some reason (concerning which Augustine will one day have his view) seemed to haunt men always? Had Homer, even, appeared unreal and affected in his poetic flight, to some of the people of his own age as seemed to happen with every new literature in turn? In any case, the intellectual conditions of early Greece had been—how different from these! (WP, 2: 104–5)

Present here are two views of the relation between historical process and the art of a given culture. One privileges the mood or Zeitgeist of a period as crucial; the other sees the poetic talent as somehow synchronic, a "touch of 'golden alchemy'" that transcends its age. To consider a given work in terms of the former is to investigate its relations to the unique spirit or attitude of an age, as Pater himself does in the essay on Johann Winckelmann, where he traces the growth and transformation of the special Greek "temperament." The other view sees these cultural events as produced by qualities that persist over time; Pater also follows this method as, for example, when he describes classicism and Romanticism as synchronic attitudes, not as specific historical events. In this passage, neither view is given priority over the other. To be sure, it may seem at first that historical process is emphasized more powerfully. Not only does Flavian experience Homer's poetry as the product of a culture so "different from" his own, but he is aware that he views this historical phenomenon within history itself, that he (and all future readers) look back to Homer under the power of the "enchanted-distance fallacy." But as we read on, we discover that certain qualities remain constant over time. This point is, characteristically, suggested rather than argued by Pater's assertion that languuour "seemed to haunt men always" and in the almost off-handed reminder that Augustine as well as Flavian (as well, presumably, as Pater himself) will "one day have his view" on these matters. Synchronicity and diachronicity alike thus mark Pater's view of the relation between cultural artifact and historical moment; as usual, he presents us not with an answer to the problems he himself has raised, but a problematic, an interpretive puzzle.

This double attitude toward history is of the greatest importance. For it not only provides one means of defining the particular habit of thought that marks British aestheticism; it also suggests a way of placing that movement in its proper literary context. In the first place, this heightened but simultaneous sense of diachronicity and synchronicity enables us to distinguish British aestheticism from a literary current with which it is often confused: "symbolism," whether we mean symbolism as it is articulated in German idealist philosophy, enacted in French poetry, or privileged in British Romantic theory. Paul de Man has suggested in a seminal essay, *The Rhetoric of Temporality*, that all these systems of thought partake of "the change that takes place in the latter half of the eighteenth century, when the word 'symbol' tends to supplant other denominations for figural language, including that of 'allegory.'"[22] For de Man, the use of "symbol" as a master trope for figurative language itself is a specious and self-defeating mystification; criticism, he suggests, needs to reinstall allegory in its place. "Allegorizing tendencies, though often in a very different form, are present not only in Rousseau but in all European literature between 1760 and 1800. Far from being a mannerism inherited from the exterior aspects of the baroque and rococo, they appear at the most original and profound moments in the works, when an authentic voice becomes audible" (205). For,

[w]hereas the symbol postulates the possibility of an identity or identification, allegory designates primarily a distance in relation to its own origin, and, renouncing the nostalgia and the desire to coincide, it establishes its language in the void of this temporal difference. In so doing, it prevents the self from an illusory identification with the non-self, which is now fully, though painfully, recognized as a non-self. It is this painful knowledge that we perceive at the moments when early romantic literature finds its true voice. (207)

De Man's suggestive revision of the Romantic symbol/allegory distinction may help us to place the rhetoric of English aestheticism in its proper literary setting. The privileging of the symbol in Romantic theory itself symbolizes that unity of dialectical opposites which is at once desired and feared by English Romantic poets. The "balance or reconciliation of opposite or discordant qualities" that Coleridge adduced as the primary "power" of the Romantic imagination is attempted repeatedly and magnificently in the great works of British Romanticism—in *Tintern Abbey* or *Frost at Midnight* or *Sartor Resartus*. All of these yearn after the impossible synthesis of a variety of contradictory phenomena (mind and nature, subject and object, time and timelessness), even though they must defer that consummation to some indefinite future moment or to some distant location imaginable by these authors but not as yet experienced by them.[23] The ways out of this dilemma are various, and have been well described by critics of the last twenty years: Wordsworth's "binding down" to nature; Coleridge's poetics of interruption and deferral; Keats's annexation of the vale of soul-making.[24] It is frequently suggested by critics who seek to fold aestheticism into the Romantic project that its valorizing of art provides a solution to the problem of realizing this desired and feared consummation. For art itself, these critics argue, may be seen as the only successful locus of unity for the oppositions, one that becomes both the ground and the outcome of the union of clashing contraries.[25]

I would suggest, in contrast, that rather than representing the moment in the project of Romanticism that permits, via the totalizing rhetoric of art for art's sake, the movement from Romanticism to modernism, British aestheticism represents an explicit turn to the allegorical, which, as de Man suggests, provides the "true voice" of Romantic practice but which the Romantics themselves devoted much of their energy to denying, evading, or recasting. Aestheticist poetry is alle-gorical not only in its frequent deployment of such explicitly allegori-cal tropes as personification (Rossetti and Swinburne are particularly persistent personifiers, but personification of a different sort can be said to be the basic method of Pater's *Renaissance*, which identifies individual historical figures as representatives of larger imaginative structures or patterns) or even in its resolute self-consciousness and self-referentiality (witness the conscious return to literary modes of the Middle Ages in "Pre-Raphaelite" poetry, or, more subtly, in Pater's adoption of the form of Victorian history writing in order to trans-form the covert agendas of Victorian historicism in *The Renaissance*). Rather, it is the renunciation of the "possibility of an identity or iden-tification" that binds aestheticism to allegory in the de Manian sense of the term. For it is precisely the spirited critique of identity thinking, of the yearning after unity in all its manifestations, that is performed almost ritualistically in work after work of the aesthetic movement. The result is that aesthetic poetry persistently creates conundrums or puzzles that are designed to elicit acts of interpretation but not to pro-vide any resolution for them. "In the world of the symbol," de Man writes, "it would be possible for the image to coincide with the sub-stance, since the substance and its representation do not differ in their being but only in their extension: they are part and whole of the same set of categories." But in the world of allegory, "it remains necessary, if there is to be allegory, that the allegorical sign refer to another sign that precedes it. The meaning constituted by the allegorical sign can then consist only in the *repetition* (in the Kierkegaardian sense of the term) of a previous sign with which it can never coincide, since it is of the essence of this previous sign to be pure anteriority" (207). It is this latter world that aestheticism inhabits—the world, in fact, that it eagerly seeks out.

Aestheticism's double treatment of time places it even more firmly in the context of de Manian allegory. Allegory "designates primarily a distance in relation to its own origin" (207), and aestheticism's double attitude toward time can be understood as a critique of the notion of origin itself. Pater, for example, flirts with the language of origin in order to demolish the notion of origination. The reader brings the desire for causal explanation to bear on the moment we have dis-cussed in *Marius*, only to discover that such explanations unravel when confronted by the recurrence or repetition of certain structures and patterns that annul his or her understanding of causation, origination, and ultimately the historical process itself. Moreover (anticipating subsequent emphases in de Man's work, emphases already present in *The Rhetoric of Temporality*), it is the fact of textuality itself that undoes these myths of origination. For, as opposed to the view that the ancient Greeks lived a poetry far greater than that of their bards, Pater argues (via the "careful student") for the notion of the "mediatorial function of the poet, as between the reader and the actual matter of his experience"; that is, Pater insists on the fact that Homer's texts themselves shaped and were shaped by the seemingly naive and unself-conscious experience of his contemporary readers who, as Pater also reminds us, are known to us only through texts of their own. It is not so much that history is undone by its contact with textuality, but that history itself is understood to be a species of textuality, known not only to the historical observer but also to the historical participant as a vertiginous sequence of signs.

To consider the allegorical dimension of British aestheticism is, in other words, to recognize not only the way in which these texts conform to the de Manian notion of "allegory" but also to see the ways in which they anticipate de Man's subsequent equation between "the rhetorical, figural potentiality of language with literature itself" in which "rhetoric radically suspends logic and opens up vertiginous possibilities of referential aberration." [26] The ease with which Pater's text lends itself to a deconstructive reading is readily apparent, as the critical responses of J. Hillis Miller and Gerald Monsman have eloquently demonstrated—and the same arguments can (and should) be made with respect to the work of Dante and Christina Rossetti, William Morris, and A. C. Swinburne, at the very least. [27] Yet at the risk of sounding naive, I wonder whether the rapidity with which a deconstructive vocabulary has emerged in the criticism of British aestheticism might not itself be drawn forth by something in that literature itself. The very ease, in other words, with which one can "deconstruct" a Paterian text like the ones I have cited, combined with Miller's own assertion that "Pater is effective today as a precursor of what is most vital in contemporary criticism," leads one to wonder whether aestheticism itself might not represent a moment within the very tradition of thought from which deconstructive praxis springs, and to which deconstructive theory then naturally refers.*

*The lines of transmission between British aestheticism and Franco-American deconstruction are traced by Miller himself in "Walter Pater"; they lead from Ruskin (and Pater) to Proust; from Proust to Benjamin; from Proust and Benjamin to Barthes and Derrida and de Man. Miller's point is that this is one possible genealogy one can construct from Pater, and that Pater's own resolute doubleness is mimicked by the

My point here is not to "ground" deconstruction in a specific moment in literary history, or to accuse it of a lingering or even a forthright aestheticism (although both of these arguments are hardly untenable). Rather, what I mean to suggest is that the ease with which British aestheticism may be incorporated into the deconstructive canon might provide us with an effective means of understanding British aestheticism itself. For example, viewing aestheticism as "allegorical" in the de Manian sense helps us understand more clearly its relations with the Romantic tradition from which aestheticism in England springs. Aestheticism represents the fullest, the most explicit, expression of what de Man would call the "negative moment" within that tradition —not merely the moment at which negativity as such is fully experienced, but the moment in which the Romantic attempt to turn from antinomy to dialectic, from the emphasis on oppositions to the understanding of the potential reconcilability of such oppositions, is explicitly understood to be a necessary and inevitable failure. Aestheticism's relation to Romanticism, at least in England, is thus essentially double. On the one hand, aestheticism ostensibly denies or even negates the seeming teleology of the Romantic project, but in doing so, it works out most fully the buried or repressed logic of that project, thereby putting the more problematic qualities of that project on display.

This point needs to be made less abstractly; let me do so by discussing the question of poetic form. For aestheticist poetry habitually inhabits the modes or forms characteristic of Romantic poetry, only to undermine them from within. Swinburne's poetry provides a number of examples of this procedure: *The Lake of Gaube*, for example, is a brilliant rewriting of the nonce form we might want to call the Romantic Alp lyric. Like Book XIV of Wordsworth's *Prelude*, or Coleridge's *Hymn Before Sunrise*, or Shelley's *Mont Blanc*, Swinburne's poem is a sublime ode to a mountain landscape; but, unlike Wordsworth or Coleridge or Shelley, Swinburne turns from the evocation and celebration of an Alpine landscape to one in the Pyrenees. This shift of physical location is performed throughout the rest of the poem, in which Swinburne evokes conventions of Romantic poetry, but alters their ontological status. The poem opens, for example, in the typical language of the Romantic sublime, with a celebration of the power of the mountain:

> The sun is lord and god, sublime, serene,
> And sovereign on the mountains: earth and air

---

doubleness of the response of subsequent critics to Pater, in Pater's paradoxical shared paternity of Eliot and de Man, Pound and Benjamin. Miller, "Walter Pater," p. 97.

> Lie prone in passion, blind with bliss unseen
>   By force of sight and might of rapture, fair
>   As dreams that die and know not what they were.
> The lawns, the gorges, and the peaks, are one
> Glad glory, thrilled with sense of unison
> In strong compulsive silence of the sun. (ACS, 6: 200, ll. 1–8)

"The sun is God," Turner is said to have cried on his deathbed, but Swinburne goes Turner one better by imagining a universe in which the sun is "lord and god" and sovereign.[28] The sublimity of this God, however, is overtly sinister: He celebrates the marriage of earth and air, their apocalyptic union into one "glad glory," but only by means of a "strong compulsive silence." This God subjugates the mountain and the sky, forcing them to "lie prone in passion, blind with bliss unseen," as if their very unity represented a perversely ordained copulation, one in which "passion" slid into its root sense of suffering and "bliss" returned to its etymological sense of wounding or crippling. The Sun is not the son-God of the New Testament, but rather a representative of God the Father: it is the very image of patriarchal authority compelling the world into order and hierarchy.[29]

The poem begins, then, with the typical drama of the Romantic sublime: an encounter with a power or entity of such transcendent, awe-inspiring strength that the poet is led by the sheer force of comparison to feel blocked, powerless, impotent. As Thomas Weiskel brilliantly argued, Romanticism prescribed various solutions to this dilemma: an identification with the landscape in which this force manifested itself, for example, or the projection of a poetic countersublime that would attempt to match rhetorically what was experienced in and beyond nature.[30] But here, Swinburne conspicuously chooses none of these canonical strategies of the English Romantic tradition. Rather, his poem turns on them by (literally) turning to a different scene, which it treats with an entirely different kind of language:

> Flowers dense and keen as midnight stars aflame
>   And living things of light like flames in flower
> That glance and flash as though no hand might tame
>   Lightnings whose life outshone their stormlit hour
>   And played and laughed on earth, with all their power
> Gone, and with all their joy of life made long
> And harmless as the lightning life of song,
> Shine sweet like stars when darkness feels them strong. (ll. 9–16)

From the sublime order of the mountain landscape, the poet's gaze shifts to the protean world at his feet, a world in ceaseless change.

From a world of causes, he turns to the world of effects, the world of flowers and salamanders glittering in the sunlight. This world is rendered in a language that is the antithesis of the language employed in the first stanza. Instead of a language that emphasizes authority, hierarchy, and silence, the language of non- or un-sublimity present in this stanza presents a kaleidoscopic set of shifting terms in which hierarchy is impossible to discern. Thus, for example, the priority of the literal over the figurative proposed in the first stanza, in which the entire stanza provides an explication of the poem's claim that "the sun is god," is replaced by a language in which literal and figurative flow into each other with chimerical volatility. Flowers are like stars, salamanders are like stars are like flowers, are like lightnings on earth, which is like the lightning life of song, which is like stars: such is how the stanza asks to be construed, each figure growing out of or referring to a previous one, climaxing with a pun on lightning that turns the poem from the "compulsive silence" of the sun to sweet music of the spheres. As if in imitation, Swinburne's language itself here becomes salamanderlike: capable of an infinity of changes of tone and mood and meaning as it eddies and scurries about on the page. And as it does so, it undermines the authority of the language of sublimity itself, proposing in its place a linguistic model that emphasizes fluidity, metamorphosis, transformation, all subversively existing under, but also ramifying beyond, the gaze of the hierarchical Sun-God.

A similar revisionary dynamic obtains not only throughout Swinburne's oeuvre, but also that of Rossetti, Pater, and even the mature Wilde. Thus Rossetti's *The Woodspurge* enters into and parodies the Romantic quest poem, turning from the quest for meaning, consolation, and presence in nature not to the typical Romantic discovery of powers of the Imagination itself, but rather to the barren recognition that "the woodspurge has a cup of three" (DGR, 1: 298, l. 16). In his essay on Wordsworth, Pater revises Wordsworth's definition of poetry as "emotion recollected in tranquility" in such a way as to transform emotion into sensation, tranquility into utter passivity, into the claim that "the end of life is not action but contemplation—*being* as distinct from *doing*—a certain disposition of the mind" (WP, 5: 62); countless other examples could be adduced. The point here, however, is not to enumerate them, but rather to suggest that the aestheticists responded to their Romantic predecessors with a complex dialectic of identification and rejection, their revisionary impulses and their sense of their own filiation at constant and ferocious war with each other. Perhaps the best way to understand this persistent sense of rebellion against a Romanticism with which the poet nevertheless identifies is to understand the generational dilemma these writers and artists felt. The aestheticists look out on a world where their own idealism seemed on the one hand silly or even monstrous and on the other wholly necessary. To put the matter in biographical terms: this generation had witnessed Wordsworth write sonnets on public execution; Coleridge turn into a hollow, shambling wreck; Keats, Shelley, and Byron die. Moreover, they lived in a time of conscious anti-Romanticism; a time when the Romantic project in all its social, political, and imaginative manifestations was understood by their culture at large to be a failure.[31] But the aestheticists found themselves equally incapable of valorizing the reaction. They did not—could not—see themselves as new Wordsworths, or even new Keatses, but by the same token, they hardly wanted to play Matthew Arnold and dismiss Shelley as a "pale, ineffectual angel beating his wings in the void," or critique Wordsworth's animism, the decline of his poetic powers, even the division of his poetry by criteria derived from mental functions rather than Greek genres.[32] Nor did they want to play Ruskin and deny the origins of their own imaginative power by critiquing the Romantic poets who served as the fundamental source of their inspiration.

What I am suggesting here is that the aestheticist solution to this dilemma, if it can be said to be a solution, is to save appearances by taking the Romantic project to its logical extreme. In poem after poem, painting after painting, Romantic themes and topoi are taken up as a self-conscious, even obsessive matter of course. But in these same works, the potential that always existed within these themes, conventions, or topoi for expressing or discovering the failure of the project itself is exploited to the fullest, and value is sought after and in the experience of those failures. Swinburne's turn from the sun to the salamander-filled shadows or Rossetti's mock voyage into nature is the pattern described by a number of aestheticist lyrics. We are led (in Geoffrey Hartman's phrase) from the sublime to the hermeneutic, and led there as in many Romantic lyrics through the detour of an imaginative failure or insufficiency. But where in Romantic lyrics the discovery of insufficiency in one arena of experience leads to the fictive quickening of another, aestheticist poetry refuses any such compensatory gain. And while the Romantic poet claims to discover a term that might guarantee the success of his project only soon to discover the insufficiency of that term—Nature, the imagination, or whatever lies in between—aestheticist writers refuse any totalizing consolation, creating instead enigmatic fictions whose only acknowledgment of value lies in the refusal to discover any such value, or, at best, to discover values that are as transitory and interpretively opaque as the life of a salamander or the flickering of a flame. Aestheticist lyrics thus establish themselves as (at best) a kind of closed interpretive network that shifts the burden of divination and imaginative understanding from the poet to the reader; they just as often present themselves as hermetic structures that resist the reader's interpretive efforts as forcefully as they invite them.

We may thus see why aestheticist fictions are so susceptible to being read in de Manian terms. Foregrounding their own artifice, figuring their own figurativeness, they establish themselves at the beginning of a chain of interpretive deductions whose end is never clear but whose importance is constantly manifest. But to say this is not to imply, as Miller begins to suggest in his "Partial Portrait" of Pater, that aestheticist writing is fully "allegorical," at least in the de Manian sense of the term. For despite its frequent recourse to the rhetoric of loss and the exploration of the mechanisms of desire, aestheticism fails fully (or even partially) to "renounc[e] the nostalgia and the desire to coincide" that constitutes the sign of allegorical "authenticity" for de Man (207). Nor does the poetry of British aestheticism, as Miller seems to suggest, serve as a sufficient model for language or art as such. Aestheticist writing does not celebrate its own figurativeness as an end in and of itself, but rather does so in order to mourn its own alienation from the literal. It does not rejoice in the play of plurisemeity, but hopes to overcome it, even as it knows it cannot. And, as I shall now suggest, it does not "prevent . . . the self from an illusory identification with the non-self, which is now fully, though painfully, recognized as a non-self," but rather experiences the alienation of self from other and responds by idealizing erotic communion as the way of partially overcoming such alienation.

The Experience of Otherness

British aestheticism's fascination with the Other structures its second major duality. On the one hand, British aestheticism habitually denies the existence or the importance of any phenomenon beyond the confines of the self. In the Conclusion to *The Renaissance*, for example, Pater asserts that no communication, much less consummation, can take place with any other person standing outside "the thick wall of personality." His vision here is radically solipsistic: "Every one of [our] impressions is the impression of the individual in his isolation, each mind keeping as a solitary prisoner its own dream of a world" (1: 236). With typical paradoxical brilliance, Pater's student Wilde translated Pater's idiom of solipsism into the language of ethics. In *The Soul of Man Under Socialism*, Wilde argues that man's sole obligation is to "real[ise] himself perfectly" (*Artist*, p. 257). Any attempt to act out of motives of disinterestedness or altruism is only, he suggests, an unwittingly coercive form of selfishness, the more insidious because it masks itself as good will.

Yet for all this polemical praise of solipsism and selfishness, British aestheticism also spends much of its time lamenting the absence of a significant Other whom, it hopes, might somehow be able to complete or reunify the fragmented, isolated self. Indeed, this habit of thought is one of the distinctive markers of the British tradition of aestheticism. For in this matter, as in its putative "symbolism," the English tradition contrasts fruitfully with the tradition of French aestheticism (or even of French *decadence* with which it has frequently found itself confused). In his famous novel *A Rebours* (1880), for example, J. K. Huysmans notoriously portrayed an immersion in the experience of the self that mirrors Pater's praise of solipsism. Des Esseintes wills himself into Pater's prison of the self: by seeking to explore and refine every possible sense experience and combination of sense experiences, he seems to live as closely as possible to Pater's ideal life of perpetual "sharp and eager observation." In one of those instances of cultural dialogue that mark the unfolding of aestheticism in England, Huysmans's text became what Swinburne called the "Golden Book" of the later, self-consciously "decadent" phases of the aesthetic movement, its canonicity confirmed when Oscar Wilde stole major portions of Huysmans's narrative in order to flesh out the skimpy plot of *Dorian Gray*. But no Englishman was inclined (or able) fully to imitate their French counterpart; quite the contrary. Instead, the aestheticists—even Wilde —passed their time lamenting the incompleteness of the solitary self and in imagining the means of approaching the mysterious, powerful, but absent Other.

The poetry of Dante Gabriel Rossetti provides a good example of this imaginative habit, and of its consequences. Rossetti's work characteristically portrays a solitary consciousness immured in its own isolation, but the drama of the typical Rossetti lyric inheres in the attempt of such a consciousness to escape its isolation, usually with the aid of an idealized but absent lover. Such a repeated portrayal might seem an expression of a particularly obsessive form of narcissism—a diagnosis frequently offered of Rossetti, as of British aestheticism itself. But such a reading severely underrates the dialectical quality of Rossetti's concerns, and therefore of aestheticism's as well. Rossetti's poetry is most crucially engaged not in the attempt to render fully the experience of isolation, but rather to give an account of the experience of otherness itself—an account that can most fully be rendered, it would seem, through the very failure of that experience.[33]

The full complexity with which this issue is handled by Rossetti is suggested by his most famous dramatic monologue, *Jenny*. Recent criticism of that monologue has been voluminous; I will only discuss it briefly by way of suggesting that Rossetti's interests in the poem lie both in delineating his protagonist's narcissism and in gesturing toward the otherness of the other that the protagonist encounters— and evades.[34] We may note both moves most concisely if we remember that this poem presents itself as a dramatic monologue in the tradition of Browning, but—in characteristic aestheticist fashion—utterly alters the conventions of the form. Like Browning's monologists, the book- ish "young man" of *Jenny* directs his musings to a subject represented by but not present in the poem; unlike those monologists, however, he addresses an audience incapable of hearing him: she remains asleep for most of the work. Throughout the poem, the speaker attempts to understand "Jenny"—a prostitute whose real name is unknown to him but is almost certainly *not* Jenny—in terms drawn from his own experi- ence, especially the texts with which he has come to understand that experience, largely drawn from classical or Biblical sources. But the harder he tries to define Jenny in terms of classical myth or through Biblical tags, the more fully she evades his mediations. Indeed, she soon "almost fades from view" and

> A cipher of man's changeless sum
> Of lust, past, present and to come,
> Is left. A riddle that one shrinks
> To challenge from the scornful sphinx. (DGR, 1: 91, ll. 278–81)

"Ashamed of [his] own shame," the speaker begins to suggest that his mockery of Jenny is really a mocking judgment on himself (l. 384). For, as he admits here, the "changeless sum / Of lust" for which Jenny is but a cipher—in that usual conjunction of economic and sexual "spending" which, as Steven Marcus has shown, pervades the Victo- rian sexual imagination—is that of the speaker's own economic and sexual power.[35] In short, the speaker's own language begins to reveal that Jenny poses a riddle to which the answer, like the sphinx's, is "man."

It is appropriate, then, that Jenny remains asleep throughout the monologue, for she never becomes fully awake, fully sentient, or even fully alive to the speaker. Despite—or perhaps because of—his persistent attempts to understand and bring her to judgment, she remains intractably, inevitably alien, existing beyond his reflections of her, and suggesting their inadequacy. By this process, the text succeeds where its speaker fails. For by showing the speaker's failure adequately to understand and encompass Jenny—by showing, in fact, that his narcissism is so great that the metaphors which fail to define her succeed only in defining himself—the text gives us a sense of Jenny's authentic being extending beyond the confines of the speaker's consciousness and imagination. Precisely because the speaker's linguistic mediations fail to render her with any justice, Jenny causes those mediations to fold back on themselves; she reminds us of the artificiality of the speaker's own awareness and that of the very form in which he expresses himself. In sum, the trick of the poem is to give us a speaker describing Jenny so inadequately that her otherness is preserved from his attempts to appropriate it one last time.

Marius the Epicurean, on the other hand, has rarely been accused of giving any sense whatsoever of the authentic or "the real." Indeed, as we have seen, critics habitually attempt to drum it out of the tradition of the British novel entirely for its lack of temporal and local specificity. But whatever its generic provenance, *Marius* extends the aestheticist concerns with the experience of otherness. Indeed, like Rossetti's poem, it understands that this experience is essentially a dialectical one—that the self itself is molded through its experiences of significant others. But where Rossetti uses that understanding to anatomize the narcissism of his protagonist and by extension the psychology of male domination itself, Pater pushes his analysis to even more disturbing ends. In the final analysis, he suggests, the self formed through its experience of others is essentially unstable—so unstable, in fact, that it yearns to overcome its boundaries at the price of embracing its own extinction.

As critics have come to realize, *Marius* is an intricately patterned novel, one structured by significant repetitions and internal correspondences.[36] One such pattern is of particular interest to our endeavor: in each section of the book, Marius encounters another character who represents possibilities to which he aspires, but from which he seems alienated. In the first section of the book, this role is performed by Marius's classmate, Flavian; in the second, by the Christian soldier

Cornelius; in the third, by Marcus Aurelius; in the fourth, Cornelius and Aurelius vie for supremacy over Marius's mind. Through each of these characters, Marius encounters certain values and experiences: Flavian introduces Marius to poetry and to the temptations of the flesh; Aurelius introduces Marius to stoic philosophy and the chastening of the flesh; Cornelius introduces Marius to Christianity and the transcendence of the flesh. Marius is attracted by each of these various positions but, in the end, remains distant from all of them. He dies a pagan, although neither wholly Epicurean nor wholly Stoic, but is given the last rites of the Church and buried in a Christian ceremony.

This pattern raises a number of possibilities that Pater explores suggestively. The process we see enacted here is proleptic of the description Freud was to give of the psychic mechanism of identification 30 years after the publication of *Marius*. For it is through the mechanism of identification, Freud comes increasingly to suggest, that the sense of self is first established, and it is through further acts of identification that it is subsequently maintained.[37] Pater both anticipates and extends Freud's analysis. At the center of the process of identification, he suggests, is the wish to replace the Other, to mimic or mirror enough aspects of another's character that one might absorb him. But such an act is ultimately unsatisfactory. To model oneself on another in this manner ultimately forces one to confront the gap between the self and the significant Other. There is a further twist to Pater's analysis. Ultimately, he implies, this act of substitution or replacement might not be impossible; in fact, he suggests with his own mixture of fascination and fear, it might prove to be all too possible— achievable through the annihilation of the very psyche that the act of identification is designed to maintain.

We can best see this mechanism in Pater's description of Marius's schoolboy crush on his older classmate, Flavian. Flavian represents all that Marius is not, and all that he aspires to be. He is a figure of both "intellectual power" and sexual experience—Flavian has already "yielded himself . . . to the seductions of that luxurious town." Marius comes under Flavian's "dominion" and sway (WP, 2: 53–54, 55). This is true in a literal sense and in a metaphorical one as well: he aspires, under Flavian's influence, to become a poet like his admired friend. Or to be more precise, he seeks to become a poet of a particular stamp, for Flavian is a first-century aesthete. In addition to his love of "dress, and dainty food, and flowers . . . [he] cultivated also that foppery of words, of choice diction" (2: 54). "Amoral" and believing "only in himself, in the brilliant and mainly sensuous gifts he had, or meant to acquire," Flavian becomes a figure symbolizing to Marius the dying world he inhabits (2: 55, 56).

Despite his feelings, however, Marius finds himself increasingly separated from his friend. Flavian, as the representative of a dying world, must himself die, and he does so through a highly symbolic plague, which emphasizes both his own morbidity and that of the culture he represents. But as Flavian grows pale, spectre thin, and dies, his relations with Marius are transformed. When sickness first descends on his friend, Marius acts, as is his wont, as Flavian's servant, but as the disease progresses, their roles reverse. Flavian lies "with a sharply contracted hand in the hand of Marius, to his almost surprised joy" (2: 121). He begins to revert to childhood; rather than acting as a servant, or at least an emotional dependent, Marius comes to serve as something like Flavian's parent; the dying youth is now wholly dependent on him. But such a reversal causes Marius some discomfort. He feels "guilty" for his own health, and, characteristically, "longed to take his share in the suffering, that he might understand so the better how to relieve it" (2: 121). At this point, however, all Marius can experience is the "alienation, this sense of distance" from Flavian that, throughout their friendship he had wished to overcome. When Flavian dies, Marius realizes with sorrow the totality, and the inevitability, of their separation.

This pattern is extended, and taken to its logical conclusion, at the end of the novel. Again, Marius's relation with another involves him with both the mechanism of identification and the fact of death; this time, however, Marius is able to effect the substitution that lies at the center of the process of identification, albeit at a fearsome cost. Marius's friendship with the Christian Cornelius, like that with Flavian, brings him in touch with possibilities he had hitherto only imagined. "Identifying himself with Cornelius in so dear a friendship, through him, Marius seemed to touch, to ally himself to, actually to become a possessor of the coming world" (3: 209–10). Cornelius, however, is seized by the superstitious countryfolk who think him somehow responsible for an earthquake and plague; to save his friend, Marius replaces him and, while in captivity, contracts a fever and dies.

Here, too, friendship leads Marius to wish to undertake an act of substitution. Pater takes pains to demonstrate that such a substitution takes place on all levels. Half in love with Cornelius's own beloved, Cecilia, Marius replaces Cornelius so that the latter may depart "on his blithe and hopeful way, as he believed, to become Cecilia's husband" (3: 213–14). Half attracted to the life of the martyr to which Cornelius aspires, Marius has, he realizes, been left to die in his place. In fact, at the moment of his death, Marius is treated by those around him as if he were Cornelius, as if he were a true Christian martyr, although at this point Marius is still as much a pagan aesthete as a Christian.

This ending is an apt climax not only to Marius's relations with Cornelius, but to the attitude toward others he takes throughout the novel. For the death of Marius reenacts the demise of Flavian as well as that planned for Cornelius. Both Marius and Flavian die of the plague, a disease whose outbreak Pater links to the superstitions of the local pagans. The patterns of the two deaths repeat each other precisely. In Marius's death, too, we see the same initial feverishness, the same defiant efflorescence of the will to live, the same slow decline towards death in which the invalid returns to childish passivity. This similarity bears two readings. On the one hand, it suggests the relative merits of paganism and Christianity. The pagan dies alone, his death coming as "a final revelation of nothing less than the soul's extinction" (2: 127). The Christian dies in a community, and with a promise of perpetual life. On the other hand, the similarity of the two deaths also suggests an opposite implication: that death is the only possible outcome of the acts of identification and substitution Marius undertakes throughout the novel. In death, the bounds of the individual ego against which Marius has been straining are released. While he remains alive, Marius can only repeatedly discover the distance between himself and his paragon of the moment. But at the moment of his death, Marius achieves his goal of unity with his friend Flavian; further, by dying in his place (reenacting, of course, the Christian sacrifice) he becomes as identical to his friend Cornelius as is possible. The mechanism of identification, Pater suggests, may be the means by which the individual ego forms and orders itself; but it is also, he implies, linked to the deepest expression of the death impulse itself. For only in such death can the ego perform the act of substitution it aspires to throughout life. Only by dying can the self itself become an Other.

Selfhood, otherness, and death all come together as well at the Gothic climax of Oscar Wilde's *The Picture of Dorian Gray*. When Dorian's body is discovered, he is revealed to be literally other than himself—a foul corpse "withered, wrinkled, and loathsome of visage" whose identity is confirmed only by the rings on its fingers, while a portrait of his youthful visage stares mockingly at his survivors (*DG*, 224).* This moment is—as Wilde might put it—profoundly shallow; Dorian's "self"—if a character already so thoroughly compromised by his author's resolute self-consciousness may be said to have a self —has become fully (if immortally) alienated into Dorian's property, into the fine things that he wears and the finer portrait that Basil Hallward made of him. And here, as throughout the novel, Wilde gives his own distinctive spin to British aestheticism's complicated play with selfhood and otherness. He suggests that the individual subject may reach through the prison bars of its consciousness not only by stretching for the absent but all-powerful Other but also by grasping rich and rare objects—a process depicted, rather interminably, in that long digression in which the narrative inventories, with the fervor of a Huysmans-drunk accountant, Dorian's jewels, wine collection, and artworks. Its horrific finale suggests, however, that the novel's hyperbolic literalization of the doctrine of possessive individualism—of the notion that you are what you own—is complemented by its interest in the human body as the source and end of authentic human identity, the notion that you are what you feel; throughout Wilde's novel the body is both the vehicle through which some more fully vibrant form of experience may be captured and, as its final tableau suggests, the means by which that experience is crucially limited.

In these ways, then, Wilde explicitly revises the aestheticist tradition, augmenting its idiom of self and Other by proposing a dialectic between body and commodity as the ultimate ground of human identity. Here, to specify further, Wilde takes issue directly with his former teacher Walter Pater. Pater argues in the Conclusion to *The Renaissance* that the isolated self may expand itself by increasing the number of fine, rich, and rare impressions it has of the world; but these impressions are predominantly visual ones, entering through the eyes and shaping subjects into little scopophiles. In *Dorian Gray*, by contrast, we extend our experience by augmenting all our sensations of the world, and these sensations importune us through every possible sensory avenue—at least until death, at which point the body remains as an emblem of the passage of those experiences and a sign of its own corruption. And in the Conclusion—as we shall see more fully below —Pater asks us to embrace a metonymic chain that leads us from one perfect moment of intense apprehension to another; Wilde, too, de-

---

* I owe this observation, and much else as well, to Laurie Edelstein.

mands that we embrace the transitoriness of desire, but he supplies us with a mass-produced consumer item with which to do so: "A cigarette is the perfect type of a perfect pleasure. It is exquisite, and it leaves one unsatisfied. What more can one want?" (79).

But Wilde's revisionary energies do not cease with this move; indeed, they extend directly into the drama of subjectivity and otherness that Rossetti and Pater had scripted so sedulously. Wilde does not jettison entirely the drama of the yearning self and all-powerful Other so crucial to Pater and Rossetti, but rather critiques and reformulates it —and then, characteristically, critiques his own critique. Wilde revises this drama and begins to solve the dilemmas it poses by compacting both its terms into the self itself. To Wilde, as Dorian's remarks suggest, the self is always a self and an Other; while the individual subject always grasps her or his selfhood in full autonomy—one is always a fully integral self *to* oneself—she or he only does so as the result of an intersubjective, discursive, social process. Much is gained by this view. The subject is not left immured in a state of monadic or melancholic solitude, as is the case with Rossetti and Pater; nor does it have to struggle to make contact with the others surrounding it. Rather, each individual subject is understood to be already permeated by otherness, to be generated and regenerated through a process of constant interaction with others. But there are problems with this expanded notion of subjectivity as well. This account of the subject represents a version of the subject as perpetually available to the manipulation of those around it. Subjectivity so constituted, that is to say, is never free from the forces of power, domination, and control. Indeed, it is rendered by its very constitution incapable of resisting the more overt power plays launched against it—power plays, in fact, that have themselves served to shape the subject.

Wilde's rewriting of the aestheticist drama of self and Other, then, is both revisionary—ostentatiously so—and, powerfully, self-critical. We can witness both aspects of this process in the novel's treatment of the intersubjective and erotic dynamic it labels "influence." This dynamic is represented to us in the novel's portrayal of the genesis of Dorian Gray's identity. For Dorian is initially presented as a *tabula rasa* who has excited the sensibilities of Basil Hallward by his sheer physical attractiveness. Basil responds to this attraction, however, by sounding a note that will ironically echo back onto Dorian through the mediation of Basil's friend and rival, Lord Henry Wotton—the note of "influence." When he first met the youth, he tells Lord Henry, he experienced "a subtle influence [that] had passed from him to me, and for the first time I saw in the plain woodland the wonder I had always looked for, and always missed" (10). "I did not want any external influence in my life," Basil proclaims. "I have always been my own master; had at least always been so, till I met Dorian Gray" (6). Although his creation of the infamous portrait attempts to deploy the powers of visual representation to "master" the figure whom he feels "masters" him, Basil nevertheless still speaks of Dorian throughout the scene in the same language of abasement and control: "As long as I live," Basil tells Wotton, "the personality of Dorian Gray will dominate me" (29).

And it is precisely this language that Lord Henry echoes in his own verbal seduction of Dorian. Ignoring Basil's plea—"don't influence him" (14)—Henry sets out to do just that; and, tellingly, he does it precisely by telling Dorian that he is doing it. "To influence a person," Lord Henry says as they stand together while Basil finishes his portrait of Dorian, "is to give him one's own soul. He does not think his natural thoughts, or burn with his natural passions. . . . He becomes the echo of some one else's music, an actor of a part that has not been written for him" (17). And Dorian responds to Wotton's words by enacting them. Dorian is "dimly conscious that entirely fresh influences were at work within him. Yet they seemed to him to have come really from himself" (18).

"Influence," then, designates that activity by which the individual subject is configured by the discursive efforts of others; in Dorian's case, as Ed Cohen has argued, two men undertake this task in spirited homosocial and homosexual competition with each other and together endow the youth with depth, with interiority, with subjectivity itself —in short, with those "influences . . . at work within him . . . [that] seemed to him to have come really from himself." [38] But as the novel progresses, so does Dorian's sense of his own ability to wield the powers of "influence." To a certain extent, this is true merely by virtue of his appearance and demeanor; by his sheer beauty, he "dominates" Basil; by his eager receptivity, he "enthralls" the jaded Lord Henry (35). But it is increasingly true of his behavior as well. Over the course of the novel, Dorian becomes progressively more aware of his powers over others, such as Sybil Vane, the artless actress he woos and abandons, or the countless young men for whom his "friendship," according to the ever-moral Basil, exerts a fatal—if melodramatically rendered— influence: "One has the right to judge of a man by the effect he has on his friends [says Basil]. Yours seem to lose all sense of honour, of goodness, of purity" (151). And he is also increasingly willing to deploy those powers to seduce, manipulate, or, in the case of Basil, murder those others—to dominate as well as be dominated in turn in the mutually constitutive game of "influence."

This reading of the novel, it should be said, brushes it ever so slightly against the grain—and does so, ironically, by reading *with* the grain, by taking its portentous tone and parodic rewriting of Victorian sensationalism all too seriously. Obviously, reckoning with the self-undermining tonalities of the text and its ostentatious artificing must qualify or at least complicate my interpretation. But Wilde, in my view, is never quite so serious as when he is at his most playful, and the very self-parodic tone of these passages is revelatory of his pronounced ambivalence on the subject of the subject. Beneath the campy sensationalism of these scenes—Dorian murdering Basil, blackmailing his former companion Alan Campbell into disposing of the corpse, frequenting opium dens, seducing innocent village maidens—lies the nub of Wilde's critique of his own meditations on subjectivity. For contained within these moments lies the recognition that something we might call, for want of a better word, will impels individual subjectivity as powerfully as do the representations of others.

"Life is not governed by will or intention" (216–17), Lord Henry tells Dorian when the latter decides that it is high time to reform himself, and I do not mean to employ the term in the reductive sense Henry mocks here. Rather, I mean to suggest that, having himself come into being through the representational efforts of others, Dorian strives to assert himself as an integral, empowered self, but he can only do so by acting with increasing aggression, irrationality, even violence toward others—especially toward those figures who constructed "Dorian" in the first place. It is not insignificant that Dorian murders one of those figures, Basil, and wearies palpably of the other, Lord Henry; his exercise of will, his assertion of his own "personality," demands that he strike out against the figures who shaped that sense of self in the first place.

But this process does not end here; it has one last, self-recoiling step to go before the novel ends. For in this process of willful self-assertion, the novel shows, Dorian can only repeat the gestures that have configured him—can only perform actions that bear all the hallmarks of those acts that shaped him in the first place. His rebellion against Lord Henry is emblematic. Late in the novel, Dorian denounces his friend: "You poisoned me with a book once. I should not forgive that. Harry, promise me that you will never lend that book to any one. It does harm" (218). And in this descent into bourgeois moralism, he rebels against Wotton and denies the inner influence his friend has exercised over him the only way he can: by playing Philistine. Yet Dorian claims his own voice here only by echoing that of another. For in his denunciation of the immoral influence of literature, Dorian sounds exactly like Basil, and particularly Basil when he is in full throat on the subject of Dorian's malign influence. In other words, having killed Basil in order to escape his relentless sermonizing, Dorian takes to intoning sermons on his own.

And there is a further irony to Dorian's deployment of a ringing moralistic rhetoric. While his accusation against Lord Henry might seem the most un-Wottonian gesture possible (Wotton himself scoffs at Dorian), it nevertheless ironically validates the point of many of Lord Henry's (and Oscar Wilde's) paradoxes—that of the primacy of art over life. Though Dorian descends into an ironic form of bourgeois moralism that would reverse the terms of that equation, he nevertheless ironically grants art the power to enthrall, the power to corrupt—endows it fully, in other words, with all the characteristics that Lord Henry imagines it to possess. (We shall see a similarly ironic linkage between the aesthete and the moralist in Henry James's story, *The Author of Beltraffio*.) In resisting Lord Henry's paradoxes and striving to affirm his own identity, in other words, Dorian paradoxically confirms those paradoxes and collapses himself into the very lineaments he had striven to escape. Like Lord Henry himself, Dorian amazes himself—and us—with his own sincerity (216).

Wilde's text, then, redefines the subject not so much as an entity or concept but rather as a complicated amalgam of powers and deficiencies, possibilities and limitations: it is at one and the same time composed of self and Other, of aggressive violence and essential passivity, of the desire to assert its own primacy and of the ironic reinscription of its own secondariness. This redefinition is admirable and important in and of itself, but it is also significant for what it tells us about his place in literary (and cultural) context. For Wilde's redefinition of the subject has dual implications, looking at once backward and forward. On the one hand, as I have suggested, it corrects the solipsistic tendencies of Pater and Rossetti: Wilde replaces the drama they obsessively script of a monadic selfhood striving to touch an inaccessible Other with a social one, creating in its place a drama of ubiquitous intersubjective strife, of grim Darwinian struggle between powerful individual subjects caught up in the game of mutually constructing, deconstructing, and reconstructing one another. On the other hand, it opens up possibilities for his successors as well. The interest in the social interplay of verbal representations of finely tuned, acutely self-aware subjectivities and—more powerfully—of the drama of influence, freedom, control, and violence they enact in their interplay with each other is one that, as we shall see, Henry James will take up and make his own: in *The Ambassadors*, with an allusion to Wilde that is one step short of explicit, and in *The Golden Bowl*, with precise reference to the tradition of British aestheticism that Wilde had come to symbolize so powerfully, if so problematically, for his own era.

Aestheticism and Social Process

The third problematic I wish to discuss is inherent in the role aestheticism came to play in late Victorian society. For if aestheticism sought to place the work of art in an ideal world existing beyond or outside the social realm, nevertheless its rhetoric of absolute aesthetic transcendence was frequently used as a tactic of considerable cunning by men (and, less overtly but no less persistently, by women) seeking to make their way in this social world. Moreover, and more importantly, the very ways that aestheticism claimed to privilege art as existing beyond, and being redemptive of, the ethos of conspicuous consumption that marred its contemporary culture served as a subtly mystified expression of that very ethos. In short, while aestheticism claimed to represent an alternative to the materialism of its contemporary world, it was wholly complicit with that very materialism.

Let me be clear: I am not attacking British aestheticism as a form of mystification, or of dishonesty, or of bad faith. To do so seems to me itself an act of bad faith, for such an attack partakes of a naive belief in the potential innocence of social institutions, if only in articulating the disillusion that follows when such a belief is discovered to be erroneous. Rather, it seems to me that a closer look at the social role and cultural ramifications of aestheticism in England may suggest the true nature of aestheticism's ambitions as well as the reasons for the failure of those ambitions. If, for example, we look at the social origins of the chief adherents of aestheticism in England, we see a remarkably consistent pattern. John Ruskin was the son of a wealthy sherry merchant. Dante Gabriel and Christina Rossetti were the children of an Italian expatriate, who made his living as a professor at Kings College, University of London (at the munificent salary of ten pounds per annum) and as a writer. William Morris's father was a successful stockbroker and later, after a lucky investment, a mine owner.

Walter Pater was the son of a surgeon in Stepney, a less than desirable
London address. Oscar Wilde was the son of a once successful but disgraced Irish doctor (knighted in 1864, Oscar's father counted among
his patients Napoleon III and his cousin, Emperor Maximillian) and
of a revolutionary Irish nationalist poet, known as "Speranza."

In other words, with the exception of Swinburne, whose father was
an admiral, the aestheticists were all children of the middle class. Indeed, they represented the full range of Victorian middle-class experience. Some, like Ruskin and Wilde, were of the generation following
the one that had procured or produced wealth; others, of families
falling into genteel poverty. Most were socially marginal: Wilde as an
Irishman, Rossetti as second-generation immigrant, Ruskin as a militantly nonconformist Scot; others, like Morris, were less so. But, again
with the exception of Swinburne, all were outsiders to the world of
privilege in which they were to move; and, for all, the adoption or exploration of the rhetoric and stance of aestheticism may be seen as a
strategic response to their status. Aestheticism became a way for children of the middle class to make their way in the increasingly fluid
social world of late-nineteenth-century England. For it helped middle-
class men and women claim authority for themselves in that world: to
establish oneself as the arbiter of the aesthetic, devotee of "the beautiful," was to proclaim oneself as a member of an elite whose standing
was based on taste and discernment, not birth, wealth, or the other
accoutrements of aristocratic privilege.

This social dimension of aestheticism—or, at the very least, this tactical deployment of the language of aestheticism—reveals itself equally
in the two seemingly antithetical ways aestheticism responded to class.
It manifested itself first in the overtly democratizing side of aestheticism, particularly, as one might suspect, in the works of Ruskin and
Morris. Ruskin's criticism, for example, can easily be read as a kind of
aesthetic Reform Act, an extension of the franchise of art appreciation from exclusively elite circles to any patient and attentive reader
of his work. Ruskin largely accomplishes this effect, ironically enough,
through his own hyperbolic claims for his own authority. For, as Elizabeth Helsinger has suggested, Ruskin's

authority as author of *Modern Painters I* . . . [ultimately] came neither from his
knowledge of painting nor from his knowledge of natural fact but from his
ability to see in a certain way, and hence to acquire knowledge. That ability
he tries to transfer to his readers through description. The implication is that
Ruskin's readers, by the time they finish *Modern Painters*, may have as much
authority as Ruskin himself lays claim to.[39]

The center of Ruskin's endeavor is the impassioned belief that *any* person possessed the ability to see clearly and hence to appreciate fine art; that, indeed, under the proper social conditions, all possessed the ability to be an artist, as every person putatively once was in twelfth-century Venice, and could and should be again in nineteenth-century England, given the right social conditions. Ruskin's assertions formed the basis of William Morris's endeavors as well: building on a Ruskinian critique of the condition of labor, Morris not only argued powerfully for a transformation of aesthetic conditions that would also provide a transformation of social conditions, but attempted through numerous public engagements to bring about such a transformation.

This democratizing function revealed itself no less powerfully in the less egalitarian side of aestheticism—the mode of aestheticism represented by Pater or Wilde in which the aesthete proclaims himself a rare and superior being, capable of acts of special perception and appreciation. The ultimate expression of this stance is the pose we associate with the later phase of aestheticism: that of the aesthete as Dandy, as devotee of the finest of sensations and launcher of the most cutting of remarks. Obviously, such a role seems far from democratic in spirit; its very existence was antithetical to the democratizing ethos of the middle classes. As Ellen Moers puts it in her classic account of Dandyism:

> What the utilitarian middle class most hated in the nobility was what the court worshipped in the dandy—a creature perfect in externals and careless of anything below the surface, a man dedicated solely to his own perfection through a ritual of taste. The epitome of selfish irresponsibility, he was ideally free of all human commitments that conflict with taste: passions, moralities, ambitions, politics or occupations.[40]

Indeed, in his dandiacal incarnation, the aesthete proclaims himself an aristocratic minority of one. His language, his gestures, his connoisseurship, all proclaim that he is a man of unique discernment, taste, and distinction—even if, like a Wilde or a Pater, he is utterly lacking in birth or wealth.

But, as this formulation suggests, even in the midst of the cult of Dandyism, the middle-class hypothesis holds. Although to a certain extent the aesthete's adoption of the stance of the Dandy mirrors the assumptions of a class-ridden society, it also shifts the criteria of value in such a way as to satirize and revise class divisions. *Plus snobbiste que les snobs*, the aesthete's assumption of the role of superiority comes to perform the most fundamental maneuver of the middle class. It

insists on the "career open to talent" in the highest reaches of society. Thrown back on his own wit, his own taste, his own discernment,
the Dandy/aesthete outdoes the aristocrat at his own game, and in so
doing, changes its rules.*

I mention the class complexities raised by Dandyism because they
bring into sharp focus the social fate of aestheticism in the late years of
the nineteenth century. For all its rhetoric of absolute aesthetic transcendence, aestheticism realized itself in social terms as a means of
upward mobility. The clearest example of this was, of course, Oscar
Wilde, who, in his own path through London society, honed the aestheticist rhetoric of Arnold, Ruskin, and Pater into a career weapon
of considerable force and subtlety. In Oxford, as Richard Ellmann observes, Wilde's initial gaucherie informed his creation of the persona
of the aesthete. "Rebuffed [socially], Wilde determined to be ahead
of rather than behind the English. His Dublin accent disappeared in
favor of that stately and distinct English, phrased in perfect sentences,
which so astonished Yeats and others later. He developed a great appetite for formal wear, and told a friend, 'If I were alone on a desert
island and had my things, I should dress for dinner every night.' "[41]
Several years later, aestheticism helped Wilde, a penniless Irishman
who worshipped those "two great gods, Money and Ambition," to
achieve notoriety in London high society.

Wilde's career testifies to an even more impressive connection between the rhetoric of aestheticism and its ambient social sphere.
Wilde's remarkable powers of self-publicization remind us as well of
the close affinities between aestheticism and the institutions of a newly
forming mass culture.[42] Wilde's social notoriety immediately brought

---

*As Moers suggests, such has been the role of the Dandy since the time of Beau Brum-
mell; the pose of the Dandy has frequently been one adopted by wealthy commoners
seeking to make their way in the highest levels of British society. Thus Brummell himself
became, through the intensity of his snobbery and perfection of his dress, an intimate
of the Prince Regent; thus, to cite a more significant example, Disraeli was able to adopt
the stance of the Dandy to transform himself from the son of a Jewish financier to the
protector of Queen and Empire. The role, however, is more than just a way for parvenus to enter high society. There is also a moment in the career of the Dandy in which
he must choose allegiances: in which he must decide whether to assert his own authority
or submit to that of the caste to which he wishes to belong. Brummell, for example,
was ultimately rejected by George IV after the latter's ascension to the throne, and,
after three glorious years of attacking his former intimate, fled to France to escape his
debtors, there eventually to die a paralytic wreck. So, too, there was a moment at which
Wilde had to choose between the unwritten rules of late Victorian society—that homosexual liaisons were tolerated but only if maintained discreetly—and his own knack for
publicity. Wilde's subsequent experience resembles Brummell's with uncanny accuracy.

him to the attention of a large reading public in England and America through the popular dissemination of George Du Maurier's satirical cartoons, which were reprinted in newspapers and mass-circulation journals, particularly in America. His American tour was cosponsored by Richard D'Oyly Carte, in order to publicize Gilbert and Sullivan's *Patience*, and by Mrs. Frank Leslie to publicize her journal, *Leslie's Illustrated Newspaper*; after the services of the invaluable Samuel Morse, the agent assigned to arrange his American tour, were withdrawn, Wilde was forced to play the role of his own advertising man, his own publicity agent—and he did so with innate skill and considerable effectiveness, in both England and America. Thereafter, Wilde's career continued to be intertwined with the worlds of drama and public performance: when he returned to England, Wilde was able to make his living for a time by lecturing on lecturing in America throughout the British Isles; then, after the failure of his play, *Vera, or the Nihilists*, as a free-lance journalist; and finally as an editor of a British ladies' magazine, *Woman's World*.

Wilde's career, while undoubtedly unique in many respects, was also more broadly paradigmatic. It suggests that aestheticism's rise from the status of a coterie concern into a broader social prominence in the 1880's accompanied the growth in organization, sophistication, and extensiveness of the mass-circulation press and the cultural formations it depended on and spawned—particularly such crucial formations as the mass-market advertising industry and that new craft, public relations. It might be said that Wilde's particular service was to vend aestheticism most effectively to the broadest segments of this new, engorged, but increasingly articulated marketplace; what, after all, is *Dorian Gray*'s placement of topoi that Wilde lifted from Pre-Raphaelite poetry, Paterian dogma, and Huysmans's fiction alongside plot devices that he stole from Gothic horror tales, sentimental fiction, and sensation novels but an attempt to make the imaginative enterprise of British aestheticism available to *all* the various segments of the Victorian reading public?

We must not overstress this moment in aestheticism's relations to the social; to focus exclusively on the social moment at which aestheticism entered the literary marketplace is to imply that aestheticism was ever able fully to separate itself either from the market or from other social formations, and, in so doing, to buy into aestheticism's own claims to transcend its historical moment. It would be far more accurate to argue instead that the entry of aestheticism into the booming literary market made clear what had been true all along: that the rise of

aestheticist criticism, painting, and literature formed an integral part
of the complex network of social and cultural transformations that
mark late-nineteenth-century English culture and society. There are
two such transformations we need to look at more carefully before
we turn to the American side of the Atlantic: the relation between
aestheticism and what an American historian aptly calls "the culture
of professionalism," and the relation between aestheticism and what
a group of historians call "the culture of consumption." We need to
spend some time with both of these; for what is at stake in each, I want
to suggest, is not merely the cultural fate of the aesthete, or even of the
privileging of art he advocates; what is ultimately at stake is nothing
less than the social fate of cultural criticism itself in a commodifying,
professionalizing world.

To begin with professionalism: the course of professional self-definition and self-assertion varied on both sides of the Atlantic in the
nineteenth century, but partook of the same impulse. As Burton Bledstein has argued, the emphasis on the rationalization of time and space
wrought by a mature capitalist culture leads to the organization of life
paths into distinct "careers," and thus to the further rationalization of
the career into the self-defining, self-privileging shape of the profession.[43] In America, the professions seem to have functioned dynami-
cally with respect to class; one finds the same impulses toward organization and claims for special professional expertise among bankers and
bricklayers, teachers and undertakers. Historians of England suggest
that there, professionalism functioned differently. It is true that British
professionals emphasized the same relation between their social function and an ethic of service as their American counterparts: British
and American teachers, bankers, lawyers, and doctors all claimed to
be performing a special function in society by using their training,
talents, and expertise to aid others (and, Magali Larson reminds us,
gained monopoly control over the services they provided by means of
this assertion).[44] But British professionals seem to have been far more
intent than their American counterparts to differentiate themselves
from what they saw as the acquisitive ethos of the mercantile classes or
orders, and far more interested in conforming to the codes of behavior
appropriate to the "gentleman":

The professional man, it was argued . . . thought more of duty than of profit.
The gratitude of the client rather than the market defined his reward, and
technically he was not paid but granted an *honorarium*. He earned his reputation by discretion, tact, and expert knowledge rather than by advertising and
financial success. He was a learned man, and his education was broad and

comprehensive. Unlike the businessman, who operated within an impersonal market situation, the professional man was involved with his clients at a personal, intimate level. . . . There was, therefore, a certain self-restraint in his manner, a gentlemanly quality which distinguished him from the brash and aggressive industrialists of the midlands and the north.[45]

The rise of aestheticism mirrored and helped fuel this discreet form of professionalism; indeed it might be said to provide its ideology, in something of the old-fashioned sense of ideology as a mode of false consciousness, a strategy of self-conscious delusion. Like Arnold's more notorious doctrine of disinterestedness, Ruskin's arguments for aesthetic transformation as a means of redeeming civilization, Pater's emphasis on the appreciation of fine or special moments of intense experience, and Wilde's claims for the priority of art over life are all implicitly or explicitly phrased challenges to the acquisitive, work-oriented ethos of the bourgeois economy, which nevertheless served the function of opening up career paths for individuals within that economy. One sign of this was the recourse many of the aestheticists had to the newly professionalizing academic life for their sustenance. Again, it was Arnold who blazed the trail his successors were to follow.

Arnold's career was entirely circumscribed by the professionalization of educational life: first and most obviously as an inspector of schools, that is, as a professional whose vocation it is to monitor (and improve) the professionalism of others; then, as a professor of English poetry; and as the first participant in a profession that has provided stability for so many twentieth-century intellectuals: academic literary criticism. This path was followed, to a certain extent, by Ruskin, who was wealthy enough to be independent of it, and a greater extent by Pater, who had to call on the university for his sustenance entirely; Wilde, too, might have followed this route had Oxford seen fit to ignore his flamboyant escapades and reward one of their most brilliant students with the expected postgraduate fellowship.* It is a path that many aesthetes and would-be or former aesthetes pursued for the next 50 years: long after the aesthetes had receded from public attention, there remained at both Oxford and Cambridge a substantial aesthetic "set" who modeled themselves, consciously or unconsciously, on the aesthetes of the 1890's, and, as we shall see, such a set was quite influential at Harvard as well.[46]

We ought not limit the professionalization of aestheticism to the academy alone. Indeed, aestheticism provided the impetus behind, or

*Tellingly, after his departure from Oxford, Wilde applied for the position of inspector of schools that Arnold had held before him.

the rationale for, a number of new professions, most of which resisted full incorporation within academic structures. For example, aestheticism's valorizing of aesthetic connoisseurship led to the creation of the profession, both within the academy and without, of the art expert, the person whose job it was to search out and authenticate great works of art for clients and to advise those clients as to which art they should and should not purchase. Ruskin and Morris's emphasis on the importance of handcrafts and a return to artisanal modes of production gave rise to a whole series of new vocations: careers for the makers of fine books, furniture, wallpaper, andirons, and other domestic goods; careers for the vendors of these goods, particularly those who could direct them to an upper-middle-class clientele; careers for the numerous cultural cicerones who sprung up in the wake of the "aesthetic mania" of the 1880's to offer advice and instruction to the aesthetically perplexed; careers for those entering the wholly new profession of "interior decoration."

Of course, the most spectacular career opened up by the example of aestheticism was that of the "artist" itself. Newly embedded in the transformed cultural marketplace, newly freed from the tyranny of the Academy and of aristocratic patronage, the artist was enabled by the discourse of aestheticism to construct him or herself as alienated, isolated, oppressed—and to find that this very assertion of alienation was a valuable but not unproblematic asset in the new cultural marketplace. For as the examples of Rossetti, Swinburne, and especially Wilde made clear, the role of the "alienated artist" could (and did) achieve a considerable degree of financial success and social status in the very world whose utilitarian and moralistic ethos those writers and artists claimed to rebel against. We might speculate that the ground of this social success was the intermeshing of the phantasmatic images that the alienated artist and the bourgeois public possessed of each other; the public could look to these writers and painters to confirm their prejudices about the nature of artists—their excessive and often perverse sexuality, their liberating but nevertheless inefficacious release from the exigencies of work and marketplace—while these writers and artists could look to the bourgeois public to confirm certain artistic prejudices about a society that so cruelly nurtured its alienated creators—its insensitivity, its cruel insistence on narrow notions of utility, its Philistinism. Without being unduly cynical here, it would nevertheless be fair to say that both parties to this transaction profited from it; that the stance of alienation and social marginality the aestheticists adopted was profoundly enabling for the artists in question, while the consumers of their work were thereby endowed with a voyeur-istic sexual thrill and a soupçon of vicarious social rebellion—until this transaction was called to conscious attention by the crossing of boundaries by either party, at which point it became acutely painful for both.[47]

In short, aestheticism itself served in British society (and, as we shall soon see, even more so in that of America as well) not just as a means toward establishing "the culture of professionalism"; aestheticism helped create the profession of culture making itself. It helped create a new caste of professionals who designated themselves as experts in cultural knowledge, and who defined their own role as that of instructing others in the lineaments of that knowledge. Here, the professionalization of cultural instruction follows precisely Bledstein's paradigm. If, as Bledstein suggests, the sign of the professional is the claim of possessing a particular, esoteric form of knowledge, and the equally fervent assertion of a vocation to impart that knowledge to an awed but appreciative public, then aestheticism itself can be seen as the highest form of professionalism:

In contrast to the tradesman or the craftsman, the professional person defined the unique quality of a subject, its special basis in an exclusive and independent circle of natural experiences. . . . The professional excavated nature for its principles, its theoretical rules, thus transcending mechanical procedures, individual cases, miscellaneous facts, technical information, and instrumental applications. Fredrick Jackson Turner, for instance, isolated the unique nature of American history, and Oliver Wendell Holmes, Jr., the unique nature of the law in America; G. Stanley Hall isolated the distinctive characteristics of "adolescence," and Jane Addams the professional woman social worker's special, natural sensitivity to injustice. (88)

So too the Pre-Raphaelite or Paterian aesthete, the interior decorator or the maker of aesthetic wallpaper, or even the alienated artist are all able to define the unique quality, the distinctive nature, of the "aesthetic," and, both by grounding themselves thoroughly in the texts that delimit, order, and define that quality and by creating those texts, to signal their expertise to an eager reading public. Like all experts, all professionals, their efforts were at once self-creating, self-defining, and self-authenticating.

The discourse of aestheticism we have been considering throughout this chapter thus enters its culture as what Bledstein calls "a symbol of professional authority" (98). Such symbols were necessary, Bledstein suggests, to "emphasiz[e] the complexity of a subject, its forbidding nature, to the layman, the uninitiated, and even the inexperienced

practitioner" (98). Bledstein's model here is that of the law, not literature or art; he discusses the way that a "nearly uncontrollable growth
in the publication of casebooks" and "technical expositions on such
specialized subjects as the laws of electric wire on streets and highways"
came to define the authority of the lawyer by placing the layman in a
position of relative ignorance (98). But, clearly, the texts of British aestheticism similarly work as a form of specialized, esoteric knowledge,
which is not only gathered, analyzed, and ordered by aesthetic professionals in any number of fields but which also serves to mystify the authority of those professionals. As a result, the nature of the "aesthetic"
itself was transformed. Despite the overtly democratizing tendencies
evident in the earlier phases of aestheticism, the result of aestheticism's
endeavors was that the perception of the beautiful was no longer held
to be a universal or a communal experience (as it is, at least in theory,
in the aesthetics of Romanticism); rather it became one that, like the
knowledge of the intricacies of electric-wire law, serves to define the
expertise of the relevant authority, which that authority then imparts
to an awed but appreciative public. Ruskin not only defines the importance of aesthetic experience, but tells the reader how to go about
gathering such experience for himself—from this artist, this natural
scene, and not from that one or that one. Pater can be read as performing a similar maneuver: it is not only that value inheres in one or
another special moment of intense experience, but also that one can
—and people did—read one's Pater in order to learn which moments
of experience are most intense, which focus the greatest amount of
aesthetic energy, and which are simply a waste of time. Oscar Wilde
raises the conflation of aestheticism and professionalism to a fine art.
His lecture tour of America, after all, was one in which he established
himself as a cultural authority—as not only a representative of aestheticism, but as an expert in what he called "The New Renaissance
of English Art"—and Wilde brought professionalism to new heights
of ingenuity when, after lecturing the Americans on British art, he
turned to lecturing his countrymen on lecturing Americans on British
art.

   I want to be very clear at this point about the nature of my analysis
of aestheticist professionalism. It may seem that the goal of this analysis is to diminish or deconstruct the claims of aestheticism. Certainly,
my rhetoric here is that of demystification. But if I am attempting
to use this rhetoric to demystify, I am attempting to do so with the
full knowledge of the deficiencies of that endeavor. To critique the
aesthetes for their professionalism, for one thing, smacks to a certain

extent of hypocrisy. Human beings, as any form of enlightened social criticism reminds us, have to put food on the table somehow, and that these aesthetes sought to put food on the table by criticizing the necessity of putting food on the table is no excuse for the critic, caught in similar exigencies, to adopt an attitude of superiority to them. "To flaunt one's superiority," Theodor Adorno reminds us, "is at the same time to feel in on the job."[48] The indictment of the aesthetes for professionalism, in other words, should not ignore the professional context in which the criticism is made—a context in which, at least in 1989, the critique of professionalism is one of the most respectable means of making one's way in the academic profession itself.[49]

But the critique of aestheticist professionalism is of no small importance, it seems to me, because to launch such a critique, and then to realize that it includes the maker of the critique within its confines, is to find oneself in something of the same position as the aestheticists themselves. For criticizing Pater or Wilde or Whistler or their confreres for making their way in a professionalized, consumption-oriented culture, and for indeed making their critique of that professionalized consumer culture into their way of making their way in such a culture, forces one into their very position; forces one, in fact, to recapitulate their dilemma. It is, for example, to yearn for a transcendent career path that would somehow enable one simultaneously to live inside and outside one's own cultural moment. It is, in other words, to see oneself, as Pater and Wilde and Whistler all saw themselves, as existing in a marginal elite or, to adopt the aestheticists' own neo-Arnoldian term, as "aliens" within a society that nourishes and rewards alienation with fame, notoriety, and even, at times, tenure.

To recognize this commonality is to understand more completely the difficulties that the aestheticists faced. They reacted to their double allegiances in ways that we recognize from our own culture, even our own experience: some by becoming as bourgeois as possible—this was particularly true of Millais, Hunt, and the other lesser Pre-Raphaelites —others by seeking to question the limits of social acceptance, by affirming and then reaffirming their own social marginality. Swinburne and Wilde in particular can be seen as devoting their lives to testing the line between tolerance and taboo: one thinks, as an emblem of this, of Swinburne reciting Sade in his drawing room to his ostensibly Bohemian friends, reveling in the looks of utter consternation on their faces, or of Wilde's determination to face Sir Edward Carson in an open court simultaneously to confront and confute the Philistinism of his public. Others, less abrasive or self-destructive than

Swinburne or Wilde, found themselves affirming and denying their
marginality at the same time: Pater, for example, lived a public life of
the utmost respectability, while in his works he conjured with a rich
world of beauty and violence—a world, indeed, in which devotees of
the beautiful are mutilated or destroyed by the pressures of the respectable; such at least, is the undersong of *The Renaissance*, in which
the violence of that world is directed at those, like Winckelmann or
Giorgione or even Leonardo, who most appreciate its beauty.

We need perforce to look sympathetically at the aestheticists, then,
and to do this we need to see their contradictory responses to professionalism as a serious attempt to deal with a serious problem: the
problem of the social place of cultural criticism itself. We must see their
responses to the changing course of late-nineteenth-century British
culture as an attempt to formulate a criticism of cultural possibilities
from within the confines of that very culture without either getting
trapped by or denying their place within it. An even clearer example
of this dilemma—and of the aestheticists' most successful attempt to
transcend it—is provided by the intimate relation between the rise
of aestheticism and the advent of a consumer society. For aestheticism may be seen as at once registering, shaping, and critiquing a
society whose cultural institutions are increasingly devoted to inciting,
celebrating, or inducing the act of consumption—first finding that its
critical impulses are wholly subsumed within its celebratory function,
then discovering a way to reassert them from within the confines of
the historical moment.

The precise determination of the onset of such a social transformation, of course, is still the subject of much debate among historians,
some arguing with merit that the eighteenth century saw the onset
of a mass culture organized around the consumption of commodities; others, emphasizing the late nineteenth century as the time of
the consummation of a mass-consumer culture; still others doubting
its predominance or its ultimate efficacy.[50] Whatever date, local habi-
tation, or name one gives to the socioeconomic advent of a consumer
society in England, its cultural manifestation is striking: the shift from
a producing to a consuming ethos is precisely the subject of mid-to late
Victorian cultural criticism. One thinks of the contrast between a Carlyle, with his insistence on the moral urgency of "work" and a Wilde,
with his emphasis on the joys of sheer idleness; or even, within aestheticism's own confines, between the emphasis of a Ruskin or a Morris
on regarding art as a form of unalienated labor and the insistence of
a Pater on valorizing the experience of art as passive perception of
intense sense stimuli.

Aestheticism may be seen, in other perhaps somewhat cynical words, as the expression in aesthetic and cultural terms of the ethos of consumption; it represents, we might say, the poetry of the culture of consumption. This argument is attractive. The Dandy, for example, is by definition the perfect consumer—a person who, for all his aristocratic pretensions, defines his identity solely on the basis of his acquisitions. Similarly, the notion of the autonomy of art as deployed by Pater, Wilde, and their successors serves the function not only of decontextualizing or dehistoricizing art objects but also that of placing art entirely in the sphere of consumption. To privilege the experience of art as an end in itself, or, more accurately, as the most intense experience available to excite the viewer's consciousness into quickened, multiplied intensity, is to deny the value of art for anything but satisfying the eager, appropriative gaze of the spectator. "The service of philosophy, of speculative culture, towards the human spirit," Walter Pater writes, "is to rouse, to startle it into sharp and eager observation," and no better phrase exists to define the passive, contemplative, or "reified" attitude inculcated by the economy of consumption and the ethos of aestheticism alike (WP, 1: 236).

But to interpret aestheticism solely as the mystified, high-cultural expression of the central tenets of a consumer culture is seriously to underestimate aestheticism's ambitions to critique consumerism itself. Indeed, aestheticism takes up in two or three different phases the question of consumption, moving through a number of critical strategies and stances in such a way as ultimately to pose the problem of the consumption of cultural criticism itself.

The first phase is that which we associate with Ruskin and Morris: the direct attack on commodification and consumerism from a position that claims to be exterior to it, that appeals to a source of transcendent value—whether represented diachronically, by a past period in history like the Middle Ages, or synchronically, by the immutable truths of moral experience and aesthetic perfection Ruskin increasingly attempted to invoke. To a certain extent, this social criticism was cogent and effective, and before we turn to its difficulties, it is perhaps wise to give it its due. Ruskin's attacks on the commodification of labor in *Munera Pulveris* and *Ethics of the Dust* or Morris's examination of the relation between the useful and the beautiful, indeed, between consumption and desire, influenced the social views of men and women not only of the nineteenth century, but also of the twentieth. Ruskin and Morris also deserve to be praised for understanding and reflecting upon the social importance of the cultural plane and of the official and unofficial organs of education that structure and transmit the cultural

—an understanding that anticipates analytic advances in twentieth-
century marxist thought we associate with figures like Gramsci and
Althusser. Finally, Ruskin can be partially and Morris fully cited as
classic and perhaps even noble examples of the engagé intellectual,
one who recognizes the provisionality of his own privilege and seeks
to move beyond the limitations imposed upon him by his own social
position to a form of effective political action.[51]

But the social critique articulated by Ruskin and Morris was ultimately fallible, it seems to me, because it failed to take into account
the subtlety and voraciousness of the forces arrayed against it. It failed
to take into account the spectacular ability of an advanced consumer
society to transform criticisms of that society into objects of consumption themselves—a process that Pater and Wilde, by contrast, reflected
upon and worked within. Such processes are clearest in the case of
Morris. William Morris and Company, the firm founded by Morris
to reform public taste, revive artisanal skills, and help train lower-
class men in an ennobling and lucrative craft, was in some sense too
successful. It managed to create wallpaper and furniture that was at
once beautiful and useful—which helped revolutionize not only the
taste, but the attitudes toward home decoration of its era. But because its methods involved a painstaking attention to craft and detail,
the company was forced to vend to an exclusively upper-middle-class
and upper-class clientele—to precisely the leisured classes, ironically
enough, whom Morris's celebration of labor was designed to critique.
As Holbrook Jackson wrote in 1908:

[Morris's] aim was to make what he was fond of calling "useful pieces of goods"
under conditions which would insure that they were also works of art, and that
these products of a new-old method should be generally accessible for common usage. But he had reckoned without his host, for when he had created
his beautiful things, only the rich could buy them.[52]

This criticism has always struck me as a trifle unfair; Morris can
hardly be held accountable for the very phenomena that he himself
tried to correct, and the criticism of Morris's enmeshment within that
system is too facilely used as an argument against change itself, as if
possibility and desirability were the same thing. Nevertheless, there is
an important theoretical and historical point to be made here: Morris's
attempts to transform a social system based on the production and exchange of commodities were themselves thoroughly commodified by
that system not despite, but rather because of, the critique they offered
of it. This process was heightened by the enthusiastic public reception
for Morris's productions in the late nineteenth century and the first

years of the twentieth. The social vogue for Morris's goods—Morris chairs, rugs, tapestries, and even stained glass windows became "expensive indicators of good taste," as Eileen Boris has shown—directed Morris's example more toward legitimating the ethos of consumption than correcting or supplementing it.[53] Consider as paradigmatic the "William Morris Room," established in 1903 in the downtown Chicago showroom of the Tobey Furniture Company. According to Boris, the room

combin[ed] Hammersmith rugs, "acanthus" design moulding, velvets, tiles, pottery, Burne-Jones stained glass, copper andirons shaped like sunflowers, along with both eighteenth century and reproduction Sheraton and Hepplewhite mahogany—"well rubbed down, with coverings in the master's [Morris's] own lovely and enduring textiles" [according to Isabell McDougall's account in the magazine, *House Beautiful*]. The room incorporated both medievalized features—such as a dais, an inglenook, and casement windows with leaded panes—and electric fixtures, which [designer Joseph Twyman] believed Morris, who hated gas, "would have approved." A portrait of Morris presided over this combined homage, crusade, and commercial venture. (59)

What is most striking about this room is its absolute defiance of most of Morris's own principles. His emphasis on restraint and harmony in interior decoration is controverted by the profusion and confusion of design elements, all of which when taken together make the room resemble nothing so much as the overstuffed Victorian living rooms Morris detested. Even more problematic is its defiance of the essence of Morris's social creed, a defiance implicit in the gesture of creating the room in the first place. For William Morris Rooms were a staple of many of the Arts and Crafts clubs or meeting halls (as were rooms named after Ruskin); in such rooms, Morris's central precept, the necessity for beautifying the place of lived experience as a means of overcoming the spiritual ugliness of capitalist society, could be put on vivid and public display. Twyman's showroom appropriates his gesture and performs a reversal of its emphasis, which could be described as elegant if it were not so crass: Morris's cultural products are here being used as a legitimation of the very attitudes he set out to critique. Indeed, further to heighten the irony, Morris's benign gaze is invoked not only in favor of "electric light" (which, indeed, Morris does seem to have approved of), but for the very act of eager and constant acquisition itself, which it is the social function of the room to induce.

The room itself thus exemplifies the problematic fate of Morris's social critique—and of the transcendent critique of consumer culture he represents. It suggests the spectacular ability of that consumer society to derail such a critique, to rob it of its critical force, first by canonizing the critic of such a society and then by employing his critical authority in order to legitimate the very patterns of experience he attacked. An even subtler, and perhaps more significant, version of the same problematic attended Ruskin's social criticism. For as his later career demonstrates, the problem faced by Ruskin was precisely the concomitant of the public's appetite for the criticisms he made of it. As George Landow has suggested (following John Holloway's useful analysis), Ruskin may profitably be read as a secular religious prophet on the model of Carlyle or George Eliot. Landow argues that Ruskin sought consciously to place himself in this position: it is, he suggests, a carefully controlled consequence of his manipulation of rhetorical ethos and Biblical echo.[54] But Ruskin's control over his audience's reading experience was never as absolute as such an analysis would imply. To a certain extent, the stance of the Victorian sage was one that was elicited by the expectations of Ruskin's audience itself, which therefore controlled *him*—as is indicated by his frequent diatribes against that audience for ignoring the burden of his social criticisms, diatribes that may have placed him in the same position as a Biblical prophet, but also frequently lodged him in the position of a Victorian crank—a "general scold," as Henry James called him.

The most important sign of this difficulty was Ruskin's inability to control the distribution of his work. That he attempted to direct his discourse at specific audiences (for the working men of England, *Fors Claveriga*; for businessmen, *Ethics of the Dust*; for travelers, *Mornings in Florence*) is evidence of his awareness of the problem, as Brian Maidment has shown.[55] But, as Maidment has also suggested, Ruskin was not able to control the activities of all the individuals and groups who were eager to appropriate his endeavor, often precisely by proclaiming themselves Ruskinians. Ruskin found his work reproduced in fragmented form in anthologies designed to show how his views could support a given position or positions; they became the subject of earnest exegesis by reading groups, the object of commemoration and memorialization by (largely middle-class) Ruskin societies and organizations. The result of this process of social celebration was the metamorphosis of Ruskin into "Ruskin," into a cultural institution, an anthologized "master," whose critical authority could be invoked when necessary but conveniently ignored, or distorted, or elided, when not. Indeed, I suspect that much of the increasingly bizarre tone of Ruskin's later writing stemmed not merely from his madness, nor even from his moving sense of the silence of the audience he wished to address, but also from his frustration at the ability of his culture to turn him into precisely what he did not want to be, a commodified authority whose advice could be quoted but not necessarily followed. Reading works like *The Storm-Cloud of the Nineteenth Century*, one suspects that Ruskin consciously chose the sublime irrelevance of the prophet rather than the canonized irrelevance of the Victorian cultural critic; chose, (if it can be said to be a choice) the discourse of madness rather than that of the culturally familiar but nevertheless socially limited language of the Victorian sage.

The ubiquity of the processes of social reception, of institutionalization, canonization, and commodification guaranteed that the social criticism of Ruskin or Morris could never remain wholly outside the phenomenon they were attacking, that their work and example would be irrevocably transformed into versions of the very commodity form they wished to critique. It is in the context of this problematic, it seems to me, that the works of Pater and Wilde deserve to be placed. It would seem, as I suggested above, that the works of these writers turn aestheticism away from the direct social engagement of their predecessors. This is undeniable but, I think, insufficient. For, I want to suggest, Pater and Wilde's works partake of the same critical impulse as those of their predecessors, but take that impulse in an opposite direction. Their social critique is an immanent rather than a transcendent one; they meditate on what it is like to live within the kind of world Ruskin and Morris attacked directly, and delineate with sharp and at times brutal clarity the aberrations of such a world. Standing on its own, of course, immanent critique is no more successful than transcendent critique, and Pater and Wilde may be justly accused of acquiescing too easily to its temptations: its tendency to become enamored of the object of critique, to limit its horizons to those of the object it seeks to question.[56] But at least it can be said that by their critiques Pater and Wilde are preserved from the problems directly faced by Morris and Ruskin; for Pater and Wilde might be most accurately said to represent not only the critique of commodification itself but also a critique of the *commodification* of the critique of commodification—and the attempt to move beyond that critique into imagining a genuine alternative.

What I am suggesting, in other words, is that the critical dimension of Pater and Wilde's endeavor can be located within the very aspects of those works we have earlier described as representing their acquiescence to or reflection on commodity culture. I suggested earlier that this movement may be located in their revision—perhaps refusal would be a better term—of the tradition of social criticism that begins with Carlyle and passes directly into Ruskin and Morris: that tradition which stresses the value of labor itself, in which the value of art lies in its expression of the labor of the artist or artisan who has produced it. Pater announces his rejection of this production-oriented, labor-centered, nostalgia-ridden tradition by adopting as his central trope "the Renaissance." For this move refutes Ruskin and Morris's mode of transcendent critique not only by turning from the Middle Ages to the Renaissance as a privileged historical locus, but also by turning from the idea of a privileged historical locus itself. Pater extends the notion of "the Renaissance" from a historical into an ontological category, a state of being present at different moments of history between the twelfth century and our own "modern" moment. Indeed, the complicated Paterian admixture of historicism and anti-historicism I described above is never more fully present in his work than in the delicate interplay between the notions of "the Renaissance" and "the modern"; Pater plays the two off against each other frequently in this text, by suggesting, for example, that Du Bellay is at once a typical "child of his age" and a practitioner of "an intensely modern sort of poetry in which the writer has for his aim the portraiture of his most intimate moods" (WP, 1: 172); by reading *La Gioconda* as at once the Renaissance "embodiment of the old fancy" and "the symbol of the modern idea" (1: 126); or—in his most spectacular act of historical assimilation—by identifying Winckelmann at once with the Renaissance, the Enlightenment, and as one of the crucial forces who created "the modern world" (1: 227).

The effect of this historical shuttling is to redefine the Renaissance not as a historical phenomenon but rather as an ideal criterion of value, an abstract standard that nevertheless exists within each historical moment—including our own modern moment. As such, it holds each moment of our existence accountable for itself; it explicitly prohibits the escape into nostalgic reverie that Ruskin and Morris's critical methodology permitted, even encouraged. Thus, in the Conclusion, Pater compacts the notion of "the Renaissance" entirely into contemporary experience; the point of including this exhortation to live passionately and experience intensely at the end of a volume entitled *Studies in the History of the Renaissance* would seem to be that the spirit of the Renaissance, the sense of renewal or "rebirth" for which "the Renaissance" serves as a useful trope exists not just in Renaissance artworks, or indeed in art itself, but rather in any moment of intense feeling encountered in a world that scientific inquiry, rational thought, "analysis" itself have reduced to a state of enervation and entropy. Through this maneuver, Pater is able to use the notion of "the Renaissance" as a delicate critical tool; he is able to deploy it in such a way as to hold a world that seems increasingly to be governed by the grim exigencies of "Necessity" to the demands of "the sense of freedom" (1: 231).

Pater's moves here are identifiably Hegelian (or to be more accurate, an audacious attempt to merge the German idealist and the British empiricist traditions) and as such are subject to the critiques of German idealism which both the marxist and analytic traditions have launched. But it is important to note that if, in his concern with the conflict between freedom and necessity, Pater is indeed a faithful post-Hegelian, he is one in the tradition of Weber, Adorno, and Foucault as well as one in that of Carlyle and Arnold (or Schopenhauer, Nietzsche, and Derrida, that other Hegelian tradition in which J. Hillis Miller wishes to place Pater). Pater's "Necessity," like Weber's "rationalization," Adorno's "enlightenment," or Foucault's "power/knowledge," plots the progress of what one might call un-spirit or the anti-*geist*: of the increasing limitation of human powers and actions not (only) by the expansive exercise of state power, but also through the increasing suppleness and self-knowledge of a disembodied, transhuman logic, which comes increasingly to excavate and control what Walter Benjamin calls the "tiny, fragile human body."[57] Pater's term for this force is sometimes "modern thought," sometimes "analysis," as well as what he calls "Necessity": but in all cases, his understanding, like that of Weber, Adorno, and Foucault, is based on the awareness that the force limiting the order, circumscribing and controlling the human scope of action stands not outside human beings, but rather within their very efforts of self-understanding—this force is therefore not susceptible to direct challenge, but rather only to subversion from within its own logical coordinates. "For us," Pater writes in the Winckelmann essay, "necessity is not, as of old, a sort of mythological personage without us, with whom we can do warfare: it is a magic web woven through and through us, like that magnetic system of which modern science speaks, penetrating us with a network, subtler than our subtlest nerves, yet bearing in it the central forces of the world" (1: 231). In the Conclusion, the "central forces" Pater calls here "necessity" are identified explicitly with what he delicately terms "the tendency of modern thought," a euphemism for the voracious process that begins within human consciousness but which has taken on an autonomous force of its own, reducing human aspirations and possibilities to a mere confluence of random forces—"birth and gesture and death and the springing of violets from the grave are but a few out of ten thousand resultant combinations"—and limiting human self-definitions to an effort of inadequate anthropomorphism: "That clear, perpetual outline of face and limb is but an image of ours, under which we group them—a design in a web, the actual threads of which pass out beyond it" (1: 234).

It is against the progress of this all-devouring rationality—and the progressive limitation of human being and action it brings with it— that Pater's arguments for aesthetic experience must be understood. And it is with these arguments that Pater deploys the method of immanent critique with the greatest of subtlety. Accepting the proposition that the process of rational, analytic thought and its hyperactive step-child, scientific inquiry, has stripped us of our self-satisfied humanism —"that naive, rough sense of [human] freedom, which supposes man's will to be limited, if at all, only by a will stronger than his, he can never have again," Pater writes in the Winckelmann essay—the question nevertheless remains whether one can discern principles within that process that one can turn against it, that can force the powers of an increasingly voracious Reason to consume themselves (1: 231). In the Winckelmann essay, such a principle is discovered in the aesthetic representation of the triumph of Necessity; in an audacious redaction of the notion of Aristotelian catharsis, Pater argues that witnessing vicariously the "network of law" gives us a kind of aesthetic mastery over Necessity which allows us to *choose* to affirm the "chain of circumstance," presumably in gratitude for its endowing us with "those great experiences" (1: 232). Although the logic is perverse, almost Emersonian in its acceptance of the inevitable in order to master inevitability, this move adumbrates Pater's next, and more audacious, move in the Conclusion, where he enters fully into the destructive operations of the scientific spirit in order to discover those principles that will transcend that spirit. If science, reason, and "analysis" have decentered the human and deconstructed the self, then it is within those coordinates that reason can be evaded, transcended, and stripped of its aggressive power, and that the decentered self can claim its own prerogatives. Thus, if the self for Pater is reduced by rational inquiry to what David Hume calls "nothing but a bundle or collection of different perceptions, which succeed each other with an inconceivable rapidity, and are in a perpetual flux or movement," then it is in the quest for the most intense of those perceptions that the destructive process of rational self-inquiry can be circumvented.[58] If "reflexion" reduces our experience to a "whirlpool . . . still more rapid, [a] flame more eager and devouring," then it is precisely in experiencing the flickeringness of our experience that "reflexion" can be transcended (1: 234). Such, of course, is the import of contemplative attitude that Pater recommends at the end of the Conclusion, where he argues that the ephemerality of experience demands that we cultivate the most intense of those sensations: "Not the fruit of experience, but experience itself, is the end. A counted number of pulses only is given to us of a variegated, dramatic life. How may we see in them all that is to be seen in them by the finest senses? How shall we pass most swiftly from point to point, and be present always at the focus where the greatest number of vital forces unite in their purest energy?" (1: 236).

It is, therefore, as part of his immanent critique of instrumental reason and its offspring, scientific inquiry, that Pater's valorizing of the aesthetic, the contemplative, must be understood. It will be doubtless objected at this point that Pater's critique pushes itself into blatant irrationalism on the one hand and apolitical quietism on the other. Indeed, considered under the sign of more rigorous social critique, Paterian aestheticism would seem to reflect in a thoroughly uncritical manner the "contemplative" or reified attitude that another Romantic post-Hegelian, Georg Lukács, defined as the essence of human experience in an exchange economy. This charge interests me less, however, than its more refined variant: the claim that Pater's newly born contemplative self may be seen as a high-cultural version of the mobile, perceptually organized self of a consumer society, a self that "fines itself down" (to use Pater's terms) to a series of sensual engagements with the world—the very process consumer culture depends on and induces. The reason that I am more struck by this assertion is that recent theoretical accounts of the experiential basis of consumer society have taken on, at least to the attentive student of British aestheticism, a remarkably Paterian air. Here, for example, is Jean-Christophe Agnew's description of the cognitive effects of consumer culture on its participants:

[In such a society] singular and discrete use values are translated into multiple and interchangeable exchange values. Commodities become, in William Leiss's words, "progressively more unstable, temporary collections of objective and imputed characteristics—that is, highly complex material-symbolic entities." This "disintegration of the characteristics of objects," as Leiss notes, produces in its turn a progressive "fragmentation of needs." Not that these needs become false needs in some moral or metaphysical sense; rather, they —like the characteristics they take as their objects—become infinitely divisible

and divorced from any cognitively stable context. Neither the commodity nor
the consumer remains definable in terms of some steady or persisting nucleus
of traits or needs. The result, according to Leiss, is a "'brownian movement'
of particular consumer needs within the fluid medium of the market."[59]

This analysis of consumerism mimics the process Pater delineates in
the Conclusion: the reduction of all seemingly stable entities to an increasingly unstable and wavering set of relations, a process that affects
not only seemingly sturdy things in the world, but their equally unvary-
ing observer. Like Pater's "analysis," Agnew and Leiss's marketplace
works to corrode any principle of stability whatsoever, both within and
without; both commodity and consumer are reduced to the state of
flux by the strategies of a commodity culture.

The echoes between Pater's language and that of Agnew and Leiss
may appear to be something of an adventitious homology. But I would
prefer to read it as something more, particularly in light of the links
I discussed above between the language and attitudes of the aesthete
and that of the culture of consumption he inhabited. I would suggest
that we can see in Pater's work, with the unfolding of the high-cultural
level of art and philosophy, a logic encountered throughout social life
in the late nineteenth and early twentieth centuries—a logic that, in
Pater's case, is not merely expressed or articulated, but also subverted.
According to Agnew, consumerism demands two different things of
the self: endlessly mobile receptiveness to an infinitely eddying succession of sensual experiences, and a cognitive organization of that flux
or welter of experiences, "the desire to master the bewildering and
predatory imperatives of the market by an acquisitive or possessive
gesture of the mind." For

each display invokes, satisfies, and reinvokes a cognitive drive, what Jean Baudrillard calls "the passion for the code." Each advertisement promises a fix
on the complexities of the market by appealing to the power of purchase as a
mental power, a matter of possession and leverage in an indeterminate situation. . . . What modern consumer culture produces, then, is not so much a way
of being (profligate, miserly, reserved, exhibitionist) as a way of seeing—a way
best characterised as visually acquisitive. (73)

Pater's redefinition of the self as a fundamentally aesthetic entity
organized by acts of constant "impassioned contemplation" (as he puts
it in his famous essay on Wordsworth) might initially seem to fit into
the coordinates Agnew describes; but when we place it there, we see
that instead it actively disrupts them (5: 60). For Pater's aesthetic
consciousness actively refuses to be captured by any one sense ex-

perience; endlessly mobile, indeed acutely hyperkinetic, it comes into being under the injunction to refuse any sense of "possession or leverage in an indeterminate situation"; to seek, instead, to profit from the very "bewildering and predatory imperatives" of the sensual world:

While all melts under our feet, we may well catch at *any* exquisite passion, or *any* contribution to knowledge that seems by a lifted horizon to set the spirit free for a moment, or *any* stirring of the senses, strange dyes, strange colours, and curious odours, or work of the artist's hands, or the face of one's friend. Not to discriminate every moment some passionate attitude in those about us, and in the brilliancy of their gifts some tragic dividing of the forces on their ways, is, on this short day of frost and sun, to sleep before evening. (1: 237; emphasis mine)

The force of Pater's argument here is that one dare not pause for the slightest moment to "acquire" the attributes one experiences, however purely cognitive and momentary that acquisition may be; at each and every moment one must be engaged in an active tracing out of the metonymic chain that leads one from one experience to another, just as Pater's text passes from one figure to another without pausing to organize them into one dominant metaphoric structure. To do otherwise is to acquiesce prematurely to the mind's grossness, the "roughness of eye that makes any two persons, things, situations, seem alike," and to refuse the moral imperative of burning "*always* with [a] hard, gemlike flame, to *maintain* this ecstasy" (1: 236–37; emphasis mine). It would also be to capitulate in the face of the transience of things and the inevitability of death, to (in Pater's remarkable phrase) "sleep before evening."

I need to be clear about what I am and am not asserting here. I am not claiming that Pater's Conclusion is a veiled attack on consumer capitalism on the order, say, of Veblen's *Theory of the Leisure Class* (1899)—written a mere generation after Pater's *Renaissance* and published only four years after his death (and, as I shall suggest below, reflecting in large part on the American consequences of Paterian aestheticism). Pater would doubtless have agreed with the thrust of Veblen's argument; from what little one can glean from accounts of his remarkably uneventful life, Pater did as much as he could to insulate himself from the middle-class world of acquisition and status seeking, and was doubtless horrified by the brisk market in Renaissance masterpieces his writings helped engineer, largely through the strenuous efforts of a self-proclaimed Paterian, Bernard Berenson.[60] Direct Veblenian assault, however, was neither Pater's methodological nor his ideological inclination. Nevertheless, if *The Renaissance* in particular and the project of Paterian aestheticism in general can be read as an intervention in the tradition of social criticism of Carlyle and Ruskin and an even more direct interrogation of the philosophical matrix of that tradition, then we can say that what Pater has done is to shift critical attention from the production to the consumption of cultural artifacts, and from issuing transcendent critiques of social formations to offering more indirect, more immanent, but nevertheless distinctly critical accounts of their cultural mediations. Pater twists the tradition of social critique aside from social criticism itself, to the undoubted detriment of that critique, it may be conceded; but at the same time, he refines its methodology and points it in directions where the blunter tools of transcendent critique could not operate.

My evidence for this rather paradoxical claim is the fact that versions of Pater's analysis have achieved a cogency in a cultural situation he could not have known. Pater's turn toward valorizing the pursuit of sense experiences as not only a reflection of but also as a response to a world bereft of all transcendent orders of value and meaning is one that has been explored further—and in ways less rigorous than Pater's—by later marxist and post-marxist theorists. Marcuse's *Eros and Civilization* (first published in 1955—the same year as E. P. Thompson's remarkably different contribution to marxist criticism, *William Morris*), for example, proposes that "the aesthetic dimension"—here understood not merely as great works of art, but as the "transformation of toil (labor) into play," the "de-sublimation of reason" and "self-sublimation of sensuousness," and "the conquest of time in so far as time is destructive of lasting gratification"—can provide a redemptive alternative to the labor-centered, reality-principled dictates of capitalist society. Despite his studied ignorance of the Anglo-American tradition Pater represents, Marcuse's effort to press German idealist philosophy into political service may be read, I think, as a remarkably Paterian effort; for both, the project of living fully and feeling intensely enables one to move through and beyond the psychic dictates of an advanced consumer society; to turn, that is, the very sensuousness such a society incites and advocates against its utilitarian, work-oriented ethos.[61]

Marcuse, to be sure, repudiated this particular version of the "Utopian dimension," although his late work suggests that he had not fully abandoned it. But a Paterian tendency is not absent from other modes of marxist thought; recent French responses to the *société de consommation* have also led to remarkably Paterian formulations, and to what one might also describe as an equally Paterian politics. I am thinking here of the work of Guy Debord and the "situationists," of Jean Baudrillard, and of Deleuze and Guattari—all of whom rather un- wittingly follow Pater by adducing the valorization of a decentered, playful, mobile, perceptually hyperactive model of the self as the only way out of the psychic binds of Western culture. Indeed, when com- pared to both Marcuse and the French libidinal radicals of the 1960's, Pater's position seems to take on a greater cogency and rigor; under- standing, as they do, the necessity to correct the progress of rationality and overcome the consequent degradation of the senses, Pater never- theless predicates his solution with tragic eloquence on precisely the hard facts that such theorists founder on: the limitation of human en- deavor, the inevitable passage of things, the depredations of time, the death's head that grins out from even the center of decenteredness.

Eloquent and precise as Pater may have been, however, it must also be admitted that the purity of his critical energies was perhaps too great for his immanent method to work successfully as a form of social critique. I want to suggest in conclusion, however, that in the hands of Pater's pupil, successor, and rival, Oscar Wilde, Pater's mode of imma- nent critique was deployed more successfully—and more subversively. Wilde's politics, unlike Pater's, may be described as persistently and at times even joyously subversive; from an early age Wilde defined him- self as a skeptical outsider to the privileged spheres he sought to enter, and his works formulate a persistent critique of that world that was all the more effective because it was predominantly comic in nature. (As far as Victorian cultural criticism goes, *The Importance of Being Earn- est* has had considerably more endurance than the works of Ruskin, Carlyle, and Morris put together.) Yet at the same time, Wilde strove ceaselessly for financial and social acceptance by the very social world he also sought to critique—which is to say that what is often taken as Wilde's hypocrisy or venality is only a slightly exaggerated version of the social position habitually occupied by Victorian cultural criti- cism and its aestheticist variants. What gives Wilde's works their special vitality, their critical edge, is his fascinating acknowledgment of—and play with—the set of contradictions, complicities, and consequences that eventuate from a recognition of these multiple commitments. In plays like *Lady Windermere's Fan, An Ideal Husband*, and, of course, *The Importance of Being Earnest*, for example, Wilde's explicit (and sur- prisingly "earnest") goal was to bring the Victorian audience face to face with their own hypocrisy—and in his mocking curtain speeches, Wilde's staging of his own hypocritical delight in his audience's equally hypocritical enjoyment of his denunciations dramatized his commonality with them along with their commonality with him. Wilde's fiction created similar effects: *Dorian Gray* is but a calculated slap at the moralistic expectations its audience and author share, even if (or especially because) its final confirmation of these expectations subverts Wilde's own efforts at subversion.

But it is in Wilde's critical prose—to my mind, his greatest achievement, and perhaps the only body of work produced by the aesthetic movement that can be called an unequivocal success—that his subversive inclinations and his literary performance come together most successfully. For in the medium of the prose essay, Wilde found a form in which he could simultaneously expound and subvert, assert and complicate, advance a thesis and explore its antithesis. "A Truth in art is that whose contradictory is also true," Wilde writes in a famous passage from *The Truth of Masks*; but only in his prose was Wilde able simultaneously to explore all the contradictories—and, for that matter, the contradictories of the contradictories—that compose the "Truth" (*Artist*, p. 432). The form of the dialogue that Wilde so frequently adopts aids his accomplishment of this task; but Wilde's work is able to perform its critical function because it is more genuinely, more fully, "dialogical" than even his persistent recourse to this form would suggest. (Indeed, the terms in which Mikhail Bakhtin valorizes the "internal dialogism of the word" are remarkably similar to those in which Wilde describes the inherent contradictoriness of "truth": "the word is born in a dialogue as a living rejoinder within it; the word is shaped in dialogic interaction with an alien word that is already in the object . . . every word is directed toward an *answer* and cannot escape the profound influence of the answering word that it anticipates.")[62] Wilde's remarkable stylistic sensitivity enables him to enter into the verbal contours of a given argument, to explore (and, frequently, to expose) its ensemble of hidden assumptions and covert claims, then to move on either to explore a contrary of that position or its parodic double (and, of course, sometimes to do both at once).

This, I argued earlier, is the formal structure of the Wildean epigram, which mimics the binary form of conventional moral sentiments and then simply (one might also say elegantly) reverses one of those terms in order to subvert that sentiment's original intention. His essays expand this habit of thought into a method of argumentation, dramatizing an aesthetic or an experiential stance, and in so doing, putting on brilliant display both its weaknesses and its strengths. *The Decay of Lying* and *The Critic as Artist* provide splendid examples of this procedure: by exploring the aesthetic and moral stances of the common

Victorian reader and his aesthete antagonist, Wilde is able to play the two off against each other, to weigh their relative merits, and to suggest their unexpected affinities and commonalities as well as to limn their divergences. When in *The Soul of Man Under Socialism* Wilde turns his attention to politics, he is able to achieve even more complicated effects; for he is able to mimic positions that were currently hegemonic in his culture with such satiric precision as to be able to undo them utterly. Thus, Wilde is able to argue for the virtues of socialism not by appealing to either religious or moral certainties, or to the inevitable course of historical development; rather, Wilde argues on the grounds that socialism is to be desired because it is the inevitable fulfillment of the central assumptions of its seeming antagonist, bourgeois individualism.

It is, in other words, as an immanent critique of individualism and its economic correlatives that Wilde's argument for the abolition of these forms works. Articulating the central contentions of individualism—that the highest good is not corporate or communal, but rather the unfettered development of individual energies—Wilde argues that the last thing that people should do is to seek to encumber themselves with what typically stands as the sole measure of individual worth and achievement, private property:

The possession of private property is very often extremely demoralising, and that is, of course, one of the reasons why Socialism wants to get rid of the institution. In fact, property is really a nuisance. Some years ago people went about the country saying that property has duties. They said it so often and so tediously that, at last, the church has begun to say it. One hears it now from every pulpit. It is perfectly true. Property not merely has duties but has so many duties, that its possession to any large extent is a bore. It involves endless claims upon one, endless attention to business, endless bother. If property had simply pleasures, we could stand it; but its duties make it unbearable. In the interest of the rich we must get rid of it. (*Artist*, p. 258)

What is most striking about this formulation is not only its witty paradoxicality but its rhetorical limberness: its ability to enter into the moral and perceptual system of the group it opposes—a group that, to be sure, comprises most of his audience—in order to demonstrate, from within, the incoherency of their positions. The argument works because of the precision of its phrasing. Since Wilde understands—again to cite Bakhtin—that "all words have the 'taste' of a profession, a genre, a tendency, a party, a particular work, a particular person, a generation, an age group, the day and hour," he savors the very language system of the property-owning classes in order to turn their own

implicit assumptions against them (*Artist*, p. 293). Wilde adopts the
drawling tones and mimics the formulaic disavowals of the wealthy—
"property is really a nuisance. . . . a bore. . . . a bother"—so as to pose
one aspect of their value system—the systematic pursuit of leisure—
against another—the systematic accumulation of wealth. His polemical
point therefore follows with stunning ease: if property *really* is such a
bore, then how much better off one would be to be liberated from the
yoke of obligations it imposes. The most indolent lord, by this argument, not only can but must be the most fervent advocate of his own
abolition—and the degree of his fervor must increase with the degree
of his indolence. Throughout the essay, a similar strategy obtains: if
we are to take the claims of individualism seriously, then we must seek
the abolition of its lowest forms, represented by capitalism, and put in
their place a higher—the highest—form of "individualism," which is,
Wilde asserts, socialism. And because Wilde understands so deeply, so
inwardly, that capitalism is not merely a form of economic organization but rather a cultural one, an ensemble of attitudes toward and
assumptions about the world that often controvert or undercut its own
official system of values, Wilde is able to turn his argument for socialism away from economic arrangements towards those affecting every
aspect of individual life. Wilde's "Socialism" will abolish, along with
private property, the entire authority structure by which his society
maintains itself: the nuclear family, the legal system, the culture industry, the penal system—but it will do so not in the name of humankind,
or in that of a class, but rather in that of the unfettered development
of the autonomous individual.

It may be objected—indeed, it often has been objected—that Wilde's
argument has the effect not only of destabilizing the position he seeks
to critique but also the position from which that critique is launched.
Just as Wilde enters into the linguistic field of individualism in order
to demonstrate its incoherencies, so too he inhabits socialism in order
first to correct it—"if the Socialism is Authoritarian; if there are Gov-
ernments armed with economic power as they are now with political
power; if, in a word, we are to have Industrial Tyrannies, then the
last state of man will be worse than the first"—then to refine it out of
existence (*Artist*, p. 257). Wilde's essay works itself around to the conclusion that in the ultimate form of socialism, human beings would be
so liberated from the grubby exigencies of labor (largely through the
advent of labor-saving devices) that they would be free ceaselessly to
fulfill themselves in acts of continuous creation. The ultimate socialist,
for Wilde, is the artist, because the artist is the individual who is most

fully able to be an individual as such; all men should be allowed to "realise [themselves] completely" in a similar manner. Admirable as such a turn may be—and, indeed, it quite closely resembles arguments made by the early, "humanistic" Marx and the middle Marcuse—one is still left wondering whether Wilde sees individualism as a subset of socialism, or socialism as a component of individualism. The essay may begin in the former position, but it ends with the latter; having pressed socialism into service in order to correct smug individualism, Wilde unleashes a revised, perfected version of individualism ("the new Individualism") on socialism itself:

Pleasure is Nature's test, her sign of approval. When man is happy, he is in harmony with himself and his environment. The new Individualism, for whose service Socialism, whether it wills it or not, is working, will be perfect harmony. It will be what the Greeks sought for, but could not, except in Thought, realise completely, because they had slaves, and fed them; it will be what the Renaissance sought for, and could not realise completely except in Art, because they had slaves, and starved them. It will be complete, and through it each man will attain to his perfection. The new Individualism is the new Hellenism. (*Artist*, p. 289)

To paraphrase Shaw, this may be magnificent, but it is not necessarily socialism.

Or is it? Again, as with Pater, the explicit tendency of Wilde's thought may lead toward political irrelevancy, but that direction is nevertheless one that has been followed by the twists and turns of political thought itself. For example, Wilde's line of argument here is unabashedly Utopian—this is the essay in which occurs Wilde's famous assertion that "a map of the world that does not include Utopia is not worth even glancing at" (*Artist*, p. 269)—but, then, again, so are recent revisionary marxisms, the most important of which probably being Frederic Jameson's repeated attempts to reinscribe Utopia onto the marxist map, climaxing with *The Political Unconscious* (1981). Wilde's individualist Utopia, while clearly less purely marxist than Jameson's apocalyptic one, also anticipates recent refinements in the marxist model—the turn in certain western European marxisms towards valorizing social movements based on principles of communal responsibility but grounded in respect for individual difference.[63]

The most important contribution of Wilde's essay toward a political criticism is his understanding of the political necessity of critique itself. Where Wilde's assertions simultaneously differentiate themselves from any other form of leftist criticism and render themselves suspect in the eyes of those more programatically pure of heart is in his eagerness to maintain a critical perspective even in the face of what seem to be concrete realizations of the goals he himself advocates. This is clearest in Wilde's enlistment of Utopian discourse in the service of critique, for it is in his arguments for a militant and persistent Utopianism—a Utopianism that extends even to Utopia—that Wilde holds his own society to account and establishes a principle by which any future one might be interrogated. The contrast with Jameson here is telling: the difference between Jameson's Utopia and Wilde's is not only the difference between a collectivist and an individualist agenda, but also the contrast between an apocalyptic and a historicist deployment of the Utopian. For Wilde, the Utopian is always available to serve a critical function because history will never be over, because history is precisely the sum of the attempts to escape from history into the Utopian, attempts that may succeed precisely because they never can. Or, as Wilde puts it in the aphorism I only partially quoted above: "A map of the world that does not include Utopia is not worth even glancing at, for it leaves out the one country at which Humanity is always landing. And when Humanity lands there, it looks out, and, seeing a better country, sets sail" (*Artist*, pp. 269–70).

With that final, marvelously paradoxical formulation, we return both to paradoxical virtues and vices of the immanent method Pater and Wilde deployed and, more generally, to those of the imaginative disposition of British aestheticism itself. If, as I have been arguing, Wilde's social criticism and Pater's more implicit form of critique acquit themselves from charges of political irrelevance by virtue of the fact that they anticipated, with unerring prescience, directions that leftist thought itself was to take, then this can suggest a way of rescuing the entire aestheticist project itself from the similar marginalization it has suffered at the hands of literary and cultural historians alike. For while aestheticism has been viewed by even its most sympathetic critics as a form of "premodernism," or as a moment of transition between English romanticism and Anglo-American modernism, I have tried to show that British aestheticism most accurately anticipates, and is most rewardingly read through the lens of, "postmodern" theory and practice. I have been suggesting this both explicitly and implicitly by attempting to place aestheticism in the context of postmodernist literary theory and in that of post-marxist marxism; and in both cases, where British aestheticism anticipates the postmodern most fully is in its sustained critique of the explanatory syntheses of nineteenth-century European thought—the "grand meta-narratives" in Jean-François Lyotard's phrase, of Wordsworth or Hegel, of Carlyle or Marx.[64] Entering into these narratives in such a way as to pay tribute to their power, the aestheticists nevertheless made it their policy to subvert or pervert them, to turn them aside from their headlong rush to conclusion or synthesis and to devote themselves to playing with the fragments that are left behind—fragments that, they increasingly discovered, were not merely aesthetically perfect shards, like Keats's Grecian urn, but also irrevocably reified, commodified, and culturally canonized ones, like "Keats's Grecian Urn." The response of the British aestheticists to the ensuing dilemmas recapitulates perfectly, in advance, the ambivalence of postmodernists: there, too, we find the volatile admixture of contempt and nostalgia for the products of the "grand meta-narratives" of the past, of admiration for and disappointment with the artifacts of mass culture that have seemed to replace them, of avant-garde alienation and self-conscious professionalism. There, too, we find the creation of unstable, often parodic, frequently fragmentary works of art that fairly shout out their inauthenticity, making this claim into an argument for their surpassing authority. The resolute paradoxicality of aestheticism—indeed, the ability of aestheticism to destabilize all stable structures of thought and priorities of value—therefore reaches into and beyond the very efforts to periodize it, casting doubt not only on the modernist project, which it reveals to be not a revolutionary one but rather a desperate attempt to breathe life into a tradition that had already been demolished, but also on the claims of the "postmodern" to be "post" anything at all.[65]

Paying tribute to the power of aestheticism to unsettle all the structures in which it is placed, however, also allows us to understand precisely why the uneasy instabilities of British aestheticism had to be evaded by the generation of modernist poets, artists, and critics who followed in its wake. This is particularly true of the modernist writers who evaded the example of Pater, Rossetti, Wilde, et al. by turning back to precisely those aspects of Romanticism that the aestheticists had experienced as already superceded. The modernist yearning for system making, for example, reads as a regressive attempt to complete a project that Coleridge and Wordsworth (not to mention Keats and Byron) had already abandoned, and the abandonment of which became both a topos and a form of praxis for Pater and Wilde. But, as I shall argue below, this process is one that has not only literary but also cultural and historical ramifications. The uneasy and unstable creation by the aestheticists of the image of the artist as mystified professional—of the image of the writer as an Artist with a capital A who experiences himself as a spiritual isolato but who is welcomed by the very literary marketplace he claims to abhor—is also one with which subsequent generations wrestled, as is the burden of the aesthetic movement's attempt to formulate a social critique from within, rather than beyond, the acknowledgment of those social deformations themselves. Much of that wrestling, as I shall try to show in the rest of this book, was performed by Henry James, who, I shall argue, emerges as a crucial figure in the transformation of British aestheticism into high Anglo-American modernism.

But before turning to James, I need to spend some time tracing the career of British aestheticism on the American shores of the Atlantic. For—to conclude the by now perhaps tiresome proliferation of ironies with which British aestheticism presents its student—some of the most vital and interesting ramifications of British aestheticism were to be found not in England itself, but rather in America. There, aestheticism did not just function as a short-lived fad—although the "aesthetic mania" that Americans experienced in the 1880's is one of the great neglected subjects in American social history; rather, it superintended a remarkably various set of cultural manifestations, ranging from cultural theories to cultural artifacts, from revolutions in poetic dogma to revolutions in advertising technique. Not the least of the cultural phenomena that it helped to shape, as we shall see at greater length below, were the novels of Henry James.

Chapter Two

British Aestheticism and American Culture

In 1907, the novelist and critic Zisha Lindau proclaimed his literary creed in the Yiddish-language periodical, *Di Yunge*:

The prophet, the preacher, the politician, have distant goals; distant and often obscure. And frequently calculation takes the place of goals. Only we, the aesthetes, have no goals and no purposes. Certainly no calculations. The tree blooms—the tree is beautiful . . . Everything that is here is beautiful; and because it is here. This is a truth known to all who live with their senses.[1]

Despite its striking eloquence and its appearance in so unexpected a milieu, Lindau's aesthetic manifesto was not unique in turn-of-the-century America. A few blocks north of the Lower East Side ghetto where *Di Yunge* was published lived such self-proclaimed "decadent" or "bourgeoisphobic" writers as James Huneker and Edgar Saltus who contributed to magazines that could trace their lineage directly back to *The Yellow Book*. A few hundred miles to the northeast, in Boston, a group of refined Harvard students also identified themselves as aesthetes, claimed that their only goal was to live for the senses, and wrote poetry in the manner of Dowson and prose in the manner of Pater. Eight hundred miles west, the Chicago house of Stone and Kimball published the works of these Harvard poets as well as translations from the French symbolists and productions of native "Bohemian" writers like Bliss Carmen. And farther west, cities like Omaha and Kansas City possessed their own Ruskin clubs, their avant-garde little magazines, and their rebellious writers, poets, and artists.

By the first years of the twentieth century, then, the tastes, the perceptions, the very attitudes of British aestheticism had thoroughly penetrated the American cultural consciousness. But the ways in which they did so were multiple, conflicting, and often—not unsurprisingly —deeply contradictory. The tradition of British aestheticism inspired poets and pottery makers, conservative cultural critics and radical socialists; it imparted to the literary and cultural elite a well-defined ideological structure that guided their attitudes not only toward art but also toward the role of high culture in a mass, consumer society; it also endowed advertisers and retailers with a marketing strategy that enabled them to put the icons of high culture to work vending commodities. It drew for artists, writers, and critics the image of the artist as a mystified authority, one who stands resolutely above the grubby demands of the new, enlarged literary marketplace; but it also helped delineate for those artists a well-defined, and increasingly profitable, niche within that very market.

In other words, as Americans contended with the shifting and contradictory tenets and tendencies that defined aestheticist thought in England, they attempted to employ its assertions to meet their own shifting ends, needs, and difficulties—with results that were often problematical, unexpected, and riddled with national misprisions, but just as often remarkably sophisticated, resonant, and productive of inspired and original cultural reworkings. Confused as this process may frequently have been, however, it rapidly took on a distinct shape, which I shall try to describe below. For, as I shall try to show in more detail there, the volatile discourse of aestheticism entered the equally volatile American cultural scene at a strategic moment: at the time when the cultural hegemony of one literary and artistic elite—the so-called "gentry elite" who controlled literary periodicals and organized educational institutions in the established centers of high-cultural life (Boston, New York, Philadelphia)—was challenged by another, less-well-defined elite largely composed of professionals, white-collar managers, their wives and children, whose augmenting wealth, status, and ambition in postbellum America allowed them to exert increasing cultural power not only in the Northeast but throughout the entire country. And on the battlefield of high-cultural taste making, different aspects of British aestheticism were enlisted by each group. The high, conservative rhetoric of Ruskinian aestheticism was of obvious appeal to the former; the subversive discourse of Paterian and Wildean aestheticism provided powerful ammunition for the latter.

The battle between old and new elites often took the form of a competition to appropriate elements of the other's aestheticist canon. The magisterially moralistic Ruskinism preached by such representatives of high New England culture as Charles Eliot Norton was challenged and, to a certain extent, confuted by the adoption of Ruskin as an authoritative tour guide by the increasing number of leisured and wealthy Americans seeking to experience authentic "culture" in

Europe. And even while "dinky" magazines modeled on the notorious *Yellow Book* proliferated in the hinterlands, the house organs of the gentry elite like *The Nation* were cautiously moving beyond their Ruskin-inspired medievalism to a new appreciation for Pater, for the Renaissance, and for the vaguely defined but nevertheless potently asserted values of "the aesthetic." Moreover, the efforts of both elites were soon challenged by the generation that followed them into prominence—the generation who were to valorize what Van Wyck Brooks called, only half ironically, "the Newness." To this generation, the efforts of the critics, writers, and artists who preceded them to normalize aestheticism—to admit it into their particular canon by denying or ignoring its subversive, erotic, or political dimensions—had the paradoxical effect of leaving British aestheticism free from the touch of moralism and bourgeois vulgarity that tainted other nineteenth-century cultural manifestations; aestheticism was thus left available as a stylistic resource and experiential guide for their own revisionary efforts.

Further to complicate the matter, it would be inaccurate to suggest that the American reworking of British aestheticism was fully encompassed by the efforts of high-culture intellectuals, writers, and artists. Indeed, one of the most remarkable aspects of the American reception of British aestheticism was the enthusiastic response on the level of popular culture. Part of this response was, admittedly, strictly satirical: the extraordinary outpouring of cartoons, bric-a-brac, songbooks, penny novels, and handbills that accompanied Oscar Wilde's 1882 tour of America painted a picture of Wilde that far exceeded the contemporaneous satires of *Punch* in malice, if not wit. But the influence of aestheticism on American popular culture was circumscribed neither by Wilde nor by the satirical American response to him. The aestheticist project of the beautification of everyday life, its privileging of sense experience, its evocation (particularly in its Paterian and Pre-Raphaelite phases) of a redemptive world elsewhere where such experiences could be ceaselessly realized—all these intersected with the dynamics of late-nineteenth- and early-twentieth-century American culture so as to exert a significant pressure on its new social and ideological configurations. For example, the concerns of British aestheticism coincided with those of mid-century American domestic ideology in such a way as to make palatable, even desirable, new, more luxuriant tastes in household decoration and ornamentation: under the guidance of Morris and, more powerfully, his popularizers, Americans were led to supplant the ideal of the "American home" with that of the

"House Beautiful." More generally, and more important, British aestheticism provided crucial stylistic resources and ideological support for the efforts of manufacturers, retailers, and advertisers to expand sales of luxury goods; indeed, aestheticism's valorizing of sense experience enabled it to serve as a foundation for those advertising men and marketing experts who helped to build, in the late nineteenth and early twentieth centuries, the culture of consumption we so proudly and so anxiously inhabit today.

In all these ways—and in many others besides—the example of British aestheticism exerted a diffuse but powerful influence on American culture and society at the particularly formative period between 1870 and 1920. Since this was exactly the moment at which Henry James reached his full artistic maturity, spurted into transitory but powerful notoriety, and then achieved his final monumentalization as the elite novelist par excellence—the internationally acclaimed but rarely read master of the art of fiction—an inquiry into the relation between James and British aestheticism is particularly relevant. It is all the more relevant because James both mirrored and crucially contributed to the cultural processes I am attempting to describe here; beginning, as a chartered member of the Boston gentry elite, with a powerful encounter with the example of Ruskin—an encounter that, I shall argue briefly below, is still resonating as late as *The Wings of the Dove*—James wholly engaged himself with the full range of the aesthetic experience in England, anticipating, recapitulating, and—most important—crucially influencing the patterns of response that were being played out across the Atlantic.

The American Ruskin

In Edith Wharton's *False Dawn* (1922), Lewis Raycie, a wealthy young New Yorker of the 1840's, is dispatched by his Philistine father on a Grand Tour of Europe, with instructions to send home the appropriate number of Old Masters for the family collection. Before he can complete his mission, however, Lewis encounters a mysterious Englishman with "deep blue eyes . . . scarred cheek and eloquent lip" who informs Lewis that he, too, is "one of the privileged beings to whom the seeing eye has been given" and inspires him to send home Italian primitives rather than the Raphaels his father craves.[2] The Englishman is none other than John Ruskin, and Lewis's encounter with Ruskin is perhaps the most crucial moment in the young man's life. When the Giottos are received in New York, Mr. Raycie disinherits Lewis for his lack of judgment and soon thereafter dies, perhaps of aesthetic grief. Lewis marries his impecunious sweetheart and dedicates his life to the art he has so rashly chosen—even opening a "Gallery of Christian Art" in the family mansion to show his collection to an indifferent New York public. The story ends ironically. Lewis dies before the true merit (and value) of the paintings is learned; they are passed from attic to attic before bringing a large fortune to a descendant of Lewis's wife who, like all those connected with the Raycie family, has no idea of their worth: she is discovered by a representative of the Louvre while trying to wash one of the dingier paintings with soap and water.

Wharton's story paints a remarkably accurate picture of the American experience of European art and aesthetic values in the middle of the nineteenth century.* For it is a matter of historical fact that this experience was shaped by a long and persistent encounter with the works and life of Ruskin. Ruskin seemed to speak to many Americans with the intimacy and authority he showed toward Lewis Raycie. "*Modern Painters*," wrote William Stillman (editor of the Ruskinian art journal, *The Crayon*, and, for a time, a close friend of Ruskin's), was "one of the sensation-books of the time" which "fell upon the public opinion of the day like a thunderbolt from the clear sky."[3] The reviews and sales of *Modern Painters I* were so favorable that Ruskin's later works were reprinted for American readers in numerous editions, often shortly after their publication in England.[4] The Ruskin vogue was not merely a phenomenon of the mid-fifties; by the end of the century, a representative of the "authorized" American publisher, John Wiley, reported that Ruskin was still one of the most popular authors in the catalog.[5]

Ruskin's pronouncements were spread by other means as well. Anthologies of selections from his writings appeared regularly, first from Wiley, then from other houses. *The True and the Beautiful in Nature, Art, Morals, and Religion* (1859) was followed by *Precious Thoughts: Moral and Religious* (1866), *Pearls for Young Ladies* (1878), and *Art and Life*

---

*Indeed, *False Dawn* is modeled on two of the most famous art collections of the mid-nineteenth century. In 1856, Thomas Jefferson Bryan opened the "New York Gallery of Christian Art" on lower Broadway to exhibit his own collection of art; the New York public was far from enthusiastic, however, and Bryan ultimately donated his collection to the New York Historical Society, where it now may be found. (Like Raycie's descendant, Bryan was notorious for washing his own paintings with soap and water.) James Jackson Jarves fell under the spell of Ruskin and A. F. Rio in his youth and founded a famous collection of Italian primitives; his works were also unappreciated, and were ultimately donated to Yale in exchange for a nominal fee. They may now be seen at the Yale University Art Gallery.

(1886). Collections of Ruskin's ruminations on specific subjects were also popular—*Readings from Ruskin: Italy* (1885), *Science: A Ruskin Anthology* (1886), and *The Communism of John Ruskin* (1891), to cite three, drawn from the enormously disparate fields in which Ruskin's influence was felt. It was, however, in the field of aesthetics that Ruskin's influence was most pervasive. Two influential art journals devoted themselves to the popularization of Ruskin's dicta (or at least those perceived as being Ruskin's). *The Crayon*, edited by Stillman and John Durand, reprinted summaries of Ruskin's lectures and portions of books that had not yet made the transatlantic journey, along with poems from Emerson and Lowell and *Letters on Landscape Painting*, by Asher Durand, John's brother. *The New Path*, edited by Clarence Cook, the caustic art critic for Horace Greeley's *New York Tribune*, continued *The Crayon*'s effort, but supplemented its commentary on art with that of contributors from other fields, including the geologist Clarence King and the architects Russell Sturgis and Peter Wight, both of whom were associated with the best Gothic revival architecture in America. Allied with *The New Path* was The Society for the Advancement of Truth in Art, which, as its name suggests, was an association formed expressly to spread the Ruskinian gospel.

Given this tumult of American activity on his behalf, it is no wonder that Ruskin wrote in *The Crayon* in 1855 that Americans possessed a "heartier appreciation and a better understanding of what I am and mean, than I have ever met in England."[6] The reasons for this popularity are multiple; indeed, the persistence of Ruskin's canonization in America was due to the different ways that different facets of his work could appeal to different members of the American cultural elite. To clergymen and religious intellectuals, for example, Ruskin offered a moral apologia for art that allayed the suspicions of aesthetic luxury and of visual representation itself lurking in the American psyche from the time of the Puritans.[7] To conservative social critics, Ruskin provided arguments for the beneficial effect of aesthetic values on the moral and spiritual fiber of a materialist nation. To artists, particularly those associated with the Hudson River School, Ruskin gave an endorsement of the kind of art Americans were already creating; Ruskin provided impassioned arguments for the turn from history painting and portraiture to landscape painting that Americans had already made. And to those Americans traveling to Europe in increasing numbers, Ruskin acted as a combination tour guide and tutor. Whether directly, through anthologies like *Readings from Ruskin: Italy*, or through the generous helpings of Ruskin that were served up in guidebooks, Americans could learn from Ruskin what monuments, artworks, and buildings they should see and—perhaps more important—what they should think and say about them. In an 1868 review of *Modern Painters V*, Russell Sturgis wrote that any visitor to Europe should "copy every piece of description and of criticism of pictures, statues, buildings, and scenery from all Ruskin's writings, classify them geographically, and study each thing commented on with the aid of the comments."[8] Many did so; those who did not could always buy the "Traveller's Edition" of *The Stones of Venice*, in which Ruskin's prose rhapsodies were rearranged according to the scene they described.

While Ruskin's specific appeal to all these groups may have been different, two general dimensions of his thought seem to have sparked the initial burst of popularity. The first—and least consequential for our concerns, although fascinating in itself—was his naturalism, a quality singled out for praise by most of the early reviewers. This understanding of Ruskin led to the first fruitful American attempt to domesticate him: the attempt of art critics like William Stillman, Asher Durand, and others associated with *The Crayon* to invoke Ruskin's authority for a militantly representationalist aesthetic which emphasized a minutely accurate recounting of natural fact. This group and the painters associated with them are sometimes known as American Pre-Raphaelites, and the works they produced fascinate in the way Pre-Raphaelite art compels: they give us accounts of natural scenes so faithfully rendered as to appear unreal, even hallucinatory. The aesthetic they produced to justify this kind of art (or, in the case of Stillman, the kind of art they produced in order to justify this aesthetic) is no less hallucinatory in its response to Ruskin. Downplaying or ignoring the development of Ruskin's thought beyond the advocacy of truth to nature found in *Modern Painters I*—ignoring the turn to the transfiguring properties of the imagination in *Modern Painters II* and *III*, for example—these writers frequently found themselves elevating eyesight over insight, nature over art. "You advocate the study of Nature in opposition to works of Art," wrote a reader of *The Crayon* to its editor, Stillman. "What is the nature and extent of the good to be derived from the *latter*?" Stillman responded with genuine perplexity:

This, again, is a subject which demands careful treating, not to produce confusion. Although it is not a matter which we feel in doubt about, it is one we cannot so easily make perfectly clear to a less experienced inquirer. There can be nothing genuine in Art which is not found in Nature first, and, therefore, much of the distinction between Nature and Art is really only to be made between Nature and bad art or false art. But we will also bear this subject in mind, and answer it at some other time.[9]

Stillman never answered his correspondent—he suffered a nervous breakdown shortly thereafter, and withdrew from the editorship—but the questions she raised continued to reverberate throughout the 1850's and 1860's. As Ruskin himself learned, and as the Americans following in his footsteps were forced to acknowledge, an aesthetic of radical naturalism must, if taken seriously, end with a questioning of the value of the aesthetic itself. This development was quite significant, for it both enhanced Ruskin's appeal to his American audience and limited it. The simplification of the complex nuances of thought that surround the notion of the "naturalist ideal" led Americans away from the splendors of Renaissance art, and led realist writers and aestheticians away from the most vital experimentation of the mid-century, particularly that which centered on Courbet and the Barbizon school. The discovery of these artists later in the century largely through the efforts of men like William Morris Hunt and John La Farge necessitated a rejection of Ruskin himself.

Problems of precisely the opposite nature were presented by the other chief school of American Ruskinians, a school that gained in influence throughout the 1860's and 1870's. Writers, critics, and connoisseurs like Charles Eliot Norton and James Jackson Jarves emphasized the crucial importance of traditional European art to the cultural situation of America. To Jarves, the problem was chiefly one of exposure and education. As he argues in the opening pages of *The Art-Idea*, no culture could be truly great that did not possess advanced and supple aesthetic sensibilities. In accordance with these beliefs, Jarves sought to expose Americans to the great artistic traditions of Europe by gathering a collection of medieval art. The unhappy fate of this collection—no institution was willing to pay Jarves what the art was worth and it was sold, for a pittance, to Yale in order to cover his debts —suggests just how necessary this education was. But the fact that, not twenty years after Jarves was forced to sell his collection, millionaires vied with each other for the remaining spoils of European art and paid sums for a single painting far greater than those Jarves expended in toto, also suggests how effective his efforts, and those of men like him, were to be.[10]

For Norton, however, the problems were greater, and the effort required to overcome them correspondingly massive. One of Ruskin's oldest and closest friends, Norton echoed Ruskin's thunderous denunciations of modern industrial society and of the corruption of tradition, culture, and value it had wrought, and turned that critique into a weapon of considerable force against what he saw as the decadence of contemporary America. Norton believed that America, lacking the sense of tradition and depth of feeling and intellect that informed the European consciousness, had fallen into a sordidness and materialism far greater than that which afflicted the Continent. Norton called America "the Paradise of Mediocrities," and fought to correct its deficiencies. This task was evident in his literary and journalistic endeavors.

Norton was one of the most influential and powerful men of letters of his time. A regular contributor to *The Atlantic*, editor for five years of *The North American Review*, cofounder of *The Nation*: Norton's writing was inescapable, and his influence on the writing of others immeasurable. Through his journalism, books like *Historical Studies of Church-Building in the Middle Ages*, and the professional encouragement he offered to other writers and critics, Norton strove continuously to expose the American public to the glories of European art, especially the art of the Middle Ages. His aim was not, like Jarves's, educational, but rather moral, social, and political. Norton followed in Ruskin's path by seeking to isolate and praise the values that informed medieval art—faith, unity, simplicity, naturalness—and to trace the presence or absence of such values in nineteenth-century society. The lack of poise and idealism evident in post-Renaissance art thus expressed the fall of civilization from its medieval state of religious faith and social unity into its present condition of anarchy and chaos—a chaos to which America, lacking utterly in traditions and the cultural institutions to propagate them, was particularly prone.

Norton's position suggests one of the most important ways the example of Ruskin was relevant to the American cultural agenda. Ruskin's conservative, hierarchical social vision and sense of the social importance of art mirrored the ideology of the group that historians refer to as the American gentry—the largely northeastern, indeed largely Bostonian elite who considered themselves the embattled proponents of culture and civilization in an increasingly materialistic and secular age.[11] Indeed, Ruskin's project was akin to that of the gentry elite in a number of important ways. Like many members of this group, Ruskin found himself torn between the demands of a rejected but nevertheless powerful religious faith and an equally powerful, and equally problematic, allegiance to Romanticism. Further, like many members of the Bostonian gentry, Ruskin turned from both of his faiths to a form of social criticism that measured the decadence of society by the decadence of its culture, and sought to revitalize public appreciation of fine art as a means of reestablishing a stable, hierarchical social order. There is, I believe, more to Ruskin's vision of the power of art and art education than a mode of enhancing social control, but it was in this project that his authority was enlisted by the Bostonian gentry—especially by the moralistic Norton. Indeed, a Ruskinism of such severity that it surprised Ruskin himself informed all of Norton's various cultural activities. In addition to his influence over the periodical press, Norton was a moving force behind many of the cultural organizations of his day—the American Archeological Society, the Dante Reading Circle, and the Dante Society, as well as, later in the century, the Arts and Crafts Movement—and served also as a scrupulous monitor of architectural rectitude: Norton engaged in a number of protracted and bitter controversies over building plans at Harvard, which he found insufficiently Gothic in spirit.

Not insignificantly, in his role as educator Norton put Ruskin's principles into action most influentially. For 25 years, Norton was one of the most popular teachers at Harvard, and his lectures were as likely to be occupied with vivid denunciations of contemporary art and society as with a careful and graceful account of art history from the Greeks to, but not through, the Renaissance: "Professor Norton lectured in Italian 4 this afternoon. The dear old man looks so mildly happy and benignant while he regrets everything in the age and the country— so contented, while he gently tells us it were better for us had we never been born in this degenerate and unlovely age." [12] Norton's most influential educational efforts, however, were extracurricular. It was Norton's study, for example, that Henry James remembered as the locus of his "consecration to letters," and Norton sought to cultivate young men like James for the rest of his life; his protégés included the likes of Bernard Berenson, Ernest Fenollosa, and Van Wyck Brooks. [13] Norton knew every major writer in England and America, and he seems to have introduced his protégés to most of them: when James first visited England as an adult in 1868, letters of introduction from Norton enabled him to meet Ruskin, Carlyle, Rossetti, and Morris. Twenty years later, Norton provided a similar service by introducing a promising young undergraduate named Berenson to his future patron, Mrs. Isabella Stewart Gardner.

Norton's generosity, however, was tempered by his severity. Berenson, for example, never forgot that

at Harvard, Charles Eliot Norton said to Barrett Wendell who repeated it, "Berenson has more ambition than ability." . . . He wrote a long review of my *Lorenzo Lotto*, taking it as a serious but mistaken effort, mistaken in method and mistaken in purpose, for Lotto was not worth the trouble. Years later, when my *Drawings of the Florentine Painters* was put on sale, he discouraged the Harvard Library from purchasing a copy. It was no satisfaction to me that afterwards they did buy it at an enhanced price.[14]

However, James remained friends with Norton for the rest of Norton's life—and was, of course, particularly close to his sister Grace, to whom some of his most affectionate and moving letters were addressed. Nevertheless, he too seems to have chafed at Norton's strenuous moralism; such at least is the impression one receives from James's 1908 memorial essay, *An American Art-Scholar: Charles Eliot Norton*.[15] For there, he affectionately but nevertheless unmistakably condescends to his friend and mentor. To James, Norton is finally a "*case* . . . of such a mixture of the elements as would have seemed in advance, critically speaking, quite anomalous or at least highly incalculable" (421–22). The anomaly of Norton's endeavor, James suggests, inhered in the odd mixture of intensity and equanimity he brought to his self-proclaimed role as a "'representative of culture'" (413). For the very Puritan self-assurance Norton brought to his "civilising mission"—to the task of inculcating "the particular civilisation that a young roaring and money-getting democracy, inevitably but almost exclusively occupied with 'business success,' most needed to have brought home to it"—was in fundamental conflict with the suppleness of consciousness and sensitivity of aesthetic apprehension true civilization demands (415). "His interest was predominantly in Art . . . his ostensible plea was for the esthetic law, under the wide wing of which we really move, it may seem to many of us, in an air of strange and treacherous appearances, of much bewilderment and not a little mystification; of terribly fine and complicated issues in short, such as call for the highest interpretive wisdom" (422). Norton was a missionary, James suggests, who failed to comprehend the faith he was preaching—a faith in which James himself was the true votary:

Nothing in fact *can* be more interesting to a haunter of other intellectual climes and a worshipper at the esthetic shrine *quand même* than to note once more how race and implanted quality and association always in the end come by their own; how for example a son of the Puritans the most intellectually transmuted, the most liberally emancipated and initiated possible, could still plead most for substance when proposing to plead for style, could still try to lose himself in the labyrinth of delight while keeping tight hold of the clue of duty, tangled even a little in his feet; could still address himself all consistently to the moral conscience while speaking as by his office for our imagination and our free curiosity. (422)

The intensity of James's effort to evade Norton's moral example and authority may suggest just how powerful the Nortonian/Ruskinian orthodoxy remained among the Boston literati of the late nineteenth century, which is to say in the high-cultural life of America as a whole. But it also suggests one way around that orthodoxy. James deftly distances himself from Norton by adopting for his own the stance of the perfervid aesthete—the "worshipper at the aesthetic shrine *quand même*"—and by imparting value to Norton's endeavor only in so far as his critical "office" enabled him to speak for the aestheticist values of "imagination and free curiosity." This tactic was hardly unique; as we shall see, an entire generation of American upper-middle-class youth similarly struck the stance of the aesthete in order to evade the moralism Norton preached and enforced. Indeed, it might be said that the cultural role of Norton's genteel Ruskinism was precisely to prepare the rebellion against it—a rebellion that, as we shall also see, impelled the movement from a nineteenth-century aesthetic and cultural order to one we recognize as distinctively modern.

Before we turn to this development, we need to note the other path that the rebellion against Norton's Ruskinism followed. This path is one we associate with men like Van Wyck Brooks—another of Norton's favorite students—who came to see Norton as the embodiment of all he distrusted in genteel American culture: moralism, effeteness, the detachment of art and criticism from "real" experience. Brook's rejection of Norton in the name of the "Newness" is most significant to our endeavor, however, for the light it casts on the continuing force of Ruskin in American consciousness. It is a tribute to the very inescapability of Ruskin that Brooks's rejection of Norton is coupled with a claim of continuing sympathy with Ruskin himself. In his *An Autobiography*, Brooks writes that it was Ruskin who provided him with his first vision of the relation between the artist or the critic and his society—of the possibility that both artist and critic might engage in a genuine social and cultural criticism: "Ruskin stood for the Utopian impulse that was deeply planted in the American mind and that awoke in me also in time; and it was this common impulse, fostered by Ruskin in both of us, that was to lead me to Lewis Mumford." Brooks places Ruskin in his own personal pantheon, along with Emerson, Tolstoy, and Romain Rolland.[16]

Brooks's Ruskinism reminds us, then, of the third great wave of Ruskinian sentiment in the United States—that which centered on his political and social thought, particularly as they were extended and revised by William Morris. Throughout the late years of the nine-

teenth century and into the early years of the twentieth, Ruskin continued to inspire American writers, artists, and intellectuals with his
critique of modern industrial society and its enfeebled culture. It was
in a Ruskin club in San Francisco that young Jack London and Carl
Sandburg first discovered socialism, and William Dean Howells found
support in Ruskin for his arguments for the necessary relation of the
arts to "the needs of the common people." Critics and social activists
like Lewis Mumford, Vernon Parrington, Jane Addams, and Emma
Lazarus were all similarly inspired by Ruskin, albeit to perform vastly
different tasks. For, recapitulating the general cultural struggle to appropriate Ruskin's cultural authority, many different groups among
late-nineteenth-century reformers and radicals explicitly sought to
claim Ruskin's heritage as their own. Utopian communitarians, for example, often cited Ruskin's extravagant attempt to reform society by
re-creating ex nihilo the social structure of the fourteenth century in
his St. George's Society; a Ruskin Commonwealth was formed in central Tennessee to experiment with this model in an American context.
(Like such illustrious predecessors as Brook Farm, this experiment
in communal living dissolved after several years as a result of personal and ideological disputes. Attempts to continue the experiment
in Georgia were similarly unsuccessful.) Socialists privileged Ruskin's
critique of the moral consequences of capitalism; one of their number
edited an anthology, *The Communism of John Ruskin*, designed to show
how Ruskin anticipated Marx. The Arts and Crafts Movement of the
late nineteenth and early twentieth century was similarly inspired by
Ruskin's thought, and by Morris's attempt to follow out its implications by seeking to revive artisanal skills. They, too, claimed Ruskin as
precedent for their attempt to cultivate handcrafts as the best way of
renewing the social and moral fiber of the country.

The Arts and Crafts Movement has been justly criticized for its failure to follow Morris beyond handcrafts to a cannier, more fully institutionalized effort at social transformation.[17] But with these developments we are getting beyond the chronological horizons of this study.
The important point to grasp, at least for our purposes, is the ubiquity of Ruskin's authority over questions of art, representation, and
the relation of each to morality for the generation that came to intellectual maturity in the 1850's and 1860's—the generation, in other
words, in which Henry James came to maturity. Left and right, aestheticians and politicians, social reformers and anxious defenders of
the status quo, nature lovers and art scholars, writers and artists: men
of differing opinions, interests, and beliefs all acknowledged Ruskin

as their prime authority on an unusually diverse number of questions, and struggled to include him in their camps.[18] This was not a universal phenomenon, to be sure. The best American landscape painters often found Ruskin's dicta either irrelevant or, at best, confirmation of their own technical or theoretical inclinations.[19] And a significant number of American critics resisted Ruskin, sometimes by adhering to neoclassical norms of generalized beauty and sometimes by focusing on Ruskin's failure to acknowledge German aesthetic theory. But these dissenters remained, until about 1870, in the minority, especially in the centers of culture, Boston and New York. Ruskin's presence on the intellectual and cultural landscape was massive and unavoidable, and helped shape American notions of artistic representation, aesthetic morality, and social obligation. Henry James put the matter with his usual eloquence when he wrote in 1868:

We have not the space to go over the ground of our recent literature, and enumerate those fading or flourishing tracts which, in one way or another, communicate with that section of the great central region which Mr. Ruskin has brought under cultivation. Sometimes the connecting path is very sinuous, very torturous, very much inclined to lose itself in its course, and to disavow all acquaintance with its parent soil; sometimes it is a mere thread of scanty vegetation, overshadowed by the rank growth of adjacent fields; but with perseverance we can generally trace it back to its starting-point, on the margin of *Modern Painters*.[20]

As James suggests, the experience of Ruskin remains at the center of the American cultural consciousness, so that even the turn away from Ruskin later in the century was made with reference to him. Indeed, James's experience was itself paradigmatic of this process. James was, from adolescence on, thoroughly imbued with Ruskin. T. S. Perry recalls that in the summer of 1858, James "fell under the influence of Ruskin" and devoted his time "to the conscientious copying of a leaf and very faithfully drew a little rock that jutted above the surface of the Lily Pond" according to Ruskin's directions.[21] His references to Ruskin in the early art criticism, like the passage I quote above, were uniformly favorable. James's attitude to Ruskin, however, soon came to be touched with ambivalence. Three years after the review of Phillip Gilbert Hamerton's art criticism, which contained the description of Ruskin's "garden," for example, James compared Ruskin's description of the Alps unfavorably with that of John Tyndall's *Hours of Exercise in the Alps*, praising the latter for its "urbanity" and criticizing Ruskin for his querulousness and for the "lack of composition" of his fiery and fervent prose. Six years later, oppressed by the extreme moralism of Ruskin's recent writing, James complained that these works are "pitched in the nursery-key, and might be supposed to emanate from an angry governess"; during the Whistler/Ruskin controversy, James criticized Ruskin's lack of critical decorum.[22]

But there is also another tone in James's descriptions of Ruskin, one usually sounded at the same time as the note of criticism. After his criticisms of Ruskin's recent writing on Italy, for example, James claims a continuing affection for his earlier works, especially *The Stones of Venice*, writing: "It is Mr. Ruskin who beyond anyone helps us to enjoy." And in the account of the Whistler/Ruskin controversy, James excuses Ruskin as a "chartered libertine" who deserves to be indulged, if not valued, as a "general scold."[23] It is true that James was always suspicious of Ruskin's moralism (although as we shall soon see, things are more complicated in this regard than they at first appear), but Ruskin's vision of the possibilities of representation does not leave James so easily. Even as James flirted with naturalism and strove to find a more organized, less idiosyncratic, theory of representation than that offered in *Modern Painters*, the central perceptions and much of the language of Ruskin both remain. Writing in 1869 about an exhibition of French painting, for example, James declares that "to satisfy the requirements of the character now represented by the term 'painter,' it is necessary to look at Nature in the most impartial and comprehensive manner, to see objects in their integrity and to reject nothing."[24] This language places its author in an intermediary position, somewhere between Ruskin's famous injunction to "go to Nature, selecting nothing, rejecting nothing" and the new French emphasis on detachment, objectivity, and impartiality. Indeed, James locates unerringly the continuity between these two visions of representation—a continuity that Ruskin himself refused to acknowledge—and attempts to stake out the common ground between them.

James's relation with Ruskin continued to unfold complexly. His responses to Ruskin demonstrate a constant impatience with his rhetoric while manifesting a deepening sympathy with his project, specifically that aspect of his project emphasized to James by the august and gloomy figure of Charles Eliot Norton—that aspect James chose to rebel against in 1908. One index of this sympathy is the recurrence of Ruskinian terminology and topoi in James's fiction; but of far greater importance is the way that the side of Ruskin that Norton emphasized to his friend provided a crucial model for the stance and achievement of the Jamesian novelist himself.

We may perhaps best note this continuing and dual importance to

James of Ruskin in *The Wings of the Dove,* for that novel is itself brooded
over by many of the most famous Ruskinian texts, and its persistent
echoing of these texts helps the novel achieve much of its sonority.
Some of these echoes have been previously noted. Miriam Allott, for
example, has observed that Kate Croy's characterization of Aunt Maud
Lowder as the "Britannia of the Market-Place" echoes directly one of
Ruskin's most famous tropes.[25] In his lecture *Traffic,* Ruskin vociferously argued that his culture, and therefore its architecture, acknowledged only one deity: "the Goddess of Getting-On," "Britannia of the
Market" (JR, 18: 433–58). "The Athenians had an 'Athena Agoraia,'
or Athena of the Market; but she was a subordinate type of their goddess, while our Britannia Agoraia is the principal type of ours" (18:
448). The relevance of Ruskin's text to James's seems obvious enough,
and James's deployment of it in the novel seems manifestly satirical.
As Kate realizes, the "Britannia Agoraia" is an appropriate name for
the deity worshipped by the Lancaster Gate society over which Maud
Lowder reigns. For all its aristocratic pretensions, this "set" believes
that human relations are identical to business transactions, and that a
beautiful, impecunious Englishwoman and a dying American exist to
be auctioned off to the highest bidders. The allusion, in other words,
tells us in a compressed way what we also learn through the novel's
plot, and serves to underscore Kate's horrified initial vision of Lancaster Gate as an "office, her counting-house . . . a toll-gate" (NY,
19: 30).

But the allusion is at once subtler and more satirical than it appears at first glance. For as we are soon to learn, Kate's parroting of
Ruskin's critique of the "Market-Place" in no way prevents her from
taking enthusiastic part in it. If Aunt Maud is the goddess "Britannia
of the Market" personified, then Kate is one of her adepts, an attendant, moreover, who possesses commercial skills superior to those of
her deity. It is Kate, in fact, who articulates explicitly the principles
that govern the Lancaster Gate market: "Everyone who had anything
to give . . . made the sharpest possible bargain for it, got at least its
value in return. The strangest thing furthermore was that this might
be in cases a happy understanding. The worker in one connection was
the worked in another; it was as broad as it was long—with the wheels
of the system, as might be seen, wonderfully oiled" (19: 179). And it
is Kate, of all the Lancaster Gate merchants, who strikes the sharpest
bargain.

The allusion, then, tells us something about the ease with which
Kate covers over her own complicity in the marketplace: in her hands,

honesty and self-exposure come to be (as they are with Lord Mark and, indeed, with all members of Mrs. Lowder's set) a subtler and more refined form of deception. But it also tells us something about the social fate of Ruskin himself. Kate's allusions to Ruskin suggest the range of her reading, but also its superficiality. She is able to employ Ruskin's tropes, but only by draining them of their moral power. To Kate, the language of Ruskin has thus become nothing more than so much drawing-room patter, so much mental chitchat, denoting its user's sophistication, perhaps, but also suggesting its own exhaustion. What is suggested in this one allusion is confirmed elsewhere in the novel. Kate, the other members of the Lancaster Gate set, and even her own family all employ the language of Ruskin and, indeed, the discourse of British aestheticism itself as an elegant and refined mode of noncommunication, an empty diction whose hollowness speaks eloquently only of the emptiness of their lives:

> "It's just why I've sent for you—that you may see me as I really am."
> "Oh, papa, it's long since I've ceased to see you otherwise than as you really are. I think we've all arrived by this time at the right word for that: 'You're beautiful—*n'en parlons plus*.' You're as beautiful as ever—you look lovely." (19: 9)

Kate and her father speak here in an Arnoldian/Ruskinian/Paterian patois that applies the language of British aestheticism—of seeing the object as it really is and judging it for its beauty or loveliness—to human relations. This diction is the lingua franca of Lancaster Gate as well, whose members also reflect the contrast between the language of beauty and the moral ugliness of Lionel Croy's demand that his daughter "work" Milly Theale. For they, too, set out simultaneously to bathe Milly in an atmosphere of aestheticist appreciation and to "work" her to the hilt.

The richness of satirical meaning generated by this discourse, however, is supplemented by other uses James finds for the language of Ruskin. *Traffic* is not the only text of Ruskin's echoed in the novel; indeed, Ruskinian echoes resound throughout, most prominently, as one might expect, in the portion that takes place in Venice. Here, James's use of Ruskin transcends the satirical; indeed, he turns to Ruskin to give resonance to the moral voice in which the novelist wishes to speak. For to Ruskin, as to James, Venice was more than a monument to its own magnificence; its history was a reenactment of the most primal drama of human history. This drama is described in the very first paragraph of the first volume of *The Stones of Venice*:

Since first the dominion of man was asserted over the ocean, three thrones, of mark beyond all others, have been set upon its sands: the thrones of Tyre, Venice, and England. Of the First of these great powers only the memory remains; of the Second, the ruin; the Third, which inherits their greatness, if it forget their example, may be led through prouder eminence to less pitied destruction.

It is glossed throughout all three volumes, and delineated again at the end of the last:

It is as needless as it is painful to trace the steps of her final ruin. The ancient curse was upon her, the curse of the Cities of the Plain, "Pride, fulness of bread, and abundance of idleness." By the inner burning of her own passions, as fatal as the fiery rain of Gomorrah, she was consumed from her place among the nations; and her ashes are choking the channels of the dead, salt sea. (JR, 9: 17, 11: 195)

The decline and fall of Venice was for Ruskin nothing less than a reenactment of the Fall of Man—*The Fall*, in fact, is the title he gives to volume three of *Stones*. It is this association James brings to his novel to give added weight and meaning to the Fall of Merton Densher. Densher, to be sure, may be said in some sense to be fallen from his first appearance in the novel, but—like the character upon whom he is modeled, Hawthorne's Donatello—Densher is curiously unaware of the implications of his own actions; he hides from himself his knowledge of his complicity in the plots on Milly's fortune, being neither truly guilty nor innocent, until he becomes aware that Milly herself is aware of his guilt. When this contact occurs, the text itself seems to imitate its protagonist; at the moment it describes the onset of Densher's awareness of Milly's consciousness of his guilt, James's novel itself becomes acutely conscious of the language of Ruskin:

It was a Venice all of evil that had broken out for them alike [i.e., for Densher and Milly's servant Eugenio], so that they were together in their anxiety, if they really could have met on it; a Venice of cold lashing rain from a low black sky, of wicked wind raging through narrow passes, of general arrest and interruption, with the people engaged in all the water-life huddled, stranded and wageless, bored and cynical, under archways and bridges. (NY, 20: 259)

The rhetoric of this passage is so deeply Ruskinian that one hardly knows where to begin specifying details. It is Ruskinian, first, in its hyperbolic application of a biblical language to the depiction of a natural phenomenon; phrases like "a Venice all of evil" or "the wicked wind" elevate this storm, as Ruskin so frequently elevated storms, into nothing less than a foretaste of the Apocalypse. It is Ruskinian, further, in its desire to connect the moral experience of an individual consciousness with such a hyperbolized natural phenomenon. The thunder clap is, of course, a spectacular coup de theatre, but it is also a magnificently grandiloquent naturalization of the sudden onset of spiritual "anxiety" into which Densher has fallen. Very much like Turner's *Slave Ship*, in which, Ruskin assures us, a storm cloud advances "like the shadow of death upon the guilty ship," James depicts a moment at which an individual consciousness finds its moral drama projected into the heavens and played out by a conscious, almost frenzied nature (JR, 3: 572). More important, it is Ruskinian in its desire to connect this interplay between individual consciousness and natural phenomenon with social being. Densher's perception of his own inner "Gomorrah," his vision of his own "pride, fulness of bread, and abundance of idleness," leads him to see for the first time the true condition of the Venetian populace. Indeed, he is able for the first time to connect his own condition with their enfeeblement: the people of Venice and Densher alike are "stranded," huddled within what James called elsewhere "the most beautiful of tombs" and finding only inadequate protection from the storm that breaks on them all. Following this train of thought to its logical conclusion, we may identify as Ruskinian its desire to find in the storm that breaks on Venice nothing less than an image of the enfeebled spiritual condition of Western civilization itself:

The wet and the cold were now to reckon with, and it was to Densher precisely as if he had seen the obliteration, at a stroke, of the margin on a faith in which they were all living. The margin had been his name for it—for the thing that, though it held out, could bear no shock. The shock, in some form, had come, and he wondered about it while, threading his way among loungers as vague as himself, as he dropped his eyes sightlessly on the rubbish in shops. There were streches of the gallery paved with squares of red marble, greasy now with the salt spray; and the whole place in its huge elegance, the grace of its conception and the beauty of its detail, was more than ever like a great drawing-room, the great drawing-room of Europe, profaned and bewildered by some reverse of fortune. (NY, 20: 261)

Densher's fall into an awareness of his own fallenness is also a fall into an awareness of the bankruptcy of a civilization in which men are nothing but "vague loungers" and cultural products are just so much "rubbish in shops." Framed by the Venetian monuments to spiritual and temporal authority—the "old columns of St. Theodore and

the lion"—the storm that breaks on Venice is nothing less than what
Ruskin calls "the storm-cloud of the nineteenth century," a visible
manifestation of the materialism, the loss of faith, the decline of morals
and of a spirit of social comity, that mark contemporary society. "Remember," thunders Ruskin in 1884, speaking for the last time with
the power and vigor of the biblical prophet, "for the last twenty years,
England, and all the foreign nations, either tempting her, or following her, have blasphemed the name of God deliberately and openly;
and have done iniquity by proclamation, every man doing as much
injustice to his brother as it is in his power to do. Of states in such
moral gloom, every seer of old predicted the physical gloom, saying,
'The light shall be darkened in the heavens thereof, and the stars shall
withdraw their shining'" (JR, 34: 40–41). It is in these tones, not those
of the urbane Venetian flaneur, that James chooses to speak at this
moment in the novel.

Like Ruskin, then, James elevates the attenuated condition of Venice
into an emblem of the attenuated condition of Western civilization itself. "He had supposed himself civilized; but if this was civilization—"
says Densher in mute horror of the goings-on in Lancaster Gate; it
is not until he reaches Ruskin's Venice—a Venice where emblems of
faith jostle with reminders of faithlessness, where signs of past artistic
glory crumble near "the rubbish in shops" that denotes present aesthetic decadence, where reminders of former temporal power loom
over symbols of the mutability of Empire—that James is able to complete his sentence (NY, 20: 44). It is this use of Venice that I want to
cite as a prime example of James's deployment not only of Ruskin, but
one crucial aspect of the entire tradition of nineteenth-century Ruskinism in this novel. What James does here is more than merely to
allude to Ruskin's terminology or characteristic figures (as is the case
with the "Britannia of the Market") or even to invoke his perceptions,
the better to add to the resonance of his own prose. Rather, what he
does in this scene is make that language and those perceptions his
own: to align his moral, aesthetic, and social vision with Ruskin's; indeed to do nothing less than strike the Ruskinian stance of the secular
prophet. Like the Ruskin of *Traffic* or *The Storm-Cloud*, James does this
by the act of fusing aesthetic, cultural, and moral forms of criticism.
And, like the Ruskin of *Stones*, it is in Venice that James finds a locus
in which these different forms of critique can be brought together, as
if in homage to the lost unity that Venice symbolizes. For James, as
for Ruskin, it is as if the integrative culture that was once achieved by

Venice can be recapitulated by the cultural criticism it inspires. But for James, as for Ruskin, it is therefore a tragic necessity that such criticism comes into being under the sign of loss, its sole task being to trace the causes and consequences of the fall into personal and cultural decadence.

The Ruskinian aspects of James's vision extend further. For James, as for Ruskin, the paradigm of human history presented by Venice is directly, even crucially, relevant to the condition of England. If Western civilization is imaged in Venice as the drawing room of a bankrupt millionaire, then another apt image for it would be the ugly drawing room of the bankrupt and disgraced Lionel Croy in London, a "vulgar little room" on a "vulgar little street" with "narrow black housefronts, adjusted to a standard that would have been low even for backs" (19: 3). Not only is the ugliness of middle-class England linked to the fall of Venice in a thoroughly Ruskinian manner (Ruskinian as well, of course, is the focus on the *ugliness* of the house and street), but so are the conditions of British social intercourse which, as Lord Mark explains them, pick up directly on the imagery of the Venetian storm: "*Was* it a set, or wasn't it, and were there no such things as sets anymore?" wonders Lord Mark; "was there anything but the groping and the pawing, that of the vague billows of some great greasy sea in mid-Channel, of masses of bewildered people trying to 'get' they didn't know what or where?" (19: 150). Thus to James, as to Ruskin, the cultural analysis he brings to the fore in Venice ultimately points directly back to London, and its central task is to articulate with power and melancholy to Britain itself "the warning which seems to me to be uttered by every one of the fast-gaining waves that beat, like passing bells, against the STONES OF VENICE" (JR, 9: 17).

What James accomplishes at this moment in the novel, then, is not only to adopt a Ruskinian rhetoric, but to attempt to reinvigorate it —to redeem it, and the critical stance it adopts, from the degradation James had anatomized earlier in the novel. His end in doing so, I think, is both to reanimate Ruskin's social critique and to articulate one of his own. For James's reinvigoration of Ruskin's rhetoric suggests how compellingly he aspires to the cultural position that goes along with it—that cultural role which, as we have seen, John Holloway eloquently names as that of the "Victorian sage."[26] Like Ruskin before him, he speaks both hyperbolically and parabolically of the conditions of his own culture, and does so with the Victorian sage's typical end of decrying the social, aesthetic, and moral transgressions of his materialist, middle-class culture. To understand this, I think, is to see with greater clarity James's position in the cultural scene of his own time, and to challenge certain widely held assumptions about his art. His adoption of this role suggests, I think, how completely James found himself achieving the status Charles Eliot Norton had envisioned for his young friend: that of the American artist as magisterial critic of culture. It was Norton, we remember, who first endowed James with his sense of a "consecration to letters," and at moments like these, we can see James giving up on his attempts to evade Norton's authority and conscientiously attempting to fill the role Norton had consecrated him for. "It was the relation of art and nature to man as a moral being for which he mainly cared," wrote Norton of his friend and mentor Ruskin, "every artistic faculty and disposition of his nature, the very delicacy and keenness of his perceptions, his very power of enjoyment of beauty, did but make his sentiment of the wrong of existing social conditions continually more and more intense." [27]

It is precisely this Ruskinian fusion of aesthetic and social criticism that James, like Norton before him, seeks to recapitulate. By creating a form that attempts to interweave the consideration of the aesthetic deficiencies and merits of an individual culture, its economic or class relations, and the moral drama enacted within it by an individual consciousness, James writes precisely the mode of fiction that those critics who position him as an ahistorical aesthete accuse him of evading. Indeed, this moment in the novel suggests that James has crafted a precise historical position for himself, and envisions a specifically engaged role for his art. It is true that neither position is necessarily a fully attractive one—like that of Norton before him, or Eliot after him, James's social criticism here is profoundly pessimistic, elitist, antidemocratic. But it is one which, unlike Norton's bitterly nostalgic critique or Eliot's ultimately horrific vision of a redeemed, reunified, "Christian culture," may not be wholly circumscribed within the ambit of the reactionary imagination. For James's critique not only rests on a profound sense of the bankruptcy of human relations in a culture governed by economic relations alone, but is also grounded in a vision very much like that of the leftist social critics who were to follow James by one generation, especially the social critics of the Frankfurt school who shared James's commitment to the institutions of high culture and his despair at their failure. James, like Adorno— I am thinking here of the Adorno of *Minima Moralia* and, especially, of the late essay, "Cultural Criticism and Society"—writes in the wake of the collapse of the programmatic valorization of high culture with which he is so frequently and so reductively associated; moreover, like Adorno, he muses on the consequences of the failure of the program of transcendent critique by which cultural critics habitually seek to interrogate their society.[28] Ruskinian as the novel might wish to be, then, it is also inevitably, and consciously, post-Ruskinian in its emphasis on the participation of cultural institutions in the very system they ought to transcend and transform; in its awareness of the degradation of even the most enlightened form of social and aesthetic criticism into drawing-room chitchat; in its awareness as well of the means by which alternatives to such a system have themselves been made into mere "rubbish in shops." As we shall see in Chapter 5, in this novel James faces directly the implications of this angle of vision: the recognition of the necessarily complicitous relation between cultural critique and the social formations such critiques seek to interrogate.

American Aestheticism

One of the most important consequences of the massive presence of Ruskin on the American cultural scene was a relative lack of interest in the first stirrings of the British "aesthetic movement." Pre-Raphaelitism enjoyed a brief vogue in the 1850's, climaxed by a major exhibition in New York in 1858, but it was the naturalist, Ruskinian dimension of Pre-Raphaelite art that drew the most attention—significantly, the artworks received with the greatest enthusiasm in New York were Ruskin's own nature sketches. And the guardians of the genteel who watched over the major literary magazines may have praised—and taken private pleasure in—the poetry of Rossetti and the Pre-Raphaelites, but they rarely reprinted it in their own magazines.[29] It should not surprise us, then, that *The Renaissance* was met with little of the interest or controversy that greeted its appearance in England. Howells's relatively respectful review in *The Atlantic* was the single positive notice in the established periodical press—and even Howells expressed a good deal of skepticism toward Pater's more imaginative passages. Stillman, who by that time had become the chief critic of *The Nation*, criticized Pater severely for his "dilettantism," "subjectivism," and ignorance of the "pure beauty of Nature," although, now in the process of moderating his more extreme views, he added that he was speaking not only of the "external and material nature," but also of the "universal human-divine nature, in which are born and nourished every aspiration and emotion, the embodiment of which becomes art."[30]

It was against this background of indifference, hostility, and neglect that Americans first encountered the high-cultural manifestations of aestheticism—although, significantly, they were already familiar with aestheticism's contribution to the world of fashion and household design. The first American encounter with an actual aesthete occurred in 1882, with Oscar Wilde's tour of America. That tour provided some of the most amusing anecdotes in both American and British cultural history, most of them recounted by Wilde himself, and most of them utterly untrue. But it also vividly suggested the extent to which the lower-cultural manifestations of aestheticism, its appearance as a "mania" or "craze," had already made their way into American consciousness. It suggested as well the ways that these aspects of British aestheticism were already beginning to shape the contours of the emerging American consumer culture.

Wilde's tour was the product of a cultural mistake. It was, as I suggested above, occasioned by Richard D'Oyly Carte's fear that the American public would have no knowledge of the actual aesthetes who were parodied in *Patience*; his plan, accordingly, was to send Wilde to acquaint this audience with a real, live aesthete, then send in his wake a touring company of *Patience* to satirize him. The tour was cosponsored by Mrs. Frank Leslie, of *Leslie's Illustrated Newspaper*, who wished to garner further publicity for her journal, which had already associated itself with aestheticism by reprinting Du Maurier's cartoons and hints for aesthetic fashion. But, as that example suggests, the American public was already quite familiar with Wilde and with British aestheticism itself—or at least with aestheticism in its manifestation as a popular craze and a subject of parody and satire. It is hardly surprising, then, that Americans were by and large disappointed with Wilde, in part because he delivered his lectures so indifferently, in part because he dressed like an English gentleman, not a Bunthornean aesthete, and in part because, far from bringing Americans anything new, Wilde preached the familiar Ruskinian gospel of the moral value of art, especially the moral importance of handcrafts—although Wilde, as practical minded as his audience, soon switched to delivering a talk on the new principles of interior decoration.

Anticipating Wilde's own recognition that life imitates art, Americans did not hesitate to recreate Wilde in their image of him. The most spectacular version of this transformation was the portrayal of Wilde as a thin, languid aesthete in *Leslie's Illustrated Newspaper*; needless to say, the stocky Wilde looked nothing like his portrait there.[31] An equally typical distortion was the conflation of Wilde with the figure he

had come to America to publicize, Gilbert and Sullivan's Bunthorne.
Bunthorne is, deep down, nothing more than an "aesthetic sham":

> This air severe
> Is but a mere
> Veneer!

> This cynic smile
> Is but a wile
> Of Guile!

> This costume chaste
> Is but good taste
> Misplaced!

> Let me confess!

> A languid love for lilies does *not* blight me!
> Lank limbs and haggard cheeks do *not* delight me!

> I do *not* care for dirty greens
> By any means.
> I do *not* long for all one sees
> That's Japanese.
> I am *not* fond of uttering platitudes
> In stained-glass attitudes.
> In short, my medievalism's affectation,
> Born of a morbid love of admiration.[32]

The American press portrayed "Oscar Wilde, the ass-thete" as if he
were Bunthorne incarnate: Wilde was described as a fraud in even
the most sympathetic accounts. *The New York Herald* wrote: "His real
position is that of a penny Ruskin at the head of a band of so-called
aesthetic enthusiasts. . . . The idea of an artistic mission [however]
is not a pretext, and Mr. Wilde, besides being in for a paying thing,
evidently enjoys the attention he receives." Less sympathetic journals
stressed Wilde's Bunthornean hypocrisy more strenuously. *The New
York Graphic* published a cartoon of Wilde kissing a bowl with a dol-
lar sign; the caption read "Aestheticism as Oscar understands it," and
verses echoing Gilbert's lyrics appeared underneath. Cruelest of all,
perhaps, was the authoritative voice of *The Nation*: "What [Mr. Wilde]
has to say is not new, and his extravagance is not extravagant enough
to amuse the average American audience. His knee breeches and long
hair are good as far as they go, but Bunthorne has really spoiled the
public for Wilde."[33]

However cruel and inaccurate *The Nation*'s account may have been
—Wilde abandoned knee breeches early in the tour, for example—it

was accurate in one sense: despite friendly receptions in many of the cities he visited, especially San Francisco, Wilde's tour failed because he was not "extravagant enough" for the taste of his public, and because he seemed to be the only one involved in the tour who took his "mission" seriously. If Wilde was trapped in his own idealist rhetoric, America to him seemed a nation of literalists who took straight the ironic aspects of Wilde's self-promotion and who refused to see beyond them to the more serious intentions of his tour. They wanted spectacle, not substance, and Wilde's surprisingly naive attempt to use spectacle to preach a gospel of aestheticism—to use his notoriety in order to expose what he took to be a benighted audience to the doctrines of Arnold, Ruskin, Morris, and Pater—was therefore doomed to failure. Needless to say, this was not a mistake he was to make again.

The Americans' concentration on Wilde's avarice and hypocrisy did not prevent them from exercising their own; indeed, the ubiquitous American view of Wilde as a commercialized self-promoter seems to have been a classic case of self-serving national projection. Before and after a Wilde appearance, local advertisers had a field day:

> Gents!
> Have you seen the Oscar Wilde shoes?
> (They are too utterly too-too)
> At B. Frank Hart's, 81 W. 4th St.[34]

The pirate companies of *Patience* that D'Oyly Carte feared—and sent Wilde to America to preempt—took to following in Wilde's wake. Thomas Nast stole a page from Du Maurier's book by using Wildean aesthetes in his cartoons of late 1882—some satirizing Wilde himself (Wilde wincing with pain after sitting on one of the American stoves whose appearance he had criticized) or portraying Americans in the guise of the aesthete (Samuel Clemens as a Bunthornesque lily-sniffing idealist in quest of an international copyright treaty). A number of popular songs were issued commemorating and satirizing Wilde: "My Aesthetic Love, or Utterly Utter, Consummate, Too, Too," for example, or the "Oscar Wilde Forget-Me-Not Waltzes."[35] A popular novel about the aesthetic beau monde, *Mrs. Geoffrey*, appeared, as did a number of racy biographies; Wilde thus found himself in the amusingly Wildean position of buying an utterly inaccurate account of his own life for ten cents.

It is difficult to tell, then, just who was exploiting whom during Wilde's American tour. His tour thus reminds us that the role aestheticism was playing in Great Britain was its part, too, in the drama of nineteenth-century American culture. For as Wilde's tour made clear, Americans were already in the midst of a hypercommercial "aesthetic craze" of their own, a craze that, as the reception of Wilde's lectures suggests, centered on the design and decoration of the home. This craze had been initially sparked by the American publication of Charles Eastlake's popularization of Ruskin and Morris's dicta on home furnishing and decoration, *Hints on Household Taste* (1867; first published in America in 1872, and in ten subsequent editions before 1888). The popularity of Eastlake may have been initially due to the ways he confirmed the governing precepts of American homemaking; his emphasis on the value of "sincerity" in home decor and on the moral importance of the well-made (or "sincere") home sorted well with the ideological lineaments of mid-century American domesticity. But Eastlake's popularity had other, more destabilizing, implications. Despite his strenuous moralism, Eastlake's emphasis on the home as a place of public self-presentation, rather than as an efficient, utilitarian locus of family nurture, and his emphasis on English ornament and furnishings as the standard of cultural value both served to undercut basic tenets of early domestic ideology—its emphasis on restraint, its rejection of displays of wealth or taste, its assertion of its own proud Americanness. Subsequent developments continued to subvert the more austere versions of domesticity. The Philadelphia Exposition of 1876 brought to the attention of the American public the actual furniture, stained glass, embroidery, and carpets of Morris and his associates, and led to a tremendous popular demand for these objects. Indeed, in the next few years, American upper-middle-class home designers displayed remarkable enthusiasm for all things quaint, picturesque, and semimedieval—an enthusiasm at once commemorated and egged on by the ladies' magazines like *Godey's Ladies' Book* and *Appletons' Journal* and by the guides to household decoration of Harriet Prescott Spofford (*Art Decoration Applied to Furniture*, 1878), Clarence Cook (*The House Beautiful*, 1878; *What Shall We Do with Our Walls?*, 1880), and scores of other, less prominent, writers on interior decoration.[36] Mrs. M. E. W. Sherwood wrote in *Appletons'* that

It has become a crime now in Boston or its elegant neighborhood to have an unbeautiful room. A horsehair sofa, which was once but a misdemeanor, has become one of the capital sins. . . . No one dares select a wall-paper which would offend the principles of William Morris, while sideboards and bookcases of medieval design, with lovely keys which Lucrezia Borgia might have worn at her girdle, and which Benvenuto Cellini might have originally designed, lock up tea and sugar from pilfering domestics.[37]

It is no coincidence that the aesthetic craze in America should have initially focused on the reform of interior decoration. The increasing wealth of the upper and upper-middle classes, the decline of republican ideals in the aftermath of the Civil War, the ebbing of the fear of luxury evident earlier in the century, and the continuing power of the cult of domesticity combined to create a wide-scale assent to the proposition that the "House Beautiful" was something to be avidly sought and painstakingly created, that the home itself could and should be seen as a work of art.* To a certain extent, the ideal of the aesthetic interior was one that could only be fully realized by the wealthiest in American society; but the late-nineteenth-century rise of a mobile, professional, and increasingly well-to-do middle class ensured that the pursuit of the House Beautiful would not be restricted to the Vanderbilts and the Whitneys. Indeed, it was widely disseminated to that class by an extraordinary profusion of artists, craftsmen and -women, entrepreneurs, and salesmen, all of whom asserted their expertise by invoking their knowledge of Morris, Ruskin, the Arts and Crafts Movement, and its successor, the Queen Anne, and "aesthetic" designs.[38] Some among this group produced a genuinely American version of British "aesthetic" designs—Candace Wheeler, the Rookwood pottery makers, and Louis Tiffany are perhaps the best known, but their efforts were supplemented by scores of less celebrated, sometimes anonymous, designers of ceramics and pottery, of metal grilles and stained-glass windows, of plush sofas and armchairs, of wallpaper and dinner plates. But these artists and craftsmen and -women were supplemented—and largely made possible by—a growing infrastructure of vendors and salesmen who made their work available to an increasingly avid public: furniture stores that both stocked and pro-

---

*The history of the trope of the "House Beautiful" suggests the extensiveness of the intersection between the British aesthetic movement and transformations in American interior design. The phrase, originally Bunyan's of course, was echoed by Eastlake in *Hints* and by Pater as a chapter heading in *Marius*, then taken by Wilde as a title of an American lecture; it thereafter metamorphosed into the title of a guidebook to household design written by Clarence Cook, the caustic art critic of the *New York Tribune*; served as a chapter title in Twain's *Life on the Mississippi*; and as a provisional title for the manuscript that became *The Spoils of Poynton*. Early in the twentieth century, the phrase —now thoroughly saturated with any number of cultural associations—was adopted by the editors of a new magazine devoted to household design, published by Herbert Stone, one of the founders of the avant-garde publishing house Stone and Kimball, discussed below. *House Beautiful*, of course, still exists today, a testimony to the link between contemporary patterns of consumption and the imaginative structures of the aesthetic movement. For details of this interchange—and for some helpful references on the figure of the "House Beautiful"—see Handlin, *The American Home*, pp. 232–329.

moted the new aesthetic designs (often, tellingly, the new department
stores, some of which sponsored classes in arts and crafts education in
order to train artisans to produce the "authentic" work they were selling) or antique dealers who purveyed the newly canonical bric-a-brac
of the aesthetic moment; cultural cicerones or guides to the aesthetically perplexed, some of whom, like Spofford and Cook, performed
their labors in print, others of whom, like practitioners of the new
profession of interior decoration, did so in person. Standing just beyond these groups and seeking to guide their efforts were the gentry
intellectuals and social reformers: Boston Brahmins like Norton who
sought to supervise the Boston Arts and Crafts Society or University
of Chicago professors who sought to guide the Industrial Arts League
of Chicago, often to the chagrin of those groups. What we witness in
the craze for aesthetic home decoration of the 1880's and early 1890's,
in other words, is the creation of both a new market for household
goods and the creation of new roles and new professions within that
market—all accomplished within, and made possible by, the ideological framework of the beautification of everyday life preached by the
aesthetic movement.

This was not a transitory phenomenon. It is true that the aesthetic
craze of the 1880's and its successor, the "Trilby mania," were soon
to fade; but the importance of aestheticism to American culture did
not fade with them. While artisans and decorators moved on to other
styles, many deeply indebted to those with which they had experi-
mented in the "aesthetic" period (art nouveau, or the modernist architecture of Frank Lloyd Wright in particular), the attitudes, indeed
often the very language, of the American marketers of the aesthetic
in the 1880's and early 1890's made their way into the next century
as well, carried there by the groups who first rose to cultural prominence at the same time as, and often in collaboration with, American
aestheticism: especially high-culture writers of fiction and poetry who,
as we shall see in more detail below, carried the essential stylistic and
ideological assumptions of the aesthetic movement forward into the
"modern" era; commentators on and guides to interior design, who
continued to promulgate the house-beautiful ethos; and, perhaps most
crucially of all, advertisers. Combining their efforts with those of other
groups, these writers and artists working on the plane of "high" and
"popular" culture alike articulated and shaped a new social ethos, one
that privileged the experience of beauty as a valuable experience in
and of itself and served, wittingly or unwittingly, to celebrate the act of
consumption. Through their influence, the terminology, the topoi, the

very imaginative disposition of aestheticism continued to exert a shaping influence on American culture and society, guiding the means by
which the culture of consumption in which we are ourselves enmeshed
were first articulated and defined.

Indeed, aestheticism played a more important role in the strategies of that culture than has previously been thought. Typically, historians named the 1920's the period of the ascendency of the ethos
of consumption, although more recent critics have suggested that it
first comes to the fore in the late 1880's and early 1890's, when what
Christopher Wilson calls "the rhetoric of consumption" first began to
appear in the new mass-circulation magazines.[39] But in the popular
American responses to the British aesthetic craze, this kind of rhetoric appears even earlier—as early as the late 1870's, four years before
Wilde's tour and eight years before the first mass-circulation magazine
appeared. In ladies' magazines like *Godey's* or *Appletons'*, for example,
not only were the new, more luxuriant designs for dress, furniture,
and interior decoration described and reprinted, but the principles
underlying this turn toward aesthetic richness were fully articulated.
Here, for example, is the distinctive voice of Mrs. Sherwood:

On all sides now we hear of household and decorative art. It is one of the
forms in which color has revived—in which a long-dormant passion for art
and beauty has awakened and taken possession of us. Why a cloud came over
the race and for so many decades obscured its sense of color and splendor,
we cannot now inquire; but it is certain that the old medieval delight in form,
and light and shadow, and pomp, has come back to us—with many modifi-
cations, of course, but with much of its old sense of beauty for beauty's sake.
It is curious to watch and see the manifestations of this latest renaissance. A
whole new literature has grown out of it; new armies of artisans have been
marshaled as its servants; and even new, or rather revived, sets of rules have
been formulated. "It is against my principles," replied an artisan, upon being
asked by one not within the radius of the new light to make for him a certain
ornament for a bookcase. . . . [R]eplied the disciple of Eastlake and Morris; "it
is my rule never to construct ornament—I only ornament construction." And
in this way the artisans, mastered by the new passion, deeply read in Owen
Jones, disciples at the feet of Eastlake, Clarence Cook, and Elliott, filled, no
doubt, with Matthew Arnold's "sweetness and light," are banishing from our
apartments ugly forms and bare walls, overthrowing white paint and colorless
washes of all sorts, and overwhelming us with the charm of their studies of
colors, their *ensemble* of sumptuous effects, their transformation of dull rooms
into paradises of beauty.[40]

What we encounter here, I want to claim, is more than just a celebration of new possibilities in interior design. What we witness is the

emergence of a rhetoric that deployed the "cultural" and the "aes-thetic" as advertising slogans, as part of a naive but nevertheless effec-tive strategy for advertising commodities that would at once glorify and efface the act of consumption itself by grounding even the most mundane acquisitive choices in the nonmaterial realm of transcen-dent value designated by the aesthetic. It is important to note that the topoi of British aestheticism are an integral part of this process. The aestheticized medievalism of the Pre-Raphaelites (there are none of Ruskin's moral concerns here), the language of "beauty for beauty's sake," the ironic use of Morris's trope of the "Earthly Paradise": all are invoked as signs of a new attitude or consciousness that manifests itself not in the creation of art or poetry nor in social criticism nor even, finally, in home decoration. Rather, this language advertises the direct availability of "culture" and the aesthetic to the diligent consumer. Although the presence of Arnold is explicitly invoked, Arnoldian "cul-ture" is redefined. It is no longer viewed as a process or an activity, an endeavor or a discipline; rather, it is something whose rules can be learned or, failing that, something that can be bought. And the witty, ironic tone of fashionable aestheticism conceals the fact that this work —the magazine itself—could itself be bought in order to achieve pre-cisely the desired goal of "being cultured." Or rather the irony *is* the message: a guarantee of the ironic, worldly attitude that is part of cul-tural sophistication, and that can be bought along with the magazine.

The aestheticized consumerism (or consumerist aestheticism) that Spofford articulated was to prove crucial indeed to the subsequent shape of American society. Many of the notions expressed half-banter-ingly by Spofford in the aesthetic craze of the 1870's and early 1880's emerged, after a period of cultural assimilation and reworking, as staples of the so-called advertising revolution of the 1920's. The *neces-sity* of the beautiful, the revival of color, the existence of aesthetic regu-lations that could and should be learned by the discerning consumer: all these notions advanced tentatively, even ironically, by Spofford and other ideologues of the aesthetic craze were rediscovered and rede-ployed seriously, even scientifically, by the advertisers of the 1920's. As Roland Marchand has shown in *Advertising the American Dream*, in the 1920's new productive processes like color lithography helped ad-vertisers devise marketing strategies that appealed to a sense of color and aesthetic values in selling consumer goods. As with Spofford and Cook, this process seems to have begun in the home, although not, as with these writers, in the living or dining room, but rather in the bathroom: towels and bath fixtures began to be advertised on the basis of their aesthetic appeal—whether, as in the case of the former, on the basis of their color, or, in the case of the latter, by the association of mundane implements with images of spectral beauty. The strategy of the Bathroom Beautiful, like its predecessor, was a paradoxical one. On the one hand, it suggested that the commodities one purchased were not so much objects for use as objects of art, to be acquired and appreciated the way a connoisseur purchases a fine oil; at the same time, the strategy was linked to mass production of these commodities: only when sinks are being produced on a mass scale is it possible—or necessary—to suggest that sinks be differentiated on the basis of their relative beauty. ("Eastlake" furniture posed the same marketing problems; Eastlake's text advocated the Ruskinian notion that each piece should be authentic, idiosyncratic, "sincere"; but because he also advocated rectilinear, unornamented designs, "sincere" Eastlake pieces were marvelously suited to mass production.) Despite (or because of) its logical flaws, this strategy was wildly successful: sales levels increased dramatically in those industries in which it was prevalent, and profit levels of individual firms adopting an aesthetic-oriented strategy increased with particular vigor.[41] It is no surprise that the strategy spread to advertising for other areas of the house—advertisements for the kitchen, the living room, even the furnace—and beyond, into the sale of a wide variety of consumer goods including, crucially, the sale of automobiles, which to this day are frequently marketed as if they were valuable works of art.

As the advertising revolution fulfilled many of the tenets of Spoffordian aestheticism, so too it frequently reactivated the very iconography of aestheticism: Pre-Raphaelite imagery suffuses the visual content of many of the "aesthetic" advertising campaigns of the 1920's. Perhaps its most famous practitioner was Maxfield Parrish, whose posters, advertisements, and illustrations provided a spectacular literalization of Morris's trope of the Earthly Paradise by filling unreal Rossettiesque space with languid, unworldly, tall, and slender women —all in the service of selling *The Century*, General Electric Edison-Mazda lamps, or Jell-O. One of Parrish's most famous posters suggests the ways that aestheticism shaped the visual contours of these advertising campaigns; an ad for General Electric, entitled *Enchantment*, poses a Pre-Raphaelite woman, complete with red hair and a flowing robe, on a stairway in a never-never-land garden. It is twilight, and she is looking toward a light somewhere beyond the frame of the picture, her face illuminated by its glow. The woman, the light, the garden: all combine to create a vivid association between the scene and the sponsor (Edison-Mazda lamps), a metonymy that places not only the woman, but the consumer looking at the ad, in that world "sublimated beyond" the transfigured worlds of Christian or pagan paradises that Pater celebrated—a transfiguration here accomplished by means of the artificial glow of an incandescent light bulb.[42]

As this example suggests, aestheticism provided American advertisers with something more important than specific strategies or specific icons. It may be said to provide for American culture the image of the Earthly Paradise itself, to offer it the imaginative structure in which the privileging of beauty, art, and the aesthetic themselves could promise a world transfigured by the sensual delights of acts of frequent and repeated consumption. It is no wonder, then, that we can hear even in the advertising of our era echoes of aestheticist slogans, see afterimages of aestheticist icons. "Great moments / Great moments / Great moments / For you on CBS": in this slogan, the cultural fate of aestheticism becomes clear, for it suggests that the Paterian doctrine of the perfect moment has been wholly engulfed within the cultural unconscious of advertisers and consumers alike.* Aestheticism, I suggested in my previous chapter, always bordered on establishing itself as the poetry of consumption; in the "magic system" of advertising, and the culture of consumption it services, aestheticism fully achieves this destiny.[43]

But to restrict the fate of aestheticism in America to this commercial function would be to neglect a more specific role aestheticism played in the transformation of American society, a role not entirely unrelated to the emergence of the "culture of consumption," but not entirely circumscribed by it, either. For aestheticism helped guide the experience of a crucial group in American culture of the twentieth century—a group whose rhetoric and self-image put them increasingly at odds with the increasingly consumerist orientation of that culture, even as they were individually to participate in and profit from its rituals; those Americans who devoted themselves with increasing avidity to their own cultural improvement—particularly, but not exclusively,

---

*There are numerous contemporary examples of the stylistic continuities between the graphic art of the aesthetic era and that of the past twenty years as well. I am thinking, for example, of the art of Peter Max, which adopted many of the stylistic features of the aesthetic movement and its graphic successor, art nouveau, to something of the same end—the glorification of consumption, here suffused by the aura of the "counterculture" but nevertheless (or thereby) remodeled into a consumer item of mass appeal —or the recent advertising campaign for Nestlé's chocolate, in which the nineteenth-century tradition of the *tableaux vivant* is revived by models reenacting Maxfield Parrish paintings while eating Nestlé's candy bars.

American writers, artists, and intellectuals. Here, too, British aestheticism played a crucial role. On the one hand, it provided a means for
the newly rising professional and managerial elites to challenge the
cultural hegemony of the established gentry elite; at the same time, it
gave a new cadre of rebellious intellectuals, writers, and artists stem-
ming from both castes a rhetoric for experiencing and expressing
their increasing sense of alienation from the culture that surrounded
them—and a socially acceptable means of playing the role of alienated
autonomy within that culture.

The crucial role played by aestheticism in America, in other words,
needs to be understood in the social context of the late nineteenth
century. This period is marked by a sharp increase in the upwardly
mobile, professional, or managerial classes, in middle-class, middle-
brow middle Americans largely, but not exclusively, living outside the
great cultural centers of the East. These newly empowered groups increasingly sought the social respectability that they associated with the
established, early-nineteenth-century "gentry" elite who dominated
the organs of high-cultural expression—the "genteel" magazines like
Scribner's, *The Atlantic*, and *The Nation*; the (largely Bostonian) prestige
publishing houses; the universities, especially, of course, Harvard. The
new elites challenged their predecessors on their own grounds, by devoting themselves to the task of cultural improvement with an extraordinary avidity. The depth of this movement might possibly escape our
notice, but it is worth considering. We remember the 1880's and early
1890's as the time of the last spasm of cultural self-assertion by the
Eastern gentry: as a time of the creation of the great public art muse-
ums in Boston, Philadelphia, and New York, and the time as well of the
consolidation of the great private art collections, whether wrought by
gentry connoisseurs (like James's friend, Mrs. Isabella Stewart Gardner) or robber barons eager to establish their respectability. But it was
also the time when the Chautauqua lecture series brought speakers
on subjects of cultural interest to middle-class Americans throughout
the country; the time when not only Wilde but also Matthew Arnold
toured the country instructing the locals on their own cultural improvement; the time when small towns throughout the country formed
their own Ruskin or Browning societies or reading circles; a time when
"little" or "dinky" magazines were springing up in smaller cities like
Omaha or small towns like Binghamton, New York, as well as established cultural centers like Boston and San Francisco; a time as well
when land-grant universities in the Midwest and the West were opening up possibilities of higher education in areas in which, 30 years
before, secondary schools had been a rarity.[44]

The result of these developments was what one might call a "culture boom": an increasing public awareness of, and interest in, high culture —not only high culture conceived as a magisterial space of aesthetic contemplation, but also high culture experienced as a site of intense social competition. What was at stake in this competition, of course, was a sense of cultural legitimacy, of cultural competence; being cognizant of or versed in the works privileged by the gentry provided a powerful means for the newer elites to grant themselves an equivalent status. But what was also, and increasingly, at stake in this competition was nothing less than cultural authority itself: who defined, guaranteed, and defended the nature and limits of the canonically cultural, and what the ends and social role of high culture might be.

In this contest, the American experience of British aestheticism played a crucial, if somewhat overdetermined, role. For British aestheticism was constructed precisely to challenge the assumptions at the core of the gentry's privileging of "culture" as a means of enforcing social and moral order; both the older and the newer elites responded to its destabilizing implications with wariness and enthusiasm. The old elites, particularly those surrounding the genteel group, responded to aestheticism with distinct distrust, all the more powerfully felt, it would seem, because aestheticism grew uncomfortably out of the British literary tradition with which they identified. The newer elites were, initially at least, more welcoming. It is no coincidence that the most creative center of "aesthetic" ceramics design was Cincinnati; or that Oscar Wilde was met with the most enthusiasm outside the established centers of cultural endeavor on the East Coast; or that dozens of little or dinky magazines, uniting consciously aesthetic graphic design and avant-garde stories and essays, were founded, flourished, and folded in larger Midwestern or Western metropolises like Omaha and Fort Worth or in even smaller cities and university towns. Indeed, the contents of many of these journals suggests that the American redaction of the aesthetic movement organized and superintended the "culture boom" itself; the American versions of British coterie periodicals gave a prestigious and public forum for the verse of local writers, the feverish prose of local university students, or papers from the local Browning society.[45]

Aestheticism soon posed a severe problem for these groups, too; while its seeming refusal of moralistic criteria was energizing and polemically suited to a battle with the moralistic cultural establishment, such attitudes were no less problematic for upwardly mobile middle Americans than they were to the gentry. Their response and the gentry's therefore came increasingly to resemble each other; each competed to normalize aestheticism, to admit it into the canon of the "cultural" by stripping it of its subversive power. But British aestheticism rather perversely refused to be so accommodated; and its very resistance to its late-nineteenth-century revision, I would suggest, allowed it to exert its greatest force in the twentieth century, helping shape the transition from a sense of high culture massively dominated by moralistic ideals and expectations to one that could play a more alert, and socially commodious, role.

The American response to Pater provides an excellent example of this complicated process. Pater's reputation rose steadily throughout the late 1880's. Following its publication in 1885, *Marius the Epicurean* received a far more favorable reception than had *The Renaissance*; for example, in *The Nation* George Woodberry described his surprise at discovering "in the evangel of aestheticism a morality of this height," although he, like most of the reviewers, remained skeptical about the merits and the historical accuracy of the novel.[46] It was not until 1888 that Pater received his first American "rave," in the pages of the liberal Congregationalist journal, the *Andover Review*, where the "infinite grace and indescribable charm" of Pater's writings were praised—even the more controversial of those writings, for the reviewer quotes approvingly Pater's infamous description of *La Gioconda*.[47] Pater's death in 1894 brought a number of respectful obituaries and memorial tributes, and the posthumous reviews of *Plato and Platonism* and *Greek Studies* were universally favorable. By the middle of the 1890's, the critical priorities of the 1870's were fully reversed. In 1896, *The Nation* suggested that, as an authority on art, Pater was Ruskin's superior; in that same year, *The Outlook* asserted that Pater "went far beyond the two other great critics of our time"—Ruskin and Arnold. Indeed, by 1897, *The Nation* had come to look on Pater so favorably that it suggested that Pater's "counsel of perfection" was one that needed "preaching" to a "gross and materialized democracy like ours."[48]

The rehabilitation of Pater seems to accomplish the accommodation of aestheticism to the ideological agenda of the gentry elite. Thus a certain defensiveness underlies even the most positive American reviews of Pater. Almost to a man, the American reviewers praise Pater for his turn from the questionable doctrines of *The Renaissance* to the religious and philosophical concerns of *Marius* and *Plato and Platonism*; *Marius* may have been a "Neo-pagan," *The Atlantic* helpfully informed its readers, but he "leave[s] upon the mind of his reader . . . [a] much more winning and persuasive impression than does the Neo-Christian of the balm, the brightness . . . brought into the diseased and moribund société of Rome by the coming of Christ." [49] But British aestheticism was constructed precisely to evade such facile attempts of moral reconciliation, and when they confronted less easily accommodated manifestations of aestheticism, American critics moved onto the attack. The *Andover Review*'s 1888 praise for Pater, for example, must be coupled with an 1884 attack, *Christianity and Aestheticism*, in which the Christian Socialist Reverend Washington Gladden discusses the problems aesthetes raised for ministers disposed to be sympathetic to any rebellion against narrow-minded Calvinism:

It is evident that the two kingdoms of Christianity and aestheticism are now in many quarters contending for the mastery. . . . The modern Paganism lays down its law . . . "Love art for art's sake, and all things that you need will be added unto you." The very words of Christ's law are travestied, and art is put in the place of righteousness as the supreme end. . . . To be a Christian disciple, it is not necessary that one should abjure the pleasures of refined taste, but it is necessary that he should make these pleasures subordinate and tributary to the service of God and men. . . . [E]very minister of the gospel who stands before the cultivated and luxurious congregations of our great cities is bound to be faithful in his testimony against this aesthetic Paganism, whose gods are set up in so many of the homes of his people, and whose degrading worship threatens the life of the church and the nation.[50]

The publication in this significant periodical—the self-appointed voice of liberal Congregationalism—of both a strenuous attack on aestheticism and a warm review of Pater suggests the uneasy position in which the gentry elite found itself when confronted with aestheticism. The defection of an increasing number of gentry youths, called by the seductive melodies of *The Renaissance*, only exacerbated the problem. During the time in which their elders struggled between their consciences and their interest in the latest British cultural development, many of their children put down their Arnold and their Ruskin and picked up their Pater—and did so without any of the earnest moral concerns their elders brought to their reading of *The Renaissance*. For example, Pater enjoyed a particular popularity among Harvard students. During the 1880's and 1890's, the Pater vogue was so intense that students wrote home for copies of *The Renaissance* because all the available editions had been stolen from the college library. One of the first and greatest enthusiasts, Bernard Berenson, was so inspired that he proselytized among his teachers as well as his fellow students. The response of those so approached suggests the continuing ambivalence or disapproval of the Boston gentry: William James commented that Pater's prose made him feel as if he were immersed in a warm bath, and Charles Eliot Norton responded simply and magisterially: "My dear boy, it won't do."[51]

Even as Pater grew more acceptable, grew even, despite the best efforts of James and Norton, somewhat respectable, the more eccentric forms of aestheticism continued of necessity to be demonized. The seeming schizophrenia of the *Andover Review* is an excellent case in point. Its publication of Woodberry's article in praise of Pater and Gladden's attack on "the new Paganism" can be read as an indication of a certain ambivalence among even the most liberal Christians on the question of aestheticism, but it can also be seen as a cultural horse trade: the acceptance of Pater—and even the most explicitly amoral aspects of Pater's thought—being permitted, but only in exchange for the rejection of Wilde. Similarly, Pater's admittance into the ranks of the "great critics of our time" in the 1890's was accompanied in the popular press and highbrow journals alike with fervid denunciations of the "decadent" or fin de siècle writers, and especially of *The Yellow Book*; *The Nation* may have come around to Pater, but it instantly condemned *The Yellow Book* as an "insult to the intelligence of the century." The popular press was even less restrained; according to the *Boston Commonwealth*, "this periodical seems to fill the function of presenting the public things that other magazines refused to publish and were better left unsaid."[52] Striking as well was the continuing denunciation of Wilde, until his trial and imprisonment in 1895, at which point the American press ceased mentioning him altogether.[53] The established American cultural machinery, in other words, was calibrated to sift through the various forms of the aestheticism it encountered to find an acceptable variant—even when this year's gold was last year's dross.

American middle-brow culture performed similar maneuvers. If aestheticism attracted its greatest interest outside the Eastern confines of the waning gentry culture, it also received more skeptical, indeed often more corrosive, scrutiny there. That scrutiny is most powerfully testified to, as it was in England, by the numerous popular satires on aestheticism, satires that, again as in England, were intimately connected to the "aesthetic crazes" they accompanied and furthered. The prevalence of satires on Oscar Wilde in the popular media is perhaps the first manifestation of this antiaesthetic impulse; and the dinky magazines that proliferated in the 1890's often took a similarly whimsical, self-denunciatory turn. The American humor magazine *The Yellow Kid* was renamed *The Yellow Book* to invoke the frisson of decadence and the aura of modernity associated with its notorious British companion, though its fundamental purpose was to print bad jokes and worse cartoons; similarly, the extremely decadent-sounding Kansas City journal, *The Lotus*, made up for its risqué title by asserting its fundamental moral purity; on the last page of its first issue, it reprinted the reassurances of the *Kansas City World*—"*The Lotus* is entirely free from decadency"—and, even more tellingly, those of the trade journal, the *American Magazine Exchange*: "I was most agreeably surprised to find a fitting wealth of intellect and soul. There has recently been too much striving after artistic effect at the expense of a sane literature, but in *The Lotus* I find nothing degenerate."[54]

Perhaps the best indication of this middle-class, middle-brow ambivalence—and of its consequences—can be found in the work of William Dean Howells. Howells, it is safe to say, represented in their most benign, least aggressive guise the challenges to gentry domination; not only as a midwesterner, but also as a sponsor of avant-garde literary movements—realism, naturalism, regionalism, and even symbolism—Howells helped pass the cultural torch from the Bostonian elite to their more fractious, indeed more rambunctious, successors.[55] The work in which he comments most thoroughly on this process is *A Hazard of New Fortunes* (1890). That novel's protagonist, Basil March, mimics Howells's own move from Boston to New York and from older forms of cultural expression like the genteel organ of the Boston gentry, *The Atlantic*, to the new experimental form of the illustrated mass-circulation periodical, which in this novel is represented by a journal entitled *Every Other Week*. It is of great relevance to our present subject that this journal is, as Roger Stein observes, also an "aesthetic periodical"—that is, a journal of unconventional design, paying close attention to artistic quality (even going so far as to give the impression of having uncut leaves), and printing new, refined fiction and sophisticated criticism.[56] Tellingly, the journal is to present itself as much as a book as a periodical; its design is intended to suggest that it attains the monumentality and high-cultural appeal of the former, that it has transcended the ephemerality and mass-market fate of the latter. It is therefore of even greater importance that this journal is not, as one might have suspected, directed at a coterie audience, but rather aspires to reach a broader middle-class public. As its guiding spirit cum marketing expert, Fulkerson, puts it, the journal is designed to appear not just "on the center tables of the millionaires—the Vanderbilts and the Astors—[but] in the homes of culture and refinement everywhere." Moreover, as Fulkerson continues, the periodical is designed, like other aestheticist commodities, to confirm the cultural legitimacy

of its middle-class readership—and to induce further demand for cultural "enlightenment" and thus sales for the journal that guarantees
that enlightenment: "It's the talk of the clubs and the dinner tables;
children cry for it; it's the Castoria of literature, and the Pearline of art,
the Won't-be-happy-till-he-gets-it of every enlightened man, woman,
and child in this vast city."[57]

The novel's attitude toward the periodical and the cultural work it
performs, however, is ambivalent at the very best. Howells's interest
here lies as much in criticizing the privileging of the aesthetic as it
does in depicting the triumph of mass-market aestheticism. In large
measure, his critique is registered through Basil March's progress in
the novel. At the beginning, Basil encounters New York with aestheticizing detachment—he and his wife, Isabel, took "a purely aesthetic
view of the facts as they glimpsed them in this street of tenement-
houses . . . they would have contented themselves with saying that it
was as picturesque as a street in Naples or Florence and with wondering why nobody came to paint it; they would have thought that
they were sufficiently serious about it in blaming the artists for their
failure to appreciate it, and going abroad for the picturesque when
they had it right under their noses" (65). The violent intersection of
the microcosm of the journal world and the macrocosm of strike-torn
New York forces Basil to confront the limitations of this impulse and
to recognize his complicity in the social and economic iniquity he had
hitherto observed with the aesthete's detached gaze.[58] The novel's portrayal of Basil's moral growth, however, is accompanied and in part
supplemented by the satirical portrayal of an actual aesthete, Angus
Beaton, and it is in its unpitying satire of Beaton that the novel places
itself most firmly in the contours of American responses to British
aestheticism. Like Howells's other aesthetes—and his fiction is extraor-
dinarily rich in these figures, from the 1880's to the first years of the
twentieth century—Beaton is as much a caricature as a character.[59]
His moral failings are ruthlessly inventoried, and would perhaps be
worrisome if he were not so deeply ineffectual. Beaton's flaws seem
initially to inhere in his March-like aesthetical attitude; Beaton gazes
at all around him with an explicitly aestheticizing detachment, viewing them as potential "studies" or sketches. But far more than Basil,
Beaton extends aesthetic detachment into moral deficiency. The most
shocking instance of this, of course, occurs when Beaton confronts
the streetcar strike, the novel's moral test and narrative crucible. Irri-
tated by the inconvenience, his only reaction to the human suffering
he witnesses is to snap at a policeman, "If you'd take out eight or ten

of those fellows . . . and set them up against a wall and shoot them,
you'd save a great deal of bother" (404). The same quality pervades
all his personal relations, in subtler but perhaps no less shocking ways.
When old Mr. Dryfoos visits him and rests on his couch, overcome by
emotion, Beaton conceives of the sorrowing man in purely aesthetic
terms, as a potential subject for a painting. Similarly, when we first encounter Beaton, the artist is modeling with rapt fascination the head
of Lindau; this head, we learn, is to be used as a portrait of Judas:

> He utilized the remorse with which he was tingling to give his Judas an expres-
> sion which he found novel in the treatment of that character—a look of such
> touching, appealing self-abhorrence that Beaton's artistic joy in it amounted
> to rapture; between the breathless moments when he worked in dead silence
> for an effect that was trying to escape him, he sang and whistled fragments of
> comic opera. (120)

Kermit Vanderbilt comments on this moment by suggesting that it
establishes Lindau as the novel's Judas, a betrayer of the principles of
nonviolence for which the Christ-like Orville Dryfoos gives his life;
but it seems to me more likely that it implies that Beaton serves this
function, that the detachment he shows toward the human suffering
he witnesses, and his attempt to transform such suffering into the stuff
of art, betrays his subjects' essential humanity—and his own.[60]

In other words, Beaton is established by Howells as a kind of
counter-Basil; possessing the same kind of aestheticizing perceptual
apparatus as Basil and Isabel, he nevertheless refuses to recognize the
deficiencies of this mode of apprehension. For this transgression he
is remorselessly punished by the novel: systematically rejected by the
woman he loves, humiliated by the woman he flirts with, elbowed out
of his job, Beaton progresses through the text to a humiliatingly unsuccessful suicide—a suicide whose very bungling denies him even the
pathos of a tragic end: he "laughed with cynical recognition of the
fact that he had got his punishment in the right way, and that his case
was not to be dignified into tragedy" (491). The Dantesque appropri-
ateness of Beaton's "punishment" places him, alone of all the novel's
characters, in a moral universe governed by the economy of right and
wrong, transgression and punishment.

This move is odd indeed; in a novel that stresses the complexity of
motive and the intertwining of disparate causes underlying any human
behavior, Beaton's systematic reduction to a simplistic caricature is
strikingly anomalous, if not an embarrassing violation of Howells's own
"ethically grounded realism." The only way to account for it, I think,

is to identify it as the result of a surge of surplus moralism rising up within Howells himself when he comes to deal with Beaton's aestheticism—a moralism that is similar in spirit and effect to old Mrs. Dryfoos's religiosity, not the New Testament morality of her son. In part, this moralism exists to defend Basil—and Howells himself—from the vengeful side of Howells's own hypertrophied authorial conscience; inculpating Beaton is a way of exculpating not only Basil but also the author for whom he so often speaks. But this moralism also speaks to the form of cultural organization that the novel elsewhere depicts with whimsey, even a certain amount of detached curiosity. It is in response to the rise of journals like *Every Other Week*—in response, that is, to the rise of aestheticism within, rather than beyond, the new mass literary market—that Howells finds it necessary to spend so much authorial energy in critiquing aestheticism itself; indeed, it is necessary for Howells to demonize Beaton's aestheticism to precisely the degree that it is elsewhere becoming normalized, neutralized, conventionalized, made part of the established cultural scene.

This moralistic response had a profoundly double effect. On the one hand, it provided an eloquent protest against what we might call the aestheticizing of American culture from within the confines of that very culture. The novel sets out to portray—and to decry—the decline of a (presumed) culture of moral strenuosity and ethical stringency, and its replacement by a culture organized around the institutions of advertising, mass-market periodicals, and the inciting and celebration of the act of consumption; through the representation of Beaton—and to a lesser extent Basil—it also extends this analysis from the cultural to the psychological sphere, to anatomize the detached, voyeuristic, personality type that such a culture engenders and shapes. Moreover, in doing so, the novel seeks to suggest the ubiquity of that personality type: to show that literary and artistic producers—the Basils and the Beatons—are fundamentally indistinguishable from the consumers of their work; that the mass reading public's fascination with their journal infiltrates and incites the same attitudes in those who write and draw for it as well.

This eloquent and impassioned critique of American aestheticism had the unexpected effect of preserving aestheticism from the normalizing massage of the mass literary market. Even as that market sought successfully to tame aestheticism—or, to put the matter less moralistically, to deploy for its own ends those aspects of British aestheticism that expressed the ethos of consumption, which the literary market sought simultaneously to instill and profit from—the critical efforts of

Howells and of the rest of the literary establishment served to maintain the association between British aestheticism and exoticism, eroticism, and moral fallibility. And, just as Howells came to embody to the following generation a kind of genteel whimsey and middle-class conservatism that was, of necessity, to be transcended, so the forms of cultural possibility he rejected took on a greater attractiveness in the eyes of those who sought to reject him and the values he advocated. In the ferment of the first years of the twentieth century, the particular aspects of aestheticism that had earlier been rejected retained a healthy charge of the forbidden, and therefore an equally powerful charge of attraction, to the generation of American writers who reached their intellectual maturity in the late years of the nineteenth century and their imaginative maturity in the first decades of the twentieth. While their parents either among the gentry or the managerial elite were beginning to accept some of the more easily sanitized forms of aestheticism, many of these young men were throwing themselves eagerly into the imitation of aestheticism's more disreputable aspects —aspects even more thoroughly disreputable than those commonly ascribed to Pater: "decadence," "degeneration," "decay." Out of this flirtation, they shaped the contours of American literary modernism.

In other words, it was precisely the resistance to aestheticism by figures like Howells in the 1880's and 1890's that allowed it to maintain cultural power in the 1910's and 1920's—in that period following the collapse of both the old gentry elite's cultural hegemony and that of the elites who had first challenged it. Again, this development may be best viewed at Harvard. The late 1880's and early 1890's witnessed many changes at that institution—President Eliot's curricular reforms; the recruiting of a distinguished faculty devoted equally to the pursuit of scholarship and the cultivation of promising students; the admission of an increasingly geographically and economically diverse student body. The tenor of student life was also transformed. As in England, where the adoption of the rhetoric and persona of the aesthete aided the entry of middle-class men and women into the existing cultural establishment, so too at Harvard the recruiting of a more diverse student body led to the rise of a distinctive set of Harvard aesthetes. Some of these aesthetes were, to be sure, far from middle class. The poets George Cabot Lodge and Trumbull Stickney, to cite two examples, were members of no fewer than three of the more distinguished families of old New England—the Cabots and Lodges of Boston, the Trumbulls of Connecticut. But they were accompanied in their adoption of an aestheticist persona by the likes of Bernard

Berenson, whose experience as a Jewish outsider at Harvard in the 1890's was nearly identical with (and quite possibly consciously modeled on) the experience of Oscar Wilde as an Irishman at Oxford in the 1870's.

These young men—supervised by young and sympathetic instructors like George Santayana—formed reading societies of their own and gradually infiltrated existing college organizations like the O.K. Society and literary magazines like the *Harvard Monthly* and the *Harvard Advocate*. Like their counterparts at Oxford, aesthetes at Harvard initially met resistance. Santayana records that his young friend, the poet Trumbull Stickney, was barred from an undergraduate poetry club because "he had mentioned the sunset and called it 'gorgeous.'"[61] Van Wyck Brooks describes the universal suspicion among students of what he called Santayana's "feline aestheticism." This distrust was shared by the college authorities, with whom Santayana was in constant trouble for excessive fraternization with undergraduates; on one occasion, only William James's intervention with his friend, President Eliot, succeeded in preserving his colleague and former student Santayana's job.[62] Over the next few decades, however, this resistance faded, and aestheticism of the more conspicuous varieties became respectable, even, perhaps, fashionable. Malcolm Cowley's description of this phenomenon is perhaps the most eloquent, but the details he records had been true for a generation:

Then, too, there was a type of aestheticism very popular during my own college years. The Harvard Aesthetes of 1916 were trying to create in Cambridge, Massachusetts an after-image of Oxford in the 1890's. They read the *Yellow Book*, they read Casanova's memoirs, and *Les Liaisons Dangereuses*, both in French, and Petronius in Latin; they gathered at tea-time in one another's rooms, or at punches in the office of *The Harvard Monthly*; they drank, instead of weak punch, seidels of straight gin topped with a maraschino cherry; they discussed the harmonies of Pater, the rhythms of Aubrey Beardsley and, growing louder, the voluptuousness of the Church, the essential virtue of prostitution. They had crucifixes in their bedrooms, and ticket stubs from last Saturday's burlesque show at the Old Howard. They wrote, too; two dozen of them were prematurely decayed poets, each with his invocation to Antinoüs, his mournful descriptions of Venetian lagoons, his sonnets to a chorus girl in which he addressed her as "little painted poem of God." In spite of these beginnings, a few of them became good writers.[63]

This increasing interest in—and imitation of—the life of the aesthete had ramifications beyond Harvard, indeed beyond the confines of New England itself. For, nurtured by former Harvard students and their contemporaries at other institutions, this more self-consciously transgressive aestheticism began to grow in popularity and literary prominence, leading directly to the creation of the "modernist" avant-garde of the early 1920's. *The Yellow Book,* for example, inspired two young Harvard graduates not only to publish in Chicago their own American avant-garde literary magazine, *The Chap-Book,* but also to found a publishing house, Stone and Kimball, that was to publish much of the best native and foreign avant-garde writing for the next twenty-five years, including early Yeats (with a frontispiece by Beardsley) and Verlaine as well as Kate Chopin and Hamlin Garland. At the same time, there began to appear a number of native-born "alienated" artists: a number of writers, in particular, took to proclaiming themselves "aesthetes" or "decadents," directing their work toward the shocking of the bourgeoisie, and generally conforming to the most outrageous patterns of aestheticist self-presentation. Significantly, those who did so could usually be found in the literary marketplace the aesthete at least claimed to abhor. Edgar Saltus, a minor novelist of this period, for example, may have signed himself as "Bourgoisphobus" and proclaimed his admiration of Baudelaire, Wilde, and Verlaine, but he achieved notoriety with a number of popular novels in the manner of Wilde's *Dorian Gray*—works, that is, that combined a frisson of exotic sense experience with plots so melodramatic as to approach the ludicrous. The aforementioned James Huneker, music critic for the *New York Tribune* and name-dropper extraordinaire, similarly achieved fame as a devotee of decadence with novels and memoirs that were as sensational as they were ineptly written. More lasting contributions, perhaps, were made by a number of poets deeply influenced by both British aestheticism and its French counterparts, the most estimable of whom were the two young Harvard poets (and close friends) George Cabot Lodge and Trumbull Stickney. Stickney in particular is an overly neglected figure; a poet of extraordinary technical skills, if a resolutely minor vision, he deserves more consideration and appreciation than he has hitherto received.

If the accomplishment of American aestheticist writers is less than compelling, however, their influence over the subsequent shape of American letters was quite significant: they helped to bring into being, for the first time, the literary institutions that we recognize as central to American literary modernism. Considered on their own, for example, the dinky magazines were ephemeral at best; but when placed next to the little magazines of the early twentieth century, they appear quite a significant phenomenon indeed. They made available to a broad reading public the very best of avant-garde European writing of their time: *The Chap-Book* printed not only the later aesthetes and their explicators, but also Maeterlinck, Ibsen, Verlaine, Huysmans, and Shaw. Other magazines, less well connected, tended toward the eccentric, the outré, and the ephemeral, but still served an important role by importing national or international writers to Kansas City or Omaha or Louisville, and providing an outlet for local writers eager to emulate them. It is not only the knowledge imparted by the dinky magazines that was to be exploited by their successors like *The Little Review* or *Poetry* or *The Dial*; they also established patterns of cultural expectation and response, and provided for the first time in American letters a successful means of matching struggling but devoted writers with a sympathetic and increasingly sophisticated audience.

Even more important, perhaps, were the ways aestheticism trained and gave shape to the experience of modernist American writers. It is important to realize, for example, that the Harvard of the 1890's and early years of the twentieth century—the Harvard of Stickney and Santayana and of the *Monthly* and the O.K. Society—was also the Harvard of Robert Frost, Edward Arlington Robinson, and Wallace Stevens, all of whom emigrated to this cultural mainland from separate "island communities" and found themselves caught up in the enthusiasm for aestheticism they found there.* The influence of this milieu may be seen in their poetry of the time—in Stevens's early sonnets, for example, which even Santayana found too fervid in their praise for beauty and art (his first published poem, significantly, was entitled *The House of Life*);[64] or in Eliot's *Prufrock*, which is nothing if not a portrait of the aesthete as an aging narcissist. But it makes its way, more lastingly, into their subsequent work.

Consider the case of Robert Frost. Critics often cite Frost's publication of *North of Boston* in 1914 as marking a break with the traditions of expression of the previous generations. Frost's spare, direct line and his unflinching response to nature, it is argued, overturn the influence of the rich, if not overripe, nature poetry of the nineteenth century— with its overabundance of imagery, its appeal to a plentitude of sense experiences, its abstraction, its langorous sentimentality. The claim for the originality of Frost's achievement, however, ignores the fact that his Harvard classmate, Trumbull Stickney, had been experimenting

---

*It was also the Radcliffe of Gertrude Stein (class of '97) who records in the voice of Alice B. Toklas: "There she had a very good time." For an account of William James's response to Stein, see Stein, *The Autobiography of Alice B. Toklas*. For the origin of the phrase "island communities," see Wiebe, *Search for Order*, esp. pp. 44–75.

with just this poetic idiom a few years earlier—in poems like *Mnemosyne*, for example, in which the landscape of the poet's memory is evoked in a series of spare, evocative stanzas punctuated by short, declarative sentences describing the "country I remember," or the equally restrained *In Summer*. To note this commonality is to remind ourselves that the origins of this sparer, more economical poetic was anticipated by the lyric of Rossetti's we discussed in Chapter 1, *The Woodspurge*, and that the most fundamental move of this poem—the subversion of the Romantic quest into nature, the recognition of the interpretive enigmas presented by the irredeemable otherness of the natural world —is the fundamental move as well of much of Frost's nature poetry: of *Design*, of *For Once, Then, Something*, of *The Most of It*, to cite three great examples.[65]

Stevens presents a similar pattern. The early influence of aestheticism passes into a more mature style shaped by a sustained engagement with an astringent and international modernism: this is the standard line of descent traced for Stevens's work. Some recrudescences of Stevens's youth as a Harvard aesthete are noted—*Tea at the Palaz of Hoon*, for example—but by and large the influence of Rossetti, Pater, et al. is thought to fade early and thoroughly. However, these writers stage frequent returns in Stevens's work, not merely on the level of overt allusion, but often at the center of Stevens's imaginative inquiry itself. To cite one famous example, *Sunday Morning* presents a sustained meditation on the themes that Pater dealt with so problematically in *The Renaissance*: the possibility of discovering a ground of value in a world of flux and ephemerality, a world where "modern thought" has dissolved all possibilities of certitude, all "complacencies of the peignoir"; where, as Pater puts it, "each mind keep[s] as a solitary prisoner its own dream of a world," and where, as Stevens would have it, "we live in / . . . island solitude, unsponsored, free, / Of that wide water, inescapable." Like Pater, Stevens's protagonist discovers that the acceptance of ephemerality itself represents the only way of living in such a world. Indeed, the final stanzas of *Sunday Morning* can profitably be read as a kind of call-and-response commentary on the final paragraphs of the Conclusion to *The Renaissance*. Pater asks: "A counted number of pulses only is given us of a variegated, dramatic life. How may we see in them all that is to be seen in them by the finest senses? How shall we pass most swiftly from point to point, and be present always at the focus where the greatest number of vital forces unite in their purest energy?" Stevens answers by asserting that the sheer abundance of sense experiences available to us ensures that we may be always present if we live in the present, even though the here and now gestures eloquently toward its own impending dissolution:

> Deer walk upon our mountains, and the quail
> Whistle about us their spontaneous cries;
> Sweet berries ripen in the wilderness;
> And, in the isolation of the sky,
> At evening, casual flocks of pigeons make
> Ambiguous undulations as they sink,
> Downward to darkness, on extended wings.[66]

But perhaps the most extensive legacy of British aestheticism may be found in the work of T. S. Eliot. Eliot's theory of poetry did not admit of much poetic achievement between the seventeenth century and his own time, but he was especially hard on Walter Pater. In *Arnold and Pater* (1930), for example, Eliot complains of Pater's conflation of religion and art (an oversimplification of Pater's endeavor, to say the least) and sniffs, "I do not believe that Pater, in this book [*The Renaissance*], has influenced a single first-rate mind of a later generation."[67] Eliot's assertion may be true, but if so, he is consigning himself to the status of the second-rate. For a number of his essays and poems reveal the influence of Pater. *The Perfect Critic* (1920), for example, explicitly rejects "aesthetic" or impressionistic criticism, which Eliot traces from Pater to Symons, in favor of a more austere, objective, impersonal criticism, yet by its end, works around to the perfectly Paterian assertion that real criticism is dependent on the quality of the reader's "sensibility" (as opposed to that reader's historical or philosophical knowledge or interests) and hints at the Wildean heresy that the best criticism of a work of art is another work of art.[68] It might be argued that this essay is less than central to the Eliotic canon, but a more influential work is also deeply reminiscent of Pater. *Tradition and the Individual Talent* (1919) develops a number of notions expressed by Pater, including that of the artist's necessary self-limitation—what Eliot calls his "continual self-sacrifice . . . continual extinction of personality,"[69] and what Pater calls "*ascêsis* . . . the austere and serious girding of loins in [artistic] youth" (WP, 1: xiii). A number of passages in Eliot's poetry are thoroughly indebted to Pater, most impressively, perhaps, these lines from *East Coker*:

> As we grow older
> The world becomes stranger, the pattern more complicated
> Of dead and living. Not the intense moment
> Isolated, with no before or after,

> But a lifetime burning in every moment
> And not the lifetime of one man only
> But of old stones that cannot be deciphered.[70]

Here Eliot alludes eloquently to Pater's ideal of living intensely, of burning "with [a] hard, gemlike flame." At first, it would seem that these lines extend the criticism Eliot offered in his 1930 essay. Pater's doctrines, Eliot writes there, led only to "some untidy lives," and these lines suggest why: they imply that to seek a single moment of intense experience is to find only isolation, if not solipsism.[71] But a closer look at the affinities between Eliot's language and Pater's suggests that in these lines Eliot is more generous than in his criticism. To remember that Pater's definition of "success in life" is to "burn *always* with [a] hard, gemlike flame, to *maintain* this ecstasy," is to recognize that Eliot and Pater are in fundamental accord. For Pater, as for Eliot, the ideal of "a lifetime burning in every moment" is the ultimate goal, and it is one to be desired as deeply as it is known to be unachievable in a world of flux and loss. For both Eliot and Pater, "success in life" so defined must be sought, but sought in the full knowledge that it is unattainable. As Eliot's poem concludes:

> Old men ought to be explorers
> Here and there does not matter
> We must be still and still moving
> Into another intensity
> For a further union, a deeper communion
> Through the dark cold and the empty desolation,
> The wave cry, the wind cry, the vast waters
> Of the petrel and the porpoise.   In my end is my beginning.

With Eliot's final, generous quotation from Pater, we seem to be in a position to account for aestheticism's role in the movement from late-nineteenth- to early-twentieth-century American literature and culture. The influence of British aestheticism seems crucial to the formation of American modernism in a number of ways. It helped create the means by which the modernists were enabled to come into contact with the best contemporary work from Britain and the Continent; it brought Eliot, and thence a generation of critics and poets, in touch with the notion of the self-sufficiency of the work of art, the autonomy or autotelic nature of the poetic object; by its very difficulty, its sheer interpretive intransigence, it accustomed public and poets alike to the valorizing of poetic difficulty we associate with high modernism. Moreover, it endowed its readers with a trove of themes, techniques, and literary and experiential structures that they were able profitably to exploit. The privileging of intense moments of special perception; the dialectical interplay of visual immediacy and representational distance; the concern with the purification of language and style; the simultaneous desire to evade or annul history and an intense, even obsessive, historicism: these are permanent gifts of aestheticism to the American modernists. Aestheticism's renegotiation of the relation between the writer and his culture proved fruitful as well. The ideology of the alienated artist, the perception of the writer as a member of a privileged avant-garde, a citizen of "Bohemia"—a recognition that becomes a potent marketing device for that author in a culture eager to purchase a depiction of its own limitations: this is the permanent contribution, for better or worse, of aestheticism to American culture itself.

By this view, Anglo-American modernism, the high canonical modernism of Eliot and Pound, of Stevens and Faulkner, even of Hemingway—for, as Hugh Kenner has observed, Hemingway too owes a strong debt to Pater and the poets of the 1890's[72]—may be read as the literary consummation of aestheticism, the full flowering of the seeds planted in the later years of the nineteenth century. I am not wholly hostile to this view, and for many reasons: it may remind us not only of the rigorously repressed and denied aestheticist origins of this species of modernism but also of the continued presence of aestheticist tendencies of thought in one particularly important vein of that modernism; of the ways, for example, that the aestheticist flirtation with the notion of the autonomy of art made its way into a critical orthodoxy in the middle years of the twentieth century. But there are dangers here as well. The notion of the autonomy of art, as we have seen, is at best a stopgap for Rossetti or Pater, but that notion becomes, through the mediation of Arthur Symons (and the valorization of the symbol he helps bequeath Anglo-American modernism), Eliot (and the theory of poetry he preaches as early as *The Perfect Critic*), and those critics who followed directly in their footsteps a critical method that is utterly antithetical to the tentativeness, to the hesitancy and the qualified paradoxicality with which the British aestheticists originally deployed it. So too the aestheticist tendency toward paradox hardens under the ministrations of critics influenced by Eliot, first into a method, then a metaphysic. The difference between the aestheticist pursuit of paradox and that of the New Critical invocation of paradox is striking: instead of presenting contradiction as a problem, as a source of interpretive struggle and experiential anxiety, American

New Criticism presents it as a solution, and a solution moreover that belies the very ambivalence for the expression of which the aestheticists sought it out.

At the same time, I find myself more than a little uneasy with the line of literary transmission I have proposed here, if only because it taints aestheticism with the certitude, the strenuous moralism, and the questionable metaphysics of canonical high modernism. Indeed, if one contrasts the classic phase of New Criticism or the less restrained writings of Eliot on art with the writing of Pater or Wilde or Rossetti, it is the former group that appears more fully composed of aesthetes in the reductive sense of the word: it is they who seem to see art as a completed object sufficient in and of itself to resolve the metaphysical, ontological, and historical problems that it is posed. The aesthetes, in contrast, appear far more interested in the problematic qualities of the well-wrought urn, in the failure of poetry to resolve the conundrums it is called upon to address; they thus appear, as I suggested in Chapter 1, far more powerfully the precursors of a postmodern aesthetic than the modernist one. We need, therefore, to rechart the genealogy of British aestheticism, to see it as representing an integral, cohesive moment in the progression of nineteenth-century poetry and prose, a moment that is neither fulfilled nor betrayed by the modernists, but rather irrevocably altered by them as they searched through the aestheticist questions for their own answers.

It is against this background that an inquiry into the relation between Henry James and the aestheticist writers takes on particular urgency. It does so because James, far more fully than any other literary figure I know, had his feet firmly placed in both worlds, and helped bring about the movement from the one to the other. On the one hand, James was thoroughly a part of Anglo-American aestheticism's social, artistic, and intellectual sphere. This was not only true of James's experience in England—where he knew, gossiped about, and read with interest and occasional horror the works of the British aestheticists—but also of his place in America as well. James was by birth, family affiliation, and intellectual tendency part of the gentry elite; he shared fully, as we have seen, its Nortonian/Ruskinian critique of the crudity, ugliness, and materialism of his society. James shared as well, we might add here, the central tenet of that elite: the notion that "culture" per se was a value missing in American society, although not to the extent or in the simple ways that most critics who have treated this aspect of his work seem to believe. However, James was also an intimate part of the aestheticist revision of gentry values. He was not only represented in the first issue of *The Yellow Book* with all that implies, but also in the third issue of its American imitator, *The Chap-Book*, and in a number of *The Chap-Book*'s own imitators. This appearance indicates something of James's status in the eyes of the generation of American writers that came of age in the 1890's and early years of the twentieth century, a generation in which James had many friends and acquaintances—Trumbull Stickney and George Cabot Lodge, the writer Logan Piersall Smith as well as Smith's brother-in-law, Bernard Berenson, to name four. To this world of American would-be writers and poets, artists, aesthetes, and "Bohemians," James was a nearly mythic figure—the "Master" or "Lion," to adopt his own terms, the greatest example of an American life successfully devoted to art and culture, and therefore a life necessarily lived in a state of willed expatriation. This position was not without its embarrassments, or its responsibilities. Saltus, who admired James as the prime "stylist" of his time, dedicated a heretical (and not particularly well written) historical romance, *Mary Magdalene*, to James. Henry Harland, *The Yellow Book*'s editor, referred to James as "mon maître," "the supreme prince of short-story writers," and "the only master of considered prose we've got."[73] Nearly all the expatriated American novelists and struggling writers paid their respects to James, demanding inspiration, advice, commentary, criticism. It is a role James seems to have willingly adopted and, for all the complaints that stories like *The Death of the Lion* register, relished.

Further, this Anglo-American aestheticist milieu was more than just a part of James's biography; it became an integral part of his fiction. We recognize the world of art collectors like Mrs. Gardner in *The Golden Bowl* and *The Spoils of Poynton*, of acolytes like Logan Smith in *The Middle Years* and *The Death of the Lion*, of expatriates dedicating themselves to art and culture in *The Portrait of a Lady* and to the fine art of living in *The Ambassadors*. More important, James's work registers a sustained interrogation of the virtues and vices of aestheticism itself. This interrogation begins as early as the first novel James thought of as canonical, *Roderick Hudson*, and continues through the very last he completed, *The Golden Bowl*. In those novels, and in many written in between, James repeatedly weighs the stance of the aesthete, dramatizing it by creating aesthete characters like Rowland Mallet, Gilbert Osmond, Mark Ambient, and Adam Verver, assessing it by placing those characters in vibrant juxtaposition with characters embodying values James wishes to affirm or deny, and ultimately remaking it by assimilating the themes, the images, the characteristic imaginative structures of British aestheticism into the commodious structure of the Jamesian novel itself.

At the same time as his work displays a sustained interest in the possibilities and problematics of aestheticism, James also played a crucial role in the formation of literary modernism. He helped shape the terms in which writers of the next century were to think about the nature and office of fiction. This is true of a number of technical devices James taught his successors: the emphasis on point of view, the unreliable narrator, and the epistemological play occasioned by both; fictional self-consciousness; and the rest of the devices that made their way to the center of American novel theory through the efforts of James-influenced critics like Percy Lubbock, R. P. Blackmur, and Wayne Booth. More important, James helped the following generations to a new understanding of the nature and purposes of narrative, the office and authority of the writer of prose fiction, and—most significant of all—the career possibilities of what can only be called a high-art professionalism. James's most immediate gift to his successors was his claim that the art of fiction was indeed an art; that the prestige and honor conventionally granted poets or painters could be extended to the writer of novels; that fiction, no less than poetry, could possess a sophistication and seriousness sufficient to merit significant technical discussion and commentary.

More profoundly, James endowed modernists of all stripes—poets as well as novelists—with the knowledge that the career of mystified professionalism that Rossetti, Pater, Ruskin, and Wilde had all sought to craft for themselves was a viable possibility, one which could lead not to (in Eliot's nasty and inaccurate phrase) "some untidy lives," but rather to a successful institutionalization of oneself in a position at once above and within the newly engorged and articulated literary marketplace. I shall have more to say below about the means by which James crafted this role—which I shall argue in Chapter 4 involved him in a series of disputes, entered into consciously and unconsciously, with that epitome of aesthetic professionalism, Oscar Wilde—and its consequences—which I shall argue in Chapter 5 led the modernist poets to adopt James as their aesthetic hero precisely in order to distinguish themselves from the generation of aestheticists upon whom they modeled themselves. What I want to point to here, rather, is what shall increasingly become my theme in the following chapters: that in creating this role, and, more specifically, by the means that he crafted it, James brought to a successful conclusion the stabilizing or normalizing efforts that American artists, writers, and intellectuals undertook as they came into contact with the imaginative example of British aestheticism; that—far more authoritatively and persuasively than any of his contemporaries—his fiction organized, structured, and brought under firm control the uneasy and often uncanny play with contradictory possibilities that marks the British aesthetic movement, and thus helped prepare for the massive appropriation and stabilization of aestheticism represented by Anglo-American modernism. For as we shall see, James's fiction seeks to separate those elements of British aestheticism of which he approved from those he found disturbing or destabilizing—this is the work that *Roderick Hudson* and *The Portrait of a Lady* perform; then moves into a series of disputes with Oscar Wilde, disputes that end with the installation of a fully tamed version of the aesthete at the center of James's literary endeavor—such is the task performed by *The Ambassadors*; then concludes by internalizing and making complex use of the entire range of the British aesthetic movement, including its self-consciously "decadent" aspects —tasks performed by *The Wings of the Dove* and *The Golden Bowl*. With that last text, James rings his final change on the aesthetic movement; there, he is able to put to rest its uncanny play of possibilities by bringing it under the control of art itself—the move that aestheticism in England flirted with but resisted, the move that the postaestheticist post-Jamesian Anglo-American high modernists performed with fervent enthusiasm.

To trace James's engagement with aestheticism, then, is to do at once two things. It is, first of all, to see how British aestheticism was shaped or bent into the contours of modernism: how aestheticism's own evasive, tentative, self-ironizing, and self-annulling rhetoric was made over into the austere formalities we discover in high, canonical, Anglo-American modernist discourse. It is also to see *why* this process was accomplished; why aestheticism's evasive and elusive angle of vision and its paradoxical understanding of time, selfhood, art, and art's relation to social process and realities *had* to give way to modernism's anxious certitudes; and, more specifically, why the valorization of art, the creation of the aesthetic as a separate, socially redemptive realm which aestheticism at once adumbrates and resists, should have been so urgent and necessary a task. Looking at James's career-long engagement with the texts, themes, obsessions, character types, and characteristic tropes of aestheticism is a way of understanding more completely the imaginative, the personal, and the social need for this transformation, the wants it begins to supply and the lack it fills. It is to this task that I now turn.

"Sad with the whole of pleasure . . . ." Titian (formerly attributed to Giorgione), *Fête Champêtre*. Cliché des Musées Nationaux—Paris.

William Stillman, *The Philosopher's Camp in the Adirondacks*. Courtesy of Concord Free
Public Library, Concord, Mass.

The American reception of
an aesthete; Oscar Wilde
at "An Aesthetic Reception."
*Frank Leslie's Illustrated News-
paper*, Jan. 21, 1882. Courtesy
of Yale University Library.

Thomas Nast on Oscar Wilde—and Oscar Wilde on "Us." *Harper's Bazar*, June 10, 1882. Courtesy of Yale University Library.

THE DAILY GRAPHIC

AN ILLUSTRATED EVENING NEWSPAPER.

39 & 41 PARK PLACE

| VOL. XXVII. | All the News. Four Editions Daily. | NEW YORK, THURSDAY, JANUARY 19, 1882. | $12 Per Year in Advance. Single Copies, Five Cents. | NO. 2744. |

BOSTON ÆSTHETICISM VERSUS OSCAR WILDE.

The Old Lady of Boston Hill:—" NO, SIR. SHODDY NEW YORK MAY RECEIVE YOU WITH OPEN ARMS, BUT WE HAVE AN ÆSTHETICISM OF OUR OWN."

(*Above*) *The Yellow Kid* becomes . . . an American *Yellow Book*. Both reproductions courtesy of Yale University Library.

(*At left*) "Boston Aestheticism Versus Oscar Wilde." Says the Old Lady of Beacon Hill: "No sir. Shoddy New York may welcome you with open arms, but we have an aestheticism of our own." *New York Daily Graphic*, Jan. 19, 1882.
Courtesy of the New York Historical Society, New York City.

An "aesthetic" advertisement: *Enchantment*, by Maxfield Parrish. Courtesy of GE Lighting, General Electric Company.

A Parrish design becomes . . . (*at left*) "The Dinky Bird," illustration from
Eugene Field, *Poems of Childhood*. Courtesy of Beinecke Rare Book and Manuscript Library,
Yale University.

. . . And (*above*) "Sweet Dreams Are Made of This": Nestlé's Alpine White
Chocolate. Courtesy of Nestlé Foods and the J. Walter Thompson Agency.

MAUDLE ON THE CHOICE OF A PROFESSION.

Maudle. "HOW *CONSUMMATELY* LOVELY YOUR SON IS, MRS. BROWN!"

Mrs. Brown (a Philistine from the country). "*WHAT!* HE'S A *NICE, MANLY BOY,* IF YOU MEAN *THAT,* MR. MAUDLE. HE HAS JUST LEFT SCHOOL, YOU KNOW, AND WISHES TO BE AN ARTIST."

Maudle. "*WHY* SHOULD HE BE AN ARTIST?"

Mrs. Brown. "WELL, HE MUST BE *SOMETHING!*"

Maudle. "WHY SHOULD HE *BE* ANYTHING? WHY NOT LET HIM REMAIN FOR EVER CONTENT TO *EXIST BEAUTIFULLY?*"

[*Mrs. Brown determines that at all events her Son shall not study Art under Maudle.*

George Du Maurier, *Maudle on the Choice of a Profession. Punch,* Feb. 12, 1881. Courtesy of Yale University Library.

FRUSTRATED SOCIAL AMBITION.

Collapse of Postlethwaite, Maudle, and Mrs. Cimabue Brown, on reading in a widely-circulated Contemporary Journal that they only exist in Mr. Punch's vivid Imagination. They had fondly flattered themselves that Universal Fame was theirs at last.

George Du Maurier, *Frustrated Social Ambition. Punch*, May 21, 1881. Courtesy of Yale University Library.

THE SIX-MARK TEA-POT.

Æsthetic Bridegroom. "IT IS QUITE CONSUMMATE, IS IT NOT?"
Intense Bride. "IT IS, INDEED! OH, ALGERNON, LET US LIVE UP TO IT!"

George Du Maurier, "A Six-Mark Tea-Pot." *Punch*, Oct. 30, 1880. All rights reserved. The Metropolitan Museum of Art.

The pre-Raphaelite woman: Rossetti, *La Pia de Tolommei*. Courtesy of the Spencer Museum of Art, University of Kansas.

Gustave Moreau, *Salomé Dancing Before Herod*. Courtesy of the Armand Hammer Collection, Los Angeles, California.

Chapter Three

James, Pater, and
the Discovery of Aestheticism

It was, appropriately enough, in Florence that Henry James first came upon Walter Pater's *Studies in the History of the Renaissance*. Despite the appositeness of the setting, however, the results of this encounter were less than earthshaking. "I saw Pater's *Studies* just after getting your letter, in the English bookseller's window," Henry wrote his brother William in 1873, "and was inflamed to think of buying it and trying a notice. But I see it treats of several things I know nothing about."[1] The very lack of interest displayed in this letter, however, is perhaps its most interesting attribute. For all its casual dismissiveness, the letter was immediately contradicted by James's actions; he must have soon bought, or at least read, *The Renaissance*, for he discussed its essay on Botticelli in the course of a travel essay published in *The Independent* of June 1874, and was soon to write a novel, *Roderick Hudson* (1875), that rang with echoes of Pater's text.[2] Moreover, James's assertion that he knew nothing about Italian Renaissance art was misleading, if not disingenuous, since he had extensively described that art in the letters he had sent his family during his 1868 journey to Italy—letters that, given their audience, were hardly less demanding or less public performances than his travel essays. (Indeed, they were read aloud to such friends of the James family as James Russell Lowell, Charles Eliot Norton, and Emerson, a fact of which the young correspondent was quite aware.) In these letters, James discussed the art of the Italian Renaissance with the enthusiasm and zeal of a new convert—as, for example, in the following effusion, addressed to his brother William:

This morning I think I definitively settled the matter with regard to Michael Angelo. . . . I have seen the Great Greek things; I have seen Raphael and I have seen all his own works. He has something—he retains something, after all experience—which belongs only to himself. This transcendent "something" invested the *Moses* this morning with a more melting, exalting power than I

have ever perceived in a work of art. It was a great sensation—the greatest
a work of art can give. . . . It's the triumph of feeling: the Greeks deny it—
poor stupid old Michael proclaims its sovereign air a regenerated world:—and
affords a magnificent pretext for making a stand against it *en suite*. (*Letters*, 1:
179–80)

This passage also serves to remind us that James's 1873 response
to Pater was odder still. For in it, James proclaims his adherence to
the same principles that Pater asserted so powerfully; he too turns
from the dominant aesthetic orthodoxies of early-nineteenth-century
neoclassicism and mid-nineteenth-century medievalism toward an explicit praise for the art of the Renaissance. In doing so, James speaks in
an idiom that is palpably Paterian. The "melting, exalting power" perceived in a work of art; the praise for a "great sensation, the greatest
sensation a work of art can give"; the discovery in art of the "sovereign
air" of a "regenerated world": all these echo the language Pater had
used in his infamous 1868 review of Morris's poetry which, as we have
seen, served as the basis for both the Conclusion to *The Renaissance*
and the essay on *Aesthetic Poetry*. More important still, these lines testify
to James's performance of the rite Pater prescribes in that review: the
discovery of value in the intense sensations elicited by a work of art
and the measuring of the amplitude of those sensations against that
of all others.

The oddity here, then, is not that James minimized his knowledge
of the Renaissance but that he minimized his own sympathy with *The
Renaissance*. I do not mean to overstress the extent of this sympathy;
James's vocabulary of aesthetic appreciation differs considerably from
Pater's in several respects: his praise for Michelangelo, for example,
centers on the more traditional language of *enargea*, of sheer aesthetic
power, a terminology Pater conspicuously turns from in his 1871 essay
on Michelangelo. (For Pater, the most important fact about Michelangelo's artistic "strength" is its surprising [and strange] "sweetness";
for James, it is characteristically his "energy—positiveness—courage"
[*WP*, 1: 57; *Letters*, 1: 181]). But despite these divergences, James and
Pater share not only a common focus of interest and a common vocabulary, but also a similar mode of response to aesthetic phenomena:
a response that brackets the moralistic concerns of the Ruskinian or
Nortonian schools currently prevailing in Boston and in London and
replaces them with a supple alertness to the "sensations" created by
these artworks, to the viewer's alertly contemplative response. This
commonality of response, however, is reflected here only in the silence
James preserves about it.

This pattern persists throughout James's subsequent responses to Pater. These responses are overtly distancing, cool, even condescending. Yet, seemingly despite themselves, they are surprisingly sympathetic in tone and oddly Paterian in diction. Here, to cite another example, is James's final tribute to Pater, contained in a letter to their mutual friend, Edmund Gosse, who had requested of James a contribution to a memorial volume to Pater:

Well, faint, pale, embarrassed, exquisite Pater! He reminds me, in the disturbed night of our actual literature, of one of those lucent matchboxes which you place, on going to bed, near the candle, to show you, in the darkness, where you can strike a light: he shines in the uneasy gloom—vaguely, and has a phosphorescence, not a flame. But I quite agree with you that he is not of the little day—but of the longer time. (*Letters*, 3: 492)

The judgment James passes here is remarkably double-edged. James gives with one hand and takes away with the other, often within a single sentence. The four adjectives that begin the passage seem to place Pater as a secondary, if not a second-rate, figure, as does the comparison of Pater to a phosphorescent matchbox, the source of a faint glow even in comparison with a bedside lamp. But mingled in with these ironic judgments are moments of praise—even if Pater's glow is pale, it illuminates the "disturbed night" of his contemporaries; he is of the "longer time." And, more significantly, James's ambivalent attitude toward Pater is expressed in language reminiscent of Pater's own most famous image, that of the "hard, gemlike flame," Pater's figure for the intensity to which the aesthete's consciousness is to aspire (WP, 1: 236). (This habit of thought begins early: compare the disingenuously Paterian verb "enflamed" with which James dismisses the possible praise of Pater in his letter to William.) The letter to Gosse thus ends with a remarkably complicated vision of Pater: he may have failed to live up to his own ideal, the passage implies, but such a failure does not vitiate the force or plangency of such an ideal—an ideal that, to follow the letter's allegory through, Pater's phosphorescent example illuminates for those more capable of full aesthetic fire than he.

The same mingled response marks James's explicit commentary on British aestheticism. On the one hand, that response is openly critical, often bitterly satirical. Aestheticism is for James always tainted by excessive self-indulgence, creative insufficiency, even, at times, criminality. But on the other hand, his condemnations always carry with them faint signs of affirmation, often concealed within qualifications, hinted at by silences, or (as in the echo of the gemlike flame in the letter to Gosse) revealed by means of allusion and implication alone.

When the attractions of aestheticism threaten to emerge in the open, however, they are suppressed, evaded, or effaced by the supple maneuverings of Jamesian prose.

This dual response structures James's frequent fictional accounts of aestheticism as well. James turned frequently in the fiction of the 1870's and early 1880's to the representation of aesthetes and the dramatic interrogation of aestheticism. In such works as *Roderick Hudson*, *The Author of Beltraffio*, and, most important, *The Portrait of a Lady* (as well as in minor efforts like *A Bundle of Letters*), aesthetes frequently play prominent roles—not the least of which being, as we shall see, that of implicating other characters in their aestheticism, of suggesting the affinities between their own problematical creed and other perceptual structures or codes of value. In these fictions the full range of James's response to aestheticism is evident. He habitually slides between overt condemnation and a covert sympathy with the means and ends of the self-conscious British "aesthetic movement"; indeed, sympathy and judgment often appear so closely tied together as to be virtually indistinguishable from each other. Such an intensely dual reaction might seem to demand to be analyzed as a form of ambivalence, as the product of an intense psychic conflict. But, while such conflicts are never far from the surface in James's work and while the difficulties that center on the figure of the aesthete also suggest larger conflicts at the center of his fictional endeavor, I think it more profitable to think of this dual response as a process of discovery—discovery in the legal as well as the imperial sense of the word: that is, as a sustained interrogation of the tradition of British aestheticism, which seeks to determine its limits and possibilities, the full range of its virtues and vices. As we shall see, what James first discerns is aestheticism's affectation, its hypocrisy, its fraudulence, its moral and aesthetic failures. But as he does so, he uncovers the ideals the British aesthetic movement expressed, and questions their necessary connection to the vices with which it seems to be contaminated. What emerges from this process is the recovery of the aestheticist valorizing of *aesthesis*, of the heightening or perfection of sense experience; only then does James encounter the aestheticist dream of the aesthetic, an autonomous realm separate from but oddly redemptive of the social sphere it inhabits. The project of James's fiction of the late nineteenth-century, I want to assert, is to bring these two modes of aestheticism together; the problem that the fiction of the twentieth faces is what happens when they are.

Roderick Hudson and the Discrimination of Aestheticisms

The first sustained record of this encounter may be found in James's first fully achieved novel, *Roderick Hudson* (1875). This work is, not insignificantly, a *künstlerroman*, the story of an American painter whose vaunting Romantic ambition and lust for achievement lead to imaginative failure and, ultimately, death. But it may also be described as an aesthete-roman: the story of a Boston dilettante who, lacking any creative spark of his own, seeks to meet the requirements of his own imagination through his sponsorship of Roderick. Indeed, the latter description is probably more accurate than the former, since not only James's narrator, Rowland Mallet, but also his artist, Roderick Hudson, learn to strike the attitude of the aesthete—indeed, Hudson learns his lesson so well as to cease to be able to create any art of his own.

But the novel is more than just a record of the relation between the aestheticism of connoisseurship and the aestheticism of creative expression; it also reflects the shape of the American social encounter with aestheticism, of the ways that aestheticism entered into the unfolding dialectic of American culture. The novel begins with an extended character sketch of the emerging social type we discussed in Chapter 2, the idle American art lover, a type whose experience, as we have seen, was informed by the increasing American exposure to the doctrines of Pater. And James's connoisseur, Rowland Mallet, defines his aspirations in terms that frequently echo Paterian pronouncements —indeed, as I suggested earlier, he echoes the pronouncements that James was at that very moment claiming to William he "knew nothing about." Rowland's belief that "a passive life in Rome, thanks to the number and the quality of one's impressions, takes . . . on a very respectable likeness to activity" (*RH*, pp. 170–71) suggests his wistful belief in Pater's "higher morality," in "not action but contemplation— *being* as distinct from *doing*—a certain disposition of mind." In Rome, too, Mallet hopes to live, like Pater's aesthete, "for the moment's sake only," or, in his own terms, with a "reconciliation to the present, the actual, the sensuous—of life on the terms that there offered themselves" (278). Aestheticism seems to offer Mallet the possibility of evading the stern morality and strenuous work ethic of his Puritan relatives —and of the Puritan side of his own character as well.

For Mallet is a walking contradiction. While he is constructed so as ceaselessly to desire a life of Paterian "impassioned contemplation," precisely those elements in his character that make this possibility seem attractive prevent him from fully indulging in it. "He was neither

an irresponsibly contemplative nature nor a sturdily practical one,"
we are told, "and he was forever looking in vain for the uses of the
things that please and the charm of the things that sustain" (176–77).
The interplay of these two impulses leads to their mutual annihilation.
Rowland's response to Cecilia's demand to "bestir yourself . . . to do
something on a large scale," for example, leads, through his "own personal conception of usefulness," to fantasies of endowing an American
art museum and, later, to "giving a reflected usefulness to my own life"
by supporting Roderick (169, 170, 199). While his "irresponsibly contemplative" impulses may assert themselves in such acts of patronage,
Rowland cannot help but feel the pull of the Protestant work ethic,
even in the midst of his acts of aesthetic contemplation (176). To his
American relatives, Rowland may appear the consummate aesthete—
"you have no duties, no profession, no home. You live for your pleasure," Mary Garland tells him at one point—but in Europe he proves
anything but (217). He promises Mary to expect "a masterpiece a year
. . . for the next quarter of a century" out of Roderick, and he seems
intent on holding his protégé to this schedule (199). "You have only
to work," he tells Roderick, and when Roderick's creative energies
begin to flag, he comforts him with such advice as "Don't heed about
your mood . . . and don't believe that there is any calm so dead that
your lungs can't ruffle it with a breeze. If you have work to do, don't
wait to feel like it; set to work and you *will* feel like it" (191, 317).

Contained within the confines of Mallet's own neurasthenic personality, then, is a particularly acute version of the conflict we saw being
raised by aestheticism within the American gentry culture—and, we
might well speculate, within Henry James himself: the conflict between
a Calvinist insistence on a life of vigorous activity and the aestheticist
privileging of a life of pure contemplation. Within Mallet, this conflict
is so intense as to lead to a state of absolute paralysis in which the
urges vigorously to act and merely to be are both so strong that neither
action nor passivity is permitted. The only form of activity agreeable
to both impulses is a certain restless wandering from scene to scene
or picture to picture that fails equally to satisfy either component of
Rowland's "awkward mixture of strong moral impulse and restless aesthetic curiosity" (177). Far from being the "idealized form of loafing"
Rowland hopes for, then, his life in Rome finally proves profoundly
disillusioning, a particularly vexing form of hyperactive indolence that
makes either outright aestheticism or rigid Puritanism seem attractive
by comparison (170).

For Mallet, as for the anxious gentry ministers and intellectuals, then, a little aestheticism serves as a welcome anodyne, but its effects on the system are paradoxically only to reinforce the disease for which it is meant to be the cure. Americans, as we have seen, dealt with the conflict created by aestheticism's refusal to keep itself within its proper bounds with a complicated cultural process of internalization and rejection; acceptable forms of aestheticism were cordoned off from those that were less assimilable, and the latter were demonized—portrayed as degenerate, dissolute, "decadent." James's novel follows the same strategy. In the shape of Roderick Hudson, it portrays for us what Malletian aestheticism would look like if it were unrestrained by the powers of his hypertrophied moral consciousness. In doing so, the novel effects the same discrimination of aestheticisms James's contemporaries in gentry magazines and religious periodicals were performing across the Atlantic.

By describing Roderick as an aesthete, I am referring not to his artistic progress (or regress) but rather to that of his connoisseurship. A shifting analogy is persistently suggested between the artistic sensibilities of Roderick and his mentor. Following their arrival in Rome, the two perform acts of aesthetic contemplation in unison, sitting "with their heads together, criticizing intaglios and etchings, water-color drawings and illuminated missals" (231–32). Initially, both Rowland and Roderick share the Ruskinian—and Bostonian—appetite for medieval religious art, but, "clamoring for a keener sensation," Roderick rapidly detaches himself from the tastes of his friend (225). Soon, he signals his own movement from the current aesthetic orthodoxies of both Boston and London to a more sophisticated preference for the Renaissance by turning from Rowland's beloved Dante to the less austere delights of Ariosto and by bragging as "all those Italian fellows in the Renaissance used to brag" (243). From here, it is not a particularly large step to the point where he declares himself an out-and-out aesthete, using the correct technical vocabulary to do so: "I never mean to make anything ugly," he proclaims at a dinner party, "The Greeks never made anything ugly, and I'm a Hellenist, I'm not a Hebraist" (242).

Roderick progresses from naiveté to artistic and cultural sophistication so rapidly that Mallet soon seems, in comparison, a failed "connoisseur," immured in the tastes of the mid-century (181). It is not long, however, before Roderick encounters his creative block, and, at this moment, comes again to resemble his patron. This time, however, it is not the beauty-loving side of Rowland's attenuated aestheticism he takes up, but rather its component of idleness. "I have lately learned

terribly well how to be idle," he exclaims early in this process, and
the ease with which he slips into Rowland's characteristic language
of self-loathing is matched by the skill with which he masters Malletian "lotus-eating" (254, 171). Indeed, Roderick rapidly becomes fero-
ciously good at doing nothing; he does nothing with an energy and an
enthusiasm that puts his patron to shame. Thus, yet again, Roderick
comes fully to embody possibilities that Rowland cannot bring himself
to explore. This is made quite clear when, in a penultimate stage in his
slide toward immobility and death, Roderick is transformed into an
aestheticist voluptuary, a parodic version of the Baudelairean dandy:

> [Rowland] went straight to Roderick's apartment, deeming this, at an early
> hour, the safest place to seek him. He found him in his sitting-room, which had
> been closely darkened to keep out the heat. The carpets and rugs had been re-
> moved, the floor of the speckled concrete was bare and lightly sprinkled with
> water. Here and there, over it, certain strongly perfumed flowers had been
> scattered. Roderick was lying on his divan in a white dressing-gown, staring
> up at the frescoed ceiling. The room was deliciously cool, and filled with the
> moist, sweet odor of the circumjacent roses and violets. All this seemed highly
> fantastic, and yet Rowland hardly felt surprised.
>   "Your mother was greatly alarmed at your note," he said, "and I came to
> satisfy myself that, as I believed, you are not ill." Roderick lay motionless ex-
> cept that he slightly turned his head towards his friend. He was smelling a
> large white rose, which he continued to press to his nose. In the darkness of
> the room he looked exceedingly pale, but his handsome eyes had an extraor-
> dinary brilliancy. He let them rest for some time on Rowland, lying there like
> a Buddhist in an intellectual swoon, whose perception should be slowly ebbing
> back to temporal matters. "Oh, I am not ill," he said at last. "I have never been
> better." (423–24)

By assuming this role of the flower-sniffing aesthete, Roderick extends
the aestheticist impulses of his patron, and thus simultaneously mirrors and mocks Rowland. His stance of absolute passivity, his "staring
at the frescoed ceiling" and "smelling a white rose," repeats in a distort-
ingly exaggerated fashion the course of Roman "Lotus-Eating" Mallet
had set for himself (171). His patient anticipation of a declaration of
love from the quintessential *belle dame sans merci*, Christina Light—a
declaration the reader knows will never come—similarly extends and
distorts Rowland's patient, suffering, but equally impossible, love for
Mary Garland.

The final result of the persistent doubling between Rowland and
Roderick, then, would seem to be a resolute indictment of aestheticism. Rowland's prediction that a life devoted to sensations in Rome
"increases ten-fold your liability to moral misery" is confirmed with

disturbing accuracy by the experience of Roderick (171). By so playing out the possibilities that remain unavailable to his patron, Roderick yokes aestheticism firmly to moral deficiency and (perhaps even worse, at least for Henry James) creative failure. But Roderick's experience serves as well a more dialectical function. It successfully serves to dis- tinguish between aestheticisms, to bear fully a taint of failure and guilt so as to leave the other relatively free of it. The very extremity of Roderick's experience may exhaust the possibilities of one form of aestheticism, that in which the aesthete pursues intense experience directly through the senses, and particularly through the heightened sense experiences of intoxication and sexuality. The young James habitually condemned this form of aestheticism—the aestheticism of Baudelaire or Swinburne—often in language that made him sound a little like an urbane prig.[3] But the very finality with which Roderick closes off these possibilities leaves room for the exploration of others —those, for example, embodied in Rowland's tentative exploration of the Paterian notion of experience undertaken—and privileged—for its own sake.

It is true that, at least in this novel, the potential of this latter form of aestheticism—that of what Pater called a "quickened, multiplied consciousness"—is barely explored before it is foreclosed. Rowland's neurasthenic temperament prevents him from embracing fully this (or any other) experience. But if we consider *Roderick Hudson* in the context of James's career as a whole, we may find that the possibili- ties Mallet explores so tentatively continue to engage James's authorial energies. Few descendents of Roderick Hudson populate the later fic- tion—Gloriani, the canny professional who makes his first appearance in this novel, becomes James's prototype for the (visual) artist—but spiritual relatives of Rowland are profuse. Hyacinth Robinson, for ex- ample, is a particularly unfortunate version of the Malletian flaneur; Lambert Strether proves a more successful one. Indeed, in a charac- ter like Strether, James collapses the values attached to Rowland and Roderick into each other. Strether is a detached Malletian observer who is freed from self-absorption by the addition of the healthiest powers of the bestowing imagination. But while Strether may be a figure of imaginative potency, he is also saved from Roderick's ex- cesses by a Mallet-like temperamental reserve. To put it in other terms: Strether is committed neither to the aestheticist value of pure contem- plative being nor to its antagonist, energetic doing; rather, he unifies these qualities into a complex amalgam of being and doing that real- izes itself in acts of detached but sympathetic contemplation. In the

world of *The Ambassadors*, merely to see is to act; moreover, in vision lies
the only possible form of moral action in a world defined on the one
hand by the crudities of Woollett, Massachusetts, and on the other by
the corruptions of Paris. The problematics of this stance await further
investigation; at this point, it is important to note that at this moment,
James's interest was excited by discovering its possibilities.

In *Roderick Hudson*, then, James performs the same labor as that
being undertaken by his compatriots across the ocean: the simultaneous acknowledgement and evasion of the example of aestheticism.
But aestheticism posed even greater problems to James than it did
for his American contemporaries—and not only because James was
encountering aestheticism directly in the salons and dinner tables of
London. As *Roderick Hudson* suggests, more was at stake for James
in Paterian aestheticism than just the evaluation of Renaissance art
or the privileging of aesthetic response; the novel suggests that the
very project of Jamesian fiction was dismayingly homologous to that
of the aestheticist writers with whom James came increasingly in contact at this time. The similarity between the imaginative project of
the Jamesian artist and that of the British aesthete is suggested most
clearly in James's explicit commentaries on his own form. Whether
or not the theory of fiction James articulated so influentially in the
late 1870's and early 1880's was directly influenced by the adherents
of aestheticism who were so vociferously active at the same moment
is somewhat disputable, although a case can be made for at least a
shadowy shaping. But what is indisputable is that there was at least the
appearance of similarity, if not identity, between James's eloquently
advanced aesthetic program and the tenets of British aestheticism—
and that such an appearance posed, at the very least, problems of
affiliation and sympathy for the young Henry James.

The best gauge of those similarities may be found in the most famous
articulation of that program, James's essay *The Art of Fiction* (1884). For
the claims he makes there for the powers of the novelist's consciousness sound strikingly similar to those Pater makes for the aesthete's
consciousness in the Conclusion to *The Renaissance*. Such an identification can be made in general terms: both James's and Pater's works
rebel against the characteristic Victorian moral demands on art; both
defend, implicitly or explicitly, aesthetic experience as a valuable end
in itself. But the resemblance goes even further. Like Pater, James
grounds his argument on a thoroughgoing and radical empiricism.
The fundamental axiom on which he rests his defense of the novelist's
freedom "to feel and say" is the value of pure experience undertaken

for its own sake—a formulation akin to the experiential idealism Pater advocates in the Conclusion. And, more Paterian still, James's arguments for the valuation of "experience for experience's sake" define that experience exclusively in terms of sense impressions. As James puts it, "if experience consists of impressions, then it may be said that impressions *are* experience, just as (have we not seen it?) they are the very air we breathe" (*LC* 1, p. 53). Further like Pater, James moves rapidly beyond impressionism to the affirmation of the value of the most vivid impressions, to the affirmation of intensity itself. James's definition of the novel as "a personal, a direct impression of life" is immediately followed by the assertion that the value of the novel is "greater or lesser according to the intensity of the impression." "[N]o intensity . . . therefore no value" (50): in its barest form, such is James's syllogism; and this syllogism, in positive terms, is central to the Conclusion to *The Renaissance*, which discovers value in an enervated, entropic universe solely within intense experience. Moreover, what is true of James's defense of the work of art is also true of his praise for the consciousness of the artist. It is the ability to respond to the swarms of sense impressions with a distinct intensity of its own that defines that special consciousness:

Experience is never limited, and it is never complete; it is an immense sensibility, a kind of huge spider web of the finest silken threads suspended in the chamber of consciousness and catching every air-borne particle in its tissue. It is the very atmosphere of the mind; and when the mind is imaginative—much more when it happens to be that of a man of genius—it takes to itself the faintest hints of life, it converts the very pulses of the air into revelations. (52)

In order to respond fully to the varied and profuse "air-borne" particles of "life," in other words, James's novelist must possess the essential qualities of Pater's aesthete: a "multiplied consciousness" and a "quickened sense of life." He must—in the phrase Pater's pupil Wilde was to pick up from James—"be one of the people on whom nothing is lost" (53).

Aestheticism, particularly the Paterian aestheticism of the 1880's, thus posed James a complex and multifaceted problem. If it was, as we have seen, dismayingly close to the center of his fictional project, the acknowledgment of that affinity would place James in an untenable position, for, as *Roderick Hudson* suggested, aestheticism represented to James either a detached but monitoring scopophilia or a self-indulgent dissoluteness. And throughout the 1880's, James confronted this problem repeatedly, presenting as he did so increasingly cunning versions of the dialectics he displayed in *Roderick* itself, the aim of which being a simultaneous exploration of the possibilities embodied in aestheticism and an exculpation of so dangerous a project. One particularly impressive response may be found in a story that embodied, and to a certain extent vented, the fear of a rampant aestheticism: *The Author of Beltraffio* (1884). In that story, F. O. Matthiessen observes, James "set himself to dramatize the aesthetic gospel of the eighties without quite indicating, perhaps without being quite sure at this stage of his development, exactly how much of it he accepted for himself."[4] Indeed, by putting much of the language from *The Art of Fiction* in the mouth of an aestheticist novelist, Mark Ambient, it questions the relation between James's stance and that of aestheticism. Contemporary reviewers were quick to make the connection, particularly in America; *The Nation* warned James against too close an identification with the "Art for Art's School," and *The Critic* wrote: "We beg to remind Mr. James of the *alter ego*—the former delightful self—and pray him not to write himself to death; not to fritter his gentility and gentle skill away, and not to patch his tunic with the cast-off purple patches of a fast-decaying Frenchy school, however great the temptation."[5]

The critics clearly had grounds for concern. The story raises questions about the aestheticism of the Jamesian novelist that go beyond mere aesthetics: the novelist's highly moralistic wife allows their child to die of diphtheria, convinced by the proofs of his latest book that Ambient's immoralism would inevitably infect their son. In this story, then, aestheticism is (as it was, paradoxically, for both the advocates and the detractors of "decadence") linked with corruption and disease, and leads inevitably to moral tragedy. But if James's story has partially worked to suggest an identification between the author himself and the adherents of aestheticism, it also works to clear both of the moralistic criticism that journals like *The Nation* and *The Critic* expressed and exemplified. For the story plots a cunning bouleversement: while suggesting the deficiencies of the author—Mark Ambient's devotion to his art at the expense of his commitment to the moral or the didactic—it also rigorously indicts that fanatical adherent of morality, his wife, for her even more fanatical pursuit of her principles. Indeed, the novel brings about a reversal of the positions held by these two. Ambient may believe in a number of immoral doctrines, but in his life he is an absolute bourgeois: a doting father, an affectionate brother, a loyal husband (at least within the troubled terms of the marriage which, with bourgeois propriety, are never acknowledged in public), and even a devoted gardener capable of sustaining a long conversation on the subject with the local vicar. His wife, by contrast, grants a potency and a power to art that even the aesthete does not claim for it. To put the matter most simply: Beatrice kills her child for the sake of a book—the proofs of which the narrator of the story naively shows her in order to prove Ambient's seriousness of purpose—and it is precisely the closing of the gap between art and life, which so dire an action implies, that Mrs. Ambient has objected to most strongly in her husband's work. To Mrs. Ambient, and Mrs. Ambient alone, art possesses the power utterly to shape the consciousness of its audience—an irony that at once inculpates and exculpates James's aesthete author and simultaneously shadows and clears James himself of the same charge.[6]

Like *Roderick Hudson*, then, this nouvelle suggests both the depth of the problem that aestheticism posed James in the 1870's and the early 1880's and the depths to which he would go to solve it, or at least to keep its destabilizing implications under control. It must be admitted that neither *Beltraffio* nor *Roderick Hudson* nor the shorter fictions can be numbered among James's great imaginative achievements. But there is another work of the same period that is indisputably one of James's most successful, and for which aestheticism is of more than passing interest: I refer, of course, to *The Portrait of a Lady* (1881). Indeed, it is in this novel that the full dimensions of James's initial confrontation with the "aesthetic movement" and its implications for the practice of his own art are most fully delineated. Aestheticism here is represented as a species of malevolence, indeed, as central to a hyperbolically understood form of evil. In the malevolent Gilbert Osmond, James creates a figure so spectacularly pestiferous as to have defined the lineaments of the aesthete for the next 50 years—fictional representations of the aesthete after James's novel inevitably imitate it: the plot of Vernon Lee's *Miss Brown* (1884) is overtly modeled on that of James's novel; George Du Maurier's Svengali (in *Trilby*, 1894) possesses many explicitly Osmondian characteristics; and Robert Herrick's malicious portrayal of a real aesthete, Bernard Berenson, in *The Gospel of Freedom* (1898) similarly replays the scenario of *Portrait*.[7] But influential as James's portrayal may have been—and, as we shall see, James's Osmond was perhaps most influential in serving as a virtual anthology of contemporary critiques of the aesthete—his work differs from that of his predecessors and its successors alike in the overdetermined and unstable quality of its response to aestheticism. James's goal is not merely hyperbolically to delineate the moral deficiencies of aestheticism—to write an entire novel, in other words, in the voice of

Mrs. Ambient. Rather, it is ultimately to perform the discrimination of aestheticisms we have seen his earlier fiction aspiring to achieve: to assert or define through the vehicle of Isabel Archer a stance in which aestheticism might be understood as being a positive, even redemptive model for the fictional act—a solution to the problems posed by aestheticism that his subsequent writings both build upon and critique.

Portrait of an Aesthete:
Gilbert Osmond and the Satire of Aestheticism

Like *Roderick Hudson*, *The Portrait of a Lady* inscribes a historically specific response to aestheticism. It is important to remember that when James arrived in London in 1880 to finish the novel, the aesthetic craze was at its height. Aestheticism had at that very moment moved from a coterie concern to a public sensation. Oscar Wilde's notoriety had reached its apogee: having come down from Oxford some two years previously, Wilde threw himself into the round of dinner parties and soirees, enthralling many and shocking the rest with his calculated outrageousness. His fame, and that of his set, extended beyond the range of dinner-party gossip. No fewer than three plays brought aestheticism to the attention of the West End public. James Albery's inept *Where's the Cat?*, a more successful farce, *The Colonel*, by the mediocre but prolific Frank Burnand, and, of course, Gilbert and Sullivan's *Patience* all opened in 1881, the latter two to spectacular public response. And, seemingly every week, *Punch* launched satirical lampoons at the aesthetes, sometimes in prose, sometimes in cartoons, most from the hand of George Du Maurier.

Aestheticism thus formed the subject matter of the plays James was seeing, the newspapers and periodicals he was reading, and, undoubtedly, the parties he was attending. It was becoming part of his professional life as well. James met Du Maurier when the latter's lampoons of the aesthetes were at their peak of popularity, and entered into protracted negotiations with him over the illustrations to *Washington Square*. And the issue of *Macmillan's* in which *Portrait* was first published was preceded immediately by one containing a venomous attack on aestheticism, entitled "The New Renaissance; or, The Gospel of Intensity," by the conservative art critic Harry Quilter; the novel's second installment was followed immediately by William Michael Rossetti's response to Quilter's assault.

It is not surprising, therefore, that aestheticism was also becoming part of James's own novel, largely through the vehicle of the malevolent

Gilbert Osmond. Indeed, the representation of Osmond is thoroughly grounded in this historical moment—far more thoroughly than critics have acknowledged.[8] Osmond resembles not only the idle American expatriate connoisseurs in Italy—of whom there were certainly enough by 1881, as James learned on his journeys there—but also the English aesthetes he was meeting, gossiping about, seeing at the theater. "What is life but an art? Pater has said that so well, somewhere" says a fatuous young American named Louis Leverett in James's 1879 story, *A Bundle of Letters*;[9] so does Gilbert Osmond, when he tells Isabel that one "ought to make one's life a work of art" (*PL*, p. 507). Osmond's taste for Japanese china and his collection of bric-a-brac place him directly in the context of the "aesthetic craze" of the late 1870's, since it was precisely these objects that the aesthetic movement prized and that its members (especially Rossetti and Whistler) collected. To nail down the association and understand its point, we need turn only to Lord Warburton's comment on what Isabel bitterly calls Osmond's "genius for upholstery"—"there is a great rage for that sort of thing now": Osmond, as collector and interior designer alike is identified with the rage or mania whose apotheosis James was witnessing in London (588). Moreover, as Richard Ellmann has reminded us, James slyly signals the connection between Osmond and the epigone of aestheticism, Oscar Wilde: the poem Osmond sends to Isabel as part of his perverse courtship, *Rome Revisited*, subtly alludes to Wilde's *Rome Unvisited*—published, along with the rest of Wilde's poems, in 1881, to a chorus of critical catcalls.[10]

Noting the precision with which Osmond's historical provenance is established helps us appreciate what James called in *The Art of Fiction* the novel's "solidity of specification," but it does something more important as well. It helps us understand not only that Osmond is partially composed in response to the aesthetes whose careers James was witnessing as he wrote the novel, but also that he is depicted along the satirical lines James was reading in magazines or seeing at the theater. Indeed, far more than being a reflection of the "real" Oscar Wilde or any of the other "real" aesthetes James knew, the representation of Osmond mirrors and mimics the satirical attacks on these aesthetes launched largely, but not exclusively, by Du Maurier and the rest of the *Punch* coterie. Their satirical portraits of the aesthete focused formulaically, even obsessively, on a limited number of issues, and James follows out the lines of this satire quite faithfully. As represented by the *Punch* satirists, the aesthete is, above all else, indolent. He is languid, weary, enervated, bored; he prefers inaction to action, passivity to assertion, all things decaying to those robust and healthy. His very demeanor implies his enervation: the characteristic pose of a Du Maurier aesthete is a cultivated slouch, and even the sunflowers and pansies he holds in his hands droop. Moreover, the aesthete believes in his own enervation. Extending Pater's praise for "*being* as distinct from *doing*—a certain disposition of the mind" as the ground of value, the Du Maurier aesthete establishes his moral superiority on the basis of his perfected being and being alone, and urges others to imitate his self-satisfied indolence. In the cartoon *Maudle on the Choice of a Profession* (1881), for example, Du Maurier's aesthete Maudle (who had come to look, as of 1881, exactly like Oscar Wilde) slouches in the direction of Mrs. Brown, "a Philistine from the country," to drawl his appreciation of her would-be artist son. "*Why* should he be an artist?" asks Maudle. "Well, he must be *something*!" replies Mrs. Brown. "Why should he *be* anything?" responds Maudle. "Why not let him remain for ever content to *exist beautifully*?"[11]

Snobbery is the basis as well of the second ground of satire: the aesthete is a creature of inexplicable enthusiasms and eccentric tastes whose values the aesthete and the aesthete alone is capable of identifying while asserting them to be transcendentally valid. Chinoiserie, medieval Italian painting, peacock's feathers, and dadoes: all are objects of delight to the aesthete and of confusion to the other members of his world, since the qualities that make such objects "aesthetic" are impossible to define except in vague, and thus ultimately absurd, terms. As Bunthorne, in Gilbert's *Patience*, says:

> If you're anxious for to shine in the high aesthetic
>   line as a man of culture rare,
> You must get up all the germs of the transcendental
>   terms, and plant them everywhere.
> You must lie upon the daisies and discourse in novel phrases of your
>   complicated state of mind,
> The meaning doesn't matter if it's only idle chatter of a
>   transcendental kind.
>   And every one will say
>   As you walk your mystic way,
> "If this young man expresses himself in terms too deep for *me*,
> Why, what a very singularly deep young man this deep young
>   man must be!"[12]

The aesthete's exaltation of taste, in other words, represents an expression of his or her will to power; and, in the terms of the social struggle in which these characters are frequently engaged, will to social power —a means of intimidating their gullible audience with recondite enthusiasms and dilettantish predilections. Moreover, there is something unnatural or perverse in the aesthete's tastes. He or she is, literally, a commodity fetishist; libidinal energies are deflected from healthy and normal outlets onto art objects, which are thus worshipped in a perverse and unhealthy manner. The most famous example of this habit of thought is Du Maurier's famous cartoon, *The Six-Mark Teapot* (1880). There, an "aesthetic bridegroom" and an "intense bride"—the term "intense" served in these satires, as it did for Quilter, as a virtual synonym for "aesthetic"—gaze reverently at a blue china teapot: "It is quite consummate, is it not?" asks the leering male (it is difficult to tell whether he is leering at the teapot or the bride); "It is, indeed! Oh, Algernon, let us live up to it!" replies his bride, a look of rapt aesthetic devotion on her face.[13]

Finally, as far as the satirists are concerned, the aesthete is a phony, a fraud, a mountebank. Some ulterior motive was necessary to explain their bizarre affectations, their mysterious enthusiasms. Such a motive was not hard to find: self-promotion, self-advancement, and pecuniary self-aggrandizement, particularly the self-aggrandizing attempts of those who by birth or wealth or both are excluded from high society to make their way into its confines. Streyke, in *The Colonel*, worms his way into the good graces of the Forester family in order to marry off his cousin and make his own fortune; when he is unmasked, we learn that the nephew is really an apothecary's assistant, not a struggling young artist, and that "the gifted master, Lambert Streyke" himself is really an accountant turned confidence man. The applications of aestheticism's valorization of the pose to the fine art of social climbing were no less obvious to Du Maurier. Throughout this period, Du Maurier's cartoons consistently portrayed aesthetes as *parvenus* seeking to climb the social ladder. In 1880, for example, his aesthete Postlethwaite avers that "the Lily had carried me through my first season, the Primrose through my second . . . what Flower of Flowers is to carry me through my next?" In 1876, one Swellington Spiff expresses the hope that his china collection will help him meet a duke.[14] Some of the more gullible members of Du Maurier's high society may be fooled by these aesthetes, but the social act Du Maurier's cartoons inscribe is that of the public revelation of their hypocrisy and fraudulence. Indeed, in one of the final cartoons in the Du Maurier aesthete series, Maudle and Postlethwaite and their favorite hostess, the *parvenue* Mrs. Cimabue Brown, learn that their fame is due to *Punch* and *Punch* alone; the title of the cartoon, and the act it seeks to perform, is "Frustrated Social Ambition."

The representation of Osmond conforms to these outlines with striking accuracy. In the first description of Osmond, James not only emphasizes the artifice of his appearance—his "thin, delicate, sharply-cut face," the "beard, cut in the manner of the portraits of the sixteenth century"—but also his resemblance to one of Du Maurier's cartoon figures. The description of Osmond he offers here is strikingly similar to the thin, pale, and indolent "aesthetic bachelors" Du Maurier drew: "he had a light, lean, lazy-looking figure, and was apparently neither tall nor short" (425).[15] Throughout this scene, it is precisely Osmond's aestheticist languor that is emphasized:

> "What epithet would properly describe me?" [Osmond asks Madame Merle].
> "You are indolent. For me that is your worst fault."
> "I am afraid it is really my best."
> "You don't care," said Madame Merle, gravely.
> "No; I don't think I care much. What sort of fault do you call that?" (435)

We can note here not only that Osmond's indolence places him in the aestheticist tradition, but that the rhetoric he uses to announce it does so as well. The paradoxical reversal of terms of value—"I am afraid it is really my best"—is, of course, a recognizable characteristic of Oscar Wilde's epigrammatic wit; and Osmond's paradoxical praise for his own capacities of indolence anticipates almost precisely Wilde's assertion that "to do nothing at all is the most difficult thing in the world, the most difficult and the most intellectual" (*Artist*, pp. 233, 381).[16]

The representation of Osmond shares other direct affinities with popular satires on aestheticism. Like Maudle, Osmond proclaims himself to be a creature beyond the mere exigencies of vocational choice: "I could do nothing. I had no prospects, I was poor, and I was not a man of genius . . . I was simply the most fastidious young gentleman living" (463). Osmond's career, of course, *is* his fastidiousness; he is solely a creature of taste, "the incarnation of taste," as Ralph Touchett puts it—partially the tastes of the aesthetic era, although not exclusively so; moreover, further like Du Maurier or Gilbert, the novel demystifies his fine taste, viewing it as nothing more than a form of affected pretension (547). As in Du Maurier's satires, it is only the naive characters who see Osmond's taste as rich, rare, and extraordinary. Osmond may be, as Isabel believes early in their courtship, "the man who had the best taste in the world," but those with greater sophistication think otherwise (631). Lord Warburton, as we have already seen, identifies Osmond's taste as a product of the more ephemeral sort of fashion; Ned Rosier is even more unsparing. "It's papa's taste; he has so much," Pansy tells him; "he had a good deal, Rosier thought; but some of it was bad" (574). As indeed it is: when Rosier walks his way through Osmond's collection, he notes for us, through the delicate modulations of the *style indiret libre*, the aesthetic gaucherie represented by the "big cold Empire clock" in Gilbert's living room, the diminished imagination registered by his collection of miniatures (574). As the novel progresses, Osmond's taste becomes progressively, even incrementally, diminished. When the reader first encounters him, Osmond is sketching the Alps and expressing quiet contentment over his "discovering . . . a sketch by Coreggio on a panel daubed over by some inspired idiot"; by the end of the novel, having been endowed with the greatest possible acquisitive scope by Isabel's wealth, he realizes the requirements of his imagination by collecting miniatures and sketching a gold coin (463). Osmond is finally attacked by the novel on the same ground on which Oscar Wilde was attacked by his critics: he is nothing more than an "aesthetic sham," or, in Ralph's words, a "sterile dilettante" (547).

More than the critique of his taste links Osmond to the satirical portraits of the aesthetes. He, like them, is finally portrayed by the novel as being nothing more than a social climber, a parvenu—even an American!—who seeks to use his aesthetic sensibilities, particularly as manifested in his choice of a wife, to mount the social ladder. Like Du Maurier's aesthetes, his stance of fastidious disdain for the social milieu is finally revealed to be only a highly developed form of hypocrisy. Ralph Touchett puts the revelation of Gilbert's worldliness for us most eloquently when, late in the novel, he realizes that

under the guise of caring only for intrinsic values, Osmond lived exclusively for the world. Far from being its master, as he pretended to be, he was its very humble servant, and the degree of its attention was his only measure of success. He lived with his eye on it, from morning till night, and the world was so stupid it never suspected the trick. Everything he did was *pose—pose* so deeply calculated that if one were not on the lookout one mistook it for impulse. Ralph had never met a man who lived so much in the land of calculation. His tastes, his studies, his accomplishments, his collections, were all for a purpose. His life on his hill-top in Florence had been a *pose* of years. His solitude, his ennui, his love for his daughter, his good manners, his bad manners, were so many features of a mental image constantly present to him as a model of impertinence and mystification. His ambition was not to please the world, but to please himself by exciting the world's curiosity and then declining to satisfy it. It made him feel great to play the world a trick. (597–98)

Indeed, Ralph's critique repeats precisely the terms of denigration employed by the popular satirists of aestheticism. For them, too, the aesthete's bizarre "tastes, his studies, his accomplishments, his collections"

serve only a "social purpose." Gilbert's Bunthorne, whose "medievalism's affectation / Born of a morbid love of admiration" (199), or the
Du Maurier aesthetes who attempt to crash high society by means of
their aesthetic refinement are all shown to possess the combination of
indifference and obsessive consideration for the social sphere Osmond
displays. "What is it to be an Aesthete?" asked Frederic Harrison, who
then proceeds to give a virtual paraphrase of Ralph's condemnation
of Osmond. "Is it not to air one's zeal for Art, not out of genuine love
of beauty, but out of fashion and love of display, in order to be like
our neighbours or to be unlike our neighbours, in the wantonness of a
noisy life and a full pocket?"[17] Gilbert and Du Maurier and Harrison
would all agree that the most galling feature of the aesthete was the
curious admixture of "impertinence and mystification" Ralph defines
as the essence of Osmondism. All join Ralph and, by extension, James,
in the satirical rejection of the aesthete, in his expulsion from the social
and moral community he seeks to join.

I don't mean to stress the satirized side of Osmond's character at
the expense of its other components, particularly that aspect critics
have tended to focus on: his massive egotism, his manipulative coldness—those qualities in Osmond that cause Isabel to think of him as
possessing "the evil eye," the "faculty for making everything wither
that he touched," the qualities that make Osmond resemble the vil-
lain of a Gothic romance (629, 628). But I also think that it is an
aspect of James's representational strategy we should not ignore. That
the novel also invites us to view Osmond satirically has consequences
not otherwise graspable if we view him in terms of the Gothic (or
even Hawthornean) romance paradigm. For it brings Osmond into
a recognizably social world. Instead of asking us to view Osmond
and Osmondism as representing a nearly supernatural form of evil
(James's version of "motiveless malignity"), or as a psychological allegory of the causes and consequences of such evil, it invites us to understand the social dimensions of his behavior: to understand its role in
the power games of the human community, to understand the ubiquity, even the banality of such games. Instead of asking us to view his
character in isolation, James's satire demands that we view the links
between Osmond's form of behavior and that of the other characters in the novel. The notorious ambivalence of satire, its tendency to
break down precisely the moral boundaries it has sought to establish,
affects this novel as well. As we are asked to view Osmond as a vehicle of malevolence, we are also led to notice the form of behavior he
so spectacularly exemplifies in all the characters who surround him—

even, or especially, those characters at whose expense he is satirized. In this, James uses satire for ends precisely the opposite of those for which we saw it deployed in *Roderick Hudson*. Instead of seeking to discriminate between an aesthete and those with whom he is surrounded, James here uses a satirized aestheticism to complicate these relations: in this novel aestheticism is understood as being an endemic—indeed epidemic—contagion, ultimately infecting even the author himself.

Ralph, Isabel, James: The Ubiquity of Aestheticism

We see this contagion most clearly in the novel's portrayal of Ralph Touchett. As virtually all critics of the novel have noted, there are numerous troubling similarities between Isabel's benefactor and her bane, and their common connoisseurship is at the center of them. R. P. Blackmur puts the matter with his customary suavity when he writes that "everyone tampers with Isabel, and it is hard to say whether her cousin Ralph Touchett, who had arranged the bequest, or the Prince, Gilbert Osmond, who marries her because of it, tampers the more deeply."[18] The link between the two inheres in more than just their common "tampering," however: it extends to the very perceptual systems that underlie such acts. Gilbert views Isabel, as he views everyone in his narrow world, as an objet d'art, a potential "figure in his collection of choice objects" (501). Osmond's particular form of what we might call the aestheticizing vision is marked both by the distance of the contemplative observer, coolly evaluating the people he encounters with an assumed—if fraudulent—disinterestedness, and by the ruthlessness with which he seeks to make them into testimonies to his taste. Such a vision carries with it an implicit notion of both self and other. In Gilbert's form of vision, the self is understood to be a smug, observing entity, a private and self-satisfied "point of view," while all others are treated as objects of this contemplative vision, to be either appreciated or rejected but always transformed into signs of the supreme taste of the observer. Gilbert's aestheticizing vision, in other words, might also be said to be a reifying vision. Despite the nobility of his rhetoric, Osmond perceives all the others he encounters as detached, deadened objects of his purely passive perception, and seeks to make those who refuse to be so into such beautiful objects.[19] And when Ralph first meets Isabel, he first resists, and then succumbs to a similar impulse:

If his cousin were to be nothing more than an entertainment to him, Ralph was conscious that she was an entertainment of a high order. "A character like that," he said to himself, "is the finest thing in nature. It is finer than the finest work of art—than a Greek bas-relief, than a great Titian, than a Gothic cathedral. It is very pleasant to be so well treated where one least looked for it. I had never been more blue, more bored, than for a week before she came; I had never expected less that something agreeable would happen. Suddenly, I receive a Titian, by the post, to hang on my wall—a Greek bas-relief to stick over my chimney piece. The key of a beautiful edifice is thrust into my hand, and I am told to walk in and admire." (254)

At first, Ralph sees Isabel as a character of pure "nature" who possesses a vital energy of her own, whose "play" transcends that of any work of art. Isabel transcends all the mental structures Ralph erects to define her, all the images he conjures up to describe her. But he is not able to sustain this vision of Isabel for long. Soon, he subtly but unmistakably metamorphoses her into that which he had previously claimed she transcended—a work of art. By so doing, he begins inadvertently to show Osmondian characteristics. Having defined the mystery that is Isabel as a painting or bas-relief, he attempts imaginatively to collect her. For after he has mentally transformed Isabel into a particularly beautiful but nevertheless static portrait of a lady, the next logical step is to hang her on the wall of his mental portrait gallery. To translate from the novel's metaphorical language back into the grammar of its plot: Ralph endows Isabel with a fortune (much as one would endow an art museum) in order to continue to contemplate her—to "gratif[y] my imagination" (382).

I mention these well-known passages not to inculpate Ralph, but rather to suggest how unwittingly he falls into Gilbert's aestheticizing vision. This judgment must be calibrated rather delicately, for many critics fall into the traps of wholly idealizing Ralph (as we are clearly meant to do, up to a certain point) or condemning him (as we are also meant to do, but again only up to a certain point). Neither approval nor condemnation, however, does justice to the tragic machine James creates out of the inevitability and the insidiousness of the process of aestheticization. Such acts are inevitable for Ralph because they are a cognitive necessity. It is impossible for even so subtle a consciousness as Ralph's to tolerate a phenomenon like Isabel, which remains so resolutely resistant to definition. Despite his own desire to do otherwise, Ralph is forced by the very structure of his perception to reify and then aestheticize Isabel, to treat her with the detached but appreciative vision of the discerning connoisseur. The novel clearly demonstrates the negative consequences of such an aestheticizing vision —even so generous a vision as one that compares Isabel to a Titian.

Ralph thinks he can respond to Isabel as he would to a work of art, with energetic detachment and consummate disinterestedness. But he is forced to discover that this is impossible, for she is neither a painting nor a bas-relief but only an extremely naive human being—prey, like all humans, to making ill-considered decisions. Isabel challenges his disinterestedness by doing what paintings cannot: by growing and changing along the idiosyncratic lines of her own character. And—in one of the bitterest ironies of this endlessly ironic book—she will exercise this freedom by marrying the one man who attempts what Ralph only imagines: to turn her into a beautiful but static and immobile work of art.

For Isabel suffers precisely the same kind of aestheticist contagion as Ralph. She, too, shares a good many of the more problematic qualities of Osmond's aestheticism, albeit in a more benign shape, and it is precisely these qualities that cause her to fall under his control. Isabel's aestheticism is signaled by James through the application of much of the characteristic language of the British aesthetic movement to his descriptions of Isabel, particularly those early in the novel. Indeed, James runs through most of the famous, if not notorious, catchphrases of the Conclusion to *The Renaissance* in depicting her. We learn that Isabel possesses a "delicate . . . flame-like spirit"; that she responds to Lord Warburton with a "quickened consciousness"; that she enjoys a number of aesthetic "pulsations" in St. Peter's; and, late in the novel, that she muses over the "infinite vista of a multiplied life" with which she first encountered Osmond (242, 257, 485, 629). To a certain extent, James employs this language to describe the eagerness with which the young Isabel partakes of the Paterian endeavor of "drain[ing] the cup of experience," a propensity Osmond appeals to in his protracted seduction: "Go everywhere," he said at last, in a low, kind voice, "do everything; get everything out of life" (345, 508). But as in the case of Ralph, Isabel's aestheticism is more deeply ingrained, and more ultimately problematic, than it appears at first glance. Isabel possesses an aestheticizing vision of her own and, as with Ralph, this vision is understood as something of a cognitive necessity. For when Isabel first meets Osmond, her reaction to him, as was Ralph's to her, is one of utter confusion:

His pictures, his carvings and tapestries were interesting; but after a while Isabel became conscious that the owner was more interesting still. He resembled no one she had ever seen; most of the people she knew might be divided into groups of half-a-dozen specimens. There were one or two exceptions to this; she could think, for instance, of no group that would contain

her Aunt Lydia. There were other people who were, relatively speaking, original—original, as one might say, by courtesy—such as Mr. Goodwood, as her
cousin Ralph, as Henrietta Stackpole, as Lord Warburton, as Madame Merle.
But in essentials, when one came to look at them, these individuals belonged
to types which were already present to her mind. Her mind contained no
class which offered a natural place to Mr. Osmond—he was a specimen apart.
(458–59)

As in the case of Ralph, Isabel's cognitive difficulties are caused by
Osmond's failure to conform to any of her preexisting mental categories. But Isabel's mistakes are even more extensive. What Isabel fails
to realize is that Gilbert's ambiguousness is a result of his limitations,
not a sign of the subtlety or fineness of his character. She cannot see
that her failure to place Osmond is utterly appropriate: that, having
no positive qualities of his own, he can only be defined in terms of
negation. This is how virtually every character in the book defines
Gilbert. Madame Merle introduces him to Isabel in the language of
negation: "No career, no name, no position, no fortune, no past, no
future, no anything" (393). After meeting Osmond for the first time
in Rome, Ralph identifies him to Warburton by name. "What is he besides?" Warburton asks. "Nothing at all," Ralph replies (495). Gilbert
himself proposes to Isabel with a declaration that, like all of Gilbert's
statements, is at once literally true and deeply false: "I have neither
fortune, nor fame, nor extrinsic advantages of any kind. So I offer
nothing" (509–10).

Isabel commits the error of mistaking Gilbert's passivity for mystery,
his fastidiousness for subtlety, his indifference for reserve. And she
responds to the mystery of his poverty in the same way as Ralph responded to that of her plentitude: by mentally transforming him into
a work of art that could meet the requirements of her imagination.
This process, again like the one Ralph undertakes with her, reaches
a climax in a moment of mental *ekphrasis*, a moment at which she
imagines Osmond as a finely drawn "picture":

She had carried away an image from her visit to his hill-top which her subsequent knowledge of him did nothing to efface and which happened to take
her fancy particularly—the image of a quiet, clever, sensitive, distinguished
man, strolling on a moss-grown terrace above the sweet Val d'Arno, and holding by the hand a little girl whose sympathetic docility gave a new aspect to
childhood. The picture was not brilliant, but she liked its lowness of tone, and
the atmosphere of summer twilight that pervaded it. (476)

Indeed, there is even a greater portion of aestheticism in Isabel's response to her mental picture than in Ralph's to his. She explicitly

adopts the attitude he unconsciously falls into, that of the connoisseur, for she stands back from her image of Osmond to nod her approval of its "lowness of tone" and the "atmosphere of summer twilight that pervaded it." Her subsequent actions extend this incipient Osmondism. Having so appreciated her own mental image of this "specimen apart," Isabel proceeds to try to add it to her own collection. Just as the greatest triumph of Gilbert's career as a collector was "discovering . . . a sketch by Coreggio on a panel daubed over by some inspired idiot," so Isabel fancies that she alone is capable of identifying the true value of the artwork that is Osmond (463). The result, needless to say, is disastrous. Her unwittingly Osmondian tendency to see Osmond as he sees himself—as a rare and fine work of art—leads to her equally unwitting Osmondian attempt to collect Osmond. By seeking to marry "the man who had the best taste in the world" for what she sees as "an indefinable beauty about him—in his situation, in his mind, in his face," Isabel finds herself transformed into a mere extension of that taste, an object for cultivated appreciation possessing "nothing of her own but her pretty appearance" (631, 632). Seeking to collect a collector, she finds herself collected.

My purpose in stressing these parallels is not merely to inculpate Isabel, but rather to suggest the universality of aestheticism in the novel. Aestheticism of one sort or another is a donnée of *The Portrait of a Lady*, a piece of perceptual equipment James issues each of his characters. In doing so, he suggests how a "sterile dilettante" like Osmond can exert so powerful a force. The plot of the novel is so constructed that Osmond's aestheticism causes Isabel's and Ralph's to rebound against them. We have seen this effect in the way that Osmond's designs on Isabel force Ralph to face the consequences of his own disingenuously disinterested vision of her; Osmond confronts Ralph with a grotesque parody of his own attempt to achieve a detached, aestheticized vision of Isabel and blatantly enacts the appropriating reification delicately implicit in Ralph's perception. We may see it even more clearly in Isabel's marriage, in which Osmond's aestheticism corresponds to her naive aestheticist propensities in just enough ways to trap her irrevocably.

Through the first two-thirds of the book, then, we witness a movement that seeks to include all characters—even (or especially) the most sensitive and richly aware characters—in a form of belief and behavior that is satirized, but not expunged, by Osmond. This movement reaches a climax at the beginning of chapter 37, when we see through the eyes of yet another aesthete, Ned Rosier, Isabel "framed in the gilded doorway . . . the picture of a gracious lady" (570). Ned sees Isabel as Ralph had unconsciously seen her and as Osmond consciously wishes to see her: a static, reified art object. But at this moment, the problematic powers of aestheticism seem to have extended even further. For by reminding us that Isabel has been converted, or has converted herself, into a person whose "function" is to "represent" her husband, James is also reminding us of the affinities between aestheticism and his own representational endeavor (597). For insofar as the novel claims to be a "portrait of a lady"—a detached, objective account of Isabel's experience—it aligns itself with the possibilities it has thoroughly criticized: with the purely disinterested aestheticizing vision of Ralph, and the ironic detachment and masked will to power of Osmond. Indeed, it would seem that Gilbert, not Ralph, would most successfully figure James's own authorial aestheticism, since Ralph's irony is qualified by deep imaginative sympathy and since his stance of disinterested observation is abandoned as early as chapter 22, and since Gilbert, not Ralph, is most intensely interested in transforming Isabel into a representation of himself.

The exploration of the problematic dimension of aestheticism reaches its climax, then, with Rosier's identification of Isabel as a portrait of a lady. At this moment, it appears that all the novel's characters and even its author are somehow implicated in one form or another of Gilbert's malevolent aestheticism, just as Roderick and Rowland were in *Roderick Hudson* and just as all the characters of *The Author of Beltraffio* will be. But this same moment also initiates a countermovement. If in the first two-thirds of the novel James is interested in linking divergent characters to Osmond, in its final part, he attempts to differentiate between them and Gilbert. If the novel suggests that even the most noble, if naive, examples of the aestheticizing vision are fatally flawed, then James's alternatives are clear: either he needs to abandon or alter his fictional project entirely, or he needs to find a way to repurify the aesthetic itself, to demonstrate that perceptual and experiential responses like intense observation and the aestheticizing vision might prove redeemable, if not redemptive. And, needless to say, it is this latter path that he chooses.

Aestheticism and the Gospel of Freedom

We may observe the first step in this process by noting the increasing interest the novel gives to discriminating between Osmond and the other characters. The most spectacular instance of this discrimination is its portrayal of the relation between Osmond and Madame Merle. During the first two-thirds of the novel, we have been asked to note their commonality: we have witnessed their combined interest in acquiring a fortune for Gilbert and a mother for Pansy by marrying Osmond to Isabel. More important, we have encountered the view of the world that can make such plots possible. Madame Merle, like Osmond, perceives herself and all those around her as things to be arranged or manipulated, and is thus able to adjust her own appearances the better to shape the actions of others in order to achieve her ends. But in the last third of the novel we discover that the two can—indeed, must—be distinguished from each other. Gilbert is finally the only character who can fully exemplify the reified self that Madame Merle so eloquently defines. This discovery opens the way to more of the novel's ironies, for, just as Gilbert uses the implicit aestheticism of Isabel Archer against her, so he employs Madame Merle's reified vision of the self to reify Madame Merle herself.

The kinds of identifications and discriminations we are asked to make between these two characters are among the subtlest and most complicated in the novel. To cite but one example, Gilbert and Madame Merle are initially united, but ultimately distinguished, by their concern for appearances. We have seen the deep duplicity of this concern throughout the novel, for we have witnessed the ways they present Mrs. Touchett, Isabel, and society at large with artfully arranged poses: Madame Merle as disinterested friend and "the cleverest woman in the world"; Osmond as devoted father and aloof aesthete who cares nothing for the opinion of the world (759). But as soon as we understand the "horror" (as Madame Merle calls it) these facades are constructed to conceal, we are asked to distinguish between their desires (389). Gilbert's concern for propriety and love of convention is shown to be one small part of his obsessive concern for "the world" and that world's opinion of him. Madame Merle's concern, while superficially similar, is ultimately antithetical to his. Her "worship of appearances" is motivated not by her love of convention or her concern for propriety but rather by her fear of the discovery of her adulterous secret. Further, this divergence between Madame Merle and her former lover provides the grounds for the final break in their relation. For, as the Countess Gemini informs Isabel, Madame Merle's "worship of appearances" became "so intense that even Osmond himself got tired of it" (751). In other words, the very ground on which stands the relation she seeks so desperately to conceal is ultimately destroyed by the tenacity with which she is compelled to conceal it.

Just as we are asked to discriminate between the attitudes of Osmond and Madame Merle toward "the world," we are also asked to differentiate between their values and perceptions throughout the rest of the novel. We are initially inclined to grant Madame Merle a stature that is denied Osmond. For one thing, Madame Merle is ultimately distinguished from the reifying aestheticism with which she has been associated for much of the novel, and Osmond alone is left to bear its taint. This particular discrimination is suggested in a number of ways throughout the last third of *Portrait*, but one of the more important is made by Isabel herself. Late in the novel, just after her ride on the Campagna, Isabel broods over Madame Merle's role in arranging her marriage, and she remembers "the wonder" of her strong "desire" for the "event." "There were people who had the match-making passion, like the votaries of art for art," Isabel reflects, "but Madame Merle, great artist as she was, was scarcely one of these" (725). This passage, of course, reflects Isabel's increasingly bitter view of Madame Merle; after all, she has just applied "the great historical epithet of *wicked*" to her "false" friend (725). And the identification of Madame Merle as a "great artist" associates art with the sinister manipulation of others. But Isabel's observation reminds us that Madame Merle does indeed seem to be granted some of the less equivocal powers of the artist, and that her qualities are therefore to be distinguished from Osmond's sterile aestheticism. Madame Merle possesses in abundance the positive qualities James habitually associated with the artist—a rich sensibility, a subtlety, a complex and ultimately tragic capacity for deep emotion—along with the admittedly less positive side of the Jamesian artist—the ability to manipulate poses and create surfaces to achieve equivocal ends. As a result of this identification, Madame Merle's stature seems to increase. We are led to view her, along with Isabel, as someone who has been trapped and betrayed by circumstance and convention, and who has therefore been forced to employ even (especially) her most positive qualities for mere manipulation—and failed manipulation at that.

Sympathetic as the novel asks us to be toward Madame Merle, however, we also acknowledge that in the final divergence between her and Osmond it traps her in its own relentlessly ironic logic. She may transcend her own definition of the self as a mere collection of reified qualities, but Gilbert does not, and his amoral aestheticism finally punishes her in a chillingly appropriate manner. If Madame Merle, along with Gilbert, has turned Isabel into a deadened object of her will—in Isabel's own words, into "a dull, un-reverenced tool"—so Madame

Merle finally discovers, she too has been used by Osmond as a mere tool, to be discarded when she is no longer useful to him (759). This dimension of their relation becomes clear in their final scene together, in which a cracked cup becomes horrifically emblematic of their relations. Madame Merle's "precious object" is established as a symbol of their relation when Gilbert sunders that relation at the same moment as he discovers "a small crack" in the cup (730). By the end of the scene, when Madame Merle turns again to her own object, it takes on an even more resonant meaning: "After he had left her, Madame Merle went and lifted from the mantel-shelf the attenuated coffee-cup in which he had mentioned the existence of a crack; but she looked at it rather abstractedly. 'Have I been so vile all for nothing?' she murmured to herself" (731).

The scene is delicate and subtle, and, as many critics have noted, it adumbrates the symbolistic later James, the James of *The Golden Bowl*.[20] But it is important to observe that the scene is also savagely satiric, and that its satire here too is again cognate with that of popular satires on aestheticism. The notion of representing human relations in terms of crockery is one which, as we have seen, exercised the moral indignation of the *Punch* satirists from the time of Du Maurier's famous 1880 cartoon on the subject of living up to one's teapot. Here, too, the aesthete's propensity to reify his relations in trivializing terms is imaged by these satiric means. But the calculated whimsy of this early cartoon is replaced in James's text by an unsparing irony: the aesthete not only demonstrates his reifying vision, but also the aesthetic flaws of the object of his contemplation. In doing so, the development of James's satire and that of Du Maurier parallel each other with uncanny accuracy. On May 14, 1881, there appeared in *Punch* a mordant sketch, probably by Du Maurier, entitled *Philistia Defiant*, "in which aestheticism, assisted by a Teapot, is the cause of a division between friends."[21] In the sketch, a Mrs. Vamp invites a friend, Betsinda Grig, to her "High-Art boudoir in South Kensington," in order to appreciate, admire, adore, and ultimately "live up to" a newly acquired antique teapot, with a small crack in it. After a long speech in praise of the teapot, Betsinda replies, "with drawlingly deliberate acerbity, 'It's dreadfully cracked, and horribly ugly; if *that's* what you mean by Unutterably Utter and all the rest of it. And, upon my word, Sara, I think you must be living up—or down—to it, for you seem to get more decidedly cracked and more utterly ugly every day.'"

My point in mentioning this sketch is not to point to a "source" for James's scene, but rather to suggest how in this scene he finds his satiri-

cal energies developing along lines parallel to those of Du Maurier.
Indeed, James outdoes the increasing acidulousness of Du Maurier's
satire. In James's hands, a "deliberate acerbity" works to punish not
only the reifying aesthete, but his reified victim as well. It is precisely
Madame Merle's own reified vision of the self as a collection of things
that is turned against her, for she has become to Gilbert nothing more
than the appurtenance she believes the self to be. She is of no more
consequence to him than an exquisite cup, to be discarded if and when
flaws are discovered in it. And, to complete the irony, we realize in her
moment of self-discovery, at her own "murmured" threnody to her
love for Gilbert and her lament for what she has done in the name of
that love, that Osmond rejects her for precisely the passionate emotion
and keen intelligence she displays in her moment of horrified recognition. In short, all the qualities that make her more than a mere object
are precisely those that cause Osmond to discard her as one.

The most important discrimination established in the last third of
the novel, however, is that between Isabel and Osmond. For as Isabel
grasps the flaws of her aestheticizing vision and begins to move beyond this form of apprehension, she progresses into a heightened and
purified form of aestheticism—a form of aestheticism superficially
similar to, but ultimately distinguishable from, the reifying aestheticism of an Osmond. It's true that Osmondian language tends to be
associated with the representation of her own thought processes—
as, for example, when she too rejects Madame Merle. The effect of
Madame Merle's unexpectedly appearing at Pansy's convent is compared by Isabel to a "sort of reduplication"; this hint of an aestheticizing temper is carried further when Isabel sees Madame Merle's
uncertainty "as distinctly as if it had been a picture on the wall" (756–
57, 759). Indeed, Isabel might be said to approach Osmondism here
—however justifiably—since her action in this scene, like Osmond's
throughout the novel, is to withdraw, to retreat into being "silent still
—leav[ing] Madame Merle in this unprecedented situation" (759). But
Isabel's aestheticizing imagination leads her in a wholly different direction than does Osmond's. In this scene, her refusal directly to confront
Madame Merle still grants her an essential otherness, still allows her
her own scope of action—grants Madame Merle the opportunity to
judge herself, to do "a kind of proud penance" (767).

What is true of Isabel's behavior in this scene is true of her perceptual apparatus as well. As her aestheticizing vision moves beyond the
reifying aestheticism so thoroughly implicated in Osmondism, it progresses to a higher form of aestheticism—if "aesthetic" is understood

as informed by the original sense of *aesthesis*, as a heightening or perfection of the act of perception. The most extended exercise in such
heightened vision is provided in the most famous moment in the novel
—the moment James claimed to have been most proud of—Isabel's
silent reverie in chapter 42. That chapter is of the utmost importance
for our endeavor, for it provides an example of a form of perception
structurally different from that we have seen associated with Gilbert
throughout the novel and in which we can implicate every other character. Isabel's visions in this scene are important because they are so
intense and because they are so personal. Like Osmond's aestheticizing vision, they are fully grounded in the self, but they are ultimately
antithetical to Osmond's. Her flickering visions in chapter 42 do not
partake of Osmond's narcissistic attempt to force the objects in the
world to serve as objects for his detached contemplation. Rather, unlike Osmond, Isabel achieves a moment of her own vision experienced
in, of, and for itself; a moment of vision that is fully detached from the
world of objects but that helps her to understand the nature of that
world. And, I would suggest, the homology between Isabel's vision and
that of Paterian *aesthesis* may be seen more clearly when we juxtapose
chapter 42 with the Conclusion to *The Renaissance*. Both Pater and
James privilege a special moment at which, under conditions of high
intensity, "a quickened, multiplied consciousness" comes into powerful
visionary being. It is quite true that there are significant dissimilarities
between the circumstances under which such an intense vision may
come into being and the uses to which it can be put. For James, the
"quickened consciousness" is (as it is always for James) attached to high
emotional drama, while for Pater such a consciousness is activated
through many forms of intense experience—"great passions" including, among others, both the "ecstasy and sorrow of love" and (first
among equals) "the poetic passion, the desire of beauty, the love of art
for art's sake" (WP, 1: 238, 239). But my point here is that for both
James and Pater the moment at which consciousness exercises itself in
heightened vision is valuable in and of itself—is the ultimate end, the
perfect end. Pater's aesthete and James's heroine both achieve a perfect moment of intense vision which, for their authors, is the highest—
perhaps the only—consummation possible in a world shadowed over
by death and human failure.

This valorization of *aesthesis*, of what James calls in the Preface to
the novel "the mere still lucidity" of Isabel's mental vision, suggests
one way that the novel recuperates a form of aestheticism (NY, 3: xxi).
But it is precisely by means of this recuperation that critics have taken

James to task for being an aesthete in the negative sense of the word. Here, the achievement of a form of transcendence by means of consciousness and consciousness alone would seem, at the very best, to associate James with a naive form of reification, and at the very worst to identify him as an arrogant connoisseur of consciousness. For this moment seems to define the transcendent self as fundamentally contemplative, passive, inert, to remove that self from any real contact with others, from any possibility of action, indeed, from history itself; it would thus seem to imprison Isabel in the prison house of consciousness as thoroughly as Osmond imprisons her in the Palazzo Roccanera. Isabel, Michael Gilmore writes, "chooses a freedom that is mental rather than experiential, a freedom uncontaminated by sensuous engagement with the world." James, he adds ominously, "makes a similar choice for his art."[22]

James, however, anticipates—and sidesteps—this critique. For there is another moment in the novel at which the aestheticizing vision is deployed, and to ends that are different from either those we see with Osmond or those we see in chapter 42. I am referring to the scene, a few chapters later, of Isabel's lonely ride on the Campagna. For we encounter in this passage yet another variant of the mode of perception Isabel shares with Osmond. As a tourist, as an observing traveler, Isabel would seem to fall into the detached, contemplative mode of Osmond; moreover she seems to perform the Osmondian task of aestheticizing the natural world she encounters, of responding to it as to a work of art:

The carriage, passing out of the walls of Rome, rolled through narrow lanes, where the wild honeysuckle had begun to tangle itself in the hedges, or waited for her in quiet places where the fields lay near, while she strolled further and further over the flower-freckled turf, or sat on a stone that had once had a use, and gazed through the veil of her personal sadness at the splendid sadness of the scene—at the dense, warm light, the far gradations and soft confusions of colour, the motionless shepherds in lonely attitudes, the hills where the cloud-shadows had the lightness of a blush. (724)

While this exercise of the aestheticizing vision may seem superficially similar to Gilbert's, it is ultimately antithetical to his vision and value system alike. Isabel may sit in Osmond's position of the detached aesthetic observer, viewing the Campagna spread out before her like a painted landscape—all motion arrested, its figures fixed in "lonely attitudes," its colors and gradations displayed in the rich muted colors of an artist's pallette—but she does not seek to detach herself from

that scene. For the "profound sympathy" between Isabel's perception
and the objects she encounters is repeatedly suggested in this passage, often by verbal repetition or by transfer of qualities from the
Campagna to Isabel's life; "the sadness of landscape" reflecting her
"sadness of mood," the "lonely attitudes" of the shepherds reflecting
her own sense of loneliness and betrayal. As she "rest[s] her weari-
ness upon things that had crumbled for centuries," as she "drop[s] her
secret sadness into the silence of lonely places," Isabel comes to recognize the "haunting sense of the continuity of the human lot" (723–24).
Having learned from Rome, a "place where people had suffered," of
the commonality of her own suffering, she rejoins the human community—not the corrupt community of Roman society that Gilbert
and Madame Merle inhabit, but a more fully human community of
shared suffering (724). Rather than possessing a reifying vision of
landscape as irrevocably other, as alien and mute objects unconnected
to human emotions and events and coldly to be appreciated as such,
Isabel achieves at this moment a humanizing vision in which her individual "sadness" and the sadness of the scene connect to form an image
of commonality and community, not one of alienation and superiority.
If in chapter 42 Isabel moves beyond her superficial Paterian aestheticism into the more valuable mode of Paterian *aesthesis*, so here she
moves beyond a superficial form of aestheticizing vision into a richer,
more meaningful one: one that emphasizes her own embeddedness in
historical process, her own participation in the human community—in
short, the very "sensuous engagement with the world" whose absence
Gilmore decries.

It is this version of the aestheticist vision that provides James with
his most deeply treasured, and most arduously won, triumph. For this
moment of detached yet meaningful perception provides a way out
of the artistic impasse James has created for himself. Isabel's vision
provides a more positive model for the stance of the detached author
than does Osmond's, one that can lead to a sense of communion, not
solipsism; to sympathy, not superiority. James signals this, I think, by
the very abstemiousness with which he treats Isabel's dilemma at the
end of the novel. If James is like Osmond in enmeshing Isabel in a
plot whose goal is to aestheticize her, to transform her into a static,
frozen portrait of a lady (the literary equivalent of the murderous aestheticization performed by the Duke in Browning's *My Last Duchess*),
he can demonstrate himself to be a non-Osmondian author only by
opening up the plot: by refusing the consolation of closure, whether
comic, ironic, or tragic. It is in response to this problematic, I am sug-

gesting, that James ends his novel with an interpretive mystery—and one of the most famous cruxes in American literature: the question of Isabel's mysteriously motivated return to Osmond. Certainly, the novel supplies by implication many reasons for this return: her loyalty to Pansy, her affirmation of convention and of social forms, her affirmation of the value of renunciation.[23] But the novel carefully refuses to choose between these various explanations. Further, it ends without giving any further indication of the success or failure of Isabel's course of action, thereby precluding any final judgment of the wisdom or folly of her choice.

It is this narrative silence that provides the final repudiation of the reifying aestheticism associated with Osmond and of the narrative problematics it initiates. James's narrative voice here may be detached, but it is hardly unsympathetic. Indeed, its failure to pass any final judgment on Isabel may be taken as an acknowledgment of James's authorial sympathy rather than as an indication of his ironic distance. For by this silence, James reminds the reader of the values that Osmond's reifying aestheticism ignores: a respect for the fundamentally mysterious otherness of human beings. The mystery with which the novel concludes indicates James's authorial acknowledgment of the otherness of others, for this gesture acknowledges Isabel's ability to transcend any one vision that tries to fix or define her—even the author's own ostensibly omniscient vision. By granting Isabel such resonant ambiguity, in other words, James endows Isabel with the powers Rossetti endows Jenny or—more relevantly—those Isabel grants Madame Merle. For the effect of this conclusion is to enable Isabel to step beyond the narrative frame within which she is enclosed, to move out of the "Portrait of a Lady"; it is—in a phrase James added to Isabel's final vision of Madame Merle in the New York edition—"like suddenly, and rather awfully, seeing a painted picture move" (NY, 4: 375).

Chapter Four

James, Wilde, and
the Incorporation of Aestheticism

If the example of Walter Pater stands powerfully and problematically behind James's fiction of the early and "middle years," a far more
disturbing presence shadows the fiction of the 1890's: Oscar Wilde.
It is true that James and Wilde had long inhabited the same social
sphere, to each other's occasional delight and frequent discomfort.
When James met Wilde for the first time in Washington during the
latter's notorious 1882 American tour, for example, his response was
less than friendly. "I went last night to the Loring's," James wrote his
friend Isabella Stewart Gardner, ". . . and found there the repulsive
and fatuous Oscar Wilde, whom, I am happy to say, no one was looking
at." James referred to Wilde in a letter to E. L. Godkin as "an unclean beast" and "a fatuous cad." Ten years later, James wrote another
friend, Mrs. Henrietta Reubell, that "Ce monsieur [Wilde] gives at last
on one's nerves," and later referred to him with snobbish disdain as
"the unspeakable one." [1]

By the 1890's, James had come to possess good reason for his pee-
vishness. The spectacular failure of *Guy Domville* intersected with the
period of Wilde's greatest success on the British stage, often directly
and embarrassingly. As is well known, James spent the opening night
of his own play attending Wilde's *An Ideal Husband* and the success
of this "thing" that seemed to him "so helpless, so crude, so bad, so
clumsy, feeble, and vulgar," served as a premonition of the failure of
Domville. James's insight proved prophetic: after the *Domville* disaster,
Sir George Alexander rushed Wilde's *Importance of Being Earnest* into
production, and, four weeks after his own opening, James witnessed
the same crowd that had hissed him cheer "the triumphant Oscar."
Wilde's success thereby came to symbolize to James the decadence of
the London theater-going public he labeled "Philistine" or "barbarian"
(*Letters*, 3: 514).

Nevertheless, James sponsored Wilde for membership in the Savile Club and, after Wilde's imprisonment, contributed a healthy sum to the support of his wife and children. But even this sympathetic response radiates a lingering resentment. James wrote his brother William that Wilde's "fall is hideously tragic—and the squalid violence of it gives him an interest (of misery) that he never had for me—in any degree—before." James came to view Wilde, in other words, as a pitiable victim, whose social downfall alone lent him a certain imaginative interest.* I can think of no more effective personal revenge.

James also seems to have taken a literary revenge. As everyone knows, the words that Lambert Strether speaks to Little Bilham in Gloriani's garden, halfway through *The Ambassadors*, "Live all you can," are quoted almost verbatim from *The Picture of Dorian Gray*. There, Lord Henry Wotton, a somewhat more sinister man than Strether, cries to Dorian Gray, a somewhat more fallible young man than Little Bilham, "Live the wonderful life that is in you. Let nothing be lost upon you. Be always searching for new sensations." It is less well known, but equally significant, that Lord Henry's remarks to Dorian echo James's advice to the aspiring novelist in *The Art of Fiction* (1884) —"Try to be one of the people on whom nothing is lost." Perhaps it is also less than common knowledge that they mimic the language of a fictional aesthete from James's novel, *The Tragic Muse* (1890), as well. "We must feel everything, everything we can. We are here for that," proclaims Gabriel Nash, anticipating both Wilde's Lord Henry Wotton and James's Lambert Strether by six months and thirteen years respectively.[2]

James's hostility to Wilde, then, is at least partially accompanied and, it is likely, occasioned by their mutual participation in an intricate intertextual chain of allusion, counterallusion, and outright theft —theft committed first by Wilde himself, but then recommitted, and with malice aforethought, by his victim. Indeed, as I shall suggest more extensively below, what Wilde appropriates from James, James reappropriates from Wilde in a disguised and somewhat ironized form. For just as Wilde's aesthete revises the nature and functions of the

---

*Edel, *Henry James*, 4: 129. James wrote Edmund Gosse about Wilde in the same terms: "He was never in the smallest degree interesting to me—but this hideous human history has made him so—in a manner." On the envelope, however, James added the notation "*Quel dommage—mais quel Bonheur—que J.A.S.* [John Addington Symonds] *ne soit plus de ce monde.*" As Richard Ellmann observes, it is in this cryptic reference that James, "a homosexual writing to a homosexual," acknowledges some of the sources of his imaginative sympathy for Wilde. See "Henry James Among the Aesthetes," p. 226; and James, *Letters*, 4: 10.

Jamesian artist, so Strether's experience in Paris transvalues the claims of Wildean aestheticism. As Strether pursues the aesthete's path in Paris, he traces out a trajectory that leads him from moralism to a sensual intoxication to its sober aftermath; the result would seem to be an equally sober weighing of the motives and costs of Wildean aestheticism. Stretherian aestheticism, unlike its Wildean forebear, is a matter of the sensibility, not the senses; it is allied with, but ultimately detached from, the games of social will-to-power in which Wilde's aesthetes were engaged; and its end brings the further enlargement of a ruefully enlightened consciousness, not the transitory fulfillments of sensual desire.

The persistence of James's critical response to Wilde thus measures the intensity of their personal and professional warfare.* But what is at stake in this battle remains, I think, somewhat unclear—and unclear, I should stress, only because so many different things *could* be at stake in it. To a certain extent, the warfare might have centered on the cultural fate of Pater—a figure who influenced both James and Wilde at a particularly formative point in their own careers. To a certain extent, it might have been occasioned by the extensive commonalities of their experience. What is most striking about the James/Wilde antagonism, after all, is the similiarity of their personal situations: James and Wilde were two marginal immigrants—an Irishman and an American—each of whom was made doubly marginal as he grappled with a homoerotic sexuality, and each of whom was nevertheless able to make his way, through the application of both a literary and a verbal genius, into the most exalted circles of British high society—circles that each man alternately admired and satirized.

However, such commonalities of experience do not, I think, fully account for James's hostility. Irritating as such similarities must have been, the equivalence between James and Wilde's professional situa-

---

*Wilde for his part may have been less overtly hostile to James, but was nevertheless far from deferential. Wilde's remarks on James's novels, like the lampoons of his contemporary Max Beerbohm, are quietly devastating: "Mr. Henry James writes fiction as if it were a painful duty, and wastes upon mean motives and imperceptible 'points of view' his neat literary style, his felicitous phrases, his swift and caustic satire." Wilde's trick here is to judge James by Wilde's own standards and to find him wanting. James, Wilde reminds us, is no satirist, no epigrammatizer: in short, no Wilde. A similar rhetorical move is performed in a letter Wilde wrote to his first male lover, continual confidant, and literary executor, Robert Ross. Having just read *The Turn of the Screw*, Wilde comments: "I think it is a most wonderful, lurid, poisonous little tale, like an Elizabethan tragedy. I am greatly impressed by it. James is developing, but he will never arrive at passion, I fear." James, one might paraphrase Wilde as saying, is developing, but will never arrive at being Wilde. (Wilde, *Artist*, p. 295; and Wilde, *Letters*, p. 776.)

tions must have been infuriating. At almost exactly the same historical moment—the rise to prominence of both an enlarged and well-defined elite audience for high culture and an even larger audience for "mass" or popular culture—both men undertook the same task: appealing to a "high-brow" audience while seeking to come to terms, if only out of financial necessity, with the demands of an increasingly remunerative mass audience. That Wilde succeeded in simultaneously speaking to both while James felt that he failed at fully addressing either is sufficient grounds for James's ire; that Wilde did so by playing a version of the high-culture "artist" to which James aspired must have doubled the antagonism.

I want in this chapter to look more closely at these three strands of interrelation—with particular attention to the third, which seems to me first among equals—not only because of the importance of the James/Wilde sibling rivalry, and not only because of what it can tell us about James's increasingly rich relation with the tradition of British aestheticism. I want to spend some time with it because it seems to me to show what is at stake in James's response to Wilde and with the tradition of aestheticism he came to represent for his own era. I want to suggest that, out of this encounter, James formulated his conception of the novelist as an elite artist—a novelist removed from yet intensely involved in gritty realities of the literary marketplace; a novelist, in fact, who makes in his own role of artist a potent marketing mechanism in that changing agora. The figure of the aesthete, as represented powerfully but not uniquely by Wilde to James, serves as both a foil and a challenge to the Jamesian novelist. Wilde first provides an infuriating example of an artist who is able successfully to appeal to both an elite and a mass audience, but then serves as an example of a self-destructive, because not sufficiently *professional*, literary career. It is this duality, I think, that structures James's fullest representation of the aesthete, that of Gabriel Nash in *The Tragic Muse,* and that, I think, shapes the complicated anti-Wildean dialectics of *The Ambassadors.* It is, further and finally, a duality James transcends in the novels of the "major phase," in which (as we shall see in the final chapter) James builds on the structures of British aestheticism to produce the great work of aestheticist art that the aesthetic movement itself conspicuously failed to create—*The Golden Bowl*—and thence to help fashion the more austere aestheticism we call modernism.

Oscar Wilde and Henry James: The Quarrels of Affinity

I have suggested above that there are three major issues at stake in James's initial response to Wilde: in all three we can locate a pattern of similarity that goes some way toward explicating not only James's particularly irritable response to Wilde but also his resolutely over-determined response to the tradition of British aestheticism. The first, and most obvious, has to do with James and Wilde's shared erotic incli-nation. It may be safely said that James and Wilde perfectly exempli-fied two distinct styles of late Victorian homoeroticism: the latent and the blatant.[3] In the early 1890's, Wilde was as flamboyant and enthu-siastic about his sexuality as James was repressed and uncomfortable about his own. James's continual emphasis on Wilde's unnaturalness might thus suggest that his increasingly uneasy feelings about his own sexuality impelled his negative response to Wilde.

This hypothesis is attractive, and would go some distance, it seems to me, in explaining the excessively *personal* quality of James's distaste for Wilde. James's own uneasy feelings about his sexuality, one might hypothesize, led him to see Wilde as the embodiment of his own im-pulses, and thus to demonize his double—to relieve himself of the burden of guilt or shame (or both) by denouncing Wilde's flamboy-ant and public flouting of sexual convention. His comments on Wilde might thus be taken as a means of self-protection, as a way of publicly demonstrating his own relative sexual conventionality.[4]

But there is a problem with such a hypothesis. Wilde was hardly the only openly homosexual or bisexual man James knew, and James's responses to such acquaintances rarely took on the intensely uncom-fortable quality that marks his reactions to Wilde. Indeed, he re-mained quite good friends with Wilde's loyal friend and first male lover, Robert Ross; although Ross was somewhat more discreet than Wilde (he was foremost among the party urging Wilde to escape to France in order to evade prosecution), he was nevertheless flam-boyantly, publicly homosexual, as were any number of James's other friends and acquaintances. One thinks here, of course, of those cir-cles of adoring young men who took James up into their midst; or of figures like James's friend Howard Sturgis, son of banker and Ruskin devotee Russell Sturgis, in whose flamboyant presence James met much of the aristocratic homosexual elite of his time. But, more significantly, one also thinks of that group of late Victorian intellec-tuals with whom James was deeply involved; for it is this group who, as Jeffrey Weeks has recently argued, essentially constructed the modern notion of homosexuality.[5] This circle included John Addington Symonds, perhaps the most notorious advocate of homoerotic desire in Victorian England and who, as open as was Wilde about his sexual orientation, differed from him only by retreating to the Continent when a public scandal erupted after the dissolution of his marriage; Edmund Gosse, equally well known for his sexual preferences, if somewhat more cautious than Symonds or Ross; and Oscar Browning, the Eton tutor whose flamboyant sexual escapades led to his dismissal.

James's relations with this circle were not entirely unvexed; as Edel suggests, James evinced equal measures of fascination and disturbance with J. A. Symonds's defenses of male-male love; and James's ambivalence is inscribed into his story, *The Author of Beltraffio*, which inflates gossip about Symonds's alienation from his horrified wife, pained by her husband's frank acknowledgment of his sexual inclinations, into a tale of Gothic horror in which a mother lets her child die rather than grow up with a homosexual father.[6] Moreover, James never publicly associated himself with those members of this circle who turned toward the articulation of a homoerotically based socialism in response to the social repression all experienced. But the point here is that toward neither Symonds nor any of his fellow "Uranians," nor toward any of their more flamboyant, less intellectual friends did James evince the sense of vociferous disapproval he consistently demonstrated toward Wilde.

The rivalry between James and Wilde demands further interrogation, then; another aspect of vexation, not entirely unconnected with the first, might be found in their differing responses to a common Paterian inheritance. As we have seen, James's early fiction initiates a complicated attempt to purify the doctrines of Paterian aestheticism; to winnow out a neo-Paterian *aesthesis* from the aesthete's deployment of it, to find within the aesthetic coordinates established by Pater a mode of praise for a purified, and redemptive, form of vision experienced as an end in and of itself. But Wilde, perhaps Pater's most notorious pupil, called these complicated efforts into question. The aestheticizing vision, which for Pater and James alike became the means to a qualified form of transcendence metamorphosed, in Wilde's work, into an enticing form of scopophilia. The Paterian quest for the privileged moment of transcendent being was transformed, in Wilde's hands, into an endless chain of sensual desire climaxing in the Gothic horror of Dorian Gray's fate. The aestheticized homoeroticism James shared with Pater was affronted by Wilde's extravagant sexuality and threatened by his social disgrace.

But again to complicate the matter, the problem of Wilde seems to have had as much to do with Wilde's social deployment of Paterian topoi as it did with his transformations of them. For while Pater himself responded negatively to Wilde's appropriation of his discourse, James's response centered on Wilde's ability successfully to appeal to an audience to which James was increasingly, and frustratingly, devoting himself: the audience of the London theater, and the larger mass or popular audience that it symbolized for James. The full dimensions of that negative response emerge in the following letter to James's friend, Mrs. Florence Bell (herself an aspiring playwright), perhaps James's longest explicit commentary on Wilde:

Oscar's play [*Lady Windermere's Fan*] . . . strikes me as a mixture that will run (I feel as if I were talking as a laundress), though infantine to my sense, both in subject and in form. As a drama it is of a candid and primitive simplicity, with a perfectly reminiscential air about it—as of things *qui ont traîné*, that one has always seen in plays. In short it doesn't, from that point of view, bear analysis or discussion. But there is so much drollery—that is, "cheeky" or paradoxical wit of dialogue, and the pit and gallery are so pleased at finding themselves clever enough to "catch on" to four or five of the ingenious—too ingenious—*mots* in the dozen, that it makes them feel quite "*décadent*" and *raffiné* and they enjoy the sensation as a change from the stodgy. Moreover they think they are hearing the talk of the *grand monde* (poor old *grand monde*), and altogether feel privileged and modern. There is a perpetual attempt at *mots* and many of them *râter*: but those that hit are very good indeed. This will make, I think, a success—possibly a really long run (I mean through the Season) for the play. There is of course absolutely no characterization and all the people talk equally strained Oscar—but there is a "situation" (at the end of Act III) that one has seen from the cradle, and the thing is conveniently acted. The "impudent" [curtain] speech at the end was simply inevitable mechanical Oscar —I mean the usual trick of saying the unusual—complimenting himself and his play. It was what he was there for and I can't conceive the density of those who seriously reprobate it. The tone of the virtuous journals makes me despair of our stupid humanity. Everything Oscar does is a deliberate trap for the literalist, and to see the literalist walk straight up to it, look straight at it and step straight into it, makes one freshly avert a discouraged gaze from this unspeakable animal. (*Letters*, 3: 372–73)

James's response is an unstable amalgam of affect—ranging from cool calculation (some of the *mots* strike their target; the "situation" at the end of Act III is acceptably dramatic) to irate condescension (in dramatic terms, Wilde's work is "infantine," of a "candid and primitive simplicity") to near-hysterical abuse (as usual, Wilde is described as a kind of unclean beast, an "unspeakable animal"—a formulation, one should note, that suggests the compulsive nature of James's denunciation, since he has just been speaking, at great length, about him). But these three divergent responses are related by James's wonder at the complicitous relation between Wilde and his audience. Both are seen as participants in an unspoken bargain. Wilde will abuse his audience, as he habitually did in his curtain speeches, and they will enjoy his impudence because it validates their seeming sophistication; Wilde will play the scornful, alienated artist to the audience at whose behest he performs, and the audience will ratify its own refinement by laughing at and then applauding their denouncer. Each participant in this drama is perfectly fulfilled because each is enabled to become a version of the other: the childish theatrical audience imagines itself to be as *raffiné* as the decadent dandy who addresses them; and the would-be dramatic artist is confirmed in his superiority by the pretensions of his gullible audience. Moreover, the admixture of parody and pandering that Wilde offers his audience is literally beyond criticism, because to criticize it is to play his paradoxical game. Thus, in the final metaphor of the passage, it is difficult to tell whether Wilde himself or his critics are the "unspeakable animal": one's first presumption is of course the former, until one remembers that in the first half of the sentence, it is Wilde himself who sets the trap for his unwary adversaries. Audience and artist, parodist and artist, cultural critic and parodist: these oppositions are collapsed into one another by the endlessly resourceful, endlessly paradoxical, and endlessly infuriating Wilde.

And, clearly, it is important to James that these oppositions be maintained, since it is precisely by means of such oppositions that he came to define his own role—often, to compound his difficulties, by speaking in language that is strikingly similar to Wilde's. In the eloquent denunciations of the British theatergoing public found in his letters to his brother or his friends, or in the more guarded but equally negative responses contained in his journalistic accounts, James sought to establish his detachment from "the regular 'theatrical public' of London which, of all the vulgar publics London contains, is the most brutishly and densely vulgar." James first defensively, then aggressively, distances himself from this audience and defines for himself a different, an elite, audience to whom his work is directed and by whom it is appreciated: "Obviously the little play, which I strove to make as broad, as gross, as simple, as clear, as British, in a word, as possible, is over the heads of the *usual* vulgar theatre-going London public—and the chance of its going on for a while . . . will depend wholly on its holding on long enough to attract the *unusual*." "The whole thing was for [the regular public] remote, and all the intensity of one's ingenuity couldn't make it anything else. It has made it something else for the *few*—but that is all." "And there was a Wednesday matinee last week as well as a Saturday, and every *raffiné* in London (I mean of course only the people who *don't* go to the usual things) has been to see it, and yet it doesn't 'go'!" (*Letters*, 3: 515, 508, 516, 517). Wilde's audience may wish to understand itself as *raffiné*, but James's is composed of the true cognoscenti, an elite that ratifies its status by its enjoyment of the complexity, the subtlety, the interpretive intransigence, of James's dramatic art. The pathos of his position lies in the insufficiency of their numbers: only the people who "don't go to the usual things" will attend James's plays, but the economics of the marketplace demand a wider, more socially commodious, appeal.

We witness the same rhetorical moves in all of James's writing of this time. In a famous letter to William Dean Howells, he describes himself as a version of the Miltonic poet, "fallen," like the Milton of book 11 of *Paradise Lost*, "upon evil days," thereby suggesting that he, too, writes for a Miltonic "fit audience though few" (3: 511). In his stories, James begins to write parables about writers at odds with their social milieu; unlike that aesthete cum country gentleman, Mark Ambient, these writers are usually ignored or misunderstood by this social world, from which they in turn exclude themselves in order to devote themselves to "the mystery of art." In his letters, he takes on the role of the beleaguered defender of civilization, standing like a Roman warrior on the walls of the city, confronting "the yelling barbarians," the "howling mob," the uncivilized (3: 508, 516). In short, at this moment in his career, James avers that his pursuit of his own art is nothing less than an epic vocation. Civilization has become his calling, culture his religion, his art at once his sacrament and his crucifixion.

To be sure, James's articulation of these sentiments in the early 1890's was not unique in his own career, even if it was at its most dramatic at this moment: his commentaries on his art were from the first phrased in the language of religious vocation, and in the later prose, such language is used with positive promiscuity. But it is important to observe here that it was far from unique in his culture as well. Indeed, the combination of an Arnoldian jargon of culture and anarchy with the language of religious devotion is to be found precisely in a specific tradition of discourse: in the works of Pater, in those of Wilde, and in aesthete or "decadent" circles and cenacles of mid-1890's Lon-

don. James sounds a good deal like Flaubert when he hymns his veiled
Muse, but when he denounces the theatrical public he sounds—irony
of ironies—exactly like Oscar Wilde: "The one thing that the public
dislike is novelty. Any attempt to extend the subject-matter of art is
extremely distasteful to the public; and yet the vitality and progress
of art depend in a large measure on the continual extension of the
subject-matter" (*Artist*, p. 272). This is Wilde, but the words might very
well have been taken from the letters Henry James was writing his
brother William after the failure of *Domville*. "In old days men had
the rack. Now they have the press. That is an improvement certainly.
But still it is very bad, and wrong, and demoralising" (276). This is
Wilde again, unmistakably so, but the sentiment from Wilde's *The Soul
of Man Under Socialism* (1891) is one with which the Henry James of
1895 would have vigorously agreed.

The situation we are confronted with, then, is doubly vexed. On the
one hand, James has established himself in a fully oppositional relation
to Wilde and to the aestheticism Wilde represented to his era; on the
other, he finds himself articulating sentiments that Wilde himself had
espoused eloquently only a few years earlier, and that were being espoused around him in the decadent circles and cenacles he profoundly
distrusted. James's response to this dilemma is, I think, significant and
problematic. Whenever he confronts Wilde, either in person or (as we
shall soon see) in his fiction, he willingly adopts Wilde's own strategy of
ironic reversal against him. James presents himself as the fulfillment
of a Wildean position or pose, Wilde, his own negation; for James
plays the true, alienated artist, the true poet insensitively abused and
scorned by his materialistic, vulgar, and inartistic society, and casts
Wilde as the embodiment of the corrupt animating principles of that
society. In short, James himself plays the *true* aesthete—"a worshipper" as he wrote in his memorial essay on Charles Eliot Norton, "at
the esthetic shrine *quand même*."[7]

To a certain extent, as I have suggested above, James's adoption
of this role was a function of the increasingly articulated marketplace in which he found himself. Thus, as Marcia Jacobson has observed, if James found himself in the 1890's increasingly less welcome
at the major periodicals—both the established ones, like *Harper's* or
The Atlantic, or the new, cheaper, and even more widely circulating
illustrated magazines, like *Munsey's* or *The Ladies Home Journal*—he
nevertheless found new outlets for his productive energies in the *elite*
magazines of 1890's aestheticism: *The Yellow Book* sought and published *The Death of the Lion* in its first issue, and *The Middle Years* in

the third; Stone and Kimball's *Chap-Book* gave the first American publication to both.* Moreover, as Michael Anesko points out, James was thereby enabled to pursue a wholly different market: "James shrewdly sensed that being *un*popular, unsalable at any price, had a cachet of its own—one that publishers, curiously, might bid for."[8] Although his works might not sell, James still brought a faint whiff of class to a publisher's list—a touch of distinction that his publication in notoriously "aesthetic" magazines like *The Yellow Book* could only enhance.†

But James's self-representation, while undeniably part of what we might describe as a persistent marketing strategy (James was seeking what we today would call an "upscale" audience), was also part of the course of his artistic self-definition. What we witness at this moment in James's career is the reformulation of his sense of his artistic identity, indeed nothing less than the forging of his own contribution to the creation of a new notion of the powers and possibilities of the literary artist: the notion of the artist as professional. Critics have recently focused on this act of Jamesian creation, suggesting that, for all his extraordinary rhetorical praise for the powers and possibilities of the artist, James was also a canny fashioner of his own literary career in a rapidly changing marketplace.[9] James was one of the first high-culture authors to make their living exclusively from their writing at a time when both the audience for that writing and the publishing world were undergoing a thorough transformation, and he brilliantly negotiated

*Here, however, is James's embarrassed response to that publication, in a letter to William: "I haven't sent you 'The Yellow Book'—on purpose; and indeed I have been weeks and weeks receiving a copy of it myself. I say on purpose because although my little tale which ushers it in ("The Death of the Lion") appears to have had, for a thing of mine, an unusual success, I hate too much the horrid aspect and company of the whole publication. And yet I am again to be intimately—conspicuously—associated with the second number. It is for gold and to oblige the worshipful [Henry] Harland." One notes in this letter the odd mixture of canniness and contempt that frequently structures James's response to the marketplace, but heightened, accentuated by his contact with Harland and the vaguely risqué project of *The Yellow Book*. One also notes how James casts Harland himself as a figure in the story he published: he is like the "worshipful" parasites who lionize James's character Neil Paraday—and thereby cause his death. James, *Letters*, 3: 482. (For examples of Harland's embarrassing idolization of James, see Mix, *A Study in Yellow*, p. 169.)

†It should also be noted, however, that American critics did not fail to notice James's connection with *The Yellow Book* and its circle, and to criticize him for it: thus a critic wrote in *Munsey's* in 1895 that "of late . . . Mr. James has been in bad company. . . . He has become one of the *Yellow Book* clique," and called on James to return home to the comfortable moral environment of America (*Munsey's* 13 [June 1895]: 311). Similarly, *The Atlantic* noted in 1897 that James's "super-subtlety of theme, for which no form of expression can be too carefully wrought . . . place[s] Mr. James inextricably in the decadent ranks" (*Atlantic* 79 [Jan. 1897]: 137).

the demands of that market—wheeling and dealing with publishers, editors, and agents; courting first one reading public, then another, then another: all the while complaining bitterly about the vulgar demands of the marketplace in which he performed so brilliantly.

What is most interesting about this course of professional self-assertion, from our point of view, is its odd symmetry with the position of that other example of aesthetic professionalism, the aesthete—and particularly with the socially and financially successful aesthete of the late 1880's and early 1890's. We can perhaps see this symmetry better if we glance briefly at James's professionalizing moves of this time, especially those tactics by which he sought to clear a space for himself in the booming literary marketplace. For there, James pursued a multi-faceted but nevertheless consistent strategy of subtle self-assertion: he claimed to represent the true exemplar of the disinterested, artistic novelist. The clearest example of this stance may be found in James's relations with Walter Besant, a prime representative of the new self-consciously professional "man of letters" and James's colleague in the Society of Authors (the organization formed in the early 1880's to rectify abuses of copyright and to advance the status of the professional writer), and of course the straw man set so splendidly ablaze in *The Art of Fiction*. For when dealing with Besant, James casts his rival as the overly professionalized professional and adopts the role of urbane sophisticate to counter him. In *The Art of Fiction*, for example, he takes issue with Besant's rather pedantic efforts to define the qualities of that new entity, prose fiction, by speaking in the eloquent tones of a French sophisticate of the breadth of possibilities open to the fictional act. His response to Besant's professionalism is equally urbane. Writing Edmund Gosse in 1895, for example, James critiques Besant's focus on the "too-iterated money question" and then suggests the limitations of the model of literary professionalism for which he speaks:

The fact is that authorship is guilty of a great mistake, a gross want of tact, in formulating and publishing its claim to be a "profession." Let other trades call it so—& let it take no notice. That's enough. It ought to have of the professions only a professional thoroughness. But *never* to have that, & to cry on the housetops instead that it *is* the grocer & the shoemaker is to bring on itself a ridicule of which it will simply die.[10]

James's disavowal of Besant's unsubtle professionalism is itself, of course, a cannily professional move, and goes a long way in helping us to understand his tactics at this point in his career. For like the professionalizing lawyers or doctors or academics of the late nineteenth century, James defines *his* professionalism in resolutely idealizing, indeed utterly mystified, terms. His is the professionalism of a gentleman; it stands in vivid opposition to the professionalism of (to use James's revealing term) "other trades," a professionalism like that of (to use his even more revealing examples) "the grocer and the shoemaker." A Jamesian literary professionalism is by contrast "tactful" or discreet; it is not directly concerned with the "money question," although it can hardly disavow all interest in that question. Rather, it is one that defines itself by its quality of "professional thoroughness": by, in other words, an abstract criterion at once objective and mystified; technical but readily discernible—at least to the eye of the Master.

In this professional situation, then, James is able to maneuver himself into a position of authority by his strenuous and influential claims for his superior knowledge of the qualities of that mysterious field, the aesthetic, and by the further claim of the disinterestedness of his dedication to that ground. Such a role was useful to James: it helped him to counter not only the rival claims of what he calls "Besantry," but also those of his more successful rivals for public attention, whether precursors like Hawthorne, or the writers of prose romances, with whom James played with equal fervor the role of the disinterested exponent of artistic merit. But the tradition of British aestheticism posed a powerful challenge to this strategy. The aesthete—particularly the popular, the successful aesthete like Wilde—represented a rival occupant of the professional niche to which James aspired. Indeed, the aesthete provides a compelling countermodel to the Jamesian artist/ novelist: dilettantish and dandyish where the Jamesian artist is dedicated; flamboyant and playful where the Jamesian artist is austere and self-effacing; and, at least in the case of Wilde, publicly and financially successful while the Jamesian artist struggles to find an audience; the aesthete nevertheless makes a powerful claim on the site of cultural authority James wishes to claim as his own: the realm, that is, of the disinterested dedication to the values of the aesthetic. When dealing with the aesthete, then, James must supplement the strategies he adopts toward his other rivals. Since James cannot out-urbane the aesthete, he must out-professional him. Instead of relying on his own sophisticated breadth of vision as warrant of his authority, he must stress the superior expertise and the superior decorousness of his commitment to the values he and the aesthete so problematically share.

Such a strategy structures his response to Wilde. James's continual emphasis on Wilde's fraudulence represents first of all an attempt to subvert the ground of Wilde's authority and to proclaim Henry James's own greater knowledge of that ground. If Wilde proclaims himself as the consummate aesthetic professional, the expert in that new, mysterious venue of "the aesthetic," it is James's role to prick his professional balloon and to aver his own, greater mastery of Wilde's field of competence. When James assesses Wilde's play, therefore, his near-hysterical rage at Wilde's success (Wilde's work, we remember, is to James "so helpless, so crude, so bad, so clumsy, feeble, and vulgar" as to be virtually unspeakable) is supplemented by what seems to be cool, objective artistic assessment. Wilde has his moments of droll wit, but the "candid and primitive simplicity" and the "situation . . . one has seen from the cradle" suggest the play's lack of aesthetic maturity. James, by contrast, speaks from the position of a fully adult expertise: indeed James speaks as the *real* theatrical expert—a judgment, needless to say, few of his critics, and none of his audiences, have shared.

James further competes with Wilde not only by stressing his own expertise as a literary professional, but also by decrying Wilde's mode of professional conduct. By this, I do not just mean Wilde's personal behavior, although one ought not underestimate how greatly Wilde's flamboyant self-promotion offended the genteel standards to which James held himself. Rather, what James focuses on is the stance Wilde adopts towards his clientele, in this case, the theatrical audience. Thus, what particularly raises James's hackles here is Wilde's refusal to adopt a proper professional attitude toward the theatrical public. Because he confirms rather than challenges the representational norms and expectations of his audience, because he tricks or fools that audience into enjoying his denunciation of them, his success is at once fraudulent and mendacious. Wilde is like a doctor who prescribes an expensive course of treatment for patients who are not ill, or the lawyer who takes on an unwinnable case in order to pocket a hefty fee. He is governed by a desire for profit and self-promotion alone, rather than by the commitment to the abstract ideals of truth and knowledge embedded in his vocation, a commitment that marks the true professional.

The uses of such a role as a pure psychic defense are, of course, obvious; but what needs to be stressed here as well is the strange corner it backs James into. For James has worked himself into an oddly self-defeating position. He seems to be suggesting in his responses to Wilde that the truest sign of professional success is professional failure. One demonstrates one's true artistic professionalism by affirming one's adherence to the abstract defining standards or qualities of the aesthetic, and then by seeking to instruct one's audience in them, to bring one's audience up to one's own level. Recognition should come from one's peers: from critics of the stature of, say, William Archer, or that bright young Irishman, George Bernard Shaw. Too great a popular success in the theater, in the literary marketplace, or in the venue of publicity and "newspaperism" that sustained both is therefore a violation of proper professional codes of behavior, an abdication of proper professional responsibilities. But, to compound the dilemma, it is precisely this tabooed success for which James simultaneously yearned with every fiber in his being—only to discover, like Ray Limbert, hero of James's ironical if self-pitying parable of the woes of the marketplace, *The Next Time*, that even when he wanted to sell out, nobody was buying.

James, then, found himself caught up in a structure of desire that was at once forced on him and frustrated by the very structure of the market he was entering. The "vulgar" theatrical world James aspired to enter in the early 1890's, or the expanded literary marketplace he sought to come to terms with before and after that time, invited one form of literary professionalism; indeed, by their demolition of older, more genteel (if equally exploitative) forms of relations between authors and publishers and their creation of newer, more remunerative publics for the writer to address, such institutions virtually required professionalism of the writer—and professionalism of the crassest, most Besant-like variety. But that world was not yet prepared for the discreet, mystified high-cultural professionalism advocated by James; there was no way of organizing, institutionalizing, or even perceiving the lineaments of that more austere, discreet mode of professional belief and behavior in the world James inhabited.

Of course, at the very same moment, Oscar Wilde was having no such difficulty; indeed, he neatly resolved the dilemmas James was facing by performing an exact reversal of them. For Wilde, as I suggested in Chapter 1, was able to make for himself precisely the career James aspired to by seeming to occupy precisely the role of high-art professionalism James desired. Wittily, parodically, and parodoxically, the Wildean aesthete enters fully into the mechanisms of the mass market—its advertising and public relations apparatus in particular —and, by vending his critique of that market on the basis of an appeal to the transcendent values of the pure aesthetic, achieves an enormous popular success in it. The aesthete, in other words, makes the commodification of literary and aesthetic value wrought by the mass market work for him—and he does so by decrying that market in the name of the mysterious, organic, and transcendent powers of art. This strategy of self-presentation, at once so similar and so different from his own, presented James with an enormously disturbing realization: that he was either in the lonely and awkward position of promulgating a professional model that failed to exist altogether, or that he was the advocate of a position that was already successfully embodied in the witty, paradoxical, resourceful, and flagrantly hypocritical form of an Oscar Wilde. Wilde was thus to Henry James something like the disturbing life-size caricature who confronts Mr. Brooke during his electoral speech in *Middlemarch*: a life-size parodic version of himself who is nevertheless too accurate a representation for comfort. And although Henry James was constitutionally more eloquent and habitually more composed than Eliot's character, this encounter with an echoing double reduced him, too, to a fit of indignant sputtering.

It is this tangle that confronts James's literary responses to aestheticism in the 1890's; indeed, I would claim, it is precisely this tangle that these responses are designed to map out, even to clear. They are perhaps most evident in James's most extensive (and most sympathetic) representation of the tradition of British aestheticism, *The Tragic Muse* (1890). In that text, James fully but somewhat benignly deploys the aesthete as an example of a life dedicated to art, but lacking the high seriousness and disciplined austerity necessary for the true pursuit of an aesthetic vocation. The aesthete here serves as a kind of beneficent foil to the career of the real artist—a career, however, whose shape and public reception James can only vaguely imagine at this point in his own professional life. By the time of *The Ambassadors*, however, James has fully worked out this problem. And to complete the chain of ironies that enmeshes any discussion of James's response to aestheticism, James himself stands there as a professionalized exponent of a purified form of aestheticism—not merely a definer of that abstract quality, art, but a retailer or even merchandiser of that value which lies behind the value system of the aesthete: the free play of consciousness.

The Tragic Muse and the Comedy of Aestheticism

The question of Jamesian professionalism and its relation to the tradition of British aestheticism is raised with particular vigor by *The Tragic Muse*, for that work is simultaneously James's most expansive and sympathetic representation of the aesthete and his most thorough treatment of the problem of vocation. The novel was written at a particularly pivotal point in James's career, and critics have suggested that it was intended to represent his farewell to the novel, and his greeting to a new, and more profitable, career as a dramatist.[11] Such an analysis is perhaps a bit facile, since the novel spends as much of its energy critiquing the theater as celebrating it, and since the representational debate it stages between theater, art, and literature is left unresolved at its conclusion. But whatever the merits of this assertion, the novel churns with a vocational anxiety of the most agonizing variety. Its hero, Nicholas Dormer, spends most of the text choosing (interminably) between a remunerative career as a politician—a choice urged upon him by his family; by his aged benefactor, Mr. Carteret; and by his beloved, Julia Dallow—and a marginal one as an artist, a portrait painter—a choice advocated only by his Oxford friend, the inescapable but ineffable aesthete, Gabriel Nash. In this vocational drama, the aesthete Nash plays a crucial—if resolutely overdetermined—role. The aesthete is first invoked in a thoroughly positive vein, as a proponent of the possibilities that inhere in a life of aesthetic vocation; but, ironically, he thereby raises in a particularly vexing manner the problems such a vocation faces in the new literary and artistic marketplace. And, I want to suggest briefly here, it is precisely to express and manage these difficulties that the most problematical aspects of the aesthete are invoked.

It is in his redemptive mode that we first encounter Gabriel. For Nash—the author of "a small book of verse which practically nobody had read"; devotee of the theater and the epigram; and, physically, an amalgam of Oscar Wilde and Henry James himself[12]—is clearly more than a loyal friend of the novel's protagonist; he also seems, as Nick's other friend, Peter Sherringham, observes, Nick's "new Mentor or oracle," or, to switch to another classical analogue, his daemon: the embodiment of impulses Nick possesses—or is possessed by—but would deny himself (*TM*, p. 70). Indeed, throughout the text Nash is endowed with mysterious and redemptive powers of insight into Nick's consciousness—even into aspects of his mind that Nick himself would rather ignore. The first scene of the novel is typical. Here, Nick is discovered struggling (as usual) between the calls of filial duty and those of his aesthetic desires. In the company of his mother and sister, duty seems to have won out, but the place in which he finds himself, Paris, calls forth all that Nick is so strenuously denying: "the place had always had the power of quickening sensibly the life of reflection and of observation" (19). It is precisely at this moment of sensible quickening that Gabriel, the advocate of a quickening sensibility, mysteriously appears as if from "Samarcand" (21). Throughout their first conversation, he possesses an equally mysterious omniscience, intuiting both Nick's vocational dilemma and the only viable solution to it —the choice of a career as an artist. The rest of their conversation continues to emphasize Gabriel's powers of insight and prophecy: "It was high time I should meet you," he tells the startled Nick, "I have an idea you need me"; Nick solemnly replies, "Upon my word, I think I do!" (22).

Gabriel's mysterious authority is similarly underlined throughout the rest of the novel; he continues either to embody or to articulate Nick's mental processes with striking accuracy. At times, the narrative acknowledges this role directly. As Nick bustles through his election campaign, for example, he still hears "two voices which told him that all this was not really action at all, but only a pusillanimous imitation of it: one of them made itself fitfully audible in the depths of his own spirit and the other spoke, in the equivocal accents of a very crabbed hand, from a letter of four pages by Gabriel Nash" (177). At others, the relation between Nash and Nick is handled more obliquely. When, to cite a more important example, Nick retires to his London studio to be alone with his paintings before his marriage to Julia, Gabriel appears in order to confirm what Nick seems to know but has not admitted to himself: that his work is of very high quality indeed. Nick acknowledges that Gabriel serves as an "ambiguous" but "excellent touchstone," but the link between Nash's enthusiastic appreciation of Nick's work and Nick's own growing awareness of its quality is greater still: Nick muses that "he had stayed in town to be alone with his imagination, and suddenly, paradoxically, the sense of that result had arrived with Gabriel Nash" (264, 265). Throughout the novel, Nash serves a similar function: articulator of the inarticulable, he continues to give voice to that in Nick that Nick will not—cannot—accept.

Gabriel's complex role in the novel is best described by Nick himself:

Nick Dormer had already become aware that he had two states of mind in listening to Gabriel Nash: one of them in which he laughed, doubted, sometimes even reprobated, and at any rate failed to follow or to accept; the other in which this contemplative genius seemed to take the words out of his mouth, to utter for him, better and more completely, the things he was on the point of saying. Nash's saying them at such moments appeared to make them true, to set them up in the world. (282–83)

In this aspect of James's multifaceted novel, the aesthete plays a redemptive role. By challenging common Victorian criteria of utility and responsibility, by calling into question the norms and expectations imposed by class and family, the aesthete opens up new vocational possibilities for the previously dormant Nick Dormer; he "sets them up in the world." But if James's deployment of aestheticism here is purely positive—aestheticism functioning as a gospel of freedom in a world justly ruled over by the muse of tragedy—aestheticism as represented by Nash is still quite problematic. On the one hand, it is not sufficient in and of itself, because it poses as being too pure for actual art making; on the other, however, it is almost disablingly critical of the compromises the novel's artists must make. Indeed, the very fastidious withdrawal of the aesthete from the world of actual artistic accomplishment enables him to critique the difficulties of that accomplishment with a startling, even paralyzing accuracy. And for performing both of these tasks, the aesthete is necessarily banished from the book—although, as I shall try to suggest here, the questions he poses are not.

The first problem raised by Nash's austere commitment to the realm of the pure aesthetic is rather easily dismissed, for it is first made into a jest, then resolved by Nick's devotion to a professionalized work ethic. The contrast between Nash's advocacy of the aesthetic and his own failure to create is one of the running jokes of the novel—as it was in many popular satires on aestheticism. "Literature, you see," he tells Nick's sister, Biddy, "is for the convenience of others. It requires the most abject concessions. It plays such mischief with one's style that really I have had to give it up" (28). In contrast to this fastidiousness stands first Miriam Rooth and then Nick himself. Both are willing to devote themselves to a single-minded craftsmanship which, while perhaps less flamboyant, bears actual fruit. For Nash, Nick tells Miriam,

the applications, the consequences, the vulgar little effects belong to a lower plane, to which one must doubtless be tolerant and indulgent, but which is after all an affair of comparative accidents and trifles. Indeed he'll probably tell me frankly, the next time I see him, that he can't but feel that to come down to the little questions of action—the little prudences and compromises and simplifications of practice—is for the superior person a really fatal descent. (500–501)

Nick and Miriam model their artistic identities on precisely the exigencies Nash scorns: "'The simplifications of practice!' cried Miriam, 'Why, they are just precisely the most blessed things on earth. What should we do without them?' 'What indeed?' Nick echoed" (501). What these "simplifications" imply, of course, is an idealized—

and un-Besant-like—form of aesthetic professionalism. In the case of Miriam, this means a constant devotion to the minutiae of her craft, a willingness painfully to refine her raw talents into the finished product of "the Tragic Muse," a painful series of efforts that climax in the complete refashioning of a maladroit, obsessional, stagestruck girl into the finest actress of her time. James quite clearly demonstrates the price this process exacts as well as the possibilities it opens up. Miriam is so deeply caught up in her theatrical self-fashioning that by the end of the novel, she has virtually no self left at all; she has wholly become her own performance in a way that seems somewhat sinister or even (as Biddy Dormer thinks) "terrible" (519). In Nick's case, such a commitment is less problematic, although it is still far from entirely benign. Like Miriam's, Nick's commitment to art means an acceptance of the professional work ethic, a willingness to slog, "a passion of work," and a willingness to sacrifice all—a political career, the hand of the beautiful and rich Lady Julia, the respect of his friends, the enrichment of his family—for the sake of his art (492). Also like Miriam's, although in a slightly lesser key, Nick's devotion to his craft is curiously obsessive, monomaniacal: he locks himself away in his London studio for major portions of the novel, for example, and expresses his distrust not only for the public, political sphere, but also for the "odious facility" of his own talent—for the very artistic abilities he has dedicated himself to fulfilling.

In contrast to both of these professional obsessives stands Gabriel, committed only to a mode of an inspired dilettantishness ("I work in such a difficult material," he tells the shocked Mrs. Dormer; "I work in life!" [106]). When Nick's sister Biddy enquires of Nash whether he is "an aesthete," his response defines the range of possibilities opened up—and closed off—by this form of aestheticism:

Ah, there's one of the formulas! That's walking in one's hat! I've *no* profession, my dear young lady. I've no *état civil*. These things are a part of the complicated, ingenious machinery. As I say, I keep to the simplest way. I find that gives one enough to do. Merely to be is such a *métier*; to live is such an art; to feel is such a career! (27)

Nash's refusal to conform to the dictates of a professionalizing world is attractive, given the obsessiveness and self-sacrifice that full artistic commitment demands; yet it is also understood by the novel to be impossible. His Paterian privileging of mere being as opposed to rigorous doing simply has no place in either the theatrical or the aesthetic spheres that the novel portrays. Gabriel's refusal to engage himself with the sordid necessities of such a world constitutes a benign form of

self-willed irrelevance—signaled in the novel by his increasingly frequent disappearances to exotic locales. "I have a notion he has gone
to India, and at the present moment is reclining on a bank of flowers
in the vale of Cashmere," Nick jestingly tells Biddy at the end of the
novel (516).

But if Cashmere or any other such exotic locale is the only place
left for a figure like Nash, this is a commentary not only on his own
character, but also on the increasing inflexibility of the aesthetic career
Nick and Miriam—and Henry James—must face. For if Nash speaks
eloquently for the possibilities opened up by a life devoted to art, he
also perceives and describes more accurately than any of the novel's
idealizing artists the aesthetic conditions under which they find themselves working. His comments on Miriam's cultural apotheosis, for
example, delineate clearly, if acidulously, the difficulties posed by her
very success in the world of the "vulgar" contemporary theater:

As Sherringham had perceived, you never knew where to "have" Gabriel
Nash; a truth exemplified in his unexpected delight at the prospect of Miriam's
drawing forth the modernness of the age. You might have thought he would
loathe that modernness; but he had a brilliant, amused, amusing vision of it,
saw it as something huge and ornamentally vulgar. Its vulgarity would rise to
the grand style, like that of a London railway station, and Miriam's publicity
would be as big as the globe itself. All the machinery was ready, the platform
laid; the facilities, the wires and bells and trumpets, the colossal, deafening
newspaperism of the period—its most distinctive sign—were waiting for her,
their predestined mistress, to press her foot on the spring and set them all
in motion. Gabriel brushed in a large bright picture of her progress through
the time and round the world, round it and round it again, from continent
to continent and clime to clime; with populations and deputations, reporters
and photographers, placards, and interviews and banquets, steamers, rail-
ways, dollars, diamonds, speeches and artistic ruin all jumbled into her train.
Regardless of expense the spectacle would be thrilling, though somewhat mo-
notonous, the drama—a drama more bustling than any she would put on the
stage and a spectacle that would beat anything for scenery. In the end her
divine voice would crack, screaming to foreign ears and antipodal barbarians,
and her clever manner would lose all quality, simplified to a few unmistakable
knock-down dodges. Then she would be at the fine climax of life and glory,
still young and insatiate, but already coarse, hard, and raddled, with nothing
left to do and nothing left to do it with, the remaining years all before her and
the *raison d'être* all behind. It would be curious and magnificent and grotesque.
(375–76)

Gabriel's amusement at Miriam's projected apotheosis and decline
may look like the snobbish indifference so often discerned in the aesthete—as Osmond reminds us, disdain is but one small step from

disinterestedness—but his vision here clarifies the novel's understanding of the cultural fate of high art. For the drama she finds herself
performing is itself part of the intrinsically theatrical world of late-
nineteenth-century mass culture. When Miriam's fine dramatic art
takes its place on the "greater stage" of the public world, it rapidly
becomes indistinguishable from the rest of the parade of frauds,
mountebanks, and one-day wonders generated by that cultural machine Gabriel synecdochically refers to as "newspaperism"—by which
he means, of course, the newly ascendent mass popular press that was
so active in publicizing the exploits of actors like Henry Irving, Ellen
Terry, and James's immediate model for Miriam, Mary Anderson, but
also those institutions like public relations and advertising that accompanied the press into prominence and, indeed, the entire nascent
consumer culture that called these phenomena into being.[13] Gabriel
understands, in other words, the limitation of even Miriam's greatest
virtue: that while she may succeed in mastering the art of dramatic
representation, she is forced by the exigencies of late-nineteenth-
century culture thereby to represent nothing at all. For Miriam—or
rather "Miriam," the culturally apotheosized "Tragic Muse"—is the
object of a social craze of limited duration and value in which, if she
represents anything, she represents merely the fact of novelty itself;
she is to be just another transient and replaceable commodity sold to
a voracious public by the insidious mechanisms of "newspaperism."

   To a certain extent, of course, the problem Nash poses forms a
part of the novel's representational debate, and its difficulties may be
seen as inhering in the theatrical medium alone; certainly, this is what
Miriam herself suggests when she praises Nick's greater promise, for
Nick's art, she believes, is free from the pressures she faces, and he
can develop in his own way, at his own pace. But particularly when
read in the context of James's maneuvers in and fulminations against
the literary marketplace, they take on a greater poignancy. For they
suggest what we have also seen in his responses to Wilde, that in such
a world, aesthetic success is even more threatening than aesthetic failure, or that aesthetic success and aesthetic failure are finally one and
the same thing. Success brings not only sordid compromises (Miriam
is particularly adroit, for example, at posing for publicity photos),
but a fundamental perversion of the professional ethos necessary for
true artistic creation to take place. Miriam has professional discipline
enough, it is true, but she lacks the opportunity to build on it—until, in
the novel's excessively benign ending, she marries her manager, buys
a theater, and (like Sybil Vane in Wilde's *Dorian Gray*) gives the perfect

performance of Juliet. But short of controlling one's own destiny in so thoroughly unrealistic a manner, in Miriam's theatrical world one's artistic fate is simply out of one's own hands, for it is governed solely by the capricious mechanisms of publicity and advertising in the "more bustling drama" played out in the popular arena.

It is this perception that Gabriel alone is in a position to articulate, for his ironic detachment enables him to perceive the potential difficulties of a popular success more clearly than characters who long for it directly—even if the aesthete is himself as completely embedded in those difficulties as are any of the novel's other characters.* But his role here is even more problematizing. For he sees the converse of the problem posed by Miriam: the brutal truth that the other route toward aesthetic success, the route that takes one away from an enlarged mass audience toward an elite public, is no more efficacious. Thus, at the end of the novel, he prophesies for Nick's iconic art an aesthetic fate that seems opposite from Miriam's theatrical art, but that is finally equally degrading:

Take care, take care, for, fickle as you may think me, I can read the future: don't imagine you've come to the end of me yet. Mrs. Dallow and your sister . . . are capable of hatching together the most conscientious, delightful plan for you. Your differences with the beautiful lady will be patched up, and you'll each come round a little and meet the other half-way. Mrs. Dallow will swallow your profession if you'll swallow hers. She'll put up with the palette if you'll put up with the country-house. It will be a very unusual one in which you won't find a good north room where you can paint. You'll go about with her and do all her friends, all the bishops and ambassadors, and you'll eat your cake and have it, and every one, beginning with your wife, will forget there is anything queer about you, and everything will be for the best in the best of worlds; so that, together—you and she—you'll become a great social institution, and everyone will think she has a delightful husband; to say nothing of course of your having a delightful wife. (507–8)

The problem here may seem to result from the machinations of Mrs. Dallow, who throughout the novel seeks to feminize Nick (it is not for nothing that Nick in Parliament is to be known as "Julia's member" [165]). But the actual difficulty has less to do with her engulfing powers, or those of the class she represents, than with the novel's failure of imagining any real career for Nick in the field it has spent so

*Nash, after all, does much to launch Miriam on the course that carries her into flagrant "newspaperism"; he and the "aesthetic people—the worldly, semi-smart ones, not the frumpy, sickly lot who wore dirty drapery" had "run after her." It is this "critical clique to which Miriam had begun so quickly to owe it that she had a vogue" (331).

much time in valorizing. Nash's prophecy may seem offensive—Nick blanches as he utters it—but it is still more concrete than anything else the text has to offer its artist. At the end of the work, the only facts we are given about the progress of Nick's actual career are that he continues to slog, that he takes the occasional trip to Paris, and that his portrait of Julia won general approval at a recent exhibition. This failure of imagination is symptomatic of the larger social failure that Nash alone is able to put his finger on: the lack of supporting or organizing institutional structures for the kind of art Nick wishes to pursue—and which the novel is clearly structured to valorize. The only alternative Nash and the novel alike can imagine to that of the mass market is the outmoded one of aristocratic patronage—here imaged as a kind of humiliating enfeeblement, a castration. But as Nash is able to see, there is no other public for Nick to appeal to, and therefore nothing left for him to do but paint portraits of his patroness.

Nash's ultimate role in the novel, then, is to suggest that the artist is caught between a rock and a hard place. He may, like Miriam, make enough of a popular success to sustain himself (even, perhaps, to buy his own theater), but at the cost of his artistic integrity; on the other hand, he can pursue a form of art that scorns such success, but will thereby inevitably fall into the very difficulties he has turned to art to escape. Nash himself moreover may escape these difficulties—but only at the cost of escaping from any commitment or accomplishment whatsoever.

Paradoxically, however, it is this very failure that enabled Nash not only to express the artist's dilemma, but also to manage it, make it more bearable. As I have suggested above, as a figure of benign excess, Nash is eminently excludable from the value system the work seems to propose—indeed, despite his partial articulation of the values of a life dedicated to the pursuit of art, he excludes himself from that pursuit. Like the more dramatic demonization of Osmond, Nash's benign irrelevance serves to focus our attention on the virtues exemplified by the other characters in the novel; he puts into sharp relief the high seriousness with which first Miriam, then Nick, pursue their craft, "awaiting [their] afflatus, and thinking only of that" (88).

This process reaches its climax at the end of the novel, in which Nash first sits for his portrait by Nick, then disappears—as does, mysteriously, the portrait itself. By means of his artistic doing, Nick alienates the advocate of mere being: he brings Nash into the "universe" he claims to stand aloof from; and Nash's response is to vanish back into the empyrean, to disappear "'without a trace,' like a personage in a fairy-tale or a melodrama" (510, 511). The unfinished portrait follows the lead of its subject; it seems to "gradually [fade] from the canvas. He couldn't catch it in the act, but he could have a suspicion, when he glanced at it, that the hand of time was rubbing it away little by little (for all the world as in some delicate Hawthorne tale), making the surface indistinct and bare—bare of all resemblance to the model. Of course the moral of the Hawthorne tale would be that this personage would come back on the day when the last adumbration should have vanished" (511–12).

This gradual disappearance of Nash's image from both Nick's portrait and James's novel is both therapeutic and suggestive. It is therapeutic because it enables the novel to master the vocational dilemma Nick faces, if only by changing the subject. The actual Nash, who presents himself as "eternal," fades away, but his image endures; and the transcendental qualities of the artwork are thereby foregrounded by James's own act of representation. This, at least, is one reading we can give to the disappearance of Nash's portrait, for it is rendered "bare of all resemblance to the model," which is to suggest that it utterly masters, assumes, and remakes the identity of the individual it attempts to represent; it effaces the historical identity of that being by transmuting his image into the consummate perfection of the artistic image (512). In this way, Nick's portrait achieves the same powers as the portraits Nick praises in the National Gallery; it, too, has become an ahistorical emblem of perfection, or, to use Nick's idealizing metaphor, the very "thread" that organizes the "pearls of history":

Empires and systems and conquests had rolled over the globe and every kind of greatness had risen and passed away; but the beauty of the great pictures had known nothing of death or change, and the ages had only sweetened their freshness. The same faces, the same figures looked out different centuries, knowing a deal the century didn't, and when they joined hands they made the indestructible thread on which the pearls of history were strung. (497–98)

But the disappearance of the portrait can be read in other, and perhaps richer, ways. The fading away of the portrait, and the disappearance of Gabriel Nash into "the ambient air," may represent not the expulsion of the aesthete from James's work, but rather his incorporation into the ambient air of James's literary consciousness (516). Nash's image may fade away, but when its effacement is complete he will return—as indeed he does in James's later, major phase novels. For Nash's advocacy of the perfection of his own being, his cultivation of a stance of enlightened, almost ironic receptivity does not disappear in

James's subsequent fiction, nor is it exclusively expressed by aesthetes alone. Rather, it is precisely this virtue that defines characters close to the heart of James's fictional project: Lambert Strether, Milly Theale, even (as we shall see in some detail) Maggie Verver. In this sense, the picture is (as the Hawthorne story James alludes to would have it) "prophetic," and what it prophesies is the return of the repressed figure of the aesthete at the very heart of James's fictional enterprise. It is a further irony that this return is accomplished in large measure through James's competitive response to Oscar Wilde's deployment of the same topos in a novel composed during the year that *The Tragic Muse* was published: *The Picture of Dorian Gray*.

We can see this process in all of its complexity most thoroughly in *The Ambassadors*, perhaps the greatest single example of the new aestheticism James built on the ruins of the old. Moreover, that novel compellingly demonstrates the debt such a Jamesian aestheticism owes to its predecessor. For in that novel, James brings his intertextual struggle with the shade of Wilde to a triumphant conclusion. Indeed, as I want to conclude this chapter by suggesting, his triumph is so complete that he almost completely effaces the traces of competition.

Strether as Aesthete

If the portrayal of Nash may be seen as a competitive gesture, it must also be acknowledged to be a relatively benign one; the representation of Nash here is affectionate, almost gentle, in comparison with James's other fictional treatments of the aesthete. But in response to this somewhat muted challenge, Wilde picked up the gage and threw down one of his own. For *Dorian Gray*—which Wilde was writing as *The Tragic Muse* languorously unfolded itself in the pages of *The Atlantic*— not only lifts from Nash a crucial phrase—"We must feel everything, everything that we can. We are here for that"—but major details of the *Muse*'s plot (25). Miriam Rooth, James's maniacally self-fashioned actress, is ironically transmuted into Wilde's Sybil Vane, whose acting skills are more natural, but who, like Miriam, is literally nothing without or beyond her own representational powers.[14] Of course, the disappearance of Nash's own portrait as his influence over Nick fades away is reflected by the central conceit of *Dorian*: the idea of an artwork with the supernatural power to metamorphose in sympathy with the fate of its subject.

The point here, however, is not to belabor Wilde's literary thievery from James, since *Dorian Gray* is little more than a collage composed of similar objets trouvés. Rather, the point is to emphasize the overdetermined qualities of James's long-delayed riposte to Wilde's response to James's own novel. Not only does James rather needlessly return to the fray in 1902—seven years after Wilde's disgrace, and two years after his death—but he does so to revise Wilde's redaction of his own text. This act of revision is, however, not performed ex nihilo; rather, James is able to accomplish it by invoking as his model Wilde's own literary progenitor, Walter Pater, and, continuing to build on his own Paterian foundations, fashions in *The Ambassadors* the final and most thoroughly realized example of a distinctively Jamesian aestheticism.

Perhaps the best way to understand this complicated intertextual interplay is to perform the paradoxical, and eminently Wildean, task of reading *Dorian Gray* through the eyes of *The Ambassadors*. When we approach Wilde's novel in this manner, we discover a remarkable similarity of perspective and intention. James's characteristic themes are articulated by Wilde with a striking similitude, although they are given a somewhat different, more disturbing twist. This is particularly true of the figure of Lord Henry Wotton, who announces himself a perverse or decadent Strether—a thoroughly European Strether, a Strether crossed with the Comte de Vionnet, say—when he praises both his own vicariousness and his careful attention to the ebb and flow of his consciousness: "How delightful other people's emotions were!—much more delightful than their ideas, it seemed to him. One's own soul, and the passions of one's friends—those were the fascinating things in life" (*DG*, p. 13). Or—as he puts the matter at his most shocking (just after Sybil Vane kills herself for the love of Dorian)— "Sometimes . . . a tragedy that possesses artistic elements of beauty crosses our lives. If these elements of beauty are real, the whole thing simply appeals to our sense of dramatic effect. Suddenly, we find that we are no longer the actors, but the spectators of the play. Or rather we are both. We watch ourselves, and the mere wonder of the spectacle enthralls us" (101). Or—as Dorian himself puts it, speaking in Wilde's most Jamesian voice—"To become the spectator of one's own life . . . is to escape the suffering of life" (110).

In short, Wilde, no less than James, was fascinated by the phenomenon of vicariousness; like Strether (or his malevolent double, the narrator of *The Sacred Fount*), Wotton adopts the stance of detached contemplation as a compensatory erotic that endows the contemplator with power over that which he sees, and relieves him of the burden of suffering that can come with more direct involvement. Moreover, Wotton's attention to the flux of his own and other's consciousnesses leads

him beyond voyeurism to what we might want to call a Stretherian phenomenology, to the highly Stretherian discovery that "the true mystery
of the world is the visible, not the invisible" (22). It leads him as well to
his Stretherian praise for the ability of youth and youth alone to take
advantage of its heightened perceptual experience of the material,
visible world. Further, both Wilde and James's novels are interested in
the failures of these notions: in the knowledge that youth is fleeting—
the knowledge that Dorian disastrously attempts to deny, the knowledge that Strether melancholically accepts—and the awareness of the
price that a life devoted to sensation exacts as well as the possibilities
it affords. "What matter what the cost was? One could never pay too
high a price for any sensations" asks Lord Henry; Dorian's Gothic fate,
like Strether's renunciation, provides a vivid riposte (57).

Moreover, to move beyond individual instances to larger structures,
Dorian Gray, like *The Ambassadors*, focuses on the problematic interrelation between sexuality, influence, and personal relations. Here again
Wotton is at the center of our concern, but now a Wotton resembling
not so much Strether as Madame de Vionnet. In Wilde's novel, as in
James's, to put oneself (as James would say) "in relation" is to open
oneself up to the dynamic interplay of the influence and counterinflu-
ence of others. And, claims Lord Henry, "To influence another person
is to give him one's own soul. He does not think his natural thoughts,
or burn with his natural passions. His sins, if there are such things as
sins, are borrowed. He becomes the echo of some one else's music, an
actor of a part that has not been written for him" (17). This rescripting
of another human being's part, this recasting of a personality by the
power of erotic domination, stands at the center of both *Dorian Gray*
and *The Ambassadors*. Both James and Wilde seek to interrogate the
ability of a significant, eroticized other to lead a young man to a vividly
experienced passional life, which alters the self so completely that
he becomes nearly unrecognizable—so much so that Dorian is transformed from an innocent young man who spends his time among the
missions in the East End into a decadent dandy, so much so that Chad-
wick Newsome is transformed from a callow American stripling into
(in a phrase that could virtually have been used by Wilde to describe
Dorian) "an irreducible young Pagan" (NY, 21: 156–57).

Indeed, to continue our endeavor of backwards reading, what *The
Ambassadors* helps us realize about *Dorian Gray* is that for Wilde, too,
the central questions posed by the drama of personal domination are
the limits as well as the possibilities of erotic influence. "She had made
him better, she had made him best, she had made him anything one

would," Strether muses near the end of *The Ambassadors*, "but it came to our friend with supreme queerness that he was none the less only Chad" (22: 284). So too Wotton makes Dorian bad, he makes him the worst—women shudder with horror when Dorian enters the room, and men stalk out—but he is none the less only Dorian: he can never escape the visible embodiment of his identity, the image painted by Basil Hallward, and when he attempts to kill it, he kills himself. "For at the end of all things they *were* mysterious: she had but made Chad what he was—so why could she think she had made him infinite?" (22: 284). The same mysterious perception of limitation, of the finitude of the self's possible transformations through the discovery of an essential core of being lying beneath an outer, metamorphosing surface is enforced somewhat self-parodically at the end of Wilde's novel.

It may seem, by this point, that I am being determinedly, willfully perverse. There is indeed something faintly ludicrous about comparing James's novel to Wilde's; between them lies the gap between cynicism and resignation, desire and regret. Indeed, while the entire plot of James's novel could be summarized by one of Wotton's more cynical epigrams—"Young men want to be faithful, and are not; old men want to be faithless, and cannot: that is all one can say"—such a suggestion only emphasizes the utter difference between the two men's worldview (29). What is for Wilde a matter of physiology is for James a matter of psychology, perhaps even ontology. But what bringing these two texts together can do is to help us see the extensiveness of the common ground they share, the thoroughness with which James follows Wilde's emotional and psychological logic—up to a point. It is at that point where our analysis of the intertextual interplay between the two must thicken; for it is at this very point that James sets out most determinedly to revise his problematic contemporary, to define his own stance against that struck by the Wildean aesthete.

James performs this task by invoking as his own direct example the very figure whose influence he and Wilde held in common, and whose texts loom large behind both his novel and Wilde's, Walter Pater. For both *Dorian Gray* and *The Ambassadors* locate themselves in a demonstrably Paterian universe, a world tending toward exhaustion and entropy in which intense experience alone can serve as respite and redemption; for both, the question thereby posed is both the possibility and the sufficiency of intensity. But it is precisely at this point that Wilde and James diverge. For Wilde, the only way to search for intense experience is to experience the greatest possible number of ecstatic sensations: "Nothing can cure the soul but the senses, just as nothing can cure the senses but the soul," says Lord Henry, speaking almost directly here for his maker (20). Wilde's solution to Pater's conundrum is to locate the hard, gemlike flame in the experiences of the body, which are to be sought after and explored with a vigorous, almost earnest gluttony. But, as Wotton's epigram indicates, Wilde knows full well that the road of sensual excess leads not only to the palace of wisdom but also to Reading Gaol: that the attempt to live a life of physical excess as a means of maintaining ecstasy must fail, because when a desire is fulfilled, it gives way to another unfulfilled desire, which is followed in its turn by another desire, and so on and so on. Another, perhaps inevitable, route to fulfillment, then, can be found through the opposite impulse: the desire to purify oneself of desire through suffering, through penitence, through self-abasement. The endeavor to redeem the body and the bodily as a means of transcendence in a world brooded over by time and loss can only end with continual quivering after new desires on the one hand or an utter annulment of desire on the other. Thus Wilde's Lord Henry can simultaneously advise Dorian that "the only way to get rid of a temptation is to yield to it" and assert that "[a] cigarette is the perfect type of a perfect pleasure. It is exquisite, and it leaves one unsatisfied. What more can one want?" (18, 79).

Wilde, then, does not resolve the conundrum posed by Pater's gospel of intensity, his valorization of the hard, gemlike flame; instead, he amplifies it, puts its unstable qualities on vivid and public display. James, by contrast, works harder at smoothing out the problematics of the gospel of intensity, at reconciling it to the limitations it faces. James, like Wilde, is a believer in both the inevitability and the failure of desire: but James nudges his own position closer to Pater's by transforming this failure itself into a mode of melancholy triumph.

Indeed, far more than Lord Henry Wotton (who is continually quoting Pater without, of course, footnoting his source), Lambert Strether may be said to be an example of Paterian man: a man, that is, vividly aware of the transience of life, of the inevitability of loss, and of his own exhaustion who finds, through a set of vivid impressions and sensations, what Pater calls "a quickened sense of life." "Great passions may give us this quickened sense of life, ecstasy and sorrow of love, the various forms of enthusiastic activity, disinterested or otherwise . . . Only be sure it is passion—that it does yield you this fruit of a quickened, multiplied consciousness," writes Pater (WP, 1: 238). It is precisely this fruit Strether is able to pluck in Paris: he leaves, one might say, with nothing *but* a quickened, multiplied consciousness.

James signals this throughout the novel by employing transparently Paterian language to describe Strether's experience. Paris itself, for example, is figured as a revised but nevertheless recognizable redaction of Pater's hard, gemlike flame—that is, as a hard, flamelike gem: "It hung before him this morning, the vast bright Babylon, like some huge iridescent object, a jewel brilliant and hard, in which parts were not to be discriminated nor differences comfortably marked. It twinkled and trembled and melted together, and what seemed all surface one moment seemed all depth the next" (NY, 21: 89).

And Paterian language continues to flare throughout Strether's Parisian perambulations. At Gloriani's party, for example, we learn that "it was as if something had happened that 'nailed' . . . Strether's impressions . . . made them more intense"; Strether spends most of the novel searching for similar moments of intense Paterian apprehension (21: 227). Discovering, in the *Comediè Français*, that "they were in the presence of Chad himself," Strether recognizes that "his perception of the young man's identity—so absolutely checked for a minute—had been quite one of the sensations that count in life" (21: 135). Later, stepping into Notre Dame for a momentary respite from "the obsession of his problem" (only, of course, to find the personification of his problem, Madame de Vionnet, sitting there), Strether finds another: "He was conscious enough that it was only for the moment, but good moments—if he could call them good—still had their value for a man who by this time struck himself as living almost disgracefully from hand to mouth" (22: 3).

James's use of Pater here teeters on parody: for the only "good moment" that Strether will allow himself (if, indeed, it can truly be called "good" rather than immoral, wicked, Romish) is that of relieving himself from his exhaustion, or seeking release from the moral dialectic in which he is entrapped only to find that the very release from that dialectic represents one pole in another. James's subsequent invocations of Pater are less comic. As Strether grows more and more familiar with his vast bright Babylon, as he becomes more and more enmeshed in the drama of Chad and Madame de Vionnet, his "impressions" are "multiplied" (22: 111), and he undertakes "frequent instinctive snatches at the growing rose of observation, constantly stronger for him, as he felt, in scent and colour, and in which he could bury his nose even to wantonness" (22: 173). Strether has become almost a parodic version of the Paterian aesthete, sniffing ever more anxiously after strange new sensations, reveling in them "even to wantonness."

As that last, loaded word suggests, Strether's Paterian aestheticism, like Wotton's, is not without its erotic dimension. This point is driven home at the moment of his greatest aestheticizing: Strether's day in the country. Indeed, in this scene Strether's Paterian quest for impressions leads to a fit of literal aestheticizing—Strether seeks to recapitulate "the only adventure of his life in connexion with the purchase of a work of art" by endeavoring to "thrill a little at the chance of seeing something somewhere that would remind him of a certain small Lambinet that had charmed him, long years before" (22: 245). Here, Strether goes Pater one better, by not only witnessing life "in the spirit of art"—the famous desideratum Pater advocates in his essay on Wordsworth—but by seeking to collapse the boundaries between the two entirely; not only does he imagine the scene as being like a Lambinet, but he fantasizes entering the frame of the painting (WP, 5: 62). Strether's aestheticism ultimately takes on something of a grandiose quality, then, but this aesthetic imperialism is ultimately reproved, for it leads Strether to witness precisely that which he has sought to aestheticize and therefore efface: Chad and Madame de Vionnet themselves, drifting sensually into his artwork. Strether's subsequent recognition, the true "impression, destined only to deepen, to complete itself," that their relation was not, as he had supposed, "intrinsically beautiful," suggests a recognition as well of the nature of his aestheticism: it suggests that his investment in perceiving beauty was only a means of evading "the deep, deep truth of the intimacy revealed" (NY, 22: 261, 266). Strether's aestheticism, we realize, idealizes but cannot fully repress the facts of sexual intimacy; indeed, that it is the very quest for such an idealized beauty that brings him by its own ineluctable logic into direct contact with that which it seeks to efface, with the fact of sexuality itself.

It would seem that, as some readings of the novel suggest, James uses Pater ironically.[15] This is true only insofar as one sees James as adopting the common Victorian reading of Pater, the reading that stresses the quest for intense sensations and ecstasies as an end in and of itself. James's evocation of the "Pater mood" is more complete than such readings suggest. For Pater, the recovery of value in intense experience is both wondrous and tragic—wondrous because it is accessible in so many forms and from so many places, tragic because it is bound by the inevitable passage of time. Pater speaks "with this sense of the splendor of our experience and of its awful brevity"; the message he has to deliver is that the best we can hope for is to give "the highest quality to [our] moments as they pass . . . simply for those moments' sake" (WP, 1: 237, 239). So too, Strether's Parisian experience suggests that even to fill one's vessel of consciousness to the point that "the cup of . . . impressions seem[s] truly to overflow" is to discover the transitoriness of such experiences: to discover that even (or especially) in a world of loss, time, and disappointment, intense experiences can suffice for a moment, but for that moment only, and that they bring us most fully into contact with loss, not fulfillment (NY, 21: 80). Strether begins to understand this late in the novel; standing in Chad's room, for example, experiencing, just before his fête champêtre, the last and perhaps most perfect of his perfect moments ("an hour full of strange suggestions, persuasions, recognitions; one of those he was to recall, at the end of his adventure, as the particular handful that had most counted" [22: 209]), the plentitude of Strether's sense of free-dom measures precisely the fullness of his loss: "the main truth of the actual appeal of everything was none the less that everything repre-sented the substance of his loss, put it within reach, within touch, made it, to a degree it had never been, an affair of the senses" (22: 211). And the lesson of the Lambinet episode is similar; every time poor Strether seeks to "nail" down his experience for all eternity, to make it withstand the "wheel of time," he is disappointed by the capacity of experience to shift and change the very terms that it presents him: to reveal within the hard, flamelike gem more facets, more dimensions, more lambent play (22: 246). It is only when he accepts that the in-evitable passage of such experiences, their ineluctable transitoriness, is the ground of their value that he achieves a tentative illumination and "sense of success, of a finer harmony in things" (22: 248). The only way Strether can irrevocably affirm the value of his experience in Paris, the only way he can fully possess what Maria Gostrey calls his "wonderful impressions," in other words, is to return to America —an awareness in which the Jamesian ethos of renunciation and the Paterian gospel of intensity become, melancholically, one (22: 326).

James's response to Pater's conundrum, then, first dismantles and then revises Wilde's. James, like Wilde, may be an adherent of the Paterian gospel of intensity, but where for Wilde that intensity must be sought through the senses, for James, it is discovered through the mobilization of the quickened, multiplied consciousness. Where Wilde literalizes Pater, insisting on the availability of the hard, gemlike flame in the lambent sensations of the body, James refiguralizes him, taking the lighting of this flame as a metaphor for the amplitude of con-sciousness that has become his chief—his only—value. Where Wilde's sensualization establishes intensity as partaking of the transitoriness of all bodily experience, for James it is precisely through the acceptance of the transitoriness and failure of sensual experience that a true intensity arrives—and lasts.

By such melancholy affirmations, it would seem that James stands closer in spirit to Pater and to the project of Paterian aestheticism than does Wilde, for he recuperates Paterianism from the sense of sensuality, self-indulgence, and flamboyant public display with which Wilde had tainted it for James. James here, as throughout his dealings with Wilde, proclaims himself as the truer aesthete, the more complete adherent of the gospel of intensity, than the man he saw as his louder, more self-advertising predecessor. Yet James does more than take back from his problematic antagonist his own words, his own thematic and formal structures; he also adopts and adapts the position of the Wildean aesthete for his own purposes—and so thoroughly as to efface the traces of competition. It is this movement I want to designate as the "incorporation" of aestheticism into James's literary project, in two senses. On the one hand it represents in a classic sense the full transumption of a problematic precursor—even if, in this case, that act is performed by invoking the precursor's precursor against him. The traces of the Wildean and, to a lesser extent the Paterian, are thoroughly effaced in James's narrative—so much so that the problematic chain of quotation that signals Wilde's presence is displaced in the novel's preface onto the manifestly un-Wildean figure of William Dean Howells, so much so that the only direct allusions to Wildean aestheticism in the novel can be found in moments of high comedy (when Waymarsh signifies his conversion to Parisian dissoluteness, for example, he places a rose behind his ear, parodying at once Wilde's habit of self-advertising through floral accoutrements and W. H. Mallock's parodic representation of Pater as Mr. Rose in his devastating satire, *The New Republic*). But they are discernible nevertheless in their disguised and transmuted forms, installed now not at the margins but, under the sign of loss, at the very center of the novel's system of value.

This movement represents "incorporation" in a more technical, economic sense as well. For in *The Ambassadors*, we witness the crystallization of the value system that will mark James's work from this moment on, and which becomes the distinctive "note" (to use a Jamesian term), or the characteristic trademark (to use a more cynical form of expression) of the Jamesian itself. For the rueful aestheticism of a Lambert Strether, reproved but reinstalled under the sign of a visionary compensation for a willingly accepted loss, becomes the defining mark of the Jamesian novelist, who dedicates himself with equal fervor (and through the acceptance of losses equally great) to similar compensations. James had been for some time hovering on the verge of such an affirmation, but after *The Ambassadors* he becomes firmer, more assertive in his advocacy of the values of a supple and wide-ranging consciousness, and more confident about his ability to make his art out of the struggle of that consciousness for its own prerogatives. *The Wings of the Dove* and *The Golden Bowl* both play out this thematic line in different venues and, as we shall see, to different ends; the Prefaces to the New York edition, to cite an even more powerful example, take as their central theme his entire oeuvre as a struggle of the novelistic consciousness with its own limitations and those of its material in order to reach the visionary perfection only gestured toward by Strether.

As that last example also suggests, it was as that kind of novelist that James was able to institutionalize and monumentalize himself; it was in that role that he was able to place himself at once above and within the competitive pressures of the marketplace. For the very monumentalizing project of the New York edition suggests that James was able finally to achieve the position he aspired to in his conflict with Wilde; that, for all his chronic complaining about his reading public, James was granted by his culture the position of the consummate artistic professional he affirmed in rivalry with the aesthetic professionalism of the aesthete. But—and the irony here is one that Oscar Wilde would have been the first to appreciate—as he did so, James also established himself as the professionalized exponent of the values of the aesthete he had spent most of his career critiquing. For as we shall see in *The Wings of the Dove* and *The Golden Bowl*, in the final turn of his career, he accepts with increasing confidence and self-assurance the *entire* burden of the aesthetic movement—internalizing and deploying not merely its praise for a highly pitched and mobile consciousness, but also its ambivalent acceptance of the commodification of that consciousness, and its even more ambivalent cultivation of the dissolute position of the "decadent." By doing so, as I shall suggest in conclusion, James helped blaze the trail that leads from British aestheticism to Anglo-American modernism—a trail that eliminated the fainter, more wandering paths of his predecessors and companions in the aesthetic movement.

Chapter Five

The Decadent Henry James: British Aestheticism and the Major Phase

To this point, I have argued that Henry James's engagement with the tradition of British aestheticism mirrored the progression of that movement itself. James's fiction and criticism both followed the same trajectory as did aestheticism in England—beginning, like Ruskin and Norton, with an attempt to understand art as a mimetic enactment of moral and social wholeness; proceeding, with Pater, to a delineation of the value of a heightened and receptive aesthetic consciousness; and climaxing in a complicated rivalry with Oscar Wilde's mastery of the mass market. But this account omits an important dimension of the British experience of aestheticism, one that was contemporary to and often coterminous with the tradition I have traced: the tradition of "dark" or "decadent" aestheticism.

I have slighted this aspect of British aestheticism for several reasons. My first inheres in the vagueness of the notion of "decadence," for the fuzziness of that term exceeds even that of "aestheticism" itself.[1] Second, the notion of decadence historically operated to open two highly misleading lines of speculation on the provenance of British fin de siècle writing, one marked by cultural provincialism (those who identified "decadence" with foreign, i.e. French, corruptions of the Anglo-Saxon literary tradition), the other by a mystifying pseudo-internationalism (those who asserted that this moment represented an invigorating importation of foreign, i.e. French, sophistication to the attenuated, provincial, and otherwise enfeebled literary culture of England). Third, and most important, the identification of aestheticism as a species of "decadence" or "dark romanticism" also accompanied a reductive dismissal of the entire aesthetic movement, whether through the diagnostic deployment of its art as a symptom of cultural decline or through the equally symptomatic association of aestheticism with tabooed forms of sexuality. These two responses were frequently linked in the contemporary responses to the aesthetic movement: in, for example, Robert Buchanan's famous denunciation of Pre-Raphaelitism as the "fleshy school of poetry"; in Max Nordau's equally famous identification of Oscar Wilde as the literal embodiment of that new social type, the "degenerate"; or in Sir Edward Carson's forensic equation of Wilde's art with the corruption of its readers.[2] But both are no less evident in the initial scholarly treatments of the aesthetic movement. Agony, degeneration, darkness, and fin de siècle perversities, leading at best to a Celtic twilight and at worst to (in Eliot's words) "some untidy lives": such has been the standard response to aestheticism from the time of the Victorians to that of the Victorianists.[3] Despite the greater theoretical sophistication recent readers have brought to the subject, "decadence" has entered our own fin de siècle carrying much the same cultural baggage.[4]

Nevertheless, there is a certain cogency to speaking about decadence in conjunction with the final turn taken by James's fiction, a turn adumbrated in *The Wings of the Dove* and performed fully in *The Golden Bowl*. For, like the idea of aestheticism, the notion of decadence was part of the cultural air that James was breathing in the 1890's and early years of the twentieth century—indeed, his friend Paul Bourget offered one of the first and most influential definitions of decadence as early as 1881, in an essay on Charles Baudelaire—and every pulse in that air was converted by James, I have been arguing, into a revelation. We should not be surprised, therefore, to see the decadent turn of the aesthetic movement in England fully reflected in James's work; to see the characteristic icons of decadent poetry and art woven with increasing frequency into the verbal texture of his fiction; to find the recognizably decadent preoccupations—cultural degeneration and deliquescence, the intertwining of sexuality and violence, the coalescence of art and madness—instituting themselves at the center of his imaginative project. *The Sacred Fount*, to cite but one example, can easily be identified as a decadent novel par excellence: in its equation between the acts of narration and sexual obsession and madness; in its imaging of human relations as a form of vampirism; even in the art that its characters gaze upon—the famous portrait of a man holding a mask that the narrator, Mrs. Server, Long, and Obert all gaze at is (as William Bysshe Stein has argued) a representation of a familiar icon of the fin de siècle, the harlequin Pierrot.[5]

James's airborne revelations, however, were never simple, and his response to the art of decadence was no exception. Thus, to continue to muse on *The Sacred Fount* in this context, James's representation

of Pierrot diverges considerably from those who populate the poetry
of Verlaine and Lionel Johnson. The Pierrot here is indeed something of a Johnsonian androgyne (the mask he has taken off, Obert
thinks, is that of a woman); and the moment does indeed ring with
Verlainesque intimations of mortality, if not morbidity (the painting,
Mrs. Server claims, ought to be called "the Mask of Death"). Yet at
the same time, James's allusion to this decadent icon places, as it were,
quotation marks around itself. This moment does not impart an interpretation of the picture so much as a reading of the reception of that
icon: a demonstration of the psychic processes that drive the novel's
fanatical overreaders to perform curious rites of appreciation in front
of this art:

> "It's the picture, of all pictures [the narrator says] that most needs an inter-
> preter. *Don't* we want," I asked of Mrs. Server, "to know what it means?" . . .
> "Yes, what in the world does it mean?" Mrs. Server replied. "One could call
> it—though that doesn't get one much further—the Mask of Death."
> "Why so?" I demanded while we all again looked at the picture. "Isn't it
> much rather the Mask of Life? It's the man's own face that's Death. The other
> one, blooming and beautiful—"
> "Ah, but with an awful grimace!" Mrs. Server broke in.
> "The other one, blooming and beautiful," I repeated, "is Life, and he's
> going to put it on; unless indeed he has just taken it off." [6]

The primary focus of the scene, of course, lies in glossing the interpretive obsessiveness of the novel's narrator; but it also seeks to place
his monomania in a broader context. The process of overreading here
includes not only the half-mad narrator but all the novel's characters,
caught up in the game of "reading" representations of Life and Death
but fully experiencing neither. It suggests as well the consequences of
this activity. In their supersubtle response to this picture, Mrs. Server
and the narrator simultaneously raise and lower the stakes of the game
of interpretation. Indeed, the stakes could hardly be higher: nothing short of Life and Death themselves seem to be at issue here. But
such matters are simultaneously deflated, rendered trivial as they are
made into aesthetic chatter, diminished further as they are reduced to
the mechanical gestures of taking a mask off or putting one on. The
scene thus moves from the hermeneutics of art appreciation to the
satire of aesthete hermeneuts, those who "want" to see everything in
this picture but the picture itself. But it also suggests, lurking behind
that satire, the larger anxieties that impel such interpretive efforts—
the unaskable and unanswerable questions of "life" and "death" such

maddening social games are meant simultaneously to raise and evade, to reveal and to mask.

As this example suggests, James's deployment of the decadent phase of aestheticism was, like his response to its predecessors, always complex and multiple, one that explores the terrain lying between high seriousness and satire, between a narrative incorporation of aestheticist impulses and insights and a critical distancing from them. These two impulses—impulses we have seen as early as *Roderick Hudson* and as late as *The Ambassadors*—battle with each other throughout the final turns of James's "major phase"; the compromises and reconciliations James effects between them create the terms on which he crafts his resolution to the problems posed by the aesthetic movement as a whole. I want here to turn to two different instances of that resolution, to *The Wings of the Dove* and *The Golden Bowl*. In these two novels, we find James attaching his narrative interrogation of aestheticism to two different manifestations of aestheticism's decadent phase: the notion of cultural decline and the association of woman with both interpretive enigmas and veiled violence. Both bring his career-long confrontation with the aesthetic movement to a vivid but dual conclusion; under the sign of decadence James first rejects and then triumphantly identifies himself with the most problematic elements of the entire range of discourse that marked British aestheticism.

The Wings of the Dove: *Aesthesis* and the Abyss

The trajectory I have traced above is perhaps most visible in *The Wings of the Dove*, for one of the most remarkable qualities of this remarkable novel is its encyclopedic range of allusions to—and its highly resonant and sophisticated deployment of—the entire imaginative achievement of British aestheticism. I have argued in Chapter 2 that the Venetian portion of the novel depends heavily not merely on direct allusions to Ruskin's vision of Venice as a mythic locus of the aspirations and decline of Western culture, but also on Ruskin and Charles Eliot Norton's gloomy diagnosis of the moral causes and consequences of that decline. But the novel's interest in aestheticism does not stop there. As I shall briefly suggest below, Milly's ekphrastic self-revelation in front of the Bronzino rewrites the scene so frequently dramatized in Pre-Raphaelite poetry: the confrontation of an individual subject with an image of a dead woman, a confrontation that leads (in Richard Stein's words) to a "fundamental reorientation of self."[7] Moreover, as I have suggested sketchily at the end of the last chapter, Milly's course of action through the novel can be understood as an extension of James's own highly Paterian exploration of the powers attained by a consciousness facing its own impending demise —the central conceit of the Conclusion to *The Renaissance*, and one which, when fully explicated by James in the Preface to *Wings*, sounds as if it could have been directly lifted from Pater's text. To conclude the catalogue, Milly's apotheosis as the "princess" is registered by an iconography of jewels, masks, and Byzantine mosaics that is both textually and historically grounded in the characteristic imagery of decadent art and poetry.

In all these cases, James's deployment of the imaginative structures of British aestheticism is self-conscious, self-defining, and—ultimately —self-critical. These allusions form, as John Goode has argued in one of the most impressive readings of *Wings*, the outlines of the distinctive "style"—literary style *and* style of life—that shape both the subject matter and the method of the novel.[8] It is the goal of these allusions, I want to suggest here, to gesture toward the complicitous relation between its characters' worldly aestheticism and that of James's own imaginative act. Steeped in the texts, the attitudes, the very *culture* of British aestheticism, the characters of this novel not only degrade its discourse into a species of cliché; they demonstrate the ways that aestheticism can allow for—can indeed accomplish—acts of imaginative and economic exploitation. This same process extends to James's text itself, whose nervous account of the return on its own narrative investment frequently figures itself in terminology and topoi lifted directly from the aestheticist tradition. In this sense, unlike *The Ambassadors* or even *The Golden Bowl*, *Wings*'s persistent echoings of aestheticist texts ring hollow; but their dull resonance helps the novel chime the true decadence only partially represented by the literary and artistic movement that identified itself with decline and decay. *The Wings of the Dove*, it might be argued, establishes itself as the ultimate decadent text because, more fully and more systematically than either the works of the British decadence or James's own *Sacred Fount*, it turns its sadomasochistic energies back on itself and ruthlessly critiques its own narrative and imaginative participation in a larger process of cultural decomposition.

However, the means through which James performs these multiple tasks are, at least initially, comic and ironic. For it is in the powerful—and persistently underrated—satirical dimension of this novel that British aestheticism first makes its presence felt. As he depicts the mores of Anglo-American bourgeois society, James demystifies the cult of "culture" and the "aesthetic" which, as we have seen, marked the emergence of the upper-middle-class elite in both England and America. The privileging of culture as a space separate from—and redemptive of—the gritty realities of the marketplace, and the simultaneous rise of market mechanisms designed to sell that culture to an increasingly large segment of the population; the social currency of the perceptions of Ruskin, Arnold, and Pater, and their corruption into a kind of meaningless mumbo jumbo that designates the user's cultural sophistication and nothing more; the increasing demand to possess—or at least possess a knowledge of—the canonized works of literature and art, and the brisk market that sprang up to supply this want: all these are brought into the novel through the enthusiastic vehicle of Mrs. Susan Shepherd Stringham.

Indeed, James's satirical energies are quite precisely aimed here. For by his portrayal of Susan, James brings into the novel a representative of the gentry elite who nourished aestheticism in fin de siècle America, and traces the arrival of that elite in the drawing rooms of late Victorian and early Edwardian England. Susan is herself an enthusiastic apparatchik in the cultural organizations that defined the American (which is to say Bostonian) gentry; she is a frequent contributor to the "best magazines" and a devoted reader of the court register of the Boston elite, *The Boston Evening Transcript.** When he deals with Susan's cultural affiliations, James often moves to the point of outright derision. "To *be* in truth literary had ever been her dearest thought, the thought that kept her bright nippers perpetually in position," he writes in his first full description of Susan (NY, 19: 107). It would seem that, in addition to being something of a second-rate Sarah Orne Jewett, Mrs. Stringham aspires to be something of a minor-league Henry James; seeking to place her "nippers" in the Jamesian position

*"When evening quickens faintly in the street, / Wakening the appetites of life in some / And to others bringing the *Boston Evening Transcript*" writes T. S. Eliot, reminding us that the *Transcript* played a powerfully defining role for the attenuated gentry for several generations after James's novel (Eliot, *The Complete Poems and Plays*, p. 66). The fortunes of that newspaper also provide a miniature history of the Boston elite; it rose to prominence along with them in the 1830's and early 1840's; gave voice to their abolitionist and Republican sentiments in the 1850's and 1860's; and continued thereafter to serve as a voice of liberal Republicanism and gentry culture. It is perhaps in the latter role that the *Transcript* is most relevant to James's text; the newspaper saw itself as an arbiter of the high-culture tradition and published some of the most sophisticated theater and music criticism of its time, although its literary criticism was more conservative. See Chamberlin, *The Boston Transcript*.

of intense gazing, however, Susan is so preoccupied with being literary
that she is incapable of doing literature.

The novel extends this satirical jab into a full-blown critique. For
the plot of the novel itself plots the demolition of Mrs. Stringham's
idealized notion of herself and her mission. Her "key of knowledge" to
Milly, we learn, "was felt to click in the lock from the moment it flashed
upon Mrs. Stringham that her friend had been starved for culture.
Culture was what she herself represented for her, and it was living
up to that principle that would surely provide the great business" (19:
109). The key of Mrs. Stringham's knowledge, however, clicks as well
on Milly's tomb, for it is as a direct result of this earnest but misguided
quest to bring "culture" to her charge that Susan Stringham delivers
Milly to the carnivores of Lancaster Gate. Moreover, the language
Susan employs here ironically adumbrates the nature of her mistake.
Mrs. Stringham is under the Arnoldian illusion that the realms of culture and commerce are wholly at odds with each other. If culture is a
great "business," it is only such in the sense of being a great "affair"—
the enterprise of expanding one's insights, honing one's perceptions,
and making the most of one's experience. "There are refinements,"
says Kate Croy, "I mean of consciousness, of sensation, of appreciation"; this, presumably, is much of what Susan means by culture (19:
99). But our awareness of the perversity of Kate's "refinements"—
which at this point in the novel include the gulling of Mrs. Lowder and
are soon to include the gulling of Milly—undercuts this exalted notion
of the cultural; her enthusiastic embrace of the commercial ethos similarly reminds us that the experience of culture, at least for the already
cultured, is part of the *real* business of life, a series of transactions in
which no holds are barred.

Through Susan, then, the novel sets out to demystify the cultural as
a criterion of value, to demonstrate what abysses lie beneath its veneer
and how complicit that culture has become—must become—in the
marketplace it claims to transcend. It is not surprising, therefore, that
from her first appearance, Susan adopts the position characteristic of
the Jamesian aesthete: she experiences Milly with the volatile mixture of detachment and involvement, appreciative disinterestedness
and thoroughgoing complicity, that we saw explored so fully in the
portrayal of characters like Gabriel Nash, Ralph Touchett, and Rowland Mallett. To make the link between this Jamesian problematic and
the tradition of British aestheticism even clearer, Susan connects her
vicarious experience of Milly with her reading of Pater when, using
the same rhetoric Ralph employs with Isabel, she claims that Milly's

"situation" transcends that of any literary or historical text: "This was poetry—it was also history—Mrs. Stringham thought, to a finer tune even than Maeterlinck and Pater, than Marbot and Gregorovius" (19: 111). Despite the fact that Milly is said to transcend no fewer than four writers (only Milton, in fact, seems adequate to figure her situation, and he is alluded to more indirectly, although no less powerfully, than are the likes of Pater and Maeterlinck), it is clear that Pater is for her first among equals, since the claim that Milly transcends Pater is made in the by now familiar Paterian diction we first saw creeping into James's work as early as *The Portrait of a Lady*. Thus, later we learn that "Mildred was the biggest impression of [Susan's] life"; that Milly gives off for Susan "impressions that of a sudden were apt to affect her as new"; that she sets off in Susan an "infinitely fine vibration" that had not "in any degree ceased"; that to learn of Milly's history was "to have had one's small world-space both crowded and enlarged" (19: 112, 115, 105, 111). Milly, in other words, plays for Susan the Paterian role of "startl[ing]" or "rous[ing]" her into acts of "sharp and eager observation"; she gives Susan impressions of such "fineness" and intensity as to arouse in her a "quickened sense of life," to give her what Pater says art gives the aesthete, "nothing but the highest quality to your moments as they pass, and simply for those moments' sake" (WP, 1: 236, 238, 239).

What I find most striking about this manifestation of the familiar Jamesian problematic of aestheticized voyeurism, however, is the edge that James gives to his critique. For in *Wings*, it is not just the observer figure who plays out the ambiguities of aestheticism; rather —even more so than in *Portrait*—it is the object of her observation who willingly—even eagerly—participates in them. For Milly no less than Susan adopts the aesthete's attitude, in a powerful if seemingly unconscious fulfillment of Susan's agenda. Thus her response to her first English dinner party rings with echoes of what Richard Ellmann memorably calls "Pater's piedpiping."[9] The scene records her "quickened perceptions," her "alertness of vision"; the way that "the very air of the place, the pitch of the occasion, had for her both so sharp a ring and so deep an undertone." "She had never," James tells us, "she might well believe, been in such a state of vibration; her sensibility was almost too sharp for her comfort" (19: 148). But its source subverts and thus satirizes Milly's English epiphany. It is one thing to resound with Paterian diction in front of St. Peter's and quite another to do so in the lair of Aunt Maud, surrounded by the likes of Lord Mark or the Bishop of Murrum, a man "with a complicated costume, a voice like an old-fashioned wind instrument, and a face all the portrait of a prelate" (19: 147).[10]

But Milly's unwitting and destabilizing fulfillment of Susan's aestheticized expectations for her does not begin with her entrance into the Manningham salon—or even with their Alpine journey, in which she plays out Susan's image of her as a Romantic traveler in the Alps; it seems, in fact, to have been initiated at some mysterious earlier point, perhaps even a point before she has met her refined friend. For, to complicate the text's rather contemptuous attitude toward Susan Shepherd Stringham, Milly seems already to have shaped herself fully in the contours of the Pre-Raphaelite imagination when Susan meets her charge:

> Mrs. Stringham was never to forget—for the moment had not faded, nor the infinitely fine vibration it set up in any degree ceased—her own first sight of the striking apparition, then unheralded and unexplained: the slim, constantly pale, delicately haggard, anomalously, agreeably angular young person, of not more than two-and-twenty summers, in spite of her marks, whose hair was somehow exceptionally red even for the real thing, which it innocently confessed to being, and whose clothes were remarkably black even for the robes of mourning, which was the meaning they expressed. (19: 105)

With her "black dress, her white face and her vivid hair" (19: 174), Milly's very appearance confirms the aestheticist epiphanies it sets off in Susan. The pallor, the haggardness, the slimness, the angularity, the dark robes, even (especially) the red hair are all the characteristic attributes of the Pre-Raphaelite woman as depicted by Millais, Burne-Jones, and, most crucially, Dante Gabriel Rossetti. Moreover, the unspoken fact that suffuses this account of Milly—that she is slowly, beautifully dying—is also thoroughly in the vein of the Pre-Raphaelite woman, who is often either dead (as in the case of Millais's *Ophelia*; Rossetti's *The Blessed Damozel*; and the anonymous subject of Rossetti's poem/painting, *The Portrait*, almost certainly his own wife, Elizabeth Siddal) or so ethereal as to be consigned to a state indistinguishable from death. The Pre-Raphaelite woman, in other words, comes to being under the sign of mortality; particularly in the death-obsessed work of Rossetti, she is envisioned as both the vehicle through which death is confronted and the means by which it may (or may not) be transcended. Milly clearly fulfills the first role throughout most of the novel; at its end, she also seems to fulfill the second.*

---

*Indeed, the language James uses here is quite similar to that he employed to describe the epitome of the Pre-Raphaelite woman, Jane Morris. Henry wrote Alice James in

Nor does this pattern limit itself to Milly's relations with Susan. Indeed, very soon after her epiphany of the dinner party, James allusively places Milly's self-fashioning within the context of British aestheticism, a process by which she acknowledges, and practically invites, the exploitation that is to follow at the hands of the novel's worldly aesthetes. I am referring to one of the great set pieces in the novel, Milly's encounter with the Bronzino portrait in the appropriately named country house, Matcham. While many critics have noted the scene's importance, few have commented on its remarkably precise allusiveness and the ways these allusions contribute to its effect.[11] For as we have seen, the transforming encounter between self and art object is a central—perhaps *the* central—topos of the aesthetic imagination in England. From Rossetti's *The Portrait* or *The Blessed Damozel* through Pater's *Renaissance* and even Wilde's *Dorian Gray*, the encounter between an alert, interrogating consciousness and a work of visual art has been a sustaining, even a defining, staple of the aesthetic movement—perhaps one of its very few characteristics that enable us to define it as an "aesthetic" movement at all.[12] And, as we also saw in Chapter 1, an entire battery of issues is brought to bear on this encounter—a series of polarities centering on the play of absence and presence, speech and silence, temporality and timelessness, ultimately even life and death. Rossetti's lyric, *The Portrait*, to cite a particularly rich example, displays in its opening stanza virtually all the qualities that define the aestheticist encounter with the artwork:

> This is her picture as she was:
>   It seems a thing to wonder on,
> As though mine image in the glass
>   Should tarry when myself am gone.
> I gaze until she seems to stir,—

1869, describing an evening spent at the Morrises' "A figure cut out of a missal . . . an apparition of fearful and wonderful intensity . . . a wonder. Imagine a tall lean woman in a long dress of some dead purple stuff, guiltless of hoops (or of anything else, I should say), with a mass of crisp black hair heaped into great wavy projections on each side of her temples, a thin pale face, a pair of strange sad, deep, dark Swinburnish eyes, with great thick black oblique brows, joined in the middle and tucking themselves away under her hair, a mouth like the 'Oriana' in our illustrated Tennyson, a long neck, without any collar, and in lieu thereof some dozen strings of outlandish beads—in fine Complete." There are a number of parallels between the details of appearance mentioned in these two descriptions—the "mass of hair, rolled and high," the long neck, the pallor, the full Tennysonian lips, the "outlandish" jewelry—but the most important similarity seems to be the two women's shared conjunction of sadness and beauty. Jane Morris's "strange, sad, deep, dark Swinburnish eyes" gaze, like Milly's eyes or like the eyes of the Bronzino portrait, on a life "unaccompanied by a joy" (*Letters*, 1: 93–94).

Until mine eyes almost aver
That now, even now, the sweet lips part
To breathe the words of the sweet heart:—
And yet the earth is over her. (DGR, 1: 240, ll. 1–9)

The portrait provides an emblem of loss, an icon of the absence of the beloved; yet somehow, transmuted in the mysterious alchemy of art and impelled by the poet's intense gaze, her memorialized image trembles on the threshold of speech, of life, of full and resonant being, only to collapse again into the frozen silence of death. The poem fully records the poet's parallel process of mourning, registering his movement from a narcissistic obsession with loss (her image is like his, frozen in a looking glass); his equally narcissistic desire to overcome it by means of a passionate, imagination-stirring gaze ("my eyes almost aver" that she is alive); and his collapse into recognition of the immutable facts of death itself ("and yet," despite his attempts imaginatively to revive his beloved, "the earth is over her").

The same process is enacted in Milly's encounter with the Bronzino:

Once more things melted together—the beauty and the history and the facility and the splendid midsummer glow: it was a sort of magnificent maximum, the pink dawn of an apotheosis coming so curiously soon. What in fact befell was that, as she afterwards made out, it was Lord Mark who said nothing in particular—it was she herself who said all. She couldn't help that—it came; and the reason it came was that she found herself, for the first moment, looking at the mysterious portrait through tears. Perhaps it was her tears that made it just then so strange and fair—as wonderful as he had said: the face of a young woman, all splendidly drawn, down to the hands, and splendidly dressed; a face almost livid in hue, yet handsome in sadness and crowned with a mass of hair, rolled back and high, that must, before fading with time, have had a family resemblance to her own. The lady in question, at all events, with her slightly Michael-angelesque squareness, her eyes of other days, her full lips, her long neck, her recorded jewels, her brocaded and wasted reds, was a very great personage—only unaccompanied by a joy. And she was dead, dead, dead. Milly recognized her exactly in words that had nothing to do with her. "I shall never be better than this." (19: 220)

Beginning, like the protagonist of Rossetti's *The Portrait*, with "tears" that seem to transform and fuse with the art object—"that *made* it just then so strange and fair"—Milly moves into a curious identification with the woman it portrays, whom indeed she views as a kind of "distant relative" of her own (this country house, indeed, is a place of "Matcham" in every sense). But Milly not only matches herself to the portrait; in doing so she paradoxically comes to what appears to be a fully individuated definition of herself. Through the recognition of the commonality between that woman's death and her own, Milly "recognized her exactly in words that had nothing to do with her"; but those words have everything to do with Milly's recognition of herself and of her existential predicament: "I shall never be better than this." The multiple ambiguity of Milly's demonstrative pronoun signifies the complexity of her realization; gesturing simultaneously toward the dead woman, the picture, and the moment at which Milly perceives both, it places all three in a complex network of similarity and difference by which Milly's deferential "recognition" of the dead noblewoman and her differential "re-cognition" of herself are irrevocably melded together.

Initially, then, we may find this moment moving and significant—a moment at which, as critics have argued of many of the aesthetic movement's ekphrases, an individual subject comes into a full recognition of the existential conditions of its own being through the heightened awareness wrought by the experience of art. Thus, Richard Stein suggests, an epiphanic moment of self-discovery is often the result of the aesthetic movement's obsessive staging of the confrontation between a witnessing subject and an aesthetic artifact. In this drama, the subject confronts an image that provokes, challenges, or forces it into a moment of insight, and through this "ritual of interpretation," the aestheticist imagination creates "a fundamental reorientation of self" —a conversion wrought through the experience of art (12). So too, it would seem, with Milly. After Milly swoons before the Bronzino—just as Rossetti's protagonist swoons before his beloved's portrait or Dorian Gray swoons before his own image—she awakens to a new sense of her self and of the world she inhabits.

None of these moments, however, are as simple as Stein's ego-oriented analytic would seem to suggest. For if in aestheticist literature the self is "discovered" or created through the confrontation between a supple and aesthetically sensitive consciousness and a work of art, then one of the things that such an obsessively replayed scene suggests is the tenuousness of the self whose creation is thus recorded. These scenes record an aesthetic version of the process Jacques Lacan refers to as the "mirror phase": a moment at which the self grasps itself as an entity by means of its perception of a specular image or double. And as Lacan has so influentially suggested, such a mechanism of identity formation perpetually places in question the "authenticity" or wholeness of that newly formed self. When the guarantee of psychic autonomy is located outside the self, the subject comes to self-awareness under the sign of paranoia, perpetually shadowed by the uneasy sense that the very source of what seems to be its genuine identity is to be located outside it. More important, the subject has good reason to be paranoid, since to Lacan the mirror stage marks the subject's movement from the "imaginary" into the "symbolic"—that is, from a purely experienced identification with an undifferentiated other to a more "mature," if equally fictive, identification with the order of "rationality" associated with language, sexual difference, and the Law.

It is precisely this paranoid scenario that marks aestheticism's scenes of ekphrastic identity formation. Thus, to return to our earlier examples, *Dorian Gray* enacts the fear of a loss of identity to a visual representation of the self—a representation that literally embodies what Lacan calls "the Law," the principles of moral behavior that Dorian has attempted to abandon. Similarly, the subjects of Rossetti's ekphrastic lyrics feel themselves overwhelmed by the greater authenticity and vitality of the absent figure represented in a work of art—whether a representation of their beloved, of a mythical God, or of a dead woman.* I want to suggest that the same scenario is played out in Milly's encounter with the Bronzino. What initially appears to be a moment of existential self-discovery actually turns out to be a moment of specular doubling, a moment in which Milly constructs her "self" in imitation of an aesthetic icon, an artistic Other. For from this moment on, she embarks on a course of specular self-imaging in imitation of that image. Milly's journey into the Symbolic, one might say, is accomplished by her increasing determination, evidenced from this moment forward, to transform herself into a symbol, a mute aesthetic signifier that can be "appreciated" and thereafter appropriated by all who encounter her. She transforms herself into the very image of the Bronzino portrait—which is to say that she initiates a process that can only climax in her re-creation of herself as a beautiful, fully aestheticized corpse.

Indeed, this process has already begun. As I have suggested with respect to *The Sacred Fount*, one of the defining characteristics of the

---

*One might also observe the prevalence among the aesthetes themselves of the paranoia that marks the Lacanian analytic of the mirror stage: Rossetti was, at the end of his life, quite literally paranoid, convinced that Robert Browning and Lewis Carroll had crafted a conspiracy against him that included virtually all the Victorian intelligentsia; Ruskin, too, suffered from paranoia in the later stages of his dementia—his particular form of mania being the conviction that his shadow would eventually overtake and then strangle him. And Wilde may be said to have brilliantly and perversely crafted his own persecution: he proved not only the truth of the apothegm that paranoids have real enemies, but also the psychoanalytic banality that they help create them.

Jamesian *ekphrasis* is James's vigilant awareness of the larger social context in which that scene takes place. Unlike the aestheticist *ekphrasis*, where the visible universe shrinks to the art observer and the artwork unified in the intensity of a transfixing gaze, James habitually emphasizes the communal nature of aesthetic reception and interpretation. So, too, in this scene Milly's "self-realization" through the experience of art is also depicted as a moment at which she is "realized" by others —at which she is made by them into a version of the artwork that she perceives. Lord Mark, after all, has led her to the Bronzino precisely as an acknowledgement of her resemblance to it; her aesthetic epiphany has hardly finished before she is herself confronted by the aggressively banal Lord and Lady Aldershaw, who look at her "quite as if Milly had been the Bronzino and the Bronzino only Milly" (19: 223). Milly's self-aestheticization mirrors, and may be said to internalize, the aestheticization of her that Aunt Maud's set performs. But at the heart of that aestheticization, as Milly so spectacularly fails to realize, lies their particular vision of art. While the inhabitants of Matcham may see Milly as a Bronzino, they also see the Bronzino as nothing more than a social signifier, a piece of party chitchat at best, a piece in a connoisseur's collection at worst. So too—and all the more powerfully—with Milly: to see her as a Bronzino is to define her as an object of cultural and economic exchange. She, like the portrait itself, is an "acquisition": the characters who "appreciate" her beauty most vociferously are those who are most eager to annex her fortune to their own. When Milly comes to see herself in these very terms, therefore, she offers herself up to the same forms of understanding and vision that are deployed to victimize her. Indeed, much of the pathos of the novel inheres in the contrast between the aestheticism Milly internalizes and that with which she is actually confronted: Milly at least seems to insist on treating herself and others in the generous and ennobled spirit of an idealized aestheticism that she has falsely introjected from those around her, not the commodifying aestheticism that Aunt Maud's circle deploys the better to exploit her.

To a certain extent, Milly remains within the ambit of this idealized aestheticism until the end of the novel, by which point she succeeds in fully transforming herself into an aesthetic sign—a "symbol of differences," to use Merton's phrase, who first signifies economic difference and then is transformed into a sign of moral difference as well (20: 219). But while the novel clearly pushes itself toward this idealizing conclusion, there is also a substantial impulse in it to demonstrate that Milly has learned to deploy the less attractive aspects of aestheticism she encounters at Matcham. The Bronzino paradigm is repeated frequently throughout the middle portions of the novel, but as Milly adapts herself to the aesthetic mediations that other characters offer her, she also comes increasingly to internalize the more equivocal elements of their aestheticism—their valorizing of artful and ambiguous surfaces; their euphemistic and hypocritical cant of "beauty"; their deployment of this idealizing jargon to further their exploitative schemes.

The clearest example of this process is offered in the novel's unfolding of its master trope, that of the dove. For when Kate renames Milly in the resonant image of the "dove"—a process that, to drive home the novel's nexus between aestheticization and commodification and to underscore the fact that Kate does, as she says late in the novel, "play fair" with Milly, follows Milly's resolute noncomprehension of the sordid truths Kate has just explained to her ("We're of no use to you. . . . You'd be of use to us. . . . You mustn't pay too dreadfully for poor Mrs. Stringham's having let you in. . . . Oh you may very well loathe me yet" [19: 281–82])—Milly breathes in that name and makes it her own: "It was moreover, for the girl, like an inspiration: she found herself accepting as the right one, while she caught her breath with relief, the name so given her. . . . *That* was what was the matter with her. She was a dove. Oh *wasn't* she?" (19: 283). Indeed, Milly sets out to remodel herself in the term of that image; she speaks to Maud in the same "tone of the fondest indulgence—almost, really, that of dove cooing to dove" with which Maud speaks to her, then sees written in her face "the measure of the success she could have as a dove" (19: 284). Here, as throughout this portion of the novel, the terms of Milly's perception of others and of her fashioning of herself are melded together; but as part of that process, Milly internalizes aspects of Kate and Aunt Maud's "dovelike" behavior that are antithetical to the seeming innocence and vulnerability suggested by that image. The signifier "dove" here suggests more than the beautiful docility Kate means by the term. That Milly can see Aunt Maud's cooing as a version of the "dovelike" suggests that the "dovelike" can mean for Milly the elegant and euphemizing hypocrisies of Lancaster Gate speech. From this moment on, Milly demonstrates how well she has learned the lesson. She adopts Kate and Maud's elegant and ambiguous diction; masters their idiom of dress and language of gesture; begins, most powerfully of all, to lie. If Milly becomes a dove—and the novelist as well as his characters insists that she does—then she not only becomes a dove of Peace, a dove of Spirit, or even a dove of Beauty: she also becomes a dove of worldly, economic power. *"Yet shall ye be as* the wings of a dove," says the Psalms, and then continues, in the admixture of economic and aesthetic language the novel grimly adopts as its own distinctive idiom: "Though ye have lain among the pots, *yet shall ye be as* the wings of a dove covered with silver, and her feathers with yellow gold" (Ps. 68:13).

With Milly's transformation into a dove, we may have seemed to have wafted downwind from the question of the novel's relation with British aestheticism. But in truth, we have only posed the question of that relation in an even more problematical form. The question we are facing here is the same we have been confronting throughout our investigation of the novel's deployment of the topoi of British aestheticism: that of the relation between aestheticization and exploitation, beauty and profit, the quickened consciousness and the quickening of worldly power. The novel grounds this relation in the cultural milieu of aestheticism first to identify with satirical specificity the social provenance of this habit of thought, then to extend that identification beyond the mere specifics of Susan Stringham or Aunt Maud's cultural affiliations to the principles underlying Milly's self-fashioning. It is thus dismayingly convenient for my purposes that the lines I have just quoted to gloss James's novel played an important role in the master text of British aestheticism itself; in the fourth edition of Pater's *Renaissance*, the line "Yet shalt ye be as the wings of a dove" was added as an epigraph.

The implications of James's and Pater's shared allusion are multiple, reminding us of the extensive commonalities of imagination and interest between James's novel and Pater's Conclusion; Milly's quest to live intensely, if vicariously, before her impending death puts her in the exact same position as the Paterian aesthete, whose quickened consciousness comes into being under the injunction to experience the greatest number of sensations "before evening" (WP, 1: 237). But this text, far more than James's earlier deployments of Pater, diverges from the powerful paradigm of the Conclusion. We can measure the extent of that diversion by remembering that James explicates the germ or "motive behind" the text in his 1907 Preface to *Wings* in terms that seem virtually to paraphrase Pater's text:

The idea, reduced to its essence, is that of a young person conscious of a great capacity for life, but early stricken and doomed, condemned to die under short respite, while also enamoured of the world; aware moreover of the condemnation and passionately desiring to "put in" before extinction as many of the finer vibrations as possible, and so achieve, however briefly and brokenly, the sense of having lived. (NY, 19: v)

Having considered the Paterian dimensions of *Portrait* and *The Ambassadors*, it would be superfluous to emphasize the extraordinary similarity between the "very old—if I shouldn't perhaps rather say a very young—motive" behind James's novel (19: v) and the carpe diem motifs of Pater's; nor would it be fully profitable at this point to underline the extraordinary verbal similarities between the Jamesian language of "finer vibrations" and that of Pater's "finer ideal" and "more intense vibrations." Rather, what I wish to underscore at this point is the extraordinary *worldliness* of this novel's Paterianism. For here, as opposed to *Portrait* or even *The Ambassadors*, aestheticism brings not only the worldly engagement of a consciousness engorged with sense data but also serves as a force to be reckoned with in the world of social power. Thus when Milly herself takes up the Paterian injunction to put in as many sensations as possible before nightfall—when she discovers that "it was more appealing, insinuating, irresistible in short, that one would live if one could"—she imagines herself not in the idealized terms of imaginative freedom or spiritual expansiveness Pater deploys and James takes over from him, but rather in the unsparingly economic terms of Kate Croy and Aunt Maud (19: 254). She compares her situation to that of the "poor girl—with her rent to pay . . . staring before her in a great city" (19: 253). The metaphor has scandalized critics—Goode is particularly harsh on it—and perhaps justifiably so; Milly's sentimental comparison of herself to a "poor girl" elides the social and economic disparities she unwittingly profits from —and whose maintenance James's equation between living fully and spending freely buys into.[13] Yet the particular shock this passage elicits results from more than just the scandal of James's social and economic deficiencies; it is elicited by the passage's undermining of the moral distinctions the novel elsewhere seems to rely upon. To witness Milly profiting from poverty of others, employing them as convenient metaphors for her own existential condition, is to recognize her indulgence in the very processes by which she is herself exploited. This recognition leads to a kind of moral slippage, an ethical indeterminacy. For the novel's emphasis on the grim economic fates facing Kate and Merton plays off Milly's economic voyeurism in this scene to suggest that Milly's particular form of vicarious exploitation is in some senses more disturbing than Kate and Merton's more overt form of profiteering; Kate, at least, never loses sight of what she is doing, and the reader never loses sight of why.

James advances this scandalous revision of the Paterian paradigm by continuing to underscore the equivocal nature of Milly's actions.

Immediately after her walk through Regent's Park, Milly performs two acts we have seen associated with the novel's worldly aesthetes. She begins to lie: first to Susan, whom she has successfully deceived in going off to Sir Luke with Kate, and whom she more generally deceives by adopting Kate as her new companion and friend; then to Kate, to whom she repeats the words of Sir Luke but not her supervening knowledge that his very solicitousness signifies to so "devilishly subtle" a patient that all is far from well (19: 253). More to the point, she uses the very euphemizing language of Lancaster Gate aestheticism to accomplish these lies: "Oh it's all right," she tells Kate, "[Sir Luke's] lovely" (19: 258); then paraphrases his advice as a call to what Pater might have called the higher hedonism:

> "I'm to go in for pleasure."
> "Oh, the duck!"—Kate, with her own shades of familiarity, abounded. "But what kind of pleasure?"
> "The highest," Milly smiled.
> Her friend met it as nobly. "Which *is* the highest?"
> "Well, it's just our chance to find out. You must help me."
> "What have I wanted to do but help you," Kate asked, "from the moment I first laid eyes on you?" (19: 260)

In this scene, as in many scenes throughout the middle of the novel, Milly and Kate seem to exchange identities; when Milly asks Kate for the help that she has already offered, she not only opens herself up to Kate's exploitative plot (the clearest gloss on "help" here), but also signals her willingness to use Kate's superior knowledge and refinement for her own ends, her own "pleasure." Milly's tone here is a bantering one, it is true, yet her playfulness ought not obviate the Kate-like nature of Milly's endeavor; she seeks to use Kate's qualities—her refinement, her friendship, even her love—to supply her with the sense of having lived that she has hitherto missed. Kate is being painfully exploitative when she offers to "help" Milly, but Milly is being equally exploitative when she helps herself to what is Kate's.

This point is driven home throughout the rest of the novel, suggested not only through the plot but through the novel's patterns of allusion and figuration. Even—indeed, especially—when it turns from London to Venice, the novel continues to invoke the terminology and topoi of British aestheticism, as if to employ the history of that movement as a kind of map on which Milly's progress through the novel may be charted. If early in the novel Milly is compared (and compares herself) to a Pre-Raphaelite woman and later is measured against the possibilities of Paterian aestheticism, in the second third of the novel,

she is problematically depicted through—and invests herself with—
the characteristic iconography of the decadent phase of British aestheticism. Here is a typical example from early in book 7, in a scene
in which Milly and Kate, newly established in Venice, encounter and
evade each other in the exquisite pas de deux that mimics the dance
of death they perform throughout the latter half of the novel:

> [Their] puttings-off of the mask had finally quite become the form taken
> by their moments together, moments indeed not increasingly frequent and
> not prolonged, thanks to the consciousness of fatigue on Milly's side when-
> ever, as she herself expressed it, she got out of harness. They flourished their
> masks, the independent pair, as they might have flourished Spanish fans; they
> smiled and sighed on removing them; but the gesture, the smiles, the sighs,
> strangely enough, might have been suspected the greatest reality in the busi-
> ness. Strangely enough, we say, for the volume of effusion in general would
> have been found by either on measurement to be scarce proportional to the
> paraphernalia of relief. It was when they called each other's attention to their
> ceasing to pretend, it was then that what they were keeping back was most
> in the air. There was a difference, no doubt, and mainly to Kate's advantage:
> Milly didn't quite see what her friend could keep back, was possessed of, in
> fine, that would be so subject to retention; whereas it was comparatively plain
> sailing for Kate that poor Milly had a treasure to hide. This was not the trea-
> sure of a shy, an abject affection—concealment, on that head, belonging to
> quite another phase of such states; it was much rather a principle of pride
> relatively bold and hard, a principle that played up like a fine steel spring
> at the lightest pressure of too near a footfall. Thus insuperably guarded was
> the truth about the girl's own conception of her validity; thus was a wonder-
> ing pitying sister condemned wistfully to look at her from the far side of the
> moat she had dug round her tower. Certain aspects of the connexion of these
> young women show for us, such is the twilight that gathers about them, in
> the likeness of some dim scene in a Maeterlinck play; we have positively the
> image, in the delicate dusk, of the figures so associated and yet so opposed, so
> mutually watchful: that of the angular pale princess, ostrich-plumed, black-
> robed, hung about with amulets, reminders, relics, mainly seated, mainly still,
> and that of the upright, restless slow-circling lady of her court who exchanges
> with her, across the black water streaked with evening gleams, fitful questions
> and answers. (20: 138–39)

This passage fairly bristles with allusions to ostentatiously decadent art and literature, capped by its knowing reference to Maeterlinck's *Blue Bird* but by no means limiting itself to that text. Indeed,
the Maeterlinck allusion is perhaps less central than those that pre-
cede and follow it. The text evokes with equal self-consciousness the
icon of the mask, which so fascinated the decadent imagination, and
its intent in doing so, which is fairly close to Oscar Wilde's when

the latter argued for what he called "the truth of masks" (*Artist*, pp. 408–32). James's text here underlies what Wilde meant by that paradoxical trope (and what Max Beerbohm meant when he made these points even more explicitly in his 1896 essay, *A Defence of Cosmetics*): "sincerity" and its correlative "truth" are themselves only the most thorough masking devices; revelation is only a more sophisticated form of deceit; the putting off of one mask is only the putting on of another, more compelling disguise. James moves from this one highly resonant trope to another favorite topos of aestheticist art, one discernable in England from Tennyson through the Pre-Raphaelites to Beardsley and Wilde (and, as we have seen, a staple of the American commercial art of Maxfield Parrish as well): that of the isolated, embowered woman—the woman locked away in a tower like the Lady of Shalott, withdrawn from the world like Mariana of the moated grange. Here again, the allusion is fairly straightforward, if somewhat ironical; the "treasure" Kate sees Milly as hiding in her dark tower is, of course, her literal treasure as well as a figuration for that which serves as the means of gaining access to it: the definitive knowledge about her fate that Milly gradually unfolds to Kate and that Kate equally gradually uses to entrap Milly. But from this allusion, the text rapidly moves on to another, more interestingly problematic version of the aestheticist woman. Bejewelled, berobed, and beplumed, Milly appears at the end of the paragraph not as a Mariana-like victim but as her more powerful sister; she appears here dressed in the costume of the decadent *belle dame sans merci*.

More than any of its companions, this allusion does complicated and multiple work. To a certain extent, of course, its implications are again ironical. If Milly appears as a somewhat more fully dressed version of Gustave Moreau or Aubrey Beardsley's Salome (or of any number of the other similarly attired women who populate fin de siècle art), she still seems as far removed as possible from the lush, cruel femininity of such a character: sexually, she is an innocent; emotionally, she is a victim. Ironically, perhaps even sardonically, it is her companion in the scene to whom the qualities of the *belle dame* seem most fully to adhere. Yet at the same time, this identification works to complicate the straightforward moral schema such a formulation invokes. This invocation of decadent iconography undercuts the facile and sentimental moralism the text elsewhere invites us to bring to Milly by reminding us that despite her impending victimization, Milly possesses to a considerable degree the most important characteristic of the *belle dame*: a considerable amount of power. Her power is emphasized in James's

narration of the scene; here, Milly remains at the center of James's
visual composition as Kate circles around her, fixed, one assumes, by
the exchange of "questions" and "answers"—by the ambiguity created
by Milly's withdrawal behind the "moat" of her silence and her own
desire for definitive knowledge of Milly's condition and affections. The
specific means of the operation of Milly's power are also delineated by
the decadent icons James alludes to. Her jewels suggest that it is economic in nature—Milly's wealth, to put the matter quite simply, gives
her the ability to control others, as she fully discovers by the end of
her life. And the mask implies that Milly's power is generated by her
ambiguous theatricality—her ability, evident from this moment in the
text on, to deploy the idiom of gesture and the language of dress to
play for Kate, for Densher, even for Lord Mark, the roles they have
cast her in without ever letting them (or the reader) know whether she
has consciously adopted these parts. Her fortune combines with her
sphinxlike mysteriousness and her retreat behind the theatrical mask
to create the paradox of Milly's power: the more she withdraws from
the social world she has entered, the more power she is able to wield in
it. Through her conflation of such attributes, Milly makes all the characters of the novel, even—especially—those who set out most fully to
exploit her, revolve around her in versions of the nervous orbit Kate
describes in this scene.

Such implications have more than a local significance. Briefly to
summarize the complicated work performed by James's invocation of
ostentatiously decadent iconography in this scene—and elsewhere in
the text—we may say that Milly is presented as at once the antithesis
and the fulfillment of the decadent *belle dame*; and that this presen-
tation sets the stage for her actions throughout the rest of the novel.
The clearest example of this occurs at the novel's end, when Milly
deploys both her economic power and her power of resonant gesticu-
lation to act from beyond the grave and endow Merton Densher with
her fortune. For at that moment, she acts as both the antitype and
the fulfillment of the decadent "dark lady." Milly seeks to employ her
wealth to endow Densher and Kate with precisely the "mercy" that the
belle dame withholds; but by doing so, she ironically deals those lovers
precisely the cruel blow it is the *belle dame*'s mission to impart. Merton's
subsequent idealization of Milly as the redemptive innocent and his
recasting of Kate in the role of the femme fatale ("I'm in your power,"
he announces to her, as if she exerted the *belle dame*'s hypnotic force
in the midst of a situation he himself has structured [20: 401]) seems
to split these two qualities apart, but by its bold conflation of the icon-

ography of the innocent American Girl and the decadent dark lady, James undermines the dichotomies Densher's moralism relies upon. Through this iconography, his text resolutely brings into taut symmetry with each other such seeming antinomies as "mercy" and "cruelty" or "love" and "revenge," suggesting thereby that Milly is to be understood as a character capable of deploying the powers of victimization even as she is victimized by power.

But the implications of this imagery do not stop here. If the invocation of decadent iconography fruitfully complicates our understanding of Milly, such a gesture also points toward a similarly complex unveiling of James's authorial powers. Its rapid-fire series of aesthetic allusions draws a close connection between James's authorial act and the acts performed by—delegated to?—his characters. If earlier in the text we have been asked to note dismissively the aestheticization of Milly performed by Susan and to note as well Milly's own eager adoption of this ritual, here we are asked to witness James's authorial indulgence in this same imaginative habit. Such a movement is of course implicit in the very proliferation of aesthetic references in the scene, which mimics both Susan's aestheticizing of Milly and Milly's aestheticizing of herself. But the point is more powerfully driven home by the text's narrative method. What is most immediately noteworthy in this moment is its suggestion that the author is enmeshed in the same epistemological predicament that faces his characters. Indeed, there is a precise correlation between his and their response to the problem of apprehending Milly. As Kate, Merton, Lord Mark, and Aunt Maud all variously discover the difficulty of fully appreciating Milly's situation and then search for literary or visual texts with which to gloss it, so too the narrator claims to be hindered or blocked in his attempt to represent Milly and to require a text to help him penetrate or illuminate the darkness that surrounds her—finding it, to heighten the irony, in the same text it has earlier so unsparingly satirized one of its characters for adopting.

Through its knowing invocations of decadent iconography and through its anatomizing of the processes whereby such iconography is invoked, the text stresses its own complicity with the acts of imaginative exploitation its characters perform. In doing so, of course, it raises one of the most fundamental questions of Jamesian fiction, one critics have been wrestling with for two generations: the precise implications of James's overt unveiling of the problematic nature of his own narrative procedures. The first and most influential of such critiques was Laurence Holland's; arguing most powerfully with respect to precisely the issues we have been discussing in *Wings*, Holland demonstrates that the text's own "framing" or aestheticizing of Milly performs a fatal and irrevocable betrayal of her similar to—and perhaps even more horrific than—Densher's, and that such acts of betrayal are implicit in the logic of James's narrative itself. More recently, Mark Seltzer has taken Holland's argument one step further, arguing that the unveilings of James's authorial will to power Holland points to are themselves only the most intricate and imaginative ruses of power —the most insidiously effective means by which power normalizes itself, portrays itself as an inevitable, impersonal feature of the order of things.[14] While I obviously agree with (and am indebted to) the thrust of both of these arguments, I would also assert that the moments we have been discussing in *Wings* complicate such critical gestures. They allow us to place James's revelation of his own authorial complicities in a broader, more historically precise context, and to delineate the peculiar valences of James's position within that context. For I would suggest that it is through its persistent allusions to, and its highly sophisticated deployment of, the art and literature of the British aesthetic movement that the novel simultaneously places itself in and comments on the tradition of Anglo-American aestheticism itself; and that doing so allows James to measure the *cultural* powers and limitations of the act his own novel inscribes.

Earlier we have seen one dimension of this process in the text's frequent citations of the Nortonian/Ruskinian rhetoric of cultural criticism. As I suggested in Chapter 2, Densher's confrontation with a "Venice all of evil" temporarily allows James to strike the Ruskinian stance of the Victorian sage, of the artist as social critic engaged in the ruthless anatomizing of the failures of his civilization and issuing the prophetic call for individual and social transformation. But moments like the one I have been discussing here suggest the difficulties implicit in such acts of transcendent cultural critique. They suggest that not only James's imaginative act but the very rhetoric that underwrites that act cannot long be sustained, because the moral assertions that such rhetoric relies upon have already collapsed. Elsewhere in the novel, James extends this problematic further, and turns it in an explicitly cultural direction that ultimately seeks to interrogate the social possibilities and deficiencies of his own fiction. He does so by supplementing both the language of moral denunciation and the destabilizing iconography of aestheticism with an explicit turn to the language that underlay the late nineteenth century's frequent invocations of both: the terms, that is, of the conflict between the values of civilization and those of barbarism.[15] If the issues of decadence are posed on the level of the subject by Milly and on the level of the social whole by the novel's Ruskinian rhetoric of cultural decline, its concern with the relation between the novelist's own act and that of the larger forces of culture and society are suggested by the complicitous links the text establishes between the journalist Merton Densher and the novelist Henry James.

For as a journalist with aspirations to profundity, Merton frequently muses throughout the novel on the question of cultural decline, and as he does so, initiates an expanding chain of complicity that includes first Densher himself and then the author who has created him. When, to pick the most spectacular example, Merton pauses to meditate, as a journalistic observer, on the "purely expeditious and rough-and-tumble nature of the social boom" occasioned by Milly's appearance in London, James simultaneously employs Merton to condemn that social world, to condemn its condemner, and to condemn himself (20: 43). "So he judged at least, within his limits," James observes, "and the idea that what he had thus caught in the fact was the trick of fashion and the tone of society went so far as to make him take up again his sense of independence. He had supposed himself civilised; but if this was civilisation—! One could smoke one's pipe outside when twaddle was within" (20: 44). James permits himself one of his many authorial intrusions here in order to remind us of Densher's manifold limitations: his weakness, his petulantly asserted but essentially specious "sense of independence," and, most important, his own "expeditious" forgetting of his complicity in the object of his critique. For of course Densher cannot so easily separate himself from the exploitative machinations of London high society. He is doubly caught up in it: caught up as a journalistic observer who helps record and promote the "boom" he despises; caught up even more powerfully in the plots and counter-plots that characterize this corrupt and violent social world by virtue of his passive participation in Kate's unfolding schemes. His recourse to silence is the sign of his evasiveness, his disingenuous distancing of himself from full consciousness of, much less acceptance of his responsibility for, the actions he himself performs. But it also suggests the impossibility of adopting any other attitude. For when civilization is defined as a perfected or fully achieved deployment of language and "barbarism" as a species of degraded or fallen speech, then the would-be cultural critic faces a situation where the only morally worthy speech is silence itself. The barbarians stand within the gates—indeed, they have occupied more than Lancaster Gate: they have captured the aesthetic, the literary, even, finally the linguistic means of expression, as the novel's systematic unveiling of the exploitative social dimension of these seemingly autonomous spheres has suggested. But silence itself has become sullied, corrupt; it represents not a protest of but an acquiescence to the very conditions one rebels against—a slippage suggested first by Densher's unfinished assertion, then his suggestion that one can (only?) signify one's contempt by moving from the drawing room to the smoking parlor. It is perhaps hardly necessary to emphasize that James's own narrative silence places him in the exact same position as his character; while he can sidestep Densher's dilemma to a certain extent by attacking him (just as Densher relieves himself of his own sense of guilty participation in Lancaster Gate by condemning it), the result of that attack is only to reinforce the homology between the positions of the author and character.

The familiar Jamesian thematic of complicity, therefore, also serves the function of cultural criticism—and a cultural criticism that includes in its purview the efforts of the cultural critic him- or herself, whose very means of expression are caught up in the phenomenon the critic wishes to decry. It is this movement I would mean to gesture toward when I identify the novel as the ultimate decadent text, for unlike so many works of so-called decadence, which with critics like Max Nordau sought to exempt themselves from this cultural deliquescence or with Wilde reveled in it, James's text simultaneously turns its energies of cultural outrage outward and inward, delineating both the dimensions of cultural decline and the inevitable participation of his own imaginative act in that deliquescence. To a certain extent, as I suggested above, such a gesture works toward the unveiling of the mystifying powers of narrative itself, or, as Seltzer would put it, the narrative ruses by which power mystifies itself. But to a larger extent, I think, it takes as its central goal the inculpation of the particular sort of narratve James was writing. It sounds the death knell for the kinds of cultural narrative central to the aesthetic movement, the narrative James himself adopted from that movement and promulgated in turn: a narrative of cultural decline and redemption which suggested that an aesthetically supple, culturally advanced, and intellectually sophisticated consciousness could escape through the very perfection of its being from the larger processes of social decomposition; that, in fact, such an educated and heightened consciousness could provide a redemptive example for its degraded world. The dream James shared with Ruskin, Pater, and Wilde of a high culture at once socially redemptive and highly pitched is shown by the novel as an empty one, confuted by the detritus of contemporary Venice, and the degeneration of the language of aestheticism into the mumbo jumbo of social exploitation. But that dream is also shown even more problematically to have become melded to its seeming opposite, a social sphere grounded in acts of acquisition and exploitation; this realization, at first limited to characters the novel overtly satirizes, extends out from them to include all of its dramatis personae and, ultimately, the author as would-be cultural critic himself.

By this analysis, the novel must finally be judged something of a failure—the very judgment James himself articulated, in his characteristic terminology of formal analysis, by suggesting that the novel's center was misplaced, its "makeshift middle" ineffectually jury-rigged (19: xviii). Yet the novel's persistent interrogation of the aestheticist tradition offers us a different, a more complicated, terminology with which to describe the peculiar awkwardnesses of this text, and to reach a more acute judgment on them. For the simultaneous identification of aestheticism with social critique (in its Ruskinian phases) and the collapse of that critique (in its decadent moments) suggests that the novel is missing more than a formal center; that it is lacking any discursive centeredness, any grounding in a larger tradition of analysis that would allow James to accomplish the acts of cultural criticism he so earnestly wishes to perform. And James faces more than just a lack of rhetorical funding; rather, his novel rather bravely faces the possibilities that the only values he can invoke to accomplish this critique are part of the problem it anatomizes. Culture, we discover in *Wings*, is anarchy; civilization is barbarism; aestheticization is exploitation; imaginative freedom is the will to control; beauty is ugliness; love —even the most radiantly sacrificial love—is indistinguishable from cruelty.[16]

It is to this series of gloomy equations that I attribute the novel's ostensible formal failures. When it seeks to bring those equivalences under its symmetrical control, to fuse them into the perfect form of the fully realized Jamesian novel, it—mercifully—cannot, for the very terms by which it has structured the argument identify this accomplishment as the means by which the very decline it anatomizes has been wrought. In other words, unlike Holland, I do not think that the novel "betrays" Milly by aestheticizing her, but rather that it remains true to its own grim vision by refusing to follow her lead, to imitate her self-aestheticization. Symmetry in this text is a temptation and beauty a lure, as the novel's hauntingly ugly ending—in which Kate rewrites Milly's text in her own language yet again and Densher transforms her generous bequest into a test for his own lover—reminds us one last time. The novel's resistance to the kind of aestheticization Milly strives for—its demonstration, in fact, of the deeply disturbing consequences of her transformation of herself into a beautiful artifact—expresses itself in the kinds of formal awkwardnesses and eccentricities James mourns in his Preface. For it is only through such formal ruptures that the novel can gesture toward its resistance to its own dark knowledge. In other words, as in so many works of the aesthetic movement itself, it is the very formal awkwardness of this text that serves as its ultimate, and most compelling, aesthetic justification.

Given the severity of James's will to symmetry, such a position was not long tenable, as his next novel, *The Golden Bowl*, demonstrates with grim zeal. In that novel, as in *Wings*, the tradition of British aestheticism is persistently and powerfully invoked; and these allusions serve to bring together a number of moral and social qualities into new, and problematic, combinations. But there is no sign of the resistance James demonstrated in *Wings* to that process; rather, he seems to revel in the very phenomena that troubled his earlier novel, and, indeed, James's entire encounter with the tradition of British aestheticism. Thus as it builds its perfectly wrought ivory tower (or pagoda) on the asymmetrical platform of *Wings*, this novel brings James's career-long dialogue with the tradition of British aestheticism to its problematical climax.

The Golden Bowl and the Triumph of Aestheticism

A full delineation of *The Golden Bowl*'s response to British aestheticism, however, would be at once daunting and superfluous. No other Jamesian text engages itself so deeply with the specifics of British aestheticism, to be sure. Yet as it does so, this novel succeeds only in perversely if brilliantly retracing the path of James's earlier investigations of the subject. The movement from connoisseurship to *aesthesis* traced by *Portrait*; the linkage between amplitude of consciousness and the experience of loss proposed by *The Ambassadors*; the nexus between aesthetic idealization and worldly power delineated by *Wings*: all these are put on full display in this novel, and, it seems, with a certain blithe serenity.

It is, accordingly, that last quality I wish to focus on here: the apparent regressiveness of this text, its desire to return—one last time—to the dimensions of British aestheticism that appear deeply to trouble James's earlier fiction. James's end in doing so is clear and clearly problematic; in this novel, James performs the move that has been impending throughout those works: the valorizing of the aesthetic as a means of addressing, and perhaps resolving, problems of morality, psychology, even epistemology. It is precisely the move that the aesthetic movement itself was largely, and I think wrongly, accused of performing; the very thoroughness of James's accomplishment of it here suggests the paradoxical formulation I wish to explore at the end of this chapter: that *The Golden Bowl* may be viewed as the great work of aestheticist art the aesthetic movement itself was unable to create. As such, then, this novel can both serve to bring the study of James's engagement with the tradition of British aestheticism to its conclusion and suggest the ramifications of that encounter. For the very success of *The Golden Bowl*'s response to the problem of aestheticism had two strikingly different effects. In terms of James's own career, the very artistic achievement of the novel ultimately proved disastrous. After *The Golden Bowl* rang down its final curtain on itself, James was unable again to complete a major work of fiction, turning instead to the revisionary efforts of the *Prefaces* or the equally retrospective velleities of the autobiographical writings. In terms of the unfolding of Anglo-American letters, however, it exerted a more positive influence. James's novel bridges the gap between the tentative aesthetic idealization of the British aesthetic movement and the more complete idealization of art performed by the Anglo-American modernists; its supple self-aestheticization suggests how the movement from one to the other was accomplished—and the price such a movement exacted. The text, therefore, both provides one final accounting of the profit and loss sustained in James's career-long engagement with aestheticism and reminds us of how eagerly the same toll was paid by his modernist successors.

In order to make my way through this novel, I wish to concentrate on the figure of Maggie Verver, despite the more obvious opportunities offered by her father, Adam. But I cannot pass Adam by entirely, for the portrayal of Adam repeats with such accuracy the issues we have seen associated with aestheticism throughout James's career. Thus, like Osmond, Adam is a man whose emotional life and connoisseurship are identical, as he demonstrates when he views the acquisition of a husband for his daughter and a wife for himself as the purchase of "representative precious objects," or late in the novel when he looks upon Charlotte and the Prince as pieces of "human furniture" whose price has been fully measured by his and Maggie's "sacrifice" of them:

The fusion of their presence with the decorative elements, their contribution to the triumph of selection, was complete and admirable; though to a lingering view, a view more penetrating than the occasion really demanded, they also might have figured as concrete attestations of a rare power of purchase. There was much indeed in the tone in which Adam Verver spoke again, and who shall say where his thought stopped? *"Le compte y est.* You've got some good things." (NY, 24: 360)

What is most remarkable about this moment, however, is the extraordinary equanimity with which it treats phenomena that James's earlier fiction found troubling. The delicate sinuosities of James's prose advance toward but then recoil from the impassioned moral commentary of *Portrait.* "A lingering view" *might* reveal the relation between the aesthetic display of the Prince and Charlotte and Adam's wealth; such a view might even grant us access to Adam's thought processes, and help us understand what it is to look at people as objects for purchase, as so much "human furniture" (24: 360). But the narrative voice, never so intrusive as when it fails fully to intrude, places itself in the same decorous relation to the demands of the "occasion" as do Charlotte and Amerigo, and declines to follow out the train of thought it has itself initiated. Similarly, earlier in the novel, the problem of Adam's Osmond-like reifying vision are both raised and dismissed by one and the same graceful gesture: "Nothing perhaps might affect us as queerer, had we time to look into it, than this application of the same measure of value to such different pieces of property as old Persian carpets, say, and new human acquisitions; all the more indeed that the amiable man was not without an inkling on his own side that he was, as a taster of life, economically constructed" (23: 196). Had we world enough and time, James implies, the question of Adam's reifying vision might be worthy of inquiry—but there are so many issues of equal importance to discuss (his abstemiousness, for example) that the problem need only be glanced at briefly, then dismissed. It is as if James wishes us to set our judgmental reflexes jangling only to set them at ease; relax, he tells us, Adam's aestheticism may appear to be cancerous, but it is fundamentally benign.

The novel's simultaneous explicitness and evasiveness on the question of Adam's aestheticism has outraged critics, who however respond to it by recapitulating the text's dual responses in their own. "Adam's failure as a father," writes John Carlos Rowe, "is the original flaw in the relations of *The Golden Bowl.* As a potential source for social and personal meaning, Adam's judgment violates the variety of human relations for the sake of his ideal vision. . . . Only when [Maggie] escapes the narrow vision of her father's religion of perfection may she begin to bear her own responsibility for life."[17] Mildred Hartsock, on the other hand, argues that such criticisms are fallaciously extratextual, grounded in an irrational prejudice against American millionaires(!); wealth, she suggests, always provided James with a complex figuration for freedom, and Adam is first and foremost to be read as a figure of visual and temperamental amplitude: given his wealth and his ease, "his freedom to see" is without limit, and, Adam thinks, "what could it do but steadily grow and grow?"[18] Both responses, however, are inadequate—and not only because they recapitulate so tidily the novel's own coy admixture of scandal and serenity. More significantly, such criticisms are ultimately beside the point, even in a discussion of the novel's deployment of aestheticism, because Adam's aestheticism becomes increasingly irrelevant to the novel. Contrary to "Adam-haters" or "Adam-lovers" alike, I would assert that the chief function of Adam's aestheticism is at once to gloss and to veil that of James's greatest, and most problematical, aesthete: his daughter, Maggie Verver. "'It came out in her by heredity,' he amused himself with declaring, 'this love of *chinoiseries*'" (23: 162), and the same may be said for all the other qualities of Adam's aestheticism: his attunement to the ebb and flow of sensations and impressions, his conflation of a passion for aesthetic perfection and serene cruelty (23: 162).* Maggie's deployment of these qualities is less obvious, and certainly less commented upon by the novel, than Adam's more outrageously serene aestheticism; nevertheless, hers far exceeds his in power and efficacy. For she is able to achieve the goal that the Jamesian aesthete habitually strives after but has not as yet attained: putting aestheticism to work in the social world. Seizing upon and deploying in that world her own versions of Adam's power tactics, Maggie provides James's final redaction of the aesthete,

---

*There exists a very complicated relation between Adam's aestheticism and Maggie's, which would take too much time fully to parse but which may be briefly mentioned here. For the close, if not incestuous, bond between Adam and Maggie seems to have much to do with their common possession of the "aesthetic principle, planted where it could burn with a cold still flame" (23: 197). According to Adam, his first wife, Maggie's mother, inhibited the development of his sensibility, limited his "freedom to see" (23: 150), in ways he delicately finds distressing: "Musing, reconsidering little man that he was, and addicted to silent pleasures—as he was accessible to silent pains—he even sometimes wondered what would have become of his intelligence, in the sphere in which it was to learn more and more exclusively to play, if his wife's influence upon it hadn't been, in the strange scheme of things, so promptly removed. Would she have led him altogether, attached as he was to her, into the wilderness of mere mistakes?" (23: 43). Maggie, by contrast, presents no such difficulties; "She was her mother, oh yes—but her mother and something more" Adam says at one point, and it is clear that one of the ways in which Maggie surpasses her mother is in the delicacy of her taste—a taste that, to heighten the hint of incest always hovering behind Adam and Maggie's relation, Adam has had every opportunity to form (23: 148).

fusing the qualities of the Paterian aesthete with those of the decadent
belle dame sans merci to produce an ambiguous entity in whose guise
we may witness the dire conflations we saw James struggling to describe in *The Wings of the Dove*: love and cruelty; passivity and power;
imaginative freedom and social control.

This process is delineated in the remarkable second half of the novel,
where, as always in James, it begins with the verbal cues of Paterian
diction—a diction here, however, that fully achieves the equivocal destiny suggested for it in *Wings*. We learn that Maggie's encounter with
her husband after he has consummated his affair with Charlotte leaves
him "*visibly* uncertain" and induces in her a "quickened sensibility"
(24: 15, 31). Like Isabel Archer, she "had a long pause before the fire
during which she might have been fixing with intensity her projected
vision," and from this moment, the thought of this "much-thinking
little person" "arrive[s] at a great intensity" which leads her to pay close
—minute—attention to the smallest fragments of sense data; which
causes her to "pluck . . . her sensations by the way, detached ner-
vously, the small wild blossoms of her dim forest" (24: 23, 44, 144). In
other words, Maggie is forced by circumstance into the position of the
Paterian aesthete: she must devote herself to the rigorous inspection
of every impression, every sensation, in order to survive. Maggie lives
in a nightmare version of the aesthete's world. "A counted number of
pulses only is given to us of a variegated, dramatic life. How may we
see in them all that is to be seen in them by the finest senses?" (WP, 1:
236). To do so is Pater's imperative, and Maggie's burden. "I go about
on tiptoe, I watch for every sound, I feel every breath, and yet I try all
the while to seem as smooth as old satin dyed rose-colour" (NY, 24:
110).

Of course, she must do more than that. She must see, but she must
also *act*. Maggie must somehow contrive to save appearances—to separate her husband from his lover, pack Charlotte off to American City,
and do this without violating her father's ostensible innocence. In performing these actions, Maggie comes increasingly to resemble the same
literary image we saw James playing with in *The Wings of the Dove*:
that of the femme fatale or *belle dame sans merci*.[19] As in *Wings*, this
identification seems paradoxical: for most of the novel we are asked
to see Maggie as anything but a femme fatale. We are asked to see
her primarily as an innocent victim—fallible, perhaps, because she is
so innocent, but no less the victim until she "takes responsibility for
her life." "I'm a small creeping thing," Maggie banteringly says to her
father early in the novel (significantly, belittling herself in comparison

to Charlotte's "courage" and "cleverness"), and it is in this light that other characters like Colonel Bob and Fanny see her, and in this way that the novel's figurative language portrays her—as a lamb, a fawn, a spaniel shaking off water (23: 181). As Maggie begins to act, however, both the attitudes of these other characters and those suggested by the novel's figurations begin to undergo a transformation. Maggie is called a "timid tigress"; she becomes, Fanny Assingham claims, "terrible"; she becomes "cold indeed, colder and colder" in her necessary detachment from Charlotte's fate (24: 10, 115, 269). It is soon the lovers, not Maggie, who are portrayed as animals, at least in Maggie's consciousness of them. She sees Charlotte as a scapegoat (explicitly bringing to mind Holman Hunt's famous picture), as a caged animal threatening to break loose; as a beast led by a silken thread emitting howls of pain. Similarly, Maggie views all of the other characters in the novel as "the cornered six whom . . . she might still live to drive about like a flock of sheep," chief among which being her husband Amerigo, whom she describes as a "precious spotless exceptionally intelligent lamb" crying "sacrifice me, my own love; do sacrifice me, do sacrifice me!" (24: 51–52, 82–83).

Moreover, as this language would suggest, Maggie sees herself as the sacrificing priest, or more vigorously, as the secular but nevertheless omnipotent authority charged with the task of bringing Charlotte and Amerigo to justice. R. P. Blackmur has written that Maggie's "psychology is peculiar: what Maggie did to her father, her friend, her husband, and herself was done in the name of love. But it sounds like the cry of the police, who are interested only in superficial order, Break it up there, break it up, together with the murmur of maternal lamentation when she buries her head in her husband's breast."[20] But Blackmur's metaphor may be taken further; Maggie not only represents the police here, but also plays the role of prosecuting attorney, judge, jury, and executioner. Having found evidence of her husband's and Charlotte's transgressions and heard testimony from the relevant witnesses (the antique dealer, Fanny Assingham, and Amerigo), Maggie sentences Charlotte to be "removed, transported, doomed"; Amerigo to be "straitened and tied," "caged," but released on promise of good behavior ("See? I see nothing but *you*.") (24: 271, 192, 338, 369). Maggie is a stern judge: she not only punishes the lovers, but also their accomplice, Fanny—a punishment whose justice Fanny herself acknowledges and to which she meekly, despairingly submits: " 'One's punishment is in what one feels, and what will make ours effective is that we *shall* feel.' She was splendid with her 'ours'; she flared up

with this prophecy. 'It will be Maggie herself who will mete it out'"
(24: 136). "More and more magnificent now in her blameless egotism,"
Maggie becomes (as Fanny puts it elsewhere) "divinely retributive,"
and so deeply so that she is transformed into a literal *Belle Dame Sans
Merci* (24: 145, 72). There is pity, there is terror, there is the awareness
that "Charlotte was in pain, Charlotte was in torment," but there is no
mercy to be had from Maggie Verver (24: 345).

It is in this judicial or executive mode that Maggie comes to resemble the figure of the enigmatic, all-powerful, and cruel femme
fatale that so fascinated the fin de siècle. We may place Maggie Verver
in this company not by virtue of her appearance or her *extravagant*
sexuality; although, alone of all of James's heroines, she is provided
by the novel with a fulfilled sexual appetancy, Maggie is nevertheless
kept virginal in appearance and passive in behavior in contrast with
the overtly sexualized and determinedly active Charlotte. Rather, it is
the way Maggie's power is specifically exercised—and valorized—that
I want to cite as the prime reason to identify her with the figure of the
femme fatale. For what distinguishes the British *belle dame sans merci*
is her particular combination of cruelty and boundless knowledge; it
is in the intersection of these qualities in a state of enigmatic ambiguity that these figures achieve their compelling power. Oscar Wilde's
Sphinx provides a master image for this fusion; it is in the nature of
sphinxes both to possess privileged but mysterious knowledge and to
veil that knowledge from their would-be interrogators; and this combination of qualities, more than anything else, allows Wilde's Sphinx
to torment its victim:

> A thousand weary centuries are thine, while I have hardly seen
> Some twenty summers cast their green for Autumn's gaudy liveries,
>
> But you can read the Hieroglyphs on the great sandstone obelisks,
> And you have talked with Basilisks and you have looked on Hippogriffs
>
> O tell me, were you standing by when Isis to Osiris knelt,
> And did you watch the Egyptian melt her union for Antony,
>
> And drink the jewel-drunken wine, and bend her head in mimic awe
> To see the huge pro-consul draw the salty tunny from the brine?
> And did you mark the Cyprian kiss with Adon on his catafalque,
> And did you follow Amanalk the god of Heliopolis?
>
> And did you talk with Thoth, and did you hear the moon-horned Io
> weep,
> And know the painted kings who sleep beneath the wedge-shaped
> Pyramid?
>
> (*Works*, 1: 291–92, ll. 33–56)

This is not one of Wilde's more successful efforts; its catalogues and singsong rhythms remind one more of a patter song from *Patience* than the poem it wants to imitate, Poe's *Raven*. But by its very sophomoric excess, *The Sphinx* limns clearly the powers deployed by the *belle dame sans merci*. As the increasingly fervid—if not ridiculous —questions of the poet would indicate, the Sphinx exerts the fascination of the very interpretive enigma it is the Sphinx's usual role to impart. The poem thus reverses the normal pattern of human/sphinx relations; and its poet is punished by its failure to answer—not by death, as in the myth, but by enduring the agony of her silence. This pattern of behavior marks most of the decadent *belles dames*. Pater's "Gioconda" is perhaps the best—and certainly the most notorious— example; she provides a similar amalgam of mysterious omniscience —of total knowledge at once suggested and withheld by the taunting perfection of her smile—and of boundless cruelty—implied by her depiction as a vampire. The same conflation is evident among Swinburne's many *belles dames—Dolores, Anactoria, Cleopatra*, Venus of *Laus Veneris*, and the like. Thus, to cite but one example, the most powerful of his dark ladies, Dolores, is interrogated by the poet in very much the same way as is Wilde's Sphinx, with the addition being that Swinburne states what Wilde leaves unsaid: the power to withhold knowledge and the power to inflict pain are one and the same, and they produce the same pleasurable torment:

> Who gave thee wisdom? what stories
>   That stung thee, what visions that smote?
> Wert thou pure and a maiden, Dolores,
>   When desire took thee first by the throat?
> What bud was the shell of a blossom
>   That all men may smell to and pluck?
> What milk first fed thee at what bosom?
>   What sins gave thee suck?
>
> We shift and bedeck and bedrape us,
>   Thou art noble and nude and antique;
> Libitina thy mother, Priapus
>   Thy father, a Tuscan and Greek.
> We play with light loves in the portal,
>   And wince and relent and refrain;
> Loves die, and we know thee immortal
>   Our Lady of Pain.
>   (ACS, 1: 285, ll. 41–56)

"O wise among women, and wisest," Dolores taunts and teases the poet with her knowledge of "sins," "deeds," "passions," "spells," and "tortures undreamt of, unheard of / Unwritten, unknown." Indeed, all the signs of her superior knowledge are "tortures," for they all enchain the poet in his desire to dream, hear, write, and know these things, and force him to bear the pain of his own ignorance.

It is this complicated awareness of the intersection between ambiguity, power, and pain that James's novel shares with the decadent phases of the aestheticist tradition. This becomes clearest, perhaps, in the problematic final pages of the novel, in which the work comes to deal with this phenomenon with a bluntness equal to its unmystified portrayal of Adam's reifying vision. The metaphorical language of enclosure, entrapment, and bondage that the novel and its characters all employ has been clear enough up until then, but what these final pages spell out is that the power that enables Maggie to enclose, enchain, and control is the combination of the possession of knowledge and the refusal to specify exactly what that knowledge may be. In the epistemologically unstable world conjured forth by the novel, in which each character possesses secrets that the other characters variously attempt to ferret out, only Maggie has been able fully to plumb the guilts or complicities of Amerigo, Charlotte, and Fanny; and she punishes them—or, more accurately, forces them to punish themselves —by signifying to each *that* she knows, but not *what* she knows. Indeed, Maggie establishes a precise ratio between the explicitness of her response and her sense of the guilt of the person she responds to; the greater the transgression, the greater the ambiguity. Fanny can and does ask questions of her sphinxlike friend and receives answers that allow her, within certain limits, to establish the extent of her knowledge, its sources, and the evidence that backs it up. Amerigo, by contrast, is shown the golden bowl, told of how Maggie learned of it, and then issued a hermeneutic challenge: "I've told you all I intended. Find out the rest—" (NY, 24: 203). Charlotte is presented with virtually no interpretive cues from Maggie at all. Fully Maggie's match in intuitive acuity, Charlotte understands that something in Maggie has changed, and the Prince's withdrawal from her compounds this knowledge, leading beyond suspicion to seeming certainty—Maggie, at least, claims late in the novel that "she knows, she knows" (24: 348). Yet, again, *that* she knows is never matched by *what* she knows, so that the greatest certainty Charlotte can attain plunges her into a vertiginous state of complete uncertainty. She never learns the degree or extent of Maggie's knowledge of her actions, and is thus unable to calculate her own countermoves with any degree of precision.

Indeed, the tactics Maggie uses against her subtlest rival are at once her most sophisticated and most problematic. "She sees it all before her—and she can't speak or resist or move a little finger. That's what's the matter with *her*," says Fanny Assingham a little earlier in the novel, getting things almost exactly wrong: Charlotte may or may not "see it all before her," but she can't ever *know* what she sees—what Maggie knows; what Adam knows; and, if both Ververs do know, what they will do; what has caused the Prince's behavior to change (24: 303). But Charlotte, who shows herself here to be as "splendid" as Maggie continually describes her, responds courageously to this condition with a series of cunning but desperate countermeasures (24: 346). Charlotte attempts to break out of her cage and (to mix two Jamesian metaphors) force Maggie into the open: inviting her at Fawns either to accuse her or proclaim her innocent, Charlotte hopes that Maggie will give her an opportunity at least to gauge the extent of her knowledge and thus a chance to prepare an explanation, a counterinterpretation, a casuistical justification (perhaps one relying on Maggie's own responsibility for the state of affairs Charlotte and the Prince were confronted with in their extraordinary marriages). Maggie's counter-counter-responses range from indirection to outright prevarication, and they are neatly and cruelly calculated to present Charlotte with a facade of disingenuous ignorance and feigned innocence so perfect that it can never be penetrated or parted; it is "a question," Maggie asserts, "of not by a hair's breadth deflecting into the truth" (24: 250–51). By the end of the novel, Charlotte is forced to respond by doing exactly what Maggie wished her to do in the first place: to play the part of the loyal wife. For only by performing, first tentatively, then regally, the role of devoted wife can she protect herself from Maggie's unspoken—and unspeakable—blackmail.

Further, in the tradition of the aestheticist *belle dame* lyric, the novel never shies from demonstrating the cruelty of this conflation of veiled knowledge and unveiled power. If "the cage [is] the deluded condition . . . Maggie, as having known delusion—rather!—understood the nature of cages" (24: 229). Having been placed there herself, Maggie knows how painful is Charlotte's entrapment in epistemological uncertainty; yet she never shies away from her encagement of her rival in precisely that condition. In the final pages of the novel, Maggie witnesses Charlotte's agony with an intensity that borders on sadism. In one of the novel's most famous and most problematical passages, she employs her preternaturally acute senses to hear Charlotte's silent cry of agony at the equally silent betrayal of Amerigo, and at her inability ever to confront her lover or his wife with her knowledge of that betrayal. But Maggie will not relent, nor is there any condemnation in the novel of her for this refusal. Instead, she is exonerated—explicitly judged, as we have seen, "more and more magnificent . . . in her blameless egoism" (24: 145).

Indeed, she is even, in some strange way, *rewarded*. For in the last pages of the novel, Maggie and Amerigo's common witnessing of Charlotte's torment becomes grounds for the reconstruction of their former intimacy—or at least as much intimacy as can be reconstructed between the two. After Maggie's relentless imagination tracks him down to his London apartment, it takes comfort in the fact that, if they are not wholly reunited, at least they are one in their sensitivity to Charlotte's pain—and to their common knowledge that they are each in their different ways the cause of her "torment." Late in the novel, she moves beyond even this renewal of sympathies with Amerigo to claim complete omnipotence over him. When the Prince seeks to assume Maggie's punitive powers by reversing her tactics and informing Charlotte of his and Maggie's mutual lie, she silences him with a gesture that asserts explicitly for the first and only time her authority over both her husband and his lover:

> "And how then is she to know?" [asks Amerigo.]
> "She isn't to know."
> "She's only still to think *you* don't—?"
> "And therefore that I'm always a fool? She may think," said Maggie, "what she likes."
> "Think it without my protest—?"
> The Princess made a movement. "What business is it of yours?"
> "Isn't it my right to correct her—?"
> Maggie let his question ring—ring long enough for him to hear it himself; only then she took it up. " 'Correct' her?"—and it was her own now that really rang. "Aren't you rather forgetting who she is?" After which, while he quite stared for it, as it was the very first clear majesty he had known her to use, she flung down her book and raised a warning hand. "The carriage. Come!" (24: 356)

Quoting Amerigo's words back to him, Maggie reminds him that his assertion of the "right" to "correct" Charlotte is inappropriate, at best; he owes not only Maggie but also Charlotte herself the maintenance of the cover story that Maggie's lies have presented her. As Ruth Yeazell reminds us, "this exchange is thus profoundly disturbing, for its terms suggest that to be truthful to Charlotte in one sense is to be false, even cruel, in another."[21] Yet the exchange is even more disturbing than Yeazell acknowledges. To allow Charlotte to adopt the fiction Maggie has crafted for her is finally to be boundlessly cruel indeed, for the basis of her assent to that fiction is the state of vertiginous ambiguity in which Charlotte is left, even at the end of the novel, to hang. Thus, as Charlotte departs to Maggie and Amerigo's accolades, Maggie's sense of triumph over her rival, mediated through as it has been wrought by her aestheticism, is absolute: "'She's beautiful, beautiful,' her sensibility reported to her the shade of a new note. It was all she might have wished, for it was, with a kind of speaking competence, the note of possession and control" (24: 365). She "sacrifices" her father in order to accomplish this triumph, it is true, but what the novel fails to mention at this point is that she and Amerigo have now become as one in "sacrificing" Charlotte—not only by forcing her to exile herself to America (where, the Prince assures Maggie, she'll "mak[e] her life,") but by keeping her in the painful cocoon of an ignorance that knows its ignorance but cannot achieve any authoritative—or even provisional —knowledge of its limits or bounds (24: 267, 349).

By the end of the novel, then, Maggie has fully invested herself with absolute punitive authority, and her infliction of punishment through the delineation of withheld knowledge is identified as the only ordering principle available in the resolutely demystified world of this novel —a world in which, in Amerigo's words, "everything's terrible, cara— in the heart of man" (24: 349). In doing so, James enters fully into the most problematic aspect of the tradition of British aestheticism, and does so in such a way as to alter it. By creating in Maggie Verver a variant of the aestheticist *belle dame sans merci*—a "timid tigress" who deploys the cruel power of withdrawn omniscience in the guise of the "American girl"—James succeeds in at once domesticating and inflating the powers of the decadent dark lady. Indeed, he quite literally domesticates that figure, turning the *belle dame*'s sadistic energies and subtle power tactics toward the establishment of marital unity and familial harmony—not, to say the least, the typical ends of the femme fatale. But it is precisely through this revision that James inflates the powers conventionally ascribed to the decadent *belle dame*. By endowing a figure like Maggie rather than the more obvious candidate, the supersubtle Charlotte, with the *belle dame*'s ability to exercise power through the creation of a "blank blurred surface . . . that ceased to signify," James suggests that such powers inhere in the very norms of domestic behavior that the *belle dame* seems to flaunt (24: 247). Maggie is able to achieve power in the domestic sphere because she does so within the very bounds of late-nineteenth-century feminine propriety. "No, I'm not extraordinary—" Maggie tells Fanny, "but I *am*, for every one, quiet"; the "timid," "mild" Maggie employs tactics of feminine deference ("I can bear anything") and self-abasement to achieve mastery (24: 217, 115). Indeed, this very role makes Maggie's success possible; the seeming "timidity" of this domesticated tigress becomes the device by which she veils her intentions and actions; it is therefore the very means by which they are accomplished. It is through her willingness to accept the limitations imposed upon her that Maggie exercises power over those who have not. She tells Fanny:

Everything that has come up for them has come up, in an extraordinary manner, without my having by a sound or sign given myself away—so that it's all as wonderful as you may conceive. They move at any rate among the dangers I speak of—between that of their doing too much and that of their not having any longer the confidence or the nerve, or whatever you may call it, to do enough . . . And that's how I make them do what I like. (24: 115)

The portrayal of Maggie does more than invoke and alter the topos of the decadent *belle dame*; she also transforms the figure of the aesthete who has been a staple of James's fiction from the time of *Roderick Hudson* on. Maggie successfully realizes the goals aimed at unsuccessfully by the male aesthete throughout James's fiction. The aesthete's valorization of surfaces and social forms; his desire actively to force life into the symmetrical perfection of art; his combination of emotional withdrawal and a severe will to power—all these are Maggie's, too, along with the ability to concretize these desires, to make them work for her in the actual, social world. It is true that Maggie's aestheticism in this novel begins with precisely the same preternaturally acute vision—the *aesthesis*—that normally supplements and corrects the aesthete's will to social power. But *The Golden Bowl* proceeds as it were backwards, to the same qualities of reification and manipulation, the same uneasy admixture of connoisseurship and control, from which this *aesthesis* is usually sifted. Maggie starts as a variant of Isabel, but ends as a more powerful Osmond—more powerful, that is, precisely because she appears to be another Isabel. Or perhaps it would be more accurate to say that she seeks to achieve Isabel-like ends through Osmondian means—the rearrangement of the "human furniture required aesthetically by such a scene," "the conquest of appearances"—but by the end of the novel is forced to learn that Osmondian means lead only to Osmondian ends: a reaffirmation of precisely the social form, marriage, that Osmond praises, and the remodeling of a husband who defers to her as totally as does Pansy Osmond to her father (24: 360).

The problematical identification of Maggie with Gilbert Osmond I have begun to suggest here is underscored by the text's deployment of its master metaphor, the golden bowl. When Maggie signifies her attempt to remake her marriage by piecing together the shattered bowl, she also performs an act we have seen associated throughout James's fiction with Osmondian aestheticism: the attempt to remold life in the perfect image of an aesthetic artifact. In a grimly ironic sense Maggie's action here, like Osmond's, is most accurately glossed by those characters in Du Maurier's *Punch* cartoon who proclaimed the importance of "living up to their china": Maggie, like those characters and like Osmond himself, seeks to shape the untidinesses and insufficiencies of life into the static perfection emblematized by the smooth, symmetrical piece of crockery—except that here, such an attempt is not only ultimately successful, but is portrayed by the novel as the only ground of human value in a social world as flawed and potentially fragmented as the cracked bowl itself.

The transformation of Maggie Verver, then, neatly reverses the movement we traced in *Portrait* and brings James's engagement with the tradition of British aestheticism full circle. That circle ends with James finally accepting the very phenomena he had scorned, demonized, or sought to revise early in his career. The nexus between aestheticization and will to power and the simultaneous valorizing of aesthetic forms and social conventions that James had satirized with such fervor in the figure of Osmond now enter his work as principles of affirmative value, as indeed the only value James can imagine. And they are accompanied in this march into respectability by a third aspect of British aestheticism: its ambivalent valorization of art itself. As critics have frequently observed, the novel's dominant metaphor of the golden bowl implies a powerful homology between James's creative efforts and those of his character Maggie: James, like his character, seeks to gather the shattered fragments of life and remake them into the smooth perfections of aesthetic form, to redeem human passions and frailties by shaping them into significant and symmetrical order. This very perfection is emphasized in the novel's last lines; by closing with an echo of Aristotle's *katharsis* in his description of Maggie's response to the Prince's embrace, James emphasizes the continuities between his own text and a finished work of tragic art—with the even more self-enclosing twist that James's novel includes the response of its audience within its own completed form.

It is precisely these kinds of authorial moves that seem to suture

James most persuasively and most problematically to the British aesthetic movement. James, it would seem, here concretizes in novelistic form the kind of high-art aestheticism we have seen him asserting in his struggles with both the moralist Charles Eliot Norton and the aesthete Oscar Wilde. By such assertions, James would seem to be positioning himself somewhere between—or to be more accurate, somewhere above—the positions held by Norton and Wilde. Vis-à-vis Norton, the discovery of value in aesthetic form rather than moral verities places James in the position of the "worshipper at the aesthetic shrine *quand même*"; but vis-à-vis Wilde, the linkage between Maggie's efforts and James's suggests that such art is to be understood as accomplishment, a striving, a doing, or a making, rather than the attitude, the state of being, or the aspect of mind it represented for Wilde and Pater alike. Indeed, in doing so, James may be said most accurately to have fused the Nortonian and the Wildean aestheticisms—to have brought together the injunction that art be moral with the injunction that morality be aesthetic to create, in the form of the Jamesian novel itself, a kind of aesthetic morality that locates in the creative impulse and the achievement of art the only source of moral possibilities in a world significantly bereft of such capacities.

In doing so, James seems to have moved through and beyond the terms bequeathed him by the tradition of British aestheticism. "Many of us will doubtless not have forgotten how we were witnesses a certain number of years since to a season and a society that had found themselves of a sudden roused, as from some deep drugged sleep, to the conception of the 'esthetic' law of life," James wrote in a 1902 essay on Gabrielle d'Annunzio. "The spectacle was strange and finally was wearisome, for the simple reason that the principle in question, once it was proclaimed . . . was never felt to fall into its place as really adopted and efficient." [22] In *The Golden Bowl*, James delineates the possibilities —and the consequences—of adhering to the " 'esthetic' law of life" not only through Maggie's attempts to reestablish order but through his own; and by the ultimate success of both endeavors, he crafts a work of art in which that law "fall[s] into its place as really adopted and efficient"—so efficient, in fact, that it turns the work of art itself into both the means by which the problem is posed and those by which it is resolved. It is in this sense that *The Golden Bowl* may be accurately said to represent the fully achieved work of art that the aesthetic movement failed to bring forth; for the capacious but finally symmetrical form of this novel brings together into a tense totality the conflicting impulses, desires, and imperatives that for the aesthetic movement itself existed only in a loose confederation; it does so by asserting authoritatively the proposition that the aesthetic movement only flirted with: that the work of art itself can provide the ontological ground on which these fragments may be reunited. "It is art that *makes* life, makes interest, makes importance, for our consideration and application of these things, and I know of no substitute whatever for the force and beauty of its process," James wrote in a famous letter to H. G. Wells in 1915; *The Golden Bowl* glosses this famous remark by suggesting not only that art shapes life in its own image—a Wildean conceit that James, here, has moved far beyond—but also that without the example of art, life would remain a shapeless, inchoate fragment—a shattered bowl, a broken vessel (*Letters*, 4: 770). Maggie's remaking of a meaningful marriage and James's reweaving of his fissured text both affirm the artistic imagination's power to reshape a fragmented world.

Even as I write these words, I am half-amused by their anachronism; the move in the chess game of criticism they represent is so old as to seem—almost—new. They seem superannuated, of course, because they once seemed so new; one cannot reread the works of those critics who privileged James's affirmation of the powers of his own art without sensing, perhaps with a certain nostalgia, their excitement at discovering so powerful an assertion of artistic—and critical —power. They seem novel because the criticism of the last generation has systematically called the equivalences they rely upon into question, emphasizing instead the political difficulties such assertions present and the extraordinary authorial narcissism they imply. Certainly, I am not invoking these aperçus in order to turn back the clock to the early days of the New Criticism. Rather, I do so here to emphasize the significance of James's turn toward the aesthetic, both for an understanding of his encounter with British aestheticism and for one of his own critical office. For it is precisely through a collapsing of James's late aesthetic-ism, his extraordinary promulgation of an ideology of art, into that of the tradition of aestheticist criticism and practice that precedes him, that the anti-Jacobites of the past three generations have launched their most powerful criticisms of his work—criticisms that have relied upon a reductive notion of aestheticism and of James's work alike, and that have systematically effaced the true complexity of their intertwining. Not only has the move the late James frequently makes toward affirming the extraaesthetic implications of his artistic powers been taken as synecdochic of his career as a whole, but James himself has been persistently denigrated as a second Osmond: an "absolute aesthete," a "commodifying dilettante," an "arachnid of art," and so on.

I have devoted the last 200 pages or so to suggesting the difficulties with this line of analysis, to attempting to put the complex interweaving of the varied and unstable tradition of British aestheticism and James's equally varied and complex aesthetic achievement in a more articulated perspective. Nevertheless, I must confess that, in dealing with this particular turn of the Jamesian screw, I am not hostile to the identification between his work and the example of aestheticism— even aestheticism at its most reductive—at least as long as this identification is put in its proper place both in terms of James's career and his role in literary and cultural history. As long as we avoid a reductive reading of James's entire career as if it were aspiring to the condition of *The Golden Bowl*, we are in a position to read James's final turn toward the aesthetic in its full complexity. In terms of James's own career, we are in a position to see that that turn provided a resolution to problems that could not be solved by any other means, a desperate attempt at bringing together, under the sign of imagination and art, the problematic qualities that have divided his fiction from the time of *Portrait* to that of *The Golden Bowl*. In this sense, the anti-Jacobites are entitled to their equivalence between James and the most reductive aspects of British aestheticism—as long as they acknowledge that this discovery on aesthetic grounds of resolutions to nonaesthetic problems failed to provide the satisfying resolution James was looking for. If the novel specifies art, and more precisely its own performance, as the ultimate ground of value in a world significantly lacking in any redemptive principle, then the resolution of the novel is at once perfect and perfectly limited. The text's circling back on itself succeeds brilliantly in solving the problems it, and James's entire career, has posed; but in doing so, it severely circumscribes that solution, instancing only itself as the means to this redemptive end. In seeking to valorize the autotelic, the novel thus succeeds only in rendering itself autistic. And, lest that metaphor seem strained in the context of an author who was nothing if not communicative, let me point out that the very perfection of *The Golden Bowl* seemed to have been powerfully inhibitory for James himself; it is not coincidental that he was never able to complete a major novel after this one, turning instead to the retrospective efforts of the autobiographical writings or the *Prefaces*, or, in *The Outcry*, to the same imaginative terrain as *The Golden Bowl*.

My point, then, is that, just as the aesthetic failure of *The Wings of the Dove* may be read as its greatest aesthetic success, *The Golden Bowl*'s very aesthetic success was paradoxically something of an aesthetic failure, not because it failed to resolve certain difficulties for James, but because it solved those problems too well. The same phenomenon marks the place of the novel in the context of nineteenth- and twentieth-century literary history, particularly in that trajectory of thought that led from British aestheticism to Anglo-American modernism. *The Golden Bowl*, we might say, presents a solution to the problems explicitly confronted in the Anglo-American aesthetic movement by turning them inward, into the dimension of aesthetic performance itself; this move, at once adumbrated and resisted by the poets and painters of British aestheticism, was subsequently performed with eager efficiency by the generation that succeeded James. The positing of art as a principle of order in a world in which such ordering principles are otherwise unavailable; the identification of ambiguity as a means of establishing this order in a debased social world; such are the lines of analysis that the modernist poets who followed James by one generation were able to take to their logical conclusion. The kinds of equivalences that shape *The Golden Bowl*, in other words, were reworked by the modernists into a well-wrought urn; in doing so, those writers were able successfully to exploit and efface the imaginative patterns they were endowed with by the tradition of British aestheticism they so adventitiously reviled.

The Lesson of the Master?

The version of literary history I have been relying upon here has become, by now, a familiar one; the claims of the modernists to "make it new" have become increasingly understood to depend on the very nineteenth-century paradigms these poets rejected.[23] In even the most eloquent and subtle examples of this revisionary history, however, two related points remain neglected which we are in a position to comment on by way of concluding this study: that at the very moment when such writers were wittingly or unwittingly rejecting their roots in British aestheticism, they were consciously adopting Henry James as an artistic model; and that the urgency with which they adopted James to their family romance has much to do with their need to mask the difference between their own mystified, high-art aestheticism and the more contradictory and destabilizing aestheticism of the poets and painters officially enrolled in the "aesthetic movement."

The former task is far from difficult, for the first of the many efforts

at rehabilitating James's reputation was performed by the founders of
the consciously post-Victorian, explicitly modernist movement itself,
especially its two most central figures, T. S. Eliot and Ezra Pound. It
was James, according to Pound, who taught him and Eliot that "poetry
should be as well written as prose"; in their critical commentary on
James, both sought to install James as at once the last Victorian and
the first modernist. Writing in a 1918 issue of *The Little Review* devoted
exclusively to James, Eliot and Pound joined the more ardent Jacobite
modernist, Ford Maddox Ford, in paying earnest, if slightly misleading, tribute to the lesson of the master—which, to sum up the matter
simply, was simply that they should be themselves. To be sure, neither
Eliot nor Pound was entirely reverent. "When he isn't being a great
and magnificent author, he certainly can be a very fussy and tiresome
one," Pound wrote John Quinn in 1918. "I think the main function
of my essay is to get the really good stuff disentangled from the in-
ferior." [24] This effort at disentanglement is accomplished not only by
both a systematic rereading of the Jamesian canon but also with lyric
effusions in the high Jamesian manner:

I take it as the supreme reward of an artist; the supreme return that his artistic
conscience can make him after years spent in its service, that the momentum
of his art, the sheer bulk of his processes, the (*si licet*) size of his fly-wheel,
should heave him out of himself, out of his personal limitations, out of the
tangles of heredity and of environment, out of the bias of early training, of
early predilections, whether of Florence, A.D. 1300, or of Back Bay of 1872,
and leave him simply the great true recorder.[25]

This passage is telling; for its extraordinary admixture of shrewdness
and sentimentality places James firmly if rather backhandedly in the
Poundian canon. The sheer heft of his devotion to his art removes
James from the limitations of his own place and time and places him
in the perpetual present of Pound's rather idiosyncratic tradition, and
thus—almost—as Pound's equal and contemporary ("the one phase of
James that one wants to *pass over* is, to me, James as contemporary of
Meredith," Pound wrote Quinn.)[26] Similarly, Pound's commentaries
portray a James hovering on the verge of Poundian modernism, but
not quite achieving it; setting the stage for analyses of the next 50
years, the expatriate Pound commends James for his systematic exploration of what was soon to be known as "the international theme"—
James spent a lifetime, Pound wrote, "trying to make two continents
understand each other, in trying, and only his thoughtful readers can
have any conception of how he had tried, to make three nations intelli-

gible one to another"—and on what we would call James's metafiction, stories about writers and artists like *The Lesson of the Master*, or comments on the art of the novel from *The Ivory Tower*.[27] Oddly, Pound has little use for the works that were soon to be known as James's "major phase": while admiring the achievement of *The Sacred Fount* ("form, perfect form, his form") Pound nevertheless warned that these novels were "not models for other writers, a caviare not part of the canon (metaphors be hanged for the moment)."[28]

Eliot's tribute is, as one might suppose, edgier, more unstable; but like Pound's, his James bears the unmistakable stamp of Eliot's own preoccupations. In his 1918 essay, Eliot praises James with faint damns (it is here that Eliot's famous assertion that James "had a mind so fine that no idea could violate it" occurs), but then turns to commend James for his expatriation in all of its many senses. "The fact of being everywhere a foreigner was probably an assistance to his native wit"; his resistance to ideas indicates the basically French, non-Anglo-Saxon, qualities of his intellect; and the audience he addressed was therefore necessarily an elite, marginal one: "[there] will always be a few intelligent people to understand James, and to be understood by a few intelligent people is all the influence a man requires."[29]

Eliot's emphasis on James's "influence"—and his denial of sustaining any specific influence from James earlier in the essay—suggests that we might best approach the modernist rereading of James as a classic case of influence anxiety. Eliot and Pound alike both misread and subtly derogate James by establishing him as an inspiring example that they have themselves transcended, as the imperfect trailblazer whose wandering path they have straightened and improved. Before proceeding further with this argument, it must be acknowledged that this rereading of James was not entirely inaccurate. While it may be a subtly amusing misrepresentation to view James as a kind of portly Stephen Daedalus, such a vision does indeed possess a certain cogency; as I have attempted to show, James did indeed powerfully define a range of vocational possibilities not only for young American but also for young English writers of the late Victorian and early Edwardian eras. But the modernist revision of James was seriously misleading in several respects. First, for all of its seeming sophistication, this view of James as an alienated but persevering artist overstates the extent of James's alienation from his audience—just as James himself overemphasized his own difficulties in finding a responsive reading public. Thus, to stick to James's most problematic audience, that of his native land,

the relations between James and his public were not only those of neglect and hostility that James depicted and the modernists emphasized.
While, as Jay Hubbell has observed, "only the few discriminating readers would care for" the novels of Henry James in late-nineteenth- and
early-twentieth-century America, the data Hubbell cites also remind
us that to the increasingly capacious, self-conscious, and well-defined
elite audience of sophisticated readers, James was the contemporary
novelist par excellence: James consistently ranked near the top of those
polls that emphasized literary prestige rather than mass popularity
—the polls for members of a new American academy, or *The Critic*'s
1893 survey of the 40 literary "Immortals," on which James ranked
a respectable thirteenth.[30] And James himself continually dwelt upon
whatever critical slights he encountered and downplayed every acclaim. Thus, to cite one richly emblematic moment, even while James
himself was complaining of public neglect in letters to more successful
friends like William Howells or Edith Wharton, an apartment house
was being named after him in New York—certainly an indication of
both the high regard in which even the late James was held, even in
his native land, and of James's ability to ignore signs of his own status.

    Second, and more important, Eliot and Pound's rereading of James
as an incipient modernist provided a misleading account of his work.
Not only did it elide those aspects of James that *were* more like George
Meredith than Ezra Pound (and begged the question, as we shall see,
of how much like George Meredith, or other late Victorians, Ezra
Pound himself may have been), it also understated, ignored, or side-
stepped much in James that was, or would have been, hostile or alien
to Pound and Eliot's literary practices—which, in fact, would have de-
stabilized the very assumptions that governed these practices. Their
James was the James of *The Figure in the Carpet*—a writer of hermetic
tales crafted precisely to be found difficult, crabbed, or uninterpret-
able by the reading public at large; or the James of *The Ivory Tower*—
a James whose energies have turned wholly inward, consuming themselves in writing fables about fable making; but not the James of *The
Wings of the Dove*, a novel that, as I have argued, subjects the kinds
of equivalences between aesthetic value and moral authority Eliot and
Pound relied upon to a spirited and critical interrogation.

    The modernist re-creation of James, then, seems to fit snugly into
the contours of an anxiety-of-influence scenario. But while this misreading of James does indeed seem classically aberrational, it must
also be admitted that it is curiously unmotivated, particularly when
the aspects of James it emphasizes are compared with the similar as-

sertions to be found among poets and critics the modernists ignore altogether.[31] I want to suggest, in other words, that the reasons for this recasting of James as a modernist poet of moderate but inadequate achievement has as much to do with the vexed relation between Eliot and Pound and their Victorian, and specifically their aestheticist, predecessors as it does with their relations with James himself. To the first generation of Anglo-American modernists, James was adduced as the privileged counterweight to the example of the aestheticists, the exemplar of the life *successfully* devoted to the making of art—but an example that, unlike that of the aestheticists, the modernist poets have successfully assimilated and moved beyond.

Thus it is particularly significant that James was regularly trotted out by Eliot as a benign alternative to the aestheticism of Pater and Wilde. In his notoriously critical essay, *Arnold and Pater*, for example, Eliot disclaims the importance of Paterian aestheticism, which symbolized the "various chimerical attempts to effect imperfect syntheses" amidst the "dissolution of thought in [the nineteenth century], the isolation of art, philosophy, religion, ethics and literature," and sets against it "the right practice of 'art for art's sake'" which he associates with Flaubert and with Henry James; Eliot defines the latter version of art for art as at once a commonplace and a profundity: "an exhortation of the artist to stick to his job."[32] To be sure, this move is something of a formulaic one—certainly, Eliot's view of the influence of Pater as leading, at best, only to "some untidy lives" was shared by most of the influential literary critics of the 1920's and 1930's. But given the extensiveness of an earlier Eliot's contact with Pater, it seems odder, more disingenuous. As we have seen, the Eliot of 1920 is capable of publishing a book, *The Sacred Wood*, that rings with Paterian echoes; the Eliot of 1930 disavows Pater altogether, choosing instead to identify himself in ethics with Newman and in craftsmanship with James. James, then, would seem to function for that later Eliot as something of an artistic equivalent of High Anglicanism: as a guarantee of canonical authority with which Eliot can identify himself, and to which he can turn in order to disavow destabilizing and disreputable former influences— and former identities.*

---

*At age 30, Eliot wrote his mother: "As it is, I occupy rather a privileged position [in the London literary scene]. . . . There is a small and select public which regards me as the best living critic, as well as the best living poet, in England. . . . I really think that I have far more *influence* on English letters than any other American has ever had, unless it be Henry James. I know a great many people, but there are many more who would like to know me, and I can remain isolated and detached" (Eliot, *Letters*, p. 280).

Similarly, Pound's emphasis on the hermetic, involuted, self-concerned James and his disavowal of the James who resembled George Meredith—by which I take it Pound means a James who delighted in word play and stylistic excess but never moved beyond the imperfect form of the novel to the chaster form of the modernist lyric—creates a James who not only anticipates Pound's own imaginative endeavor but also blocks from view the affinities between that endeavor and those of Pater, Swinburne, and Wilde. "[James] did not begin his career with any theory of art for art's sake," wrote Pound in 1918, "and a lack of this theory may have damaged his earlier work."[33] Pound thereby implies first that James's later fiction and criticism did indeed provide such a theory; second, that such a theory is a desirable thing to possess; and third—more tenuously but nevertheless distinctly— that Pound himself speaks as one who possesses such a fully theorized notion of art for art. He thus grounds his own valorization of art in James's less fully realized one, simultaneously establishing James as Pound's slightly bumbling precursor and effacing the link between his own assertions and the powerful, if more problematic, valorization of art found in the works of Pater, Wilde, or Swinburne—the last being, of course, the first to use "art for art's sake" in English criticism.

Yet again, I must confess that I cannot be wholly hostile to this modernist recasting of literary history, since, however inadvertently, it achieves a kind of accuracy. It may remind us of the relative modesty of the claims that the British aestheticists themselves made for the powers of art in comparison with those proffered by Eliot, Pound, and their more fervid followers among the academic New Critics. It reminds us as well of the comparative virtue of the aestheticists' foregoing of elaborate and totalizing syntheses, their spirited embrace of the ephemeral, the fragmentary, the contradictory, in comparison with the lust for synthesis displayed among the High Modernists. Eliot's diagnosis of the "problem" of aestheticist art, its tendency to propose "*imperfect* syntheses" (emphasis mine) is a precisely accurate commentary not only on the aestheticists but also on Eliot and Pound themselves. I have tried to suggest that the most impressive and valuable attribute of aestheticist poetry inhered in its ability to pose the problems Eliot, Pound, et al. wished to face without propounding totalizing or regressive solutions to these problems; one can turn this assertion around by saying that when Eliot or Pound or their fellow modernists took from the aestheticists their privileging of art, their doctrines of intensity, their simultaneous valorization of temporality and timelessness, they forced these complicated and contradictory patterns of imaginative response into syntheses that can be described as premature and unsatisfying at best. Moreover, and more important, in doing so they essentially reaestheticized aestheticism; they found the ground for these resolutions in the notion of art itself. Pound's definition of the "image" as an "emotional and intellectual complex in an instant of time" is fundamentally homologous to Pater's perfect moment of intense experience, but Pound simplifies and stabilizes the Paterian doctrine of intensity by locating it in the static and perfect form of the lyric poem itself (an outcome Pater's delicate evocation of the idea of art for art in the Conclusion adumbrates but resists). Similarly, Eliot's notion of the "tradition" as an ideal order of Western letters, and his subsequent attempt to ground a theory of society as well as an aesthetic in that notion of tradition, refracts the complex aestheticist vision of the simultaneous value of temporality and timelessness into an invocation of the static and perfect order of art (again a move Pater's *Marius* anticipates and resists). Indeed, when placed next to the work of the aestheticists themselves, Eliot and Pound's perfervid searches after synthesis look (at least to my admittedly prejudiced eyes) timid and weak—and, after they turn from the virtues of the aesthetic per se to more elaborate, if equally aestheticized, forms of belief, somewhat frightening.

This tendency was further accentuated by the American New Critics who followed directly in the wake of the modernist poets; in their own valorization of the well-wrought urn, they received Pound and Eliot's transformation of aestheticist speculation into hardened dogma as a form of revealed religion. By similarly locating in the aesthetic per se a completely autonomous, self-enclosed system that would provide some form of privileged knowledge and moral coherence in a world governed by social anarchy and scientific pseudoknowledge, they transformed the aestheticist flirtation with the autonomy of art into a consecrated marriage. Thus, when John Crowe Ransom unwittingly (?) echoes Pater's Preface to *The Renaissance*, we can ourselves see quite clearly that the claims for vision and for art that Pater advanced so cautiously, so tentatively there as elsewhere in that volume have become inflated beyond any Paterian measure:

The true poetry has no great interest in improving or idealizing the world, which does well enough. It only wants to realize the world, to see it better. Poetry is the kind of knowledge by which we must know what we have arranged that we shall not know otherwise. . . . What we cannot know constitutionally as scientists is the world which is made of whole and indefeasible objects, and this is the world which poetry recovers for us.[34]

Eliot, Pound, and the American New Critics who followed directly in their wake privileged the aestheticist aspects of James with such fervor, I am suggesting, because this James provided an example to these poets that was at once empowering and unthreatening, particularly in comparison with the more immediate, if more unstable, tradition of British aestheticism. If "the question [in 1908] was still: where do we go from Swinburne? and the answer appeared to be, nowhere," as T. S. Eliot wrote in 1946, then another part of the answer was: continue to build on the foundations Swinburne, Pater, and Wilde gave you, but do so under the sign of James.[35] The reasons for this strategy of simultaneous engagement with and disavowal of the example of British aestheticism are not difficult to understand. For, as C. K. Stead has argued, the early poetry and criticism of the modernists were consistently denigrated by the more hostile elements in the press as a second go-round of the aesthetic movement, particularly of its publicly disgraced "decadent" aspects.[36] But more important, the model of aestheticism itself that these poets followed out did not satisfy, because they were unable to tolerate its embrace of contradiction, its tantalizing suggestion of the possibilities of establishing a satisfactory synthesis in the valorization of art and its stubborn refusal to make good on its own promises. To writers of this imaginative disposition, the late, hermetic James could suggest not only a pattern of thematic preoccupation or formal devices, but also a structure of strategic response. He could show the writers who were to follow him how the aestheticist privileging of intense experience in general and of art in particular as the most efficient avenue toward such experience, the aestheticist nexus between cruelty and ambiguity, and the aestheticist emphasis on a cultural criticism grounded in the analysis and appreciation of art could be normalized, its diffusive energies tamed as they were brought within the venue of aesthetic performance itself, as they were concretized in self-affirming works of art.

Even more important, James demonstrated how the normalizing of aestheticist practices and procedures could be made part of a successful literary career. Eliot's emphasis on the failures of the aesthetic poets to produce art, on their leading, instead, to only a few "untidy lives" suggests how enthusiastically this aspect of James was adopted by the modernists: by his powerful performance (in every sense of the word) on the London literary scene in the first decades of the twentieth century, James vividly demonstrated that the paradigm of inadequate aesthetic professionalism exemplified by a Pater or a Wilde could be supplemented, even perfected, by a mystified—and productive—high-art professionalism. By the single-mindedness of his dedication to his art, his visible and public quest after public acclaim, his bitter denunciations of that public for failing to appreciate his aesthetic achievements, James brought into concrete being the role Pater, Wilde, and their confreres cultivated: that of the professional artist/hero— one who dedicates himself to his craft in equal defiance of bourgeois complacency and bohemian exclusiveness; and he did so without the lapses of productivity, the marginalization of literary effort, or the personal scandal that Pater, Wilde, and the decadents all displayed. Further, James provided for Eliot and Pound (and especially the former) an example of a successful *American* literary professionalism in a world that still took London as the center of the English-speaking literary universe; he showed them how an American might be able to amass and deploy his cultural capital in such a way as to establish himself as a magisterial aesthetic authority even in the aggressively provincial world of English letters. Richard Aldington wrote of Eliot that "by merit, tact, prudence, and pertinacity he succeeded in doing what no other American has ever done—imposing his personality, taste, and even many of his opinions on literary England"; but as Eliot's own essay suggests, and as any reader who is not inclined to begin literary history in 1914 knows, it was Henry James who provided the first and perhaps best example of this act.[37]

And it should be added to this rather idealizing list that by the sneaky but astute eye he kept on his public, James was also able to provide an example of a cannily *managed* literary reputation to a generation of writers who excelled in nothing if not the adroit packaging of both their poetry and their personae. W. H. Auden—a modernist of a distinctively different stripe, and one far more generously appreciative of James than were Pound or Eliot—wrote in 1948 that James's most eccentric and American quality was his concern with public opinion:

The European . . . has always been completely bewildered by the way in which James, being the kind of writer he was, worried so about his lack of popular appeal. Since coming to this country, I have realized how American in this respect he was; for I have never encountered a writer here, however highbrow, who was not seriously concerned with reviews and sales, while, on the other hand, I have never met a serious European writer who, outside of the need to pay his creditors, took the slightest interest in the opinion of any but a few friends whose critical minds he admired and trusted. There are cases in this country where the concern for public opinion does not appear on the surface. But its presence reveals itself in messianic claims and the demand for a select, uncritically adoring circle.[38]

By Auden's definition, Pound and Eliot were American in just this Jamesian way, sharing with him the need both for artistic success and popular—or at least elite—acclaim; a dalliance with the avant-garde and yet a profound yearning for respectability; and a brilliant cultivation of a high-art persona, which disavowed any contact with the increasingly large audience eager for cultural respectability but which nevertheless achieved canonical status in the eyes of the most influential members of that audience—first among the more advanced literati, then, as the later years of the twentieth century were to show, in the academy that "rediscovered" James and privileged High Modernism on precisely the same grounds.[39]

The consequences of this modernist recasting of literary history are still with us, even—especially—when we claim to disavow them. Indeed, James's reputation and that of British aestheticism for most of the twentieth century can be plotted against the critical fortunes of High Modernism in both its pre- and postacademic phases, leading to the distortions and evasions it has been the goal of this study to correct. This linkage is most immediately evident in the case of James. It is to this modernist canonization of the internationalist, formalist James that we owe our most influential reckonings of his achievement: critics of the 1940's and 1950's themselves focused both their attacks and defences on precisely the linked questions of James's formalism and his cosmopolitanism. It is no coincidence that the academics responsible for the institutionalization of the critical embodiment of modernist principles, New Criticism, were extensively involved in managing the James revival. F. O. Matthiessen is an ambivalent example of this, as William Cain has recently shown; Austin Warren provides a more enthusiastic one—and that the anti-Jacobites have almost invariably positioned themselves in direct opposition to the interpretive codes of the New Criticism.[40] But the critical fate of the aestheticists has been equally, if less obviously, linked to that of modernist formalism; first in the standard denigration of the aestheticists in the Eliotic phase of the New Criticism, then in the excavation of aestheticism through the application of New Critical principles undertaken in the 1960's, and finally in the revival of aestheticism under the aegis of post-New Critical procedures evident in the 1970's and 1980's.

The flood tide of modernist formalism has, it would seem, receded, yet it has left behind peculiar flotsam, particularly on the shores of

James scholarship. One of its more discouraging residues has been the effacement of the intersection between or crossing among the work of Henry James and the British aestheticists—Jacobites on the one hand strewing misleading comments about aestheticism in order to cover over any possible "taint" of excessive aesthetic fervor on the part of James; anti-Jacobites piling an excessively moralistic, reductive, and inadequate notion of the tradition of aestheticism on James in order to bury him beneath the shifting sands of critical fashion. The result of both these maneuvers has been to distort both the importance of aestheticism to James and the importance of James's career-long dialogue with that tradition itself. This dialogue, I have been trying to suggest here, brought these bodies of work into sharper focus; it delineated clearly the possibilities and limitations of each, and can therefore suggest to a contemporary reader a more fluid, more complicated response to both. Reading James's work through and against the tradition of British aestheticism can help us understand more clearly, less polemically, the intellectual, social, and imaginative qualities that shaped the turn toward aestheticism in the British tradition and in James's work alike; this view can also allow us, perhaps, to forgive both for the excesses and insufficiencies of their undertaking. Freed from the modernist narrative of late-nineteenth-century decline, we can understand the turn toward aestheticism as a turn toward possibilities that are only now being fully explored; freed from the modernist privileging of the formalist, aestheticist James and thus liberated from the antimodernist counterreactions, we can respond with some perspective to James's attempts to work out the problematics and paradoxes of the rich, if fragmentary, vision with which he was endowed by the British aestheticist tradition.

And more is at stake here—as I have been arguing throughout this book—than just a new way of viewing Henry James, British aestheticism, modernism, or the complicated entanglement of all three. What is ultimately at issue is our understanding of "the aesthetic" itself—our understanding of the nature, provenance, and implications of those doctrines and their attendant social practices that placed the experience of beauty or pleasure in a sphere either autonomous or morally and socially redemptive, or both. This sense of the aesthetic is now understood to be fatally compromised, and from the start. It consummated, as Raymond Williams has taught us, the separation between "culture" and "society" by delineating a zone of high, self-privileging art-making amidst the welter of practices and productions that constitute culture in the fullest sense of the word. In so doing, it mystified, as

Pierre Bourdieu has more recently argued, the criterion of "taste" and prescribed its display as a means of asserting and reproducing forms of class domination and social control. And finally, as I have tried to suggest, it generated an ideology for the full pursuit of aesthetic professionalism whose final destiny was the rise of new career paths for the writer and the critic alike—the former through high modernism, the latter (as I have only begun to argue above) through the academic institutionalization of New Criticism.

And this indeed is one story that this book has to tell. The tentative and volatile privileging of the aesthetic performed by the aestheticists in England and America; their mutually modifying interplay with late-nineteenth-century consumer culture; the aestheticists' willing—and at times unwilling—professionalization; their role in the creation of new markets for the production and the reception of high-art aesthetic commodities; the subsequent crystallization of aestheticism into both a formalist dogma and a canny career path under the ministrations first of James and then of his modernist successors—all of these might be seen as one unified story marching toward a conclusion as inevitable as it is doleful. But I have tried to tell another story here as well. This story emphasizes the discontinuities, contradictions, and problematics of aestheticist theory and practice, and it foregrounds as well the discontinuities that we must ourselves encounter as we retell and in so doing recreate the career of aestheticism in Anglo-American culture.

Indeed, I have tried to tell both of these stories at once, and for several reasons. To tell the first story alone is not only to understate the heterogeneity of Anglo-American aestheticism's textual performance or its social practices, but also to reinforce the social logic that one would wish to critique. To emphasize a heterogeneity of aestheticisms and foreground the possibilities as well as the limitations of the social critique embedded within some of them, by contrast, is to suggest that there is more than one possible outcome to the social drama aesthetic movement was itself part of, and indeed in part superintended, the rise of those new styles of consumption, new strategies of aesthetic movement was itself part of, and indeed in part it superintended, the rise of those new styles of consumption, new strategies of professionalization, and new modes of advertising that reconfigured the landscape of cultural possibilities in the early twentieth century— and it goes without saying that it is this terrain we find ourselves still exploring. To try to tell both stories at once, then, is to bow to the historical without fully reproducing its logic; to analyze a historical process without treating its outcome as either natural or necessary— or, for that matter, as final.

And hence my own final point. The privileging of a fully autonomous aesthetic sphere may have breathed its last, at least conceptually; and the older forms of institutionalized aestheticism may have passed away, at least academically—and to both of them, one wants to say good riddance. But this is not to say, I hope, that their passing does not also create space for new imaginings, new understandings, of all the things to which the contradictory doctrines and diverse social performances of Anglo-American aestheticism gave such vivid and so problematic expression. It may well be that the forging of a new idiom to reckon with the experiences of beauty and pleasure is the next challenge that awaits us; in any event, the reimagining and rearticulation of these experiences will doubtless pose as difficult and as necessary a task for our profession as it does for our taste.

Reference Matter

Notes

Complete authors' names, titles, and publication data are given in the Abbreviations, pp. ix–x, or in Works Cited, pp. 281–92.

Introduction

1. Here are some of the major works of this effort of contextualization: Anderson, *The Imperial Self*; Armstrong, *The Phenomenology of Henry James*; Brodhead, *The School of Hawthorne*; P. Brooks, *The Melodramatic Imagination*; Donadio, *Nietzsche, Henry James, and the Artistic Will*; Egan, *Henry James: The Ibsen Years*; Fogel, *Henry James and the Structure of the Romantic Imagination*; Gervais, *Flaubert and Henry James*; Grover, *Henry James and the French Novel*; Jacobson, *Henry James and the Mass Market*; Long, *The Great Succession*; Nettels, *James and Conrad*; Posnock, *Henry James and the Problem of Robert Browning*; Powers, *Henry James and the Naturalist Movement*; Stowell, *Literary Impressionism*.

2. Of all the treatments of this vast and complex issue, the most helpful for my purposes has been Raymond Williams's seminal essay "Base and Superstructure in Marxist Cultural Theory," in *Problems in Materialism and Culture*. For a more rigorously marxist treatment of the issues I discuss below, see Haug, *Critique of Commodity Aesthetics*.

3. V. W. Brooks, *The Pilgrimage of Henry James*, p. 130. Further citations in the text will refer to this edition.

4. Parrington, *The Beginnings of Critical Realism in America, 1860–1920*, pp. 239–40.

5. Geismar, *Henry James and the Jacobites*, pp. 410–11.

6. Gilmore, "The Commodity World of *The Portrait of a Lady*," p. 74.

7. Porter, *Seeing and Being*; Seltzer, *Henry James and the Art of Power*, p. 148.

8. Sherman, *On Contemporary Literature*, pp. 253, 238. In *The Pilgrimage of Henry James*, V. W. Brooks, too, uses highly Paterian language to describe James's imaginative procedures, although Brooks's elaboration of Pater's trope of the hard, gemlike flame both exaggerates James's lust for Pater-like intense impressions and suggests that James's capacity for registering those sensations was more developed and variegated than was his predecessors': "There was no

doubt about the spoils [the 'impressions' James brought back from America]. There was no doubt about the crackling twigs—armfuls of them and how they crackled!—that he had been able to pile up on the altar of perception; it had been a game of feeding the beautiful iridescent flame, ruddy and green and gold, blue and pink and amber and silver, with anything he could pick up, anything that would burn and flicker, and he had scarcely been able to move for the brush that clogged his feet" (164–65). For more on James's own use of this trope, see Chapters 4 and 5.

9. In addition to the works of Porter and Seltzer I cite above, I am thinking here of the subtle and suggestive marxist analysis of John Goode, for whom James is also to be understood under the sign of aestheticism. See Goode's fine essay, "The Pervasive Mystery of Style: *The Wings of the Dove*," pp. 244–300.

10. See Peckham, *The Triumph of Romanticism*, pp. 218ff.

11. Adorno, *Aesthetic Theory*, p. 336. Further citations in the text will refer to this edition.

12. Indeed, the ironies here are even more extensive. James and Du Maurier were able to attract early in their careers the enthusiasm of the broad reading public by writing in, and helping to shape, the new popular genre of aesthete satire; and the subsequent course of their careers—Du Maurier toward the best-sellerdom by means of writing about aesthetes, James in the direction of attracting an elite audience of cognoscenti by writing hermetic aestheticist fiction—suggests the two fates of aestheticist discourse in the brave new world of the literary marketplace: tending on the one hand toward affectionate satirization by a mass audience, on the other toward ambivalent canonization by the elite. In both cases, however, aestheticism both critiques and participates in the commodification of the aesthetic sphere; and frequently —as in the case of the widespread audience for satires of commodifying aesthetes on the one hand and the increasing size and self-regard of the elite audience of aestheticist commodifiers on the other—critique and complicity rapidly become inseparable from each other.

13. Norris, *Paul de Man: Deconstruction and the Critique of Aesthetic Ideology*.

14. De Man, *The Resistance to Theory*, p. 64, as quoted in Norris, *Paul de Man*, p. 41. For Bourdieu, see *Distinction: A Social Critique of the Judgement of Taste*.

Chapter One

1. Beerbohm, "1880," pp. 278–79.

2. See, for example, Starkie, *From Gautier to Eliot*, esp. pp. 26–85. Here is a sample of Starkie's claims: "The writers who exercised most influence in the propagation of the theories of Art for Art's Sake in England were Algernon Swinburne and Walter Pater . . . Swinburne was the first Decadent in England, owing much to French example; while Pater was the first Aesthete, also much indebted to France" (40). A similar genealogy is traced by Rosenblatt, *L'idée de l'art pour l'art*, and, more recently, by Conlon, *Walter Pater and the French Tradition*.

3. And then, it should be added, back into the German critical tradition; see Iser, *Walter Pater: Die Autonomie des Asthetischen*, translated as *Walter Pater:*

The Aesthetic Moment by David Henry Wilson. For the introduction of German philosophy to Britain, see Ashton's helpful *The German Idea*.

4. It has been traced most thoroughly by Hough, *The Last Romantics*, and Bloom, *Yeats*, pp. 23–51. For a thorough survey of the uses and abuses of the term aestheticism, see Temple, "Truth in Labelling."

5. And thence made into a separate essay in the first edition of *Appreciations* (1889), but suppressed in subsequent editions. I take my citations from this edition, not from *The Works of Walter Pater*, otherwise my source. Other portions of the Morris essay appeared as part of the Conclusion to *The Renaissance*. Pater, *Appreciations*, p. 213.

6. Newsome, *Two Classes of Men*, p. 95.

7. This poem first appeared in *Songs Before Sunrise* (1871).

8. After writing these pages, I had occasion to read Jonathan Dollimore's treatment of the same issue under the sign of "transgressive reinscription." For Dollimore, Wilde's epigrams express in reverse binary form the essential value-structures of his culture and hence avoid the pitfalls both of naive essentialism and of an equally naive anti-essentialism. Dollimore, like many recent gay critics, sees Wilde as the founder of a new gay male subjectivity; far more than most, he also positions Wilde as the questioner, via the mechanisms of "transgressive reinscription," of established Western metaphysics, epistemologies, and ontologies. My own view is somewhat less sanguine; while Wilde's ambitions in this direction are not to be doubted, his success in stepping outside of cultural determinations is: the pathos of Wilde's implication in the value systems he attempts to reject ought not be ignored. But neither should the political advantages of rereading—however transgressively—Wilde's example itself. See Dollimore, "Different Desires." For brilliant effort at transgressive reinscription for the purpose of establishing the position of a gay reader, see Koestenbaum, "Wilde's Hard Labor and the Birth of Gay Reading."

9. Chesterton, *The Victorian Age in Literature*, p. 71.

10. To these Linda Dowling has impressively sought to add the rise of Germanic philology, whose comparative technique and emphasis on the arbitrariness of the signifier loosened the Victorian mooring of moral and national hierarchies in the presumed order of language. While I find Dowling's arguments impressive, I also find her linguistic immanence somewhat questionable; the question is not, in my opinion, what philological theory did to Victorian society, or even what such theory did to literary practice, but rather what the interplay of social and intellectual forces working together wrought in the sphere of philological discourse and literary practice alike and why it is that those two spheres were sutured together so thoroughly in large part in precisely this period. See Dowling, *Language and Decadence in the Victorian Fin-de-Siècle*.

11. Bürger, *Theory of the Avant Garde*, p. 46. Further citations in the text will refer to this edition.

12. Buckley, *The Triumph of Time*.

13. The first citation of each poem will give volume, page, and line numbers; subsequent citations will give line numbers only.

14. Prince, "D. G. Rossetti," p. 369.

15. See Wittgenstein, *Philosophical Investigations*, p. 194e.

16. Indeed, the power of Lessing's formulation has remained, until virtually the current moment, absolute, influencing aestheticians, critics, and poets alike—even those who wished to revise Lessing's terms by turning to literature's capacities for "spatial form." Recently, however, it has come under more successful attack, one that all accounts of the interrelation of visual and verbal arts will, in my opinion, have to reckon with. The crucial text in this process is W. J. T. Mitchell's chapter on Lessing in *Iconology*, pp. 95–115, to which I am much indebted here. (Further citations in the text will refer to this edition.) For the tradition of *ekphrasis*, I have relied on Hagstrum's classic, *The Sister Arts*; for the ekphrastic tradition in the nineteenth century, I have consulted Park, "'*Ut Pictura Poesis*': The Nineteenth-Century Aftermath," pp. 155–64, and Richard Stein, *The Ritual of Interpretation*. My thinking on this subject has also been much stimulated by Bryan Wolf's unpublished essay, *Confessions of a Closet Ekphrastic*.

17. Richard Stein, *The Ritual of Interpretation*, p. 19.

18. For the best recent treatment of this topic, see Culler, *The Victorian Mirror of History*.

19. Knoepflmacher, *Religious Humanism and the Victorian Novel*, p. 233; Fleishman, *The English Historical Novel*, pp. 169–76.

20. Eliot, "Tradition and the Individual Talent" in *Selected Essays*, p. 4.

21. Fleishman, *The English Historical Novel*, p. 176.

22. De Man, "The Rhetoric of Temporality," p. 188. Further citations in the text will refer to this edition.

23. Coleridge, *Biographia Literaria*, vol. 2, p. 12.

24. I am thinking here of such works as Hartman, *Wordsworth's Poetry, 1787–1814*, and Bloom, *The Visionary Company*.

25. See, for example, Kermode, *Romantic Image*.

26. De Man, *Allegories of Reading*, p. 10.

27. See, in particular, Miller, "Walter Pater: A Partial Portrait," pp. 97–113, and a fine reading of the passage from *Aesthetic Poetry* I discuss above in Miller, *The Linguistic Moment: From Wordsworth to Stevens*, pp. 229–33; see also Monsman, *Walter Pater's Art of Autobiography*. For the general question of the application of deconstruction to Victorian poetry see Slinn, "Consciousness as Writing: Deconstruction and Reading Victorian Poetry."

28. The story was frequently repeated by John Ruskin; see, for example, *Fors Claveriga*, Letter 45, in *Works*, vol. 28, p. 147.

29. See Paulson, "Turner's Graffiti: The Sun and Its Glosses," for a psychoanalytic and psychohistorical account of Turner's deployment (and deconstruction) of the sun along similar lines to my analysis of Swinburne here. My sense of Swinburne is that he wished to out-Turner Turner in his celebration/rejection of the creating/castrating Father-God sun.

30. Weiskel, *The Romantic Sublime: Studies in the Structure and Psychology of Transcendence*.

31. The best explication of this sense of post-Romanticism is Murfin's *Swinburne, Hardy, Lawrence, and the Burden of Belief*.

32. Arnold, "Shelley," p. 327; Arnold, "Wordsworth," pp. 36–55.

33. For a further exploration of this dynamic, largely focusing on *The House of Life*, see Spector, "Love, Unity and Desire in the Poetry of Dante Gabriel Rossetti."

34. I have learned the most from Daniel Harris, "D. G. Rossetti's 'Jenny': Sex, Money, and the Interior Monologue." See also Hersey, "Rossetti's 'Jenny': A Realist Altarpiece," and Lackey, "A Scholar-John: The Speaker in 'Jenny.'"

35. Marcus, *The Other Victorians*, pp. 21–22.

36. See Monsman, *Pater's Portraits*, p. 76.

37. Freud discusses the problem most fully and interestingly in "Group Psychology and the Analysis of the Ego" (1921), where identification, as both the most primitive of psychic mechanisms and as the one that provides a successful resolution to the Oedipal crisis, is seen as the basis of not only the formation of the ego but also of such "neuroses" as romantic love and hypnosis. See Freud, "Group Psychology," esp. pp. 105–111.

38. Cohen, "Writing Gone Wilde," p. 806.

39. Helsinger, *Ruskin and the Art of the Beholder*, pp. 15–16.

40. Moers, *The Dandy*, pp. 12–13.

41. Ellmann, *Oscar Wilde at Oxford*, p. 9; this material is reworked in Ellmann, *Oscar Wilde*, p. 38.

42. These affinities have been admirably discussed by Gagnier, *Idylls of the Marketplace: Oscar Wilde and the Victorian Public*, and Wicke, *Advertising Fictions: Literature, Advertisement, and Social Reading*, esp. pp. 83–86.

43. Bledstein, *The Culture of Professionalism*. Further citations in the text will refer to this edition.

44. Larson, *The Rise of Professionalism*.

45. Sheldon Rothblatt, *The Revolution of the Dons: Cambridge and Society in Victorian England*, pp. 91–92. For more on the conflict between professionalism and the *ethos* of the gentleman, see Engel, *From Clergyman to Don: The Rise of the Academic Profession in Nineteenth-Century Oxford*, pp. 10–12.

46. Green's freewheeling but fascinating *Children of the Sun: A Narrative of "Decadence" in England After 1918* argues that the conflict between the descendants of the aesthetes and their antagonists structured British cultural history for the next twenty years.

47. The rise of the alienated artist and his or her complicitous relation with an increasingly assertive bourgeois audience has been thoroughly dissected by students of nineteenth-century French culture, especially Seigel, *Bohemian Paris*, and Graña, *Bohemian Versus Bourgeois*. Studies of similar phenomena in England are rarer, a sign of the greater power Paris exerted over the nineteenth-century avant-garde, perhaps, but also of a valorization of the oppositional possibilities of the aesthetic sphere not entirely absent from British cultural criticism of this moment.

48. Adorno, "Cultural Criticism and Society," in *Prisms*, p. 20.

49. To cite only two of the most recent examples of the newly institutionalized genre of professionalized institution-critique, see Bové, *Intellectuals in Power: A Genealogy of Critical Humanism*, and Graff, *Professing Literature: An Institutional History*. The most interesting examples of this concern center on

the work of Stanley Fish; for a representative sample of his sprightly and thoroughly unmystified contribution to the debate, see "Profession Despise Thyself: Fear and Self-Loathing in Literary Studies," and for a classic statement of the problems with the Fish position, see Edward Said, "Response to Stanley Fish." I must confess here that, while I find Fish's exuberance refreshing, I find his argument puzzling. On the one hand, he celebrates academic professionalism as an end in and of itself, not as a means to the affirmation of certain timeless humanistic values—e.g., the pursuit of truth or the establishment of immutable aesthetic standards. But on the other hand, he praises "professionals whose business it is to make and remake . . . culture" (364)—an appeal, in other words, to a variant of Arnoldian rhetoric that Fish has just been attacking, one in which academic intellectuals serve as the prime arbiters of culture itself. As Bledstein points out in *The Culture of Professionalism*, no profession, no matter how cynical its participants, can escape the desire to justify itself on larger social grounds; Fish's yearning for the cultural hegemony of English professors bears out the cogency of his assertion—as, more obviously, do the aspirations of Graff and Said for the rise of a new form of cultural criticism in the place of "traditional" literary studies.

50. By "consumer culture," I mean those cultural transformations that accompanied the phenomenon historians refer to as "the consumer revolution" —the supply side, as it were, of the industrial revolution, as Derek Brewer puts it (in McKendrick, Brewer, and Plumb, *The Birth of a Consumer Society*, p. 3). Here is a fine summary of this "revolution," offered by a historian of nineteenth-century France, Rosalind Williams: "Its characteristics are a radical division between activities of production and of consumption, the prevalence of standardized merchandise sold in large volume, the ceaseless introduction of new products, widespread reliance on money and credit and ubiquitous publicity. . . . In the wealthier societies the manifestations of mass consumption—department stores, discount houses, supermarkets, chain stores, mail-order houses, and perpetual advertising in newspapers and magazines and on television, radio, and billboards—are so pervasive that we hardly realize how thoroughly both private and collective life have been transformed into a medium where people habitually interact with merchandise" (*Dream Worlds*, p. 3). As this description suggests, a consumer economy is one whose cultural apparatus itself has been doubly transformed: transformed first because it has become an essential part of the process of selling consumer goods; and transformed again because its products, too, are available to being understood, bought, and sold as forms of "merchandise."

The rise of consumer culture has been a subject of particular interest to students of eighteenth-century England and nineteenth-century and twentieth-century America and France; it seems to have been of somewhat less interest for historians of nineteenth-century England, although (or because) a rich vein of British cultural criticism centers on the moral defects of consumption —the discourse of Ruskin and Morris in particular, but also of leftist intellectuals like George Bernard Shaw and, ultimately, of E. P. Thompson and Raymond Williams. For the consumer revolution in eighteenth-century England, see McKendrick, Brewer, and Plumb, *The Birth of a Consumer Society*. For the rise of a mass consumer society in nineteenth-century France, see Rosalind Williams, *Dream Worlds*.

As Williams observes, America has been frequently viewed as the first, most complete, and hence archetypal consumer society; and this tendency of thought is reflected as well in the profusion of critiques of consumer culture offered by twentieth-century American cultural historians and critics, many of whom treat consumerism and its ancillaries—abundance, leisure, the rise of advertising, mass media, and so on—as foundational to "the American character" or national identity. Classic moments in this tradition include Veblen, *The Theory of the Leisure Class*; from the 1950's, Reisman, *The Lonely Crowd*, and Potter, *People of Plenty*; and, more recently, Ewen, *Captains of Consciousness*. The best recent analyses of American consumer culture are to be found in Fox and Lears, *The Culture of Consumption*.

The most elegant theorist of consumer culture is, however, French: Jean Baudrillard. See especially *La Société de Consommation: Ses mythes, Ses Structures* and *La Système des Objets*, although the totality of Baudrillard's work might be seen as a reflection on the semiotic, ideological, psychological, and aesthetic consequences of consumerism. For a fine Baudrillardian account of the rise of consumer society and its role in the construction of the female subject as shopper, see Bowlby, *Just Looking: Consumer Culture in Dreiser, Gissing, and Zola*.

51. Thompson's famous biography, *William Morris: Romantic to Revolutionary*, pays eloquent tribute to this aspect of his endeavor; Perry Anderson's response in *Arguments Within English Marxism* represents a brilliant attempt to appropriate Morris for a less "humanistic," more "scientific" marxism. Both need to be read as attempts to discover a genuinely English marxist tradition, one as theoretically sophisticated and tactically shrewd as those of France and Germany. At times, then, an American reader may find an irritatingly nationalistic cast to these endeavors, even as he admires the eloquence and brio with which they are performed.

52. Jackson, *William Morris*, p. 152.

53. Boris, *Art and Labor: Ruskin, Morris, and the Craftsman Ideal in America*, p. 58. Further citations in the text will refer to this edition. See also Jackson, *William Morris*, pp. 152–53, and, of course, Veblen, *The Theory of the Leisure Class*, p. 162, for witty and slightly unfair discussions of Morris and Ruskin's "exaltation of the defective" as an exaltation of the expensive as well, and hence as a prime example of pecuniary canons of taste that mark "conspicuous consumption."

54. Landow, "Ruskin as Victorian Sage: The Example of *Traffic*," pp. 89–110.

55. Maidment, "Interpreting Ruskin, 1870–1914," pp. 159–71.

56. I adopt these terms from Adorno, who offers the most accessible account of the principles of immanent and transcendent criticism of culture in "Cultural Criticism and Society" (in *Prisms*, pp. 17–34).

57. Benjamin, "The Storyteller," in *Illuminations*, p. 84.

58. Hume, *A Treatise of Human Nature*, p. 252.

59. Agnew, "The Consuming Vision of Henry James," p. 71 (further citations in the text will refer to this edition). Agnew is quoting from Leiss, *The Limits to Satisfaction*, pp. 88–89, 93.

60. For Berenson's Paterianism, see Chapter 2. Michael Levey recounts that Pater refused Berenson's request to sit in on his lectures at Oxford, a rebuff that Berenson rather typically resented for the rest of his life. Levey, *The Case of Walter Pater*, pp. 186, 221.

61. Marcuse, *Eros and Civilization*, p. 193. Further citations in the text will refer to this edition.

62. Bakhtin, *The Dialogic Imagination*, pp. 279–80. Gagnier also notes Wilde's dialogism (*Idylls of the Marketplace*, pp. 31–32), which however she links to Guy Debord's discussion of plagiarism as "the revolutionary and dialectical style of diversion." My interest here, rather, is in the ways Wilde's dialogism simultaneously enables and inhibits critique.

63. For a sophisticated theoretical extrapolation from these movements, see Laclau and Mouffe, *Hegemony and Socialist Strategy*. Their formulation is unlike Wilde's in rejecting the notion of the individual or subject along with their Wilde-like rejection of reifications like "workers" or even "class" itself; but it is eminently Wildean in its refusal to conform to the language of any given political tradition and in its movement through socialism to a flirtation with libertarianism and anarchism. Wilde, Laclau, and Mouffe might all be said to occupy that territory where leftism becomes so far left as to move off the political map completely.

64. Lyotard, *The Postmodern Condition: A Report on Knowledge*.

65. Claims about which post modernism itself is properly skeptical. In *The Postmodern Condition*, Lyotard reminds us that "*post modern* [has] to be understood according to the paradox of the future (*post*) anterior (*modo*)," a suggestion that might be taken as implying that the postmodern, like the "modern" it supplements and subverts, is potentially to be found at any moment that theorizes its own modernity (81). (This is perhaps what Lyotard means by the even more enigmatical claim that "a work can become modern only if it is first postmodern" [79].) For a further exploration of this and other issues in the theory of postmodernism, see Wicke's fine review essay, "Postmodernism: The Perfume of Information."

Chapter Two

1. As translated by Irving Howe, this excerpt appears in *World of Our Fathers*, p. 431. My thanks to Dana Brand for this reference.

2. Wharton, *Old New York*, p. 36.

3. Stillman, "Modern Painters V," p. 239.

4. Much of the data presented here has been gleaned from Roger Stein, *John Ruskin and Aesthetic Thought in America, 1840–1900*, esp. pp. 13–24. Stein's account of Ruskin's influence on American culture from 1850 through 1875 or so is encyclopedic in its scope and range of evidence. Other treatments of the subject, less thoroughly researched but nevertheless helpful, include Townsend, "The American Estimate of Ruskin, 1847–1860," and Dickason,

The Daring Young Men: The Story of the American Pre-Raphaelites.

5. Since Ruskin refused to recognize any American house as his official publisher, technically all American editions were pirated. But Wiley has the best claim to be the authorized publisher, since it was the first firm to publish Ruskin here and consistently offered him royalties, which he equally consistently refused. See Roger Stein, *John Ruskin and Aesthetic Thought in America, 1840–1900,* pp. 263–65.

6. *The Crayon* 1 (May 2, 1855): 283.

7. For this suspicion, see Neil Harris, *The Artist in American Society,* esp. pp. 28–53.

8. Sturgis's review of *Modern Painters V* is in *The Nation* 7 (Aug. 27, 1868): 173–74.

9. *The Crayon* 1 (May 9, 1855): 298–99.

10. For the fate of Jarves's collection, see Steegmuller, *The Two Lives of James Jackson Jarves.*

11. "For the Puritan faith in a theocracy of sober men, the New England moralists had substituted, by the 1870's, a faith in moral suasion and a proper education for the masses as the best elements of social control," writes Dee Garrison in *Apostles of Culture: The Public Librarian and American Society, 1876–1920,* p. 11. Garrison provides a vivid sketch of the gentry elite in action; for more expansive accounts, see Persons, *The Decline of American Gentility,* and Tomsich, *A Genteel Endeavor: American Culture and Politics in the Gilded Age.*

12. The recollections of Josephine Peabody, as quoted in Vanderbilt, *Charles Eliot Norton,* pp. 133–34.

13. James, *Notes of a Son and Brother,* in *Autobiography,* p. 477; for Berenson's experience with Norton, see below; and for Fenollosa's, see Chisolm, *Fenollosa: The Far East and American Culture,* pp. 27–28, and V. W. Brooks, *Fenollosa and his Circle,* pp. 3–4. Brooks's account of evenings at Norton's Shady Hill home deserves to be quoted here, if only as a reminder of the oppressiveness of Norton's aesthetic veneration: "There, in the presence of 'Dante Meeting Beatrice,' the picture that Rossetti had painted for Norton, half a dozen young men, interested, curious, or devout, listened with copies of the *Paradiso* open in their hands. They followed the text while Norton read aloud, like a learned, elegant, and venerable priest dispensing sacred mysteries to a circle of heretics, perhaps, who were unworthy of them. One felt that there was something sacramental even in the sherry and the caraway cakes that a maidservant placed in our hands as we were about to depart" (*An Autobiography,* p. 120).

14. Berenson, *Sketch for a Self-Portrait,* pp. 51–52. "So much for the present time about Professor Norton," writes Berenson, but over the course of the next ten pages, Berenson worries repeatedly over the accuracy of Norton's description.

15. Reprinted in James, *Notes on Novelists,* pp. 412–23. Further references in the text will refer to this edition.

16. V. W. Brooks, *An Autobiography,* pp. 90, 371.

17. Especially by Lears's invigorating, if shrill, *No Place of Grace,* pp. 60–96.

18. Many of them mentioned the protean quality of Ruskin's thought in doing so. In an *Atlantic* article, "On the Relation of Art to Nature," J. Eliot Cabot mentions that "Mr. Ruskin might be quoted on both sides [of the issue]" (that is, either as a naturalist or an antinaturalist aesthetician) and eventually enlists Ruskin on his own. *Atlantic* 13 (Feb. 1864): 183.

19. Barbara Novak shows, for example, how Cole anticipated Ruskin's technical advice and aesthetic assumptions. See *Nature and Culture*, pp. 88–89.

20. James, *The Painter's Eye*, pp. 33–34.

21. Perry's account of the Newport summer of 1858 was reprinted by Lubbock in *The Letters of Henry James*, vol. 1, p. 7.

22. James, *Italian Hours*, pp. 4–5.

23. Ibid., p. 4; James, *The Painter's Eye*, p. 174.

24. James, *The Painter's Eye*, pp. 38–39.

25. Allott, "A Ruskin Echo in *The Wings of the Dove*."

26. Holloway, *The Victorian Sage*; see also Landow, "Ruskin as Victorian Sage."

27. Norton, Introduction to *The Crown of Wild Olive*, p. ix.

28. A similar argument is made in more depth (chiefly with reference to *The American Scene*) in Posnock, "Henry James, Veblen, and Adorno: The Crisis of the Modern Self."

29. A number of the "genteel critics" showed a good deal of sympathy with Rossetti, Swinburne, and Morris; Stedman's *Victorian Poets* (pp. 379–414), for example, concludes with a generous account of Swinburne and remarks favorably on Rossetti and Morris. Stedman takes Swinburne to task for the racier elements of his earlier poetry, but suggests that he has grown out of this indulgence. Further, as Tomsich has shown in *A Genteel Endeavor* (esp. pp. 113–66), the aesthetics of the genteel group can be seen as a slightly attenuated version of the aestheticist turn in English Romanticism. Tomsich also shows that George Boker shared more than aesthetic interests with Swinburne; it seems that he too was quite interested in pornography and found Swinburne's efforts interesting, if somewhat difficult to reprint.

30. *The Nation* 17 (Oct. 9, 1873): 243–44.

31. Jan. 21, 1882; reprinted in Lewis and Smith, *Oscar Wilde Discovers America*, p. 48. Note how the illustration accentuates American confusions about Wilde's gender. He is placed between the group of men and of women, and the elongation of his features and frame alike make Wilde appear far more androgynous than he in fact was, before, during, or after his American tour.

32. Gilbert, *Plays and Poems*, pp. 198–99.

33. Lewis and Smith, *Oscar Wilde Discovers America*, pp. 61, 53.

34. Ibid., p. 191.

35. For more of these song titles, see Mason, *Oscar Wilde and the Aesthetic Movement*.

36. For a bibliographical survey of the publications of the "aesthetic mania" of the 1880's, see Burke et al., *In Pursuit of Beauty*, pp. 488–502.

37. According to Russell Lynes, in whose book this quotation appears, these "claims should be discounted." But Sherwood's very hyperbole suggests how

these magazines simultaneously served as both reporters of and shills for the crazes they described. Lynes, *The Tastemakers*, p. 106.

38. For a broad cultural overview of this movement, see Roger Stein, "Artifact as Ideology: The Aesthetic Movement in Its American Cultural Context" in Burke et al., *In Pursuit of Beauty*, pp. 22–51. Other essays in this volume provide helpful accounts of the "aesthetic revolution" in different crafts: ceramics, metalwork, furniture, architecture, etc. For an account of the cognate phenomenon, the Arts and Crafts Movement, see Boris, *Art and Labor*, and Lears, *No Place of Grace*. In this work, I am less interested in the morally strenuous Arts and Crafts Movement, and more in the loosening of the moralistic impulse represented by American aestheticism.

39. Wilson, "The Rhetoric of Consumption: Mass-Market Magazines and the Demise of the Gentle Reader, 1880–1920," pp. 39–64.

40. *Appletons'*, n.s., 2 (May 1877): 473.

41. Marchand, p. 123.

42. Parrish's art was remarkably true to Pre-Raphaelite principles: it refused art nouveau curvilinear forms and adhered to a Pre-Raphaelite aesthetic of placing a photographic realism in the service of representing phantasmagorical subjects. The sources of such a style are somewhat mysterious; when Parrish enrolled in classes with the American most influenced by Pre-Raphaelite design principles, Howard Pyle, he was turned away on the grounds that Pyle had nothing to teach him. The effects of Parrish's style were spectacular; not only Parrish's advertising work but his prints became staples of middle-class design for many years. In 1936, for example, *Time* noted: "As far as the sale of expensive color reproductions is concerned, the three most popular artists in the world are van Gogh, Cézanne, and Maxfield Parrish" (Feb. 17, 1936, pp. 34–35). The inclusion of Parrish's kitschy illustrations with newly kitschified modernists like van Gogh and Cézanne in popular esteem is symptomatic of the kinds of connections I am trying to draw in this chapter between aestheticism and the popularization of "high culture."

43. For advertising as a "magic system," see Raymond Williams, *Problems in Materialism and Culture*, pp. 170–95.

44. The complicated changes in late-nineteenth-century American society and its culture have been described by Wiebe, *The Search for Order: 1877–1920*, esp. pp. 111–32, and Trachtenberg, *The Incorporation of America*, esp. pp. 140–81. For the rise of the university, see Veysey, *The Emergence of the American University*, and Bledstein, *The Culture of Professionalism*, esp. pp. 203–331. For the official Browning Societies and the unofficial Browning clubs and reading circles, see Greer, *Browning and America*.

45. See Limpus, *American Criticism of British Decadence, 1880–1900*, pp. 117–35, and Ziff, *The American 1890s*, pp. 120–45, for two accounts of what Gelett Burgess referred to as a "little riot of Decadence" (quoted in Ziff, p. 139). Most of the best-known, best-established, and longest-lasting periodicals were to be found, it must be admitted, in the larger metropolises like New York and San Francisco; Gelett Burgess's *The Lark* and James Huneker and Vance Thompson's *M'lle New York*, both of which are discussed extensively by Ziff, for example, were published in these two cultural centers. But what is most

striking about this process, it seems to me, is the extraordinary proliferation of these journals in wholly unexpected areas of the country—a facet to which Ziff pays relatively little attention.

46. *The Nation* 41 (Sept. 10, 1885): 220. *The Atlantic* review of Aug. 1885 is also quite favorable, but it remains dubious of Pater's descriptions of late Roman society and culture; see *The Atlantic* 66, p. 277.

47. Gamaliel Bradford, Jr., "Walter Pater," *Andover Review* 10 (Aug. 1888): 154.

48. *The Outlook* 53 (Jan. 1896): 160; *The Nation* 62 (April 9, 1896): 292, and 64 (March 4, 1897): 167.

49. *The Atlantic* 79 (May 1897): 711.

50. *Andover Review* 1 (Jan. 1884): 23–24.

51. Samuels, *Bernard Berenson: The Making of a Connoisseur*, pp. 37–40.

52. *The Nation* 59 (1894): 193; *Boston Commonwealth* (Aug. 9, 1894). I was guided to these expostulations by Limpus, *American Criticism of British Decadence*, pp. 102, 104.

53. But not American ministers, if Thomas Beer is to be believed. Beer estimates that Wilde was "mentioned" (unfavorably, one assumes) "in at least nine hundred known sermons" between 1895 and 1900. See *The Mauve Decade*, p. 129, and take with a grain of salt.

54. *The Lotus* 1 (Nov. 1895): 58.

55. For a fine treatment of Howells's own responses to the Bostonian elite, see Simpson, "The Treason of William Dean Howells" in his *The Man of Letters in New England and the South*, pp. 85–128.

56. Roger Stein, "Artifact as Ideology," p. 38.

57. Howells, *A Hazard of New Fortunes*, p. 221. Further citations in the text will refer to this edition.

58. For a splendid treatment of these issues in the context of Howells's representational response to the city, see Kaplan, "'The Knowledge of the Line': Realism and the City in Howells's *A Hazard of New Fortunes*."

59. I am thinking of such figures as Phillips in *The Undiscovered Country*, (1880), Ludlow in *The Coast of Bohemia* (1893), and even Bromfield Corey in *The Rise of Silas Lapham* (1885). For more on Howells's collision with American aestheticism and its ramifications, see my 1985 dissertation, "The Quickened Consciousness: Aestheticism in Howells and James."

60. Vanderbilt, *The Achievement of William Dean Howells*, p. 164.

61. Santayana, *The Middle Span*, p. 103.

62. V. W. Brooks, *An Autobiography*, p. 107.

63. Cowley, *Exile's Return*, p. 35.

64. Stevens's early sonnets, with their echoes of Rossetti and Morris as well as "adolescent echoings of Keats and Shelley," may be found in Holly Stevens, *Souvenirs and Prophecies: The Young Wallace Stevens*. The sonnet criticized by Santayana may be found on p. 33; Santayana's reply is in his *Complete Poems*, p. 131.

65. For Stickney, see *Mnemosyne* and *In Summer* in his *Poems*, pp. 22–25, 29–30. Frost, *Complete Poems*, pp. 396, 276, 451.

66. Stevens, *Collected Poems*, p. 70.

67. Eliot, "Arnold and Pater" in *Selected Essays*, p. 392.

68. Eliot, "The Perfect Critic" in *The Sacred Wood*, pp. 1–16. Louis Menand catalogs other Paterisms in the *Sacred Wood* essays in *Discovering Modernism*, pp. 194–95. Menand finds in these borrowings "only another instance of Eliot's general practice of appropriating whatever is available to suit his own uses"; my own view is, of course, that these may be read as one of the more important "instances" of the career-long negotiation between Eliot and the tradition that he grew out of and ambivalently rejected. The impact of Pater and of the tradition of British aestheticism on Eliot has become something of a commonplace in recent criticism; see, in addition to Menand, Levenson, *A Genealogy of Modernism*, pp. 10–22, and Monsman, *Walter Pater*, pp. 185–86. Monsman also presents a complete and sophisticated account of Pater's influence on the entire generation of Anglo-American modernists, pp. 160–86. The best overview of the general question of the indebtedness of modernist poetry and criticism to its immediate forbears is Christ, *Victorian and Modern Poetics*. I have also relied on Stead, *The New Poetic*.

69. Eliot, "Tradition and the Individual Talent" (first published 1919) in *Selected Essays*, p. 7. We might note as well that the dominant metaphoric structure of Pater's Preface, that of comparing aesthetic responses to scientific experimentation, recurs in Eliot's famous metaphor of the catalyst in "Tradition and the Individual Talent."

70. Eliot, *The Complete Poems and Plays*, p. 129.

71. Eliot, "Arnold and Pater" in *Selected Essays*, p. 392.

72. Kenner, *A Homemade World*, pp. 140–42. Kenner sees Pater's Conclusion, with its "appreciative intensities," as the "key to innumerable Hemingway pages" and compares Hemingway's suicide to Oscar Wilde's self-destruction as "an aesthetic necessity."

73. Mix, *A Study in Yellow: The Yellow Book and Its Contributors*, pp. 169–70.

Chapter Three

1. James, *Letters*, vol. 1, p. 391. Pater changed the title of his work in the second and subsequent editions to *The Renaissance: Studies in Art and History*.

2. James's discussion of Pater here is shot through with his characteristic ambivalence: "It is difficult to speak adequately, perhaps even intelligibly, of Sandro Botticelli. An ingenious critic (Mr. Pater, in his 'Studies on [sic] the Renaissance') has lately done so, more eloquently than coherently" ("Old Italian Pictures," p. 3). James here simultaneously distances himself from Pater and affirms his essential community with him: both strive, unsuccessfully, for adequate response to Botticelli's genius. (James is being quite immodest here, since Pater was the first great English critic to write appreciatively of Botticelli, as Pater himself noted with no little pride; see *Letters of Walter Pater*, p. 41.) For a complete inventory of James's responses to Pater, and an interesting treatment of his response to Botticelli as symptom of his reactions to British aestheticism, see Tintner, *The Book World of Henry James*, pp. 143–64.

It is quite possible that James's acquaintance with Pater predates his discovery of *The Renaissance*. An avid reader of British periodicals, James might well have followed the essays collected as *The Renaissance* as they appeared in the *Fortnightly* and *Westminister Reviews* between 1868 and 1871 (Pater's essay on Botticelli appeared in 1870). Some of his writing of this time suggests that he did so; in the 1870 story *Travelling Companions*, for example, James's German narrator describes his journey through Italy (and the progress of his love for a young American) in terms that explicitly reject Ruskin and echo Pater's revelings in intense visual experience: "Every step distilled a richer drop into the wholesome cup of pleasure. . . . There had been moments . . . when I fancied myself a clever man; but it now seemed to me that for the first time I really *felt* my intellect. Imagination, panting and exhausted, withdrew from the game; and Observation stepped into her place, trembling and glowing with open-eyed desire. . . . 'We must forget all our cares and duties and sorrows. We must go in for the beautiful' " (*Complete Tales*, vol. 2, pp. 175, 182). But, despite enjoying "Palladio's palaces . . . in defiance of reason and Ruskin" (186), neither the narrator nor the story evade Ruskinism or moralism; the former's aesthetic reveries quite rapidly find Ruskinian lessons in the social and moral dimensions of art ("I found in [Northern Italian towns] an immeasurable instruction and charm. . . . I have never elsewhere got so deep an impression of the social secrets of mankind" [184]), and the latter turns on the most un-Paterian circumstance of a young lady and gentleman bringing scandal on themselves by inadvertently spending the night in the same hotel.

3. For James on Baudelaire, see *LC* 2, pp. 152–58; for James on Swinburne, see "Essays and Studies" (1875), included in *LC* 1, pp. 1278–82.

4. "Henry James's Portrait of the Artist," in James, *Stories of Writers and Artists*, p. 2.

5. *The Nation* 40 (March 12, 1885): 226; *The Critic* n.s. 3 (May 2, 1885): 207.

6. *The Nation* demonstrates the depth of James's problem by unerringly missing his point. "Rightly or wrongly," it wrote, "fiction with us [Anglo-Saxons] must be *virginibus puerisque*, and we fear that we are still so profoundly moral, at any rate in this respect, that ninety-nine out of a hundred English or American readers will have less sympathy for the author of 'Beltraffio' than for his wife." The reviewer goes on to prove his own point by omitting mention of Beatrice Ambient's murder, euphemistically describing the story as one of a "tragic breach between" husband and wife. *The Nation* 40 (March 12, 1885): 226.

7. I have commented on the similarities between Du Maurier's text and James's in "An Aestheticism of Our Own: American Writers and the Aesthetic Movement" in Burke et al., *In Pursuit of Beauty*, p. 396.

8. See, as examples of the sporadic discussion of this grounding, Ellmann, "Henry James Among the Aesthetes," and Stambaugh, "The Aesthetic Movement and *The Portrait of a Lady*."

9. James, *Complete Tales*, vol. 4, p. 441.

10. Ellmann, "Henry James Among the Aesthetes," p. 215. Sara Stambaugh's contention that Oscar Wilde's mother, "Speranza," served as a model for Osmond's mother strikes me as more tenuous.

11. *Punch* 80 (Feb. 12, 1881): 62.

12. Gilbert, *Plays and Poems*, pp. 199–200. Further citations in the text will refer to this edition.

13. *Punch* 79 (Oct. 30, 1880): 194.

14. These examples were suggested to me by Ormond, *George Du Maurier*, p. 307.

15. In the New York edition, James extends the comparison between Osmond and the aesthete by noting: "He was dressed as a man dresses who takes little other trouble about it than to have no vulgar things" (3: 329).

16. Osmond tends to the epigrammatic throughout the novel, as, for example, with the comment later in this scene: "I prefer women like books— very good and not too long" (NY, 3: 331). And here, too, his aestheticist tendency to conflate his life as a connoisseur and his life as a lover is what the epigram emphasizes.

17. Harrison, "The Aesthete," reprinted in *The Choice of Books and Other Literary Pieces*, p. 291. Harrison's representative aesthete—whom he dubs Young Osric, an obvious thrust at Wilde—is also recognizably Osmondian.

18. Blackmur, "*The Portrait of a Lady*" in *Studies in Henry James*, p. 193.

19. It is at this point that I need to acknowledge my greatest debt to Porter, *Seeing and Being*.

20. The best explication of it may be found in Holland, *The Expense of Vision: Essays on the Craft of Henry James*, p. 48.

21. *Punch* 80 (May 14, 1881): 221.

22. Gilmore, "The Commodity World of *The Portrait of a Lady*," p. 73.

23. To Gilmore, however, none of these explanations is sufficient; rather, Isabel "spurns the chance of leaving Osmond for the more rarefied liberation of 'motionlessly *seeing*'" (73). This strikes me as perhaps the least credible of possible explanations, since it ignores entirely the possibility that Isabel might be returning as an active participant in her marriage, particularly with respect to Pansy's future—an interesting omission for so strenuously moralizing a critic as Gilmore to make.

Chapter Four

1. James, *Letters*, 2: 372; Edel, *Henry James*, 3: 31, 4: 45.

2. Citations are from the following editions: James, *The Ambassadors* (NY, 21: 217), *The Tragic Muse* (*TM*, p. 25; the Penguin edition gives the original 1890 text), and *The Art of Fiction* (*LC* 1, p. 53); Wilde, *The Picture of Dorian Gray* (*DG*, p. 39). Two of the best treatments of this chain of quotations are Charlesworth, *Dark Passages*, pp. 56–57, and Stone, *Novelists in a Changing World*, p. 59.

3. The question of James's sexuality is one that has obsessed Jamesians from his own time to the present day. That James was erotically attracted to (if not obsessed by) attractive younger men (Green's *Children of the Sun*) is incontestable; that James pushed this attraction into actual sexual performance is dubious. Edel's delicate probings of this issue strike me as admirable for their tact but somewhat lacking in their sense of the historical specificity of James's inclination. For this idealized, if not necessarily chaste, eroticizing of the ado-

lescent male is precisely the form taken by upper- and upper-middle-class British homosexual discourse of the late nineteenth century, for a complex chain of reasons that historians are only beginning to investigate. The question of James's sexual inclination, it therefore appears, needs to be approached by an analysis that places sexuality in the context of class and social setting. For a fine reading of this issue that begins to perform this work but shifts to the equally compelling question of "homosexual panic," see Sedgwick, "The Beast in the Closet," pp. 148–86.

4. This is the position, for example, that Ellmann suggests with regard to James's responses to Pater as well as to Wilde; see "Henry James Among the Aesthetes," pp. 211, 226.

5. Weeks, *Coming Out: Homosexual Politics in Britain.*

6. Edel, *Henry James*, 4: 127–28ff. Following James's own lead, Edel suggests that James instinctively divined the facts behind Symonds's separation; given James's characteristic self-veiling on precisely this issue, I am less willing to credit mere imagination.

7. James, "An American Art-Scholar: Charles Eliot Norton," reprinted in *Notes on Novelists*, p. 422.

8. Anesko, *"Friction with the Market": Henry James and the Profession of Authorship*, p. 143.

9. Although the classic account of this issue remains Charvat, *The Profession of Authorship in America, 1800–1870*, critics have focused on it with increasing theoretical depth and rhetorical zest for the last decade. Sundquist's "The Country of the Blue," the introduction to *American Realism*, places this concern in a larger cultural context. These issues are taken up with respect to James by Anesko, *"Friction with the Market"*, and Culver, "Representing the Author: Henry James, Intellectual Property, and the Work of Writing," pp. 114–36. For a treatment of the professionalization of authorship with a broader historical view and a more specific focus on the creation of an elite reading public, see Brodhead, *The School of Hawthorne*. For a subtle treatment of the literary professionalism in the context of Anglo-American modernism, see Menand, *Discovering Modernism*, pp. 97–132. Valuable, too, is Wilson, *The Labor of Words*, esp. pp. 1–91. My own understanding of these issues owes a substantial debt to Brodhead and to Amy Kaplan.

10. This letter was discovered by Anesko and is quoted on p. 232 of *"Friction with the Market."*

11. See, for example, Powers, "James's *The Tragic Muse*."

12. This point is made by Edel, *Henry James*, 4: 259.

13. See Gordon and Stokes, "The Reference of *The Tragic Muse*," p. 120, and Jacobson, *Henry James and the Mass Market*, p. 66.

14. Standing behind both characters is doubtlessly George Eliot's Alcharisi, from *Daniel Deronda*. But given the relatively little attention paid Eliot in Wilde's work, and the relatively greater influence shown in James's, it seems more apposite to trace this strand of influence directly through James here.

15. See Bellringer, *The Ambassadors*, p. 34.

Chapter Five

1. Here are the most entertaining instances of the rather dreary attempts to define "decadence" from the period in question: Johnson, "A Note Upon the Practice and Theory of Verse" (1891); Symons, "The Decadent Movement in Literature" (1893); and Lang, "Decadence" (1900). The subsequent (and voluminous) scholarly commentary includes: Ryals, "Toward a Definition of *Decadent*" (1958); Peters, "Toward an 'Un-definition' of Decadent" (1959); Harris, "Identifying the Decadent Fiction of the Eighteen-Nineties" (1962); and Gilman, *Decadence* (1979).

2. Buchanan, "The Fleshy School of Poetry"; Nordau, *Degeneration*, p. 317; Carson, "Opening Speech for the Defence," pp. 164–69.

3. The classic text in this tradition is Praz, *The Romantic Agony*; see also Charlesworth, *Dark Passages*.

4. This is not to imply that much exciting work has not been recently done on decadent poetry under the influence of psychoanalytic, feminist, and historicist criticisms, only that none of this work has challenged the associations that decadence brings with it.

5. See William Stein, "*The Sacred Fount* and British Aestheticism." Tintner makes the same identification in *The Museum World of Henry James*, pp. 137–38.

6. James, *The Sacred Fount*, pp. 55–56. Further citations in the text will refer to this edition.

7. Richard Stein, *The Ritual of Interpretation*, p. 12.

8. Goode, "The Pervasive Mystery of Style," pp. 244–300.

9. Ellmann, "Henry James Among the Aesthetes," p. 215.

10. In a fascinating and idiosyncratic article, William Bysshe Stein ("*The Wings of the Dove*: James's Eucharist of *Punch*") traces the origin of this manifestly satiricial scene, and indeed much of the novel's satire, to Du Maurier's *Punch* cartoons. Thus Kate, the "handsome girl," or the Bishop of Murrum, or the fatuous Lord Mark, or even Milly herself (a "case of American intensity") resemble the stock figures with which Du Maurier populates his drawing rooms. Stein's essay is itself a bravura stylistic performance matching in wit and bile anything the aesthetic movement produced; but it fails, however, to distinguish between the satirical responses to aestheticism and James's own response to Pater, Wilde, et al. Thus for Stein, the novel is itself something of a Du Maurier cartoon, a slash-and-burn demolition of the forests of aestheticist high society, rather than (as I shall argue below) an ambivalent satire that understands and explores its own imaginative participation in the things it condemns.

11. The interest of most critics focuses on identifying the painting in question, not on tracing the provenance of the scene in which the painting is encountered. See Allott, "The Bronzino Portrait in Henry James's *The Wings of the Dove*," and Rowe, *Henry James and Henry Adams*, pp. 185–90. Rowe's reading of the scene is first-rate, as is Laurence Holland's eloquent treatment of Milly's aestheticization, to which I am much indebted here. See Holland, *The Expense of Vision*, pp. 302–3ff.

12. This is the central argument of Richard Stein, *The Ritual of Interpretation*. Further citations in the text will refer to this edition.

13. Goode, "The Pervasive Mystery of Style," p. 265.

14. Seltzer, *Henry James and the Art of Power*. Further citations in the text will be to this edition.

15. For the relation between "decadence" and the jargon of "civilization," see Dowling, *Language and Decadence in the Victorian Fin-de-Siècle*, pp. 34–45.

16. My argument differs considerably here from Seltzer's (*Henry James and the Art of Power*), who argues that the "discourse of [James's] fiction is a double discourse that at once represses and acknowledges a discreet continuity between literary and political practices" (15), a "two-tiered writing: on one level, an aesthetic resistance to the exercises of power, on another, a discreet reinscription of strategies of control . . . [that] enables the institution of the novel to act as a relay of mechanisms of social control at the same time that it protects itself against the shame of power" (148–49). Unlike Seltzer, whose interest centers on James's discourse, my focus is on the dynamic unfolding of James's own understanding of the conflations Seltzer describes and on what I take to be James's evasion of this understanding.

17. Rowe, *Henry James and Henry Adams*, p. 208.

18. Hartsock, "Unintentional Fallacy: Critics and *The Golden Bowl*," pp. 273–74; James, *The Golden Bowl*, 23: 150.

19. This line of inquiry was suggested to me in conversation by Robert Caserio, to whom thanks are due.

20. Blackmur *Studies in Henry James*, p. 224.

21. Yeazell, *Language and Knowledge in the Late Novels of Henry James*, p. 111.

22. James, *Notes on Novelists*, pp. 246–47.

23. See my catalog of this criticism in Chapter 2.

24. Pound, *Letters*, p. 138.

25. Pound, *Literary Essays*, pp. 299–300.

26. Pound, *Letters*, pp. 137–38.

27. Pound, *Literary Essays*, p. 296.

28. Ibid., pp. 327, 326.

29. Eliot, "In Memory," pp. 46, 44.

30. Hubbell, *Who Are the Major American Writers?*, pp. 128, 86. Contemporary critical notices of James, while increasingly exasperated with his baroque manner, were consistently respectful. Indeed, in many of the American estimates of his work, exasperation and respect were intimately connected with one another; James's increasing narrative indirection was found by many critics of his native land to be particularly distressing because of the pride these critics took in James's international prestige. And Americans were his harshest critics; while British literary critics may have evinced some of the same irritation with James's late manner, they never failed to show respect for his ambition and something approaching reverence for his personal presence.

31. It is true that the influence of James on the actual poetic performance of Eliot and Pound is a capacious and, to my knowledge, not yet fully explored issue. The classic account of Eliot's poetic response to James is Matthiessen's:

"The more one thinks of Eliot in relation to James," Matthiessen writes in *The Achievement of T. S. Eliot*, "the more one realizes the extent of the similarities between them" (p. 70). According to Matthiessen, Eliot's early dramatic monologues owe much to James's exploration of point-of-view narration, particularly (in *The Waste Land*) that of enfeebled or limited "reflectors" (p. 60); Eliot's own "sense of the past" owes much to James (which, we may remember, Eliot distinguishes from Hawthorne's as "the sense of a sense"); and his *Family Reunion* explicitly poses itself as a Jamesian ghost story. Thematically, there is much that is Jamesian in Eliot's work, according to Matthiessen: Prufrock's "rankling inability to give himself to life," for example, or more impressively, "the realization that the qualities of spirit . . . rise above frustration," which Matthiessen traces to *Portrait* and *Wings* (p. 70). One is nevertheless struck in even Eliot's explicitly Jamesian work with how manifestly un-Jamesian Eliot's imagination proves to be. To cite one example: there is an enormous gap indeed between the aging Bostonian J. Alfred Prufrock and the aging Woolettite, Lambert Strether; Prufrock accepts mournfully what Strether affirms actively—the necessity of renunciation—and Strether achieves the very sense of visionary amplitude whose absence Prufrock mourns. The question of James's presence in Pound is equally complicated. While Pound's *Personae* or *Hugh Selwyn Mauberly* do indeed enlist a Jamesian cast of characters, the Jamesian note is not expanded into a full chord, much less a cadence; and while the example of James is cited in the *Cantos*, it is less influentially adduced as an index to his performance than those of, say, Fenollosa or Browning.

32. Eliot, *Selected Essays*, pp. 392–93.

33. Pound, *Literary Essays*, p. 299.

34. Ransom, *The World's Body*, pp. x–xi.

35. Eliot, "Ezra Pound," p. 17.

36. Stead, *The New Poetic*, p. 34.

37. Aldington, *Life for Life's Sake*, p. 199. I was led to this text by Menand.

38. Auden, "Henry James and the Artist in America," p. 39. I was led to this essay by Hubbell, *Who Are the Major American Writers?*, pp. 128–29.

39. "To all American writers," Auden continues, "the knowledge that James suffered as they do, without succumbing either to the crowd or the clique, should make him a tower of strength in their dark, discouraged hours" ("Henry James and the Artist in America," p. 39). Auden's own version of James, like Eliot's and Pound's, thereby romances James into the status of the very embodiment of artistic sufficiency he himself aspires to.

40. Cain, "Criticism and Politics," and Warren, "Henry James."

Works Cited

Frequently cited primary texts are listed in the Abbreviations, pp. ix–x.

Adorno, Theodor. *Aesthetic Theory.* Tr. C. Lenhardt. London: Routledge and Kegan Paul, 1984.
———. *Minima Moralia. Reflections from Damaged Life.* Tr. E. F. N. Jephcott. London: New Left Books, 1974.
———. *Prisms.* Tr. Samuel Weber and Shierry Weber. Cambridge, Mass.: MIT Press, 1981.
Agnew, Jean-Christophe. "The Consuming Vision of Henry James." In *The Culture of Consumption: Critical Essays in American History, 1880–1980,* edited by Richard Wightman Fox and T. J. Jackson Lears. New York: Pantheon, 1983.
Albery, James. *Where's the Cat?* In *The Dramatic Works of James Albery: Together with a Sketch of His Career, Correspondence Bearing Thereupon, Press Notices, Etc.* Ed. Wyndham Albery. London: P. Davis, 1939.
Aldington, Richard. *Life for Life's Sake: A Book of Reminiscences.* London: Cassell, 1941.
Allott, Miriam. "The Bronzino Portrait in Henry James's *The Wings of the Dove.*" *MLN* 68 (1953): 23–25.
———. "A Ruskin Echo in *The Wings of the Dove.*" *Notes and Queries* 201 (1956): 87.
Anderson, Perry. *Arguments Within English Marxism.* London: NLB, 1980.
Anderson, Quentin. *The American Henry James.* New Brunswick, N.J.: Rutgers University Press, 1957.
———. *The Imperial Self: An Essay in American Literary and Cultural History.* New York: Knopf, 1971.
Anesko, Michael. *"Friction with the Market": Henry James and the Profession of Authorship.* New York: Oxford University Press, 1986.
Armstrong, Paul. *The Phenomenology of Henry James.* Chapel Hill: University of North Carolina Press, 1983.
Arnold, Matthew. "Shelley." In *The Last Word.* Vol. 11 of *The Complete Prose Works of Matthew Arnold,* edited by R. H. Super. Ann Arbor: University of Michigan Press, 1977.
———. "Wordsworth." In *English Literature and Irish Politics.* Vol. 9 of *The*

Complete Prose Works of Matthew Arnold, edited by R. H. Super. Ann Arbor: University of Michigan Press, 1973.

Ashbery, John. *Self-Portrait in a Convex Mirror: Poems*. New York: Viking, 1975.

Ashton, Rosemary. *The German Idea: Four English Writers and the Reception of German Thought, 1800–1860*. Cambridge, Engl.: Cambridge University Press, 1980.

Auden, W. H. "Henry James and the Artist in America." *Harper's*, July 1948, pp. 36–40.

Bakhtin, Mikhail. *The Dialogic Imagination: Four Essays*. Ed. Michael Holquist. Tr. Caryl Emerson and Michael Holquist. Austin: University of Texas Press, 1981.

Baudrillard, Jean. *La Société de Consommation: Ses Mythes, Ses Structures*. Paris: Gallimard, 1974.

———. *La Système des Objets*. Paris: Gallimard, 1968.

Beer, Thomas. *The Mauve Decade: American Literature at the End of the Nineteenth Century*. New York: Knopf, 1926.

Beerbohm, Max. "A Defence of Cosmetics." *The Yellow Book* 1 (Apr. 1894): 65–82.

———. "1880." *The Yellow Book* 4 (Jan. 1895): 275–83.

Bellringer, Alan. *The Ambassadors*. London: Allen and Unwin, 1984.

Benjamin, Walter. *Illuminations*. Tr. Harry Zohn. New York: Harcourt Brace, 1968.

Berenson, Bernard. *Sketch for a Self-Portrait*. New York: Pantheon, 1949.

Bewley, Marius. *The Complex Fate: Hawthorne, Henry James, and Some Other American Writers*. London: Chatto and Windus, 1952.

Blackmur, R. P. *Studies in Henry James*. Ed. Veronica Makowsky. New York: New Directions, 1983.

Bledstein, Burton. *The Culture of Professionalism: The Middle Class and the Development of Higher Education in America*. New York: Norton, 1976.

Bloom, Harold. *The Visionary Company: A Reading of English Romantic Poetry*. Ithaca, N.Y.: Cornell University Press, 1961.

———. *Yeats*. Oxford: Oxford University Press, 1970.

Boris, Eileen. *Art and Labor: Ruskin, Morris, and the Craftsman Ideal in America*. Philadelphia, Pa.: Temple University Press, 1986.

Bourdieu, Pierre. *Distinction: A Social Critique of the Judgement of Taste*. Tr. Richard Nice. Cambridge, Mass.: Harvard University Press, 1984.

Bourget, Paul. "Théorie de la Décadence," in "Psychologie Contemporaine, Notes et Portraits, Charles Baudelaire." *Nouvelle Revue* 13 (1881): 412–16.

Bové, Paul. *Intellectuals in Power: A Genealogy of Critical Humanism*. New York: Columbia University Press, 1986.

Bowlby, Rachel. *Just Looking: Consumer Culture in Dreiser, Gissing, and Zola*. New York: Methuen, 1985.

Brodhead, Richard. *The School of Hawthorne*. New York: Oxford University Press, 1986.

Brooks, Peter. *The Melodramatic Imagination: Balzac, Henry James, Melodrama and the Mode of Excess*. New Haven, Conn.: Yale University Press, 1976.

Brooks, Van Wyck. *An Autobiography*. New York: Dutton, 1965.

————. *Fenollosa and His Circle; with Other Essays in Biography.* New York: Dutton, 1962.

————. *The Pilgrimage of Henry James.* New York: Dutton, 1925.

Buchanan, Robert. "The Fleshy School of Poetry: Mr. D. G. Rossetti." *Contemporary Review* 18 (Oct. 1871): 334–50.

Buckley, Jerome. *The Triumph of Time: A Study of the Victorian Concepts of Time, History, Progress, and Decadence.* Cambridge, Mass.: Harvard University / Belknap Press, 1966.

Bürger, Peter. *Theory of the Avant Garde.* Tr. Michael Shaw. Minneapolis: University of Minnesota Press, 1984.

Burke, Doreen Bolger, et al. *In Pursuit of Beauty: Americans and the Aesthetic Movement.* New York: The Metropolitan Museum, 1986.

Burnand, Frank. *The Colonel.* Unpublished ms. British Library, London.

Cain, William. "Criticism and Politics: F. O. Matthiessen and the Making of Henry James." *The New England Quarterly* 60 (1987): 163–86.

————. *F. O. Matthiessen and the Politics of Criticism.* Madison: University of Wisconsin Press, 1988.

Carson, Edward. "Opening Speech for the Defence." In *The Trials of Oscar Wilde,* edited by H. Montgomery Hyde. London: William Hodge, 1948.

Chamberlin, Joseph. *The Boston Transcript: A History of Its First Hundred Years.* Boston: Houghton Mifflin, 1930.

Charlesworth, Barbara. *Dark Passages: The Decadent Consciousness in Victorian Literature.* Madison: University of Wisconsin Press, 1965.

Charvat, William. *The Profession of Authorship in America, 1800–1870: The Papers of William Charvat.* Ed. Matthew J. Bruccoli. Columbus: Ohio State University Press, 1968.

Chesterton, G. K. *The Victorian Age in Literature.* London: Williams and Norgate, 1913.

Chisolm, Lawrence. *Fenollosa: The Far East and American Culture.* New Haven, Conn.: Yale University Press, 1963.

Christ, Carol. *Victorian and Modern Poetics.* Chicago: University of Chicago Press, 1984.

Cohen, Ed. "Writing Gone Wilde: Homoerotic Desire in the Closet of Representation." *PMLA* 102 (Oct. 1987): 801–13.

Coleridge, Samuel Taylor. *Biographia Literaria.* 2 vols. 1907. Reprint: Ed. J. Shawcross. Oxford: Oxford University Press, 1973.

Conlon, John. *Walter Pater and the French Tradition.* Lewisburg, Pa.: Bucknell University Press, 1982.

Cowley, Malcolm. *Exile's Return: A Literary Odyssey of the 1920s.* New York: Viking, 1951.

Culler, A. Dwight. *The Victorian Mirror of History.* New Haven, Conn.: Yale University Press, 1985.

Culver, Stuart. "Representing the Author: Henry James, Intellectual Property, and the Work of Writing." In *Henry James: Fiction as History,* edited by Ian F. A. Bell. London: Vision Press, 1984.

De Man, Paul. *Allegories of Reading.* New Haven, Conn.: Yale University Press, 1979.

———. *The Resistance to Theory*. Minneapolis: University of Minnesota Press, 1986.

———. "The Rhetoric of Temporality." In *Blindness and Insight: Essays in the Rhetoric of Contemporary Criticism*. 2d ed. Minneapolis: University of Minnesota Press, 1983.

Dickason, David. *The Daring Young Men: The Story of the American Pre-Raphaelites*. Bloomington: Indiana University Press, 1953.

Dollimore, Jonathan. "Different Desires: Subjectivity and Transgression in Wilde and Gide." *Genders* 2 (July 1988): 24–41.

Donadio, Stephen. *Nietzsche, Henry James, and the Artistic Will*. New York: Oxford University Press, 1978.

Dowling, Linda. *Aestheticism and Decadence: A Selective Annotated Bibliography*. New York: Garland, 1977.

———. *Language and Decadence in the Victorian Fin-de-Siècle*. Princeton, N.J.: Princeton University Press, 1986.

Dowson, Ernest. *The Poems of Ernest Dowson, with a Memoir by Arthur Symons, Four Illustrations by Aubrey Beardsley, and a Portrait by William Rothstein*. London: J. Lane, 1905.

Du Maurier, George. *Trilby*. New York: Harper's, 1894.

Eastlake, Charles. *Hints on Household Taste in Furniture, Upholstery, and Other Details*. With notes by Charles Perkins. 1st American ed., from the revised London ed. Boston: J. R. Osgood, 1872.

Edel, Leon. *Henry James*. 5 vols. Philadelphia, Pa.: Lippincott, 1953–72.

Egan, Michael. *Henry James: The Ibsen Years*. London: Vision, 1972.

Eliot, T. S. *The Complete Poems and Plays, 1909–1950*. New York: Harcourt, Brace, 1952.

———. "Ezra Pound." In *Ezra Pound: A Collection of Critical Essays*, edited by Walter Sutton. Englewood Cliffs, N.J.: Prentice Hall, 1963.

———. *The Letters of T. S. Eliot*. Vol. 1, 1898–1922. Ed. Valerie Eliot. London: Faber and Faber, 1988.

———. "In Memory." *Little Review* 5, no. 4 (Aug. 1918): 44–47.

———. *The Sacred Wood*. 2d ed. London: Methuen, 1928.

———. *Selected Essays*. New ed. New York: Harcourt, Brace, 1950.

Ellmann, Richard. "Henry James Among the Aesthetes." In *Proceedings of the British Academy*, vol. 69 (1983). London: Oxford University Press, 1984.

———. *Oscar Wilde*. New York: Knopf, 1988.

———. *Oscar Wilde at Oxford*. Washington, D.C.: Library of Congress, 1984.

Engel, A. J. *From Clergyman to Don: The Rise of the Academic Profession in Nineteenth-Century Oxford*. Oxford: Oxford University Press, 1983.

Ewen, Stuart. *Captains of Consciousness: Advertising and the Social Roots of the Consumer Culture*. New York: McGraw-Hill, 1976.

Fish, Stanley. "Profession Despise Thyself: Fear and Self-Loathing in Literary Studies." *Critical Inquiry* 10 (1983): 349–64.

Fleishman, Avrom. *The English Historical Novel*. Baltimore, Md.: Johns Hopkins University Press, 1971.

Fogel, Daniel. *Henry James and the Structure of the Romantic Imagination*. Baton Rouge: Louisiana State University Press, 1981.

Fox, Richard W., and T. J. Jackson Lears, eds. *The Culture of Consumption: Critical Essays in American History, 1860–1960.* New York: Pantheon, 1983.

Freud, Sigmund. "Group Psychology and the Analysis of the Ego." In *The Standard Edition of the Complete Psychological Works of Sigmund Freud,* vol. 18. Tr. James Strachey. London: Hogarth Press, 1955.

Frost, Robert. *Complete Poems of Robert Frost.* New York: Henry Holt, 1956.

Gagnier, Regenia. *Idylls of the Marketplace: Oscar Wilde and the Victorian Public.* Stanford, Calif.: Stanford University Press, 1986.

Garrison, Dee. *Apostles of Culture: The Public Librarian and American Society, 1876–1920.* New York: The Free Press, 1979.

Geismar, Maxwell. *Henry James and the Jacobites.* Boston: Houghton Mifflin, 1963.

Gervais, David. *Flaubert and Henry James: A Study in Contrasts.* New York: Macmillan, 1978.

Gilbert, W. S. *Plays and Poems of W. S. Gilbert.* New York: Random House, 1932.

Gilman, Richard. *Decadence: The Strange Life of an Epithet.* 1st ed. New York: Farrar, Straus, and Giroux, 1979.

Gilmore, Michael. "The Commodity World of *The Portrait of a Lady.*" *New England Quarterly* 59 (1986): 51–74.

Goode, John. "The Pervasive Mystery of Style: *The Wings of the Dove.*" In *The Air of Reality: New Essays on Henry James,* edited by John Goode. London: Methuen, 1972.

Gordon, D. J., and John Stokes. "The Reference of *The Tragic Muse.*" In *The Air of Reality: New Essays on Henry James,* edited by John Goode. London: Methuen, 1972.

Graff, Gerald. *Professing Literature: An Institutional History.* Chicago: University of Chicago Press, 1987.

Graña, César. *Bohemian Versus Bourgeois: French Society and the French Man of Letters in the Nineteenth Century.* New York: Basic Books, 1964.

Green, Martin. *Children of the Sun: A Narrative of "Decadence" in England After 1918.* New York: Basic Books, 1976.

Greer, Louise. *Browning and America.* Chapel Hill: University of North Carolina Press, 1952.

Grover, Phillip. *Henry James and the French Novel: A Study in Inspiration.* New York: Harper and Row, 1973.

Hagstrum, Jean. *The Sister Arts: The Tradition of Literary Pictorialism and English Poetry from Dryden to Gray.* Chicago: University of Chicago Press, 1958.

Hamilton, Sir Walter. *The Aesthetic Movement in England.* London: Reeurs and Turner, 1882.

Handlin, David. *The American Home: Architecture and Society, 1815–1915.* Boston: Little, Brown, 1979.

Harris, Daniel A. "D. G. Rossetti's 'Jenny': Sex, Money, and the Interior Monologue." *Victorian Poetry* 22 (1984): 197–215.

Harris, Neil. *The Artist in American Society: The Formative Years, 1790–1860.* New York: George Braziller, 1966.

Harris, Wendell. "Identifying the Decadent Fiction of the Eighteen-Nineties." *English Literature in Transition* 5, no. 5 (1962): 1–13.

Harrison, Frederic. *The Choice of Books and Other Literary Pieces*. London: Macmillan, 1886.

Hartman, Geoffrey. *Wordsworth's Poetry, 1787–1814*. New Haven, Conn.: Yale University Press, 1971.

Hartsock, Mildred E. "Unintentional Fallacy: Critics and *The Golden Bowl*." *Modern Language Quarterly* 35 (1974): 272–88.

Haug, Wolfgang Fritz. *Critique of Commodity Aesthetics: Appearance, Sexuality and Advertising in Capitalist Society*. Tr. Robert Bock. Minneapolis: University of Minnesota Press, 1986.

Helsinger, Elizabeth. *Ruskin and the Art of the Beholder*. Cambridge, Mass.: Harvard University Press, 1982.

Herrick, Robert. *The Gospel of Freedom*. New York: Macmillan, 1898.

Hersey, G. L. "Rossetti's 'Jenny': A Realist Altarpiece." *Yale Review*, n.s., 69 (1979): 17–32.

Holland, Laurence. *The Expense of Vision: Essays on the Craft of Henry James*. Princeton, N.J.: Princeton University Press, 1964.

Holloway, John. *The Victorian Sage: Studies in Argument*. London: Macmillan, 1953.

Hough, Graham. *The Last Romantics*. London: George Duckworth, 1949.

Howe, Irving. *World of Our Fathers*. New York: Harcourt Brace Jovanovich, 1976.

Howells, William Dean. *A Hazard of New Fortunes*. Bloomington: Indiana University Press, 1976.

Hubbell, Jay. *Who Are the Major American Writers?: A Study of the Changing Literary Canon*. Durham, N.C.: Duke University Press, 1972.

Hume, David. *A Treatise of Human Nature*. Ed. A. Selby-Bigge. Oxford: Oxford University Press, 1978.

Hungerford, Margaret Wolfe. *Mrs Geoffrey*. Philadelphia: J. B. Lippincott's, 1881.

Huysmans, J. K. *A Rebours*. Paris: G. Charpentier et cie, 1884.

Iser, Wolfgang. *Walter Pater: The Aesthetic Moment*. Tr. David Henry Wilson. Cambridge, Engl.: Cambridge University Press, 1987.

Jackson, Holbrook. *William Morris*. London: Jonathan Cape, 1926.

Jacobson, Marcia. *Henry James and the Mass Market*. University: University of Alabama Press, 1983.

James, Henry. *The Complete Tales of Henry James*. 12 vols. Ed. Leon Edel. Philadelphia: Lippincott, 1962–64.

———. *Henry James: Novels, 1881–86*. New York: Library of America, 1985.

———. *Italian Hours*. Boston: Houghton Mifflin, 1909.

———. *Notes of a Son and Brother*. In *Autobiography*, edited by Frederick W. Dupee. New York: Criterion, 1956.

———. *Notes on Novelists, with Some Other Notes*. New York: Charles Scribner's Sons, 1914.

———. "Old Italian Pictures." *The Independent* 26 (June 11, 1874): 2–3.

———. *The Painter's Eye*. Ed. John Sweeney. Cambridge, Mass.: Harvard University Press, 1956.

———. *The Sacred Fount*. New York: Grove, 1953.

————. *Stories of Writers and Artists*. Ed. F. O. Matthiessen. New York: New Directions, 1945.

Jameson, Frederic. *The Political Unconscious: Narrative as a Socially Symbolic Act*. Ithaca: Cornell University Press, 1981.

Jarves, James Jackson. *The Art-Idea: Sculpture, Painting, and Architecture in America*. 2d ed. New York: Hurd and Houghton, 1865.

Johnson, Lionel. "A Note Upon the Practice and Theory of Verse at the Present Time Obtaining in France." *The Century Guild Hobby Horse* 6 (1891): 61–66.

Kaplan, Amy. "'The Knowledge of the Line': Realism and the City in Howells's *A Hazard of New Fortunes*." *PMLA* 101 (1986): 69–81.

Kenner, Hugh. *A Homemade World: The American Modernist Writers*. New York: Knopf, 1975.

Kermode, Frank. *Romantic Image*. London: Routledge and Kegan Paul, 1957.

Knoepflmacher, U. C. *Religious Humanism and the Victorian Novel: George Eliot, Walter Pater, and Samuel Butler*. Princeton, N.J.: Princeton University Press, 1965.

Koestenbaum, Wayne. "Wilde's Hard Labor and the Birth of Gay Reading." In *The Question of Male Feminist Criticism*, edited by Joseph Boone and Michael Cadden. London: Routledge, 1990.

Lacan, Jacques. *Ecrits: A Selection*. Tr. Alan Sheridan. New York: Norton, 1977.

Lackey, Kris. "A Scholar-John: The Speaker in 'Jenny.'" *Victorian Poetry* 21 (1983): 425–31.

Laclau, Ernesto, and Chantal Mouffe. *Hegemony and Socialist Strategy: Towards a Radical Democratic Politics*. Tr. Winston Moore and Paul Cammack. London: Verso, 1985.

Landow, George. "Ruskin as Victorian Sage: The Example of *Traffic*." In *New Approaches to Ruskin: Thirteen Essays*, edited by Robert Hewison. London: Routledge and Kegan Paul, 1981.

Lang, Andrew. "Decadence." *The Critic* 37 (Aug. 1900): 171–73.

Larson, Magali Sarfatti. *The Rise of Professionalism: A Sociological Analysis*. Berkeley: University of California Press, 1977.

Lears, T. J. Jackson. *No Place of Grace: Antimodernism and the Transformation of American Culture, 1880–1920*. New York: Pantheon, 1981.

Lee, Vernon. *Miss Brown*. Edinburgh: William Blackwood and Sons, 1884.

Leiss, William. *The Limits to Satisfaction: An Essay on the Problem of Needs and Commodities*. Toronto: University of Toronto Press, 1976.

Levenson, Michael. *A Genealogy of Modernism: A Study of English Literary Doctrine, 1908–1922*. Cambridge, Engl.: Cambridge University Press, 1984.

Levey, Michael. *The Case of Walter Pater*. London: Thames and Hudson, 1978.

Lewis, Lloyd, and Henry Justice Smith. *Oscar Wilde Discovers America, 1882*. New York: Harcourt Brace, 1936.

Limpus, Robert. *American Criticism of British Decadence, 1880–1900*. Chicago: University of Chicago Libraries, 1939.

Long, Robert Emmet. *The Great Succession: Henry James and the Legacy of Hawthorne*. Pittsburgh, Pa.: University of Pittsburgh Press, 1979.

Lubbock, Percy, ed. *The Letters of Henry James*. 2 vols. New York: Charles Scribner's Sons, 1920.

Lynes, Russell. *The Tastemakers*. New York: Harper and Bros., 1949.

Lyotard, Jean-François. *The Postmodern Condition: A Report on Knowledge*. Tr. Geoff Bennington and Brian Massumi. Minneapolis: University of Minnesota Press, 1984.

Maidment, Brian. "Interpreting Ruskin, 1870–1914." In *The Ruskin Polygon: Essays on the Imagination of John Ruskin*, edited by John Dixon Hunt and Faith Holland. Manchester, Engl.: Manchester University Press, 1982.

Marchand, Roland. *Advertising the American Dream: Making Way for Modernity, 1920–1940*. Berkeley: University of California Press, 1985.

Marcus, Steven. *The Other Victorians: A Study of Sexuality and Pornography in Mid-Nineteenth-Century England*. New York: Basic Books, 1964.

Marcuse, Herbert. *Eros and Civilization: A Philosophical Inquiry into Freud*. Boston: Beacon Press, 1966.

Mason, Stuart. *Oscar Wilde and the Aesthetic Movement*. Dublin, 1920.

Matthiessen, F. O. *The Achievement of T. S. Eliot: An Essay on the Nature of Poetry*. 2d ed. New York: Oxford University Press, 1947.

———. *Henry James: The Major Phase*. New York: Oxford University Press, 1944.

———. Preface to *Stories of Writers and Artists*, by Henry James. New York: New Directions, 1945.

McKendrick, Neil, John Brewer, and J. H. Plumb. *The Birth of a Consumer Society: The Commercialization of Eighteenth-Century England*. Bloomington: Indiana University Press, 1982.

Menand, Louis. *Discovering Modernism: T. S. Eliot and His Context*. Oxford: Oxford University Press, 1987.

Miller, J. Hillis. *The Linguistic Moment: From Wordsworth to Stevens*. Princeton, N.J.: Princeton University Press, 1985.

———. "Walter Pater: A Partial Portrait." *Daedalus* 105, no. 1 (Winter 1976): 97–113.

Mitchell, W. J. T. *Iconology: Image, Text, Ideology*. Chicago: University of Chicago Press, 1986.

Mix, Katherine. *A Study in Yellow: The Yellow Book and Its Contributors*. Lawrence: University of Kansas Press, 1960.

Moers, Ellen. *The Dandy: Brummell to Beerbohm*. New York: Viking Press, 1960.

Monsman, Gerald. *Pater's Portraits: Mythic Pattern in the Fiction of Walter Pater*. Baltimore, Md.: Johns Hopkins University Press, 1967.

———. *Walter Pater*. Boston: Twayne, 1977.

———. *Walter Pater's Art of Autobiography*. New Haven, Conn.: Yale University Press, 1980.

Murfin, Ross. *Swinburne, Hardy, Lawrence, and the Burden of Belief*. Chicago: University of Chicago Press, 1978.

Nettels, Elsa. *James and Conrad*. Athens: University of Georgia Press, 1977.

Newsome, David. *Two Classes of Men: Platonism and English Romantic Thought*. London: John Murray, 1974.

Nordau, Max. *Degeneration*. Trans. from 2d ed. of German work. 5th ed. New York: D. Appleton, 1895.

Norris, Christopher. *Paul de Man: Deconstruction and the Critique of Aesthetic Ideology.* New York: Routledge, Chapman, and Hall, 1988.

Norton, Charles Eliot. *Historical Studies of Church-Building in the Middle Ages, Venice, Siena, Florence.* New York: Harper and Bros., 1880.

―――. Introduction to *The Crown of Wild Olive*, by John Ruskin. New York: Charles E. Merrill and Co., 1891.

Novak, Barbara. *Nature and Culture: American Landscape Painting, 1825–1875.* New York: Oxford University Press, 1980.

Ormond, Leonée. *George Du Maurier.* Pittsburgh, Pa.: University of Pittsburgh Press, 1969.

Park, Roy. "'Ut Pictura Poesis': The Nineteenth-Century Aftermath." *Journal of Aesthetics and Art Criticism* 28 (1969): 155–64.

Parrington, Vernon. *The Beginnings of Critical Realism in America, 1860–1920. Completed to 1900 Only.* Vol. 3 of *Main Currents in American Thought: An Interpretation of American Literature from the Beginnings to 1920.* New York: Harcourt, Brace, 1930.

Parrish, Maxfield. *Maxfield Parrish: The Early Years, 1893–1930.* Los Angeles: Nash Publishing, [1973].

Pater, Walter. *Appreciations, with an Essay on Style.* London: Macmillan, 1889.

―――. *Letters of Walter Pater.* Ed. Laurence Evans. Oxford: Clarendon Press, 1970.

Paulson, Ronald. "Turner's Graffiti: The Sun and Its Glosses." In *Images of Romanticism: Verbal and Visual Affinities*, edited by Karl Kroeber and William Walling. New Haven, Conn.: Yale University Press, 1978.

Peckham, Morse. *The Triumph of Romanticism: Collected Essays.* Columbia: University of South Carolina Press, 1970.

Persons, Stow. *The Decline of American Gentility.* New York: Columbia University Press, 1973.

Peters, Robert. "Toward an 'Un-definition' of Decadent as Applied to British Literature of the Nineteenth Century." *Journal of Aesthetics and Art Criticism* 18 (1959): 258–64.

Porter, Carolyn. *Seeing and Being: The Plight of the Participant Observer in Emerson, James, Adams, and Faulkner.* 1st ed. Middletown, Conn.: Wesleyan University Press, 1981.

Posnock, Ross. *Henry James and the Problem of Robert Browning.* Athens: University of Georgia Press, 1985.

―――. "Henry James, Veblen, and Adorno: The Crisis of the Modern Self." *Journal of American Studies* 21 (1987): 31–54.

Potter, David. *People of Plenty: Economic Abundance and the American Character.* Chicago: University of Chicago Press, 1954.

Pound, Ezra. *The Letters of Ezra Pound, 1907–1941.* Ed. D. D. Paige. New York: Harcourt, Brace, 1950.

―――. *Literary Essays of Ezra Pound.* Ed. T. S. Eliot. New York: New Directions, 1954.

Powers, Lyall. *Henry James and the Naturalist Movement.* East Lansing: Michigan State University Press, 1971.

———. "James's *Tragic Muse*: Ave atque Vale." *PMLA* 73 (1958): 270–74.

Praz, Mario. *The Romantic Agony*. 2d ed. Tr. Angus Davidson. London: Oxford University Press, 1951.

Prince, Jeffrey R. "D. G. Rossetti and the Pre-Raphaelite Conception of the Special Moment." *Modern Language Quarterly* 37 (1976): 349–69.

Quilter, Harry. "The New Renaissance; or, The Gospel of Intensity." *Macmillan's Magazine* 42 (Sept. 1880): 391–400.

Ransom, John Crowe. *The World's Body*. New York: Scribner's, 1938.

Reisman, David, in collaboration with Reuel Denney and Nathan Glazer. *The Lonely Crowd: A Study of the Changing American Character*. New Haven, Conn.: Yale University Press, 1950.

Rosenblatt, Louise. *L'idée de l'art pour l'art dans la littérature anglaise pendant la période victorienne*. Paris: H. Champion, 1931.

Rothblatt, Sheldon. *The Revolution of the Dons: Cambridge and Society in Victorian England*. New York: Basic Books, 1968.

Rowe, John Carlos. *Henry James and Henry Adams: The Emergence of a Modern Consciousness*. Ithaca, N.Y.: Cornell University Press, 1976.

———. *Theoretical Dimensions of Henry James*. Madison: University of Wisconsin Press, 1984.

Ryals, Clyde. "Toward a Definition of *Decadent* as Applied to British Literature of the Nineteenth Century." *Journal of Aesthetics and Art Criticism* 17 (1958): 85–92.

Said, Edward. "Response to Stanley Fish." *Critical Inquiry* 10 (1983): 371–73.

Samuels, Ernest. *Bernard Berenson: The Making of a Connoisseur*. Cambridge, Mass.: Harvard University / Belknap Press, 1979.

Santayana, George. *The Complete Poems of George Santayana: A Critical Edition*. Ed. with an introd. by William Holzberger. Lewisburg, Pa.: Bucknell University Press, 1979.

———. *The Middle Span*. Vol. 2 of *Persons and Places*. New York: Scribner's, 1945.

Sedgwick, Eve. "The Beast in the Closet: James and the Writing of Homosexual Panic." In *Sex, Politics, and Science in the Nineteenth-Century Novel*, edited by Ruth Yeazell. Baltimore, Md.: Johns Hopkins University Press, 1986.

Seigel, Jerrold. *Bohemian Paris: Culture, Politics, and the Boundaries of Bourgeois Life, 1830–1930*. New York: Viking, 1986.

Seltzer, Mark. *Henry James and the Art of Power*. Ithaca, N.Y.: Cornell University Press, 1984.

Sherman, Stuart. *On Contemporary Literature*. New York: Holt, 1917.

Simpson, Lewis. *The Man of Letters in New England and the South: Essays on the History of the Literary Vocation in America*. Baton Rouge: Louisiana State University Press, 1973.

Slinn, E. Warwick. "Consciousness as Writing: Deconstruction and Reading Victorian Poetry." *Victorian Poetry* 25 (Spring 1987): 67–81.

Spector, Stephen J. "Love, Unity and Desire in the Poetry of Dante Gabriel Rossetti." *ELH* 38 (1971): 432–58.

Stambaugh, Sara. "The Aesthetic Movement and *The Portrait of a Lady.*" *Nineteenth Century Fiction* 30 (1976): 495–510.

Starkie, Enid. *From Gautier to Eliot: The Influence of France on English Literature, 1851–1939.* London: Hutchinson, 1960.

Stead, C. K. *The New Poetic: Yeats to Eliot.* Rev. ed. Philadelphia: University of Pennsylvania Press, 1987.

Stedman, Edmund Clarence. *Victorian Poets.* Boston: Houghton Mifflin, 1875.

Steegmuller, Francis. *The Two Lives of James Jackson Jarves.* New Haven, Conn.: Yale University Press, 1951.

Stein, Gertrude. *The Autobiography of Alice B. Toklas.* New York: Harcourt Brace, 1933.

Stein, Richard L. *The Ritual of Interpretation: The Fine Arts as Literature in Ruskin, Rossetti, and Pater.* Cambridge, Mass.: Harvard University Press, 1975.

Stein, Roger. *John Ruskin and Aesthetic Thought in America, 1840–1900.* Cambridge, Mass.: Harvard University Press, 1967.

Stein, William Bysshe. "*The Sacred Fount* and British Aestheticism: The Artist as Clown and Pornographer." *Arizona Quarterly* 27 (1971): 161–73.

———. "*The Wings of the Dove*: James's Eucharist of *Punch.*" *The Centennial Review* 21 (1977): 236–60.

Stevens, Holly. *Souvenirs and Prophecies: The Young Wallace Stevens.* New York: Knopf, 1977.

Stevens, Wallace. *The Collected Poems of Wallace Stevens.* New York: Knopf, 1954.

Stickney, Trumbull. *The Poems of Trumbull Stickney.* Ed. with an introd. by Amberys R. Whittle. New York: Farrar, Straus, and Giroux, 1966.

Stillman, William. "Modern Painters V." *The Atlantic* 6 (Aug. 1860): 239–42.

Stone, Donald. *Novelists in a Changing World: Meredith, James, and the Transformation of English Fiction in the 1880s.* Cambridge, Mass.: Harvard University Press, 1972.

Stowell, H. Peter. *Literary Impressionism: James and Chekhov.* Athens: University of Georgia Press, 1980.

Sundquist, Eric. *American Realism: New Essays.* Baltimore, Md.: Johns Hopkins University Press, 1982.

Symons, Arthur. "The Decadent Movement in Literature." *Harper's,* Nov. 1893, pp. 858–67.

Temple, Ruth Z. "Truth in Labelling: Pre-Raphaelitism, Aestheticism, Decadence, Fin-de-Siécle." *English Literature in Transition* 17 (1974): 201–22.

Thompson, E. P. *William Morris: Romantic to Revolutionary.* London: Lawrence and Wishart, 1955.

Tintner, Adeline. *The Book World of Henry James: Appropriating the Classics.* Ann Arbor, Mich.: UMI Research Press, 1987.

———. *The Museum World of Henry James.* Ann Arbor, Mich.: UMI Research Press, 1986.

Tomsich, John. *A Genteel Endeavor: American Culture and Politics in the Gilded Age.* Stanford, Calif.: Stanford University Press, 1971.

Townsend, Francis G. "The American Estimate of Ruskin, 1847–1860." *Philological Quarterly* 32 (1953): 69–82.

Trachtenberg, Alan. *The Incorporation of America: Culture and Society in the Gilded Age*. New York: Hill and Wang, 1982.

Vanderbilt, Kermit. *The Achievement of William Dean Howells: A Reinterpretation*. Princeton, N.J.: Princeton University Press, 1968.

———. *Charles Eliot Norton: Apostle of Culture in a Democracy*. Cambridge, Mass.: Harvard University / Belknap Press, 1959.

Veblen, Thorstein. *The Theory of the Leisure Class: An Economic Study of the Evolution of Institutions*. New York: Random House, 1934.

Veysey, Laurence. *The Emergence of the American University*. Chicago: University of Chicago Press, 1965.

Warren, Austin. "Henry James: Symbolic Imagery in the Later Novels." In *Rage for Order: Essays in Criticism*. Chicago: University of Chicago Press, 1948.

Weeks, Jeffrey. *Coming Out: Homosexual Politics in Britain from the Nineteenth Century to the Present*. London: Quartet, 1977.

Weiskel, Thomas. *The Romantic Sublime: Studies in the Structure and Psychology of Transcendence*. Baltimore, Md.: Johns Hopkins University Press, 1976.

Wharton, Edith. *False Dawn*. In *Old New York*. New York: D. Appleton, 1924.

Wicke, Jennifer. *Advertising Fictions: Literature, Advertisement, and Social Reading*. New York: Columbia University Press, 1988.

———. "Postmodernism: The Perfume of Information." *The Yale Journal of Criticism* 1, no. 2 (1988): 145–60.

Wiebe, Robert. *The Search for Order: 1877–1920*. New York: Hill and Wang, 1967.

Wilde, Oscar. *The Letters of Oscar Wilde*. Ed. Rupert Hart-Davis. New York: Harcourt Brace, 1962.

Williams, Raymond. *Problems in Materialism and Culture: Selected Essays*. London: NLB, 1980.

Williams, Rosalind. *Dream Worlds: Mass Consumption in Late-Nineteenth-Century France*. Berkeley: University of California Press, 1982.

Wilson, Christopher P. *The Labor of Words: Literary Professionalism in the Progressive Era*. Athens: University of Georgia Press, 1985.

———. "The Rhetoric of Consumption: Mass-Market Magazines and the Demise of the Gentle Reader, 1880–1920." In *The Culture of Consumption: Critical Essays in American History, 1860–1960*, edited by Richard W. Fox and T. J. Jackson Lears. New York: Pantheon, 1983.

Wittgenstein, Ludwig. *Philosophical Investigations*. Tr. G. Anscombe. New York: Macmillan, 1953.

Wolf, Bryan. *Confessions of a Closet Ekphrastic*. Unpublished essay.

Yeazell, Ruth Bernard. *Language and Knowledge in the Late Novels of Henry James*. Chicago: University of Chicago Press, 1976.

Ziff, Larzer. *The American 1890s: Life and Times of a Lost Generation*. New York: Viking, 1966.

Index

In this index an "f" after a number indicates a separate reference on the next page, and an "ff" indicates separate references on the next two pages. A continuous discussion over two or more pages is indicated by a span of page numbers, e.g., "57–59." *Passim* is used for a cluster of references in close but not consecutive sequence.

Academic professionalism, xvii–xxviii, 53f, 266. *See also* Literary academics

Addams, Jane, 91

Adorno, Theodor, xx, xxii, xxix, 57, 65, 100–101, 267

Advertising: Wilde and, xxii, 50–51, 104, 181–82, 200; Aestheticism and, 13–14, 82, 104, 109–11, 271

Advertising the American Dream (Marchand), 109

Aesthesis, 136, 163–64f, 172, 205–28, 240–41

"Aesthetic Idealism of Henry James" (Sherman), xv

Aestheticism, xxvii–xxx, 1–78; James and, xiii–xxvii *passim*, 3, 11, 47, 78, 82, 90, 95, 131–255 *passim*, 262; Anglo-American vs. Continental, xix, 9, 12f, 36; French, xix, xxi, 36, 262, 265; critics of, xx–xxii, xxvii–xxix; definition of, 3–14; American, 53, 79, 88, 101–32; James's "incorporation" of, 200–201. *See also* British aestheticism; "Decadence"; Professionalism, aesthetic

"Aesthetic mania/craze," in America, 13–14, 54, 78, 102–10 *passim*

"Aesthetic Movement," definition of, 4, 11. *See also* British aestheticism

Aesthetic Movement in England (Hamilton), 4

Aesthetic Poetry (Pater), 4–5, 134

Aesthetic Theory (Adorno), xx

Agnew, John, 67–68

Albery, James, 146

Aldington, Richard, 253

Alexander, George, 167

Alienation, 2–3, 35, 54–55, 57, 77; Wilde and, 42, 57; Americans and, 112, 123, 128; James and, 247–48. *See also* Otherness; Solipsism

Allegory, theory of, 27–31 *passim*, 35

Allott, Miriam, 94

Ambassadors (James), xxv, 130, 182, 205; and Wilde, xxv, 47, 132, 168, 170, 192–201; vision in, 142; Lambert Strether in, 168, 192–201, 279; and *Wings of the Dove*, 206, 218

America: and British aestheticism, xxiii–xxvi, 13–14, 78–132, 142, 271; and high culture, xxiii–xxv, 80f, 90, 100–101f, 107, 113–18 *passim*, 207n; and Ruskin, xxiii, 79–101, 105–15 *passim*, 268–69; press of, xxiv, 81, 84, 87, 101–24 *passim*, 176–77, 207, 270–72; and commodity culture, 13–14, 80, 81–82, 102–11 *passim*, 267; Wilde's tour in, 51, 56, 81, 102–5, 112f, 167, 270, 272; popular culture of, 81, 102, 104, 107, 248, 271; and James's work, 137f, 207, 278; literary professionalism in, 253. *See also* Gentry elite, American; Modernism, Anglo-American

American Archeological Society, 88
American Art-Scholar (James), 89
American Magazine Exchange, 117
Anderson, Perry, 267
Anderson, Quentin, xvi, xviii
Andover Review, 114ff
Anesko, Michael, 177
Appletons' Journal, 105, 108
Archer, William, 181
Architecture, 84, 88, 94, 107
A Rebours (Huysmans), 36
Ariosto, Ludovico, 139
Aristotle, 10, 66, 241
Arnold, Matthew, 34, 53, 266; Wilde and,
 50; Pater and, 65; Americans and,
 109, 112, 114f; James and, 175–76,
 208
Arnold and Pater (Eliot), 126, 249
Art: commodification of, xii, xix–xxvii
 passim, 2–3, 50–52, 86; fiction as, xxii,
 131, 142–43, 170; and society, 1, 11–
 12, 255–56; autonomy of, 9, 11–12,
 59, 112, 127f; painting, 20–23, 84,
 92f; medieval, 25, 29, 64, 81, 134, 139;
 Renaissance, 64–65, 69, 81, 86, 133–
 34, 139; Americans and European,
 82–87 *passim*, 124; theater, 167, 173,
 174–75, 180–92 *passim*; *Golden Bowl*
 and, 241–45. *See also* Aestheticism;
 "Art for art's sake"; High culture
Art and Life (Ruskin), 83–84
Art criticism, *see* Criticism
Art Decoration Applied to Furniture (Spof-
 ford), 105
"Art for art's sake," xviii–xxii, 3–4, 9–10,
 115, 249f, 262
Art-Idea, 86
Artisanship, 54, 60–61, 91, 102, 105–7
"Artist": career of, 54–55, 77–78. *See also*
 Professionalism
Art nouveau, 107, 111n, 271
Art of Fiction (James), xxv, 142, 144, 147,
 168, 178
Arts and Crafts Movement, 88, 91, 106,
 271
Ashbery, John, 24
Atlantic, 112, 117; Norton and, 87; and
 Pater, 101, 114; James and, 176, 177n,
 192; and Ruskin, 270
Auden, W. H., 253–54, 279

Augustine, 26f
Author of Beltraffio (James), 46, 136,
 144–45, 158, 172
Autobiography (Brooks), 90
Automobile advertising, 110
Autonomy, theories of, 9, 11–12, 25, 59,
 112, 127f
Avant-gardism, xxiii, 1, 13, 77; Ameri-
 cans and, 106n, 117, 123–24, 128

Bakhtin, Mikhail, 72f
Barbarism, rhetoric of, 225–26f
Barbizon School, 86
Barthes, Roland, 30n
Baudelaire, Charles, 123, 140, 141, 203
Baudrillard, Jean, 71, 267
Baumgarten, Alexander, 10
Beardsley, Aubrey, 123, 221
Beauty, 1, 5, 58, 227
Beer, Thomas, 272
Beerbohm, Max, 1, 169n, 221
Bell, Florence, 173
Belle dame sans merci, 205–6, 221–22,
 232–40
Benjamin, Walter, 30n–31n, 65
Berenson, Bernard, 121–22; Pater and,
 69, 115, 268; Norton and, 88–89, 269;
 James and, 130; Herrick's portrayal of,
 145
Besant, Walter, 178, 181
Bewley, Marius, xvi
Blackmur, R. P., xiv, xvi, 131, 153, 233
Blake, William, 9, 16
Bledstein, Burton, 52, 55–56, 266
Blessed Damozel (Rossetti), 210f
Blue Bird (Maeterlinck), 220
Body, Wilde and, 42–43, 196
Bohemianism, xxiii, 128, 130
Boker, George, 270
Booth, Wayne, 131
Boris, Eileen, 61
Boston, 80, 107, 112–17 *passim*, 121;
 James and, 82, 129, 139, 207; and
 Ruskin, 87–92 *passim*; moralism in, 90,
 134. *See also* Gentry elite, American
Boston Commonwealth, 116
Boston Evening Transcript, 207
Botticelli, Sandro, 133, 273
Bourdieu, Pierre, xvii, 256
Bourgeois society: and autonomy of

art, 11–12; moralism of, 45–46; professionalization and, 53–58 *passim*; individualism of, 73; Americans and, 81, 123; James and, 206–7. *See also* Middle class; Social criticism
Bourget, Paul, 203
Brewer, Derek, 266
"Britannia Agoraia," 94
British aestheticism, xi–xii, xviii–xxvii *passim*, 1–3, 265; James and, xiv–xviii *passim*, xxv–xxvii, 11, 47, 78, 82, 95, 131–257 *passim*; American response to, xxiii–xxvi, 13–14, 78–132, 142, 271; definition of, 3–14; and temporality, 9, 14–35; and otherness, 9, 35–47; vs. "aestheticism," 11; and social process, 47–78. *See also* "Decadence"
Brook Farm, 91
Brooks, Van Wyck, xiii–xvii *passim*, 81, 88, 90–91, 122, 261–62, 269
Browne, Thomas, 6
Browning, Oscar, 172
Browning, Robert, 4, 16, 37, 112, 165, 214n, 279
Brummell, Beau, 50n
Bryan, Thomas Jefferson, 83n
Buchanan, Robert, 203
Buckley, Jerome, 14
Bundle of Letters (James), 136, 147
Bunyan, John, 106n
Bürger, Peter, 11–13
Burgess, Gelett, 271
Burnand, Frank, 146
Burne-Jones, Edward, 210
Byron, G., 34, 77

Cabot, J. Eliot, 270
Cain, William, 254
Calvinism, 115, 138
Capitalism, xix–xx, 52, 70, 74, 91
Careers, 52–57 *passim*, 252–53. *See also* Professionalism, aesthetic
Carlyle, Thomas, 58, 62, 64f, 70f, 77, 88
Carmen, Bliss, 79
Carroll, Lewis, 214n
Carson, Edward, 57, 203
Cézanne, Paul, 271
Chap-Book, 123f, 130, 177
Chautauqua lecture series, 112
Chesterton, G. K., 8

Chicago, 61, 107, 123
Chopin, Kate, 123
Christianity, 41, 115f, 138. *See also* Puritanism
Christianity and Aestheticism (Gladden), 115
Cincinnati, 113
Civilization, rhetoric of, 175, 224–27. *See also* Culture
Class, 48–53 *passim*, 60, 106, 256. *See also* Bourgeois society; Gentry elite, American; Middle class
Cohen, Ed, 44
Cole, Thomas, 270
Coleridge, Samuel Taylor, 6, 28, 31, 34, 77
Colonel (Burnand), 146, 149
Color lithography, 109–10
Comedy, 182–92, 200. *See also* Satire
Commodification, 59–64; of art, xii, xix–xxvii *passim*, 2–3, 50–52, 86, 181–82, 262 (*see also* Literary market); of critique of commodity culture, xxix–xxx. *See also* Commodity; Marketing strategies
Commodity, 67–68; "commodity culture" and, xii; "absolute," xx; "aesthetic," 13; and body, 42–43. *See also* Commodity culture
Commodity culture, xi–xiii, xx, xxvi–xxvii, 58–71 *passim*, 256; Wilde and, xx, 42–43, 58–64 *passim*; commodification of critique of, xxix–xxx; in America, 13–14, 80, 81–82, 102–11 *passim*, 267; James and, 188–89, 207f; defined, 266–67. *See also* Commodification; Literary market
Communism of John Ruskin, 84, 91
Community, 41, 165. *See also* Society
Congregationalism, 115
Connoisseurship, 137, 139, 147, 153–57 *passim*, 229–30, 240–41, 275
"Consumer revolution," 266–67. *See also* Commodity culture
Contemplation, 59, 67, 137–42 *passim*, 153–54, 164, 193–94
Cook, Clarence, 84, 105–9 *passim*
Courbet, Gustave, 86
Cowley, Malcolm, 122
Crayon, 83ff
Critic, 144, 248

Critic as Artist (Wilde), 72–73

Criticism, xxi–xxii, xxviii–xxix, 5, 126, 128, 243–44, 278; "Frankfurt school," xix–xx, 100; New, xxvi, xxviii, 128–29, 243, 250–56 *passim*; Ruskin and, 12, 92, 100–101

Cruelty, 227, 237–39

"Cult of Beauty," 1

Culture, xii, 59–60, 255–56; professionalism and, 55, 58, 266; America and, 111–14; James and, 129–30, 175–76, 205–9 *passim*, 224–27. *See also* Commodity culture; High culture; Mass culture; Social criticism

Daisy Miller (James), xxi–xxii

Dandyism, 49–50, 59, 140

D'Annunzio, Gabriele, xx, 242

Dante Alighieri, 139

Dante Reading Circle, 88

Dante Society, 88

Dark Glass (Rossetti), 16

Death, 40f

Death of the Lion (James), 130, 176

Debord, Guy, 71, 268

"Decadence," 1f, 4, 36, 277; Americans and, xxiv, 79, 116–17, 123, 139, 252; James and, 132, 139, 175–76, 201–45, 253

Decay of Lying (Wilde), 72–73

Deconstruction, 30–31

Defence of Cosmetics (Beerbohm), 221

Deleuze, Gilles, 71

De Man, Paul, xvii, 27–31 *passim*, 35

Democratization, 48–49, 56

Derrida, Jacques, 30n, 65

Design (Frost), 125

Desire, 35, 42–43, 196

Diachronicity, 25, 27

Dial, 124

Dialogue, 72, 268

Disraeli, Benjamin, 50n

Di Yunge, 79

"Doing," vs. "being," 137–42 *passim*, 147–48, 164

Dollimore, Jonathan, 263

Dolores (Swinburne), 235–36

Domesticity: American, 81–82, 106. *See also* Home decoration

Domville (James), 167, 176

Donne, John, 6

Dorian Gray, see *Picture of Dorian Gray*

Doubleness, 15–24 *passim*, 57–58, 213–14, 278

Dove, as signifier, 216–17

Dowling, Linda, 263

Dowson, Ernest, 8, 79

D'Oyly Carte, Richard, 51, 102, 104

Du Maurier, George, xx–xxi, xxii; in *Punch*, 1, 146–49 *passim*, 161, 241, 277; and Wilde, 51, 102, 104, 148; James and, 145–52 *passim*, 161–62, 241, 262, 277

Durand, Asher, 84f

Durand, John, 84

Earthly Paradise (Morris), 5

East Coker (Eliot), 126–27

Eastlake, Charles, 105, 106n, 110

Edel, Leon, 172, 275–76

Edelstein, Laurie, 42n

Edwardian England, 207, 247

Ego, 41, 265. *See also* Self

Ekphrasis, 19–24, 156–57, 205, 214–15

Eliot, Charles William, 121f

Eliot, George, 62, 182, 276

Eliot, T. S., xxvi, 124–31 *passim*, 207n; and Pater, 26, 31n, 126–27, 273; and James, 100, 246–54 *passim*, 278–79

Ellmann, Richard, 50, 147, 168n, 209

Emerson, Ralph Waldo, xiii, 66, 84, 90, 133

Empiricism, 65, 142–43

England, *see* Great Britain

Enlightenment, 64

Eros and Civilization (Marcuse), 70

Eroticism, *see* Sexuality

Essentialism, 263

Ethics of the Dust (Ruskin), 59, 62

Europe: Anglo-American aestheticism vs. aestheticism of, xix, 9, 12f, 36; avant-garde of, 13, 124; Americans and art of, 82–87 *passim*, 124. *See also individual countries*

Evil, 145, 152

Experience, *see* Sense experience

Failure, 3, 31–38 *passim*, 180, 188, 190, 245

False Dawn (Wharton), 82–83

Fashion, and aestheticism, 1–3, 9, 102

Faulkner, William, 128
Fenollosa, Ernest, 88, 279
Fête Champétre (Giorgione), 20
Fiction, as art, xxii, 131, 142–43, 170
Figure in the Carpet (James), 248
Fish, Stanley, 266
Flaubert, Gustave, 176, 249
Fleishman, Avrom, 25f
"For a Venetian Pastoral by Giorgione" (Rossetti), 20–24
Ford, Ford Maddox, 246
Formalism, 254–55
For Once, Then, Something (Frost), 125
Fors Claveriga (Ruskin), 62
Foucault, Michel, xiv, 65
France: aestheticism and, xix, xxi, 36, 262, 265; poetry of, 27; and commodity culture, 70–71; and "decadence," 202
"Frankfurt school," xix–xx, 100
Freedom, 47, 65–66, 158–66, 185, 227
Freud, Sigmund, 39, 265
Frost, Robert, 124–25

Gagnier, Regenia, 268
Gardner, Isabella Stewart, 88, 112, 130, 167
Garland, Hamlin, 123
Garrison, Dee, 269
Geismar, Maxwell, xiv–xvii *passim*
Gender, 22–24, 38. *See also* Sexuality; Woman
Genesis (Swinburne), 6–7
Gentry elite, American, 80, 82, 101, 112–21 *passim*, 269f; and Ruskin, 87–88; James and, 138–39, 207
George, Stefan, xix
Georgia, 91
Germany: aestheticism and, xix, 92; idealist, 4, 27, 65, 70; philology, 263
Gestalt psychology, 19
Gilbert and Sullivan, 1, 51, 102ff, 146–52 *passim*, 235
Gilmore, Michael, xiv, xx, 164, 275
Gioconda, Pater and, 64, 114, 235
Giorgione, 20–23, 58
Gladden, Washington, 115f
Godey's Ladies' Book, 105, 108
Godkin, E. L., 167
Golden Bowl (James), xvii, xxv, 130, 161, 170, 201, 206; and Wilde, xxv, 47,

242–43; and "decadence," 132, 203, 205, 228–45
Goode, John, 206, 262
Gospel of Freedom (Herrick), 145
Gosse, Edmund, 135, 168n, 172, 178
Graff, Gerald, 266
Great Britain: and consumer culture, 58, 61, 63, 266–67; Edwardian, 207, 247. *See also* British aestheticism; London; Modernism, Anglo-American
Greek poetry, 26–27, 30
Greek Studies (Pater), 114
Greeley, Horace, 84
Green, Martin, 265
Guattari, Felix, 71
Guy Domville (James), 167, 176

Hamerton, Phillip Gilbert, 92
Hamilton, Walter, 4
Handcrafts, 54, 60–61, 91, 102
"Hard, gemlike flame" (Pater), 18–19, 69, 127, 135, 196–200 *passim*, 261
Harland, Henry, 130, 177n
Harper's, 176
Harrison, Frederic, 152
Hartman, Geoffrey, 34
Hartsock, Mildred, 230–31
Harvard, 112; aesthetes at, 53, 79, 88, 121–25 *passim*; architecture at, 88; and Pater, 115–16
Harvard Advocate, 122
Harvard Monthly, 122, 124
Hauser, Arnold, 12
Hawthorne, Nathaniel, 179, 191f, 279
Hazard of New Fortunes (Howells), 117–20
Hazlitt, William, 6
Hegel, G. W. F., 4, 65, 77
Helsinger, Elizabeth, 48
Hemingway, Ernest, 128
Hermeneutics, 34, 204–5
Herrick, Robert, 145
High culture, xii–xiii, xxvi–xxix *passim*, 2; Americans and, xxiii–xxv, 80f, 90, 100–101f, 107, 113–18 *passim*, 207n; James and, xxv–xxvii, 170, 181, 226–27; Wilde and, 2, 80f, 102, 116, 170, 181; Pater and, 67f, 80, 114–16. *See also* Fashion; Modernism, Anglo-American
Hints on Household Taste (Eastlake), 105, 106n

Historical Studies of Church-Building in the Middle Ages (Norton), 87

Historicism, xvi, 25–30 *passim*, 64–65, 76, 128

History painting, 84

Hoffmannsthal, Hugo von, xix

Holland, Laurence, xvi, 223–24, 227

Holloway, John, 62, 99

Home decoration, 54, 60–61, 81–82, 102–10 *passim*

Homer, 26f, 30

Homosexuality, 2; James's, xvi, 168n, 169–73 *passim*, 275–76; Wilde's, 50n, 168n, 169–73 *passim*, 263

Hours of Exercise in the Alps (Tyndall), 92

"House Beautiful," 105–10. *See also* Home decoration

House Beautiful (Cook), 105

House Beautiful magazine, 106n

House of Life (Rossetti), 16ff

House of Life (Stevens), 124

Howells, William Dean, 91, 101, 117–21, 175, 200, 248

Hubbell, Jay, 248

Hudson River School, 84

Hume, David, 66

Huneker, James, xxiv, 79, 123, 271

Hunt, Holman, 233

Hunt, William Morris, 57

Huysmans, J. K., 36, 42, 51, 124

Hymn to Chamounix (Coleridge), 31

Ibsen, H., 124

Ideal Husband (Wilde), 71, 166

Idealism, 34, 143, 215–16; German, 4, 27, 65, 70

Identification, 29, 35, 39ff, 213–14, 265

"Imaginary," mirror stage and, 214

Immigrants, James and Wilde as, 169

"Immortals," *Critic's*, 248

Importance of Being Earnest (Wilde), 71, 167

Impressionism, 143

Independent, 133

Indolence, the aesthete's, 138, 147–48, 150

Influence, 43–47 *passim*, 194–95, 247–48

In Summer (Stickney), 125

Intensity: Pater and, 9, 58f, 64–67 *passim*, 196–200 *passim*, 217, 251, 261; James and, 195–200 *passim*, 217, 261,

274; Wilde and, 195–200 *passim*; Pound and, 251

Interior decoration, 54, 60–61, 81–82, 102–10 *passim*

Isolation, 35–37, 42, 54, 78, 127. *See also* Alienation; Solipsism

Italy, 133–34, 147

Ivory Tower (James), 247f

Jackson, Holbrook, 60

"Jacobitism," xiii–xviii *passim*, 243–44, 246, 254f

Jacobson, Marcia, 176

James, Alice, 210n–11n

James, Henry, xi–xii, xiii, xxvi–xxvii, 78, 82, 129–31; and aestheticism, xiii–xxvii *passim*, 3, 11, 47, 78, 82, 90, 95, 131–255 *passim*, 262; and Pater, xv, xxv, xxvi, 131–76 *passim*, 186–87, 193–202 *passim*, 206–11 *passim*, 217–19, 232, 242, 250, 253, 261–62, 273–74; and modernism, xvii, xviii, xxv–xxvi, 11, 78, 129–32, 170, 201, 209, 245–55, 278–79; and Wilde, xvii, xxv, xxvi, 47, 131f, 143, 147, 150f, 167–202 *passim*, 211, 214, 220–21, 242f, 250, 253; and moralism, xviii, 46, 89–97 *passim*, 137–46 *passim*, 218, 221, 223, 230, 242, 274; and Ruskin, xxvi, 62, 91–101 *passim*, 129, 131, 139, 202, 205, 224, 274; and Norton, 88–93 *passim*, 100, 129, 133, 176, 202, 205, 242; and "decadence," 132, 139, 175–76, 201–45, 257; and Eliot (George), 182, 276; "major phase," 202–47 *passim*. *See also individual works*

James, William, 115–16, 122, 124n; Henry's letters to, 133, 168, 176, 177n

Jameson, Frederic, 75f

"James revival" (1940's/1950's), xv–xvi

Jarves, James Jackson, 83n, 86

Jenny (Rossetti), 37–38

Jews, at Harvard, 122

Johnson, Lionel, 204

Jowett, Benjamin, 4

Kansas City World, 117

Kant, Immanuel, xxvii–xxviii, 5

Keats, John, 4, 6, 28, 34, 77

Kenner, Hugh, 128

Kierkegaard, S., 29

King, Clarence, 84
Knoepflmacher, U. C., 25

Labor, 64, 70, 74–75
Lacan, Jacques, 213–14
Laclau, Ernesto, 268
Ladies Home Journal, 176
Lady Windermere's Fan (Wilde), 71, 173
La Farge, John, 86
Lake of Gaube (Swinburne), 31–33
Landow, George, 62
Landscape painting, 84, 92
Larson, Magali, 52
Lazarus, Emma, 91
Lee, Vernon, 145
Leiss, William, 67–68
Leonardo da Vinci, 58
Leslie, Mrs. Frank, 51, 102
Leslie's Illustrated Newspaper, 51, 102
Lessing, G. E., 19–24 *passim*, 264
Lesson of the Master, 247
Letters on Landscape Painting (Durand), 84
Levey, Michael, 268
Libertarianism, 268
Lifanda-Freedman, Rebecca Aweli-
    sande, vi
Life on the Mississippi (Twain), 106n
Lindau, Zisha, 79
Literary academics, xxvii–xxviii, 254. *See
    also* New Criticism
Literary criticism, *see* Criticism
Literary market, xii; James and, xii,
    xxi–xxii, 176–82, 207; mass, 117–21
    passim, 181–82
Literary modernism, *see* Modernism,
    Anglo-American
Literature, *see* Literary market; Novel;
    Poetry
Lithography, color, 109–10
Little Review, 124, 246
Lodge, George Cabot, xxiv, 121, 123, 130
London: James and, 146–47, 167, 173–
    76 *passim*, 252–53. *See also* British
    aestheticism
London, Jack, 91
Loss, rhetoric of, 14–22 *passim*, 35
Lotus, 117
Love, 15–17, 227
Lowell, James Russell, 84, 133
Lubbock, Percy, 131
Lukacs, Georg, 67

Lynes, Russell, 270–71
Lyotard, Jean-François, 77, 268

Macmillan's, 146
Maeterlinck, Maurice, xx, 124, 209, 220
Maidment, Brian, 62
Mallock, W. H., 200
Marchand, Roland, 109
Marcus, Steven, 37
Marcuse, Herbert, 70–71, 75
Marginality, aestheticism and, 54–58
    passim. See also Alienation
Marius the Epicurean (Pater), 17–18f,
    25–29 *passim*, 38–41, 106n, 114–15,
    251
Market economy, xii, xx. *See also* Capi-
    talism; Commodification; Literary
    market
Marketing strategies: American, 13–14,
    82, 109–10, 128; James's, 177. *See also*
    Advertising
Marx, Karl, 75, 77, 91
Marxism, 76; and commodity culture,
    xii, xix–xx; and James, xiv, xvi, 262;
    "Western," xiv; Morris and, 59–60,
    267; Ruskin and, 59–60, 91; and
    Pater, 65, 70–71; and Wilde, 75
Mary Magdalene (Saltus), 130
Mask, 220–21
Mass culture, 58, 170; Wilde and, 50–
    51, 81, 102, 104, 170; American, 81,
    102, 104, 107, 248, 271; and literary
    market, 117–21 *passim*, 181–82; James
    and, 170, 181–82, 188–89, 248. *See
    also* Commodity culture
Materialism, 9, 47–78. *See also* Com-
    modity; Fashion; Market economy
Matthiessen, F. O., xvi, 144, 254, 278–79
Maudle on the Choice of a Profession (Du
    Maurier), 148
Max, Peter, 111n
Medievalism/Middle Ages, 25, 29, 64, 81,
    134, 139
Memory, 17–18
Menand, Louis, 273
Meredith, George, 246, 248, 250
Meta-narratives, 76–77
Michelangelo, 134
Middle class: American, xxiv–xv, 81, 90,
    105f, 112–23 *passim*, 207, 271; alien-
    ation from, 2; aestheticists from, 48,

Middle class (*Continued*)
90; Dandyism and, 49–50; artisanship and, 60, 105. *See also* Gentry elite, American
Middlemarch (Eliot), 182
Middle Years (James), 130, 176–77
Millais, J. E., 10, 57, 210
Miller, J. Hillis, 30, 35, 65
Milton, John, 175, 209
Minima Moralia (Adorno), 100–101
"Mirror phase," in *Wings of the Dove*, 213–14
Miss Brown (Lee), 145
Mitchell, W. J. T., 22, 264
Mnemosyne (Stickney), 125
Modernism, Anglo-American, xii, xxiv–xxv, 11, 76, 77–78, 107, 121–32 *passim*, 245–57; James and, xvii, xviii, xxv–xxvi, 11, 78, 129–32, 170, 201, 209, 245–55, 278–79; and contradiction, 11, 24–25, 128–29, 252; and Ruskin, 11, 90, 129, 131; and Pater, 77, 121, 125–29 *passim*, 249–52 *passim*, 273
Modern Painters series (Ruskin), 10, 12, 48, 83, 85, 92f
Moers, Ellen, 49, 50n
Monsman, Gerald, 3
Mont Blanc (Shelley), 31
Moralism: Americans and, xviii, 81–93 *passim*, 102, 105, 113–20 *passim*, 129, 134, 269, 271; James and, xviii, 46, 89–97 *passim*, 137–46 *passim*, 218, 221, 223, 230, 242, 274; Ruskinian, xxiii, 84–97 *passim*, 102, 134, 274; Wilde and, 45–46, 72, 102
Mornings in Florence (Ruskin), 62
Morris, Jane, 210n–11n
Morris, William, 8, 30; Pater and, 4–5, 134; and politics, 12; medievalism of, 25, 64; and social position, 47ff, 54, 58; and commodity culture, 59–64 *passim*, 266–67; home decoration by, 60–61, 81–82, 105; and social criticism, 63f, 71; Americans and, 81–82, 90f, 105–10 *passim*, 270; James and, 88, 134
Morris (William) and Company, 60–61
Morris (William) Rooms, 61–62
Morse, Samuel, 51
Most of It (Frost), 125
Mouffe, Chantal, 268

Mrs. Geoffrey, 104
Mumford, Lewis, 90f
Munera Pulveris (Ruskin), 59
Munsey's, 176, 177n
My Last Duchess (Browning), 165

Narcissism, 36–37, 38, 124, 243–44
Nast, Thomas, 104
Nation, 81, 112, 116; and Pater, 81, 101, 114, 116; and Wilde, 103; and James, 144, 274
"Naturalism," 85–86, 93, 101, 117
Necessity, 65–66, 109
Negativity, 31
Neoclassicism, 92, 134
New Criticism, xxvi, xxviii, 128–29, 243, 250–56 *passim*
New historicism, xvi
New Path, 84
"New Renaissance" (Quilter), 146
New Republic (Mallock), 200
Newsome, David, 6
Newspapers, *see* Press; *individual papers*
New York, 80, 83n, 92, 101, 112, 118, 271–72
"New York Gallery of Christian Art," 83n
New York Graphic, 103
New York Herald, 103
New York Historical Society, 83n
New York Tribune, 84, 106n, 123
Next Time (James), 181
Nietzsche, F., 65
Nordau, Max, 203, 226
Norris, Christopher, xxvii
North American Review, 87
North of Boston (Frost), 124–25
Norton, Charles Eliot, xxiii, 86–93 *passim*, 107, 269; moralism of, xxiii, 80, 86–93 *passim*, 116, 134, 242; James and, 88–93 *passim*, 100, 129, 133, 176, 202, 205, 242; and Pater, 115–16
Norton, Grace, 89
Novak, Barbara, 270
Novel, xxii, 131, 142–43, 170, 201, 245, 277

Objects, 3, 42, 153–62 *passim*, 211, 215, 229–30. *See also* Connoisseurship; Reification
O.K. Society, 122, 124
Origination, 29–30

Otherness, 9, 35–47, 153, 166. *See also* Objects
Outcry, 244
Outlook, 114
Oxford, aesthetes in, 53, 122, 268

Paganism, 41, 115f
Painting, 20–23, 84, 92f
Paradise Lost (Milton), 175
Paradox, 128–29
Paranoia, 213–14
Parrington, Vernon, xiii–xvii *passim*, 91
Parrish, Maxfield, 110, 111n, 221, 271
"Partial Portrait" (Miller), 35
Pater, Walter, xxv, 1–10 *passim*, 22, 77, 262; James and, xv, xxv, xxvi, 131–76 *passim*, 186–87, 193–202 *passim*, 206–11 *passim*, 217–19, 232, 242, 250, 253, 261–62, 273–74; and temporality, 9–10, 14–19 *passim*, 25–33 *passim*, 64–65, 125, 127; personification by, 29; and self, 35–46 *passim*, 66–69 *passim*; and otherness, 38–46 *passim*; and social position, 48–58 *passim*; and commodity culture, 58–68 *passim*; social critique of, 63–71, 75f; and *Gioconda*, 64, 114, 235; and Berenson, 69, 115, 268; modernists and, 77, 121, 125–29 *passim*, 249–52 *passim*, 273; Americans and, 79ff, 101, 114–16, 121, 125–29 *passim*; and "House Beautiful," 106n
Patience (Gilbert and Sullivan), 1, 51, 102, 104, 146, 148, 235
Pearls for Young Ladies (Ruskin), 83–84
Peckham, Morse, xviii, 10
Perception, 10, 128, 153, 163–65. *See also* Sense experience; Vision
Perfect Critic (Eliot), 126, 128
Perfect moments, 9–10, 15–20, 199
Periodicals, *see* Press; *individual periodicals*
Perry, T. S., 92
Personification, 29
Philadelphia, 80, 105, 112
Philadelphia Exposition (1876), 105
Philistia Defiant (Du Maurier), 161
Philology, German, 263
Philosophy, German, 4, 27, 65, 70
Picture of Dorian Gray (Wilde), 10, 36, 41–46, 51; and ekphrasis, 19, 214; and moralism, 72; Americans and, 123; James and, 168, 192–96, 211, 214

Pierrot, 203–4
Plagiarism, 268
Plato and Platonism (Pater), 114
Poe, E. A., 235
Poetry, 4–5f, 22, 23–24, 29–35 *passim*; political, 12; Greek, 26–27, 30; French, 27; quest, 33; American, 124–31 *passim*; modernist, 131, 246–52. *See also* Pre-Raphaelitism
Poetry magazine, 124
Political Unconscious (Jameson), 75
Politics, 12f, 70–76 *passim*, 207n, 268; socialist, 12, 73, 74–75, 91, 172, 268; anarchist, 175–76, 227, 260
Popular culture, *see* Mass culture
Pornography, 270
Porter, Carolyn, xiv–xv
Portrait (Rossetti), 210, 211–12
Portrait of a Lady (James), xxii, 130, 132, 136, 145–66; Gilbert Osmond in, xiii–xvii *passim*, 145–66 *passim*, 187–88, 190, 240–41, 275; as satire, xxi, 146–53, 157–62 *passim*; Ralph Touchett in, 150–58 *passim*; Isabel Archer in, 152–66 *passim*, 240–41, 275; Madame Merle in, 159–66 *passim*; *Golden Bowl* and, 161, 230, 240–41, 244; and *Wings of the Dove*, 209, 218
Portraiture, 84, 158, 166, 191
Postmodernism, xviii, 24–25, 76–77, 129, 268
Pound, Ezra, xxvi, 30n, 128, 246–54 *passim*, 278–79
Power, 23, 43; Romanticism and, 28, 31–32; and influence, 43–44; *Wings of the Dove* and, 224; *Golden Bowl* and, 239–40. *See also* Social power
Precious Thoughts (Ruskin), 83–84
Prefaces (James), 229, 244
Prelude (Wordsworth), 31
Pre-Raphaelitism, 2, 4, 10, 15–24 *passim*, 29; Wilde and, 51; and professionalization, 55, 57; Americans and, 81, 85, 101, 109, 110–11, 271; and "decadence," 203, 205–6, 210–12, 221
Press: American, xxiv, 81, 84, 87, 101–24 *passim*, 176–77, 207, 270–72; British, 13; and modernists, 252
Professionalism, aesthetic, xii, xix–xxviii *passim*, 52–58, 77–78, 256, 266; James and, xii, xxvi, 131, 170, 178–92, 201,

Professionalism (*Continued*)
247–48, 252–54; professionalization
of critique of, xxix–xxx, 57; mod-
ernists and, 252–54. *See also* Literary
market
Proust, Marcel, 30n
Prufrock (Eliot), 124, 279
Psalms, 217
Psychology, Gestalt, 19
Punch, 81, 146f; Du Maurier in, 1, 146–
49 *passim*, 161, 241, 277
Puritanism, 89, 137–38, 269
Pyle, Howard, 271

"Queen Anne" design, 106
Quest poems, 33
Quilter, Harry, 146, 149
Quinn, John, 246

Radcliffe, 124n
Rahv, Phillip, xvi
Ransom, John Crowe, 251–52
Raven (Poe), 235
Readings from Ruskin: Italy, 84
Realists/Realism, 86, 117, 119, 271
Regionalism, 117
Reification, xix, xx, 3, 59, 67, 153–66
passim, 230, 240–41, 268
Renaissance, 64–65, 69, 81, 86, 133–34,
139
Renaissance (Pater), *see Studies in the
History of the Renaissance*
Renunciation, 166, 199
Repetition, allegory and, 29
Republicanism, 207n
Reubell, Henrietta, 167
Rhetoric of Temporality (de Man), 27, 30
Robinson, Edward Arlington, 124
Roderick Hudson (James), xvii, xxv, 130–
46 *passim*, 153, 158, 205, 240
Roland, Romain, 90
Romanticism, 2–3, 77, 137; European,
xxvii–xxviii; British, 4, 24–34 *passim*,
56, 76, 87, 125, 270; "late," 10; anti-,
34; "dark," 202–3
Rome Revisited (Wilde), 147
Rookwood pottery, 106
Ross, Robert, 169n, 171
Rossetti, Christina, 30, 47
Rossetti, Dante Gabriel, 1–2, 8, 10; and
politics, 12; and temporality, 14–25

passim, 29–34 *passim*; and otherness,
36–38, 43, 46; and self, 36–38, 43,
46; and social position, 47f, 54; James
and, 88, 131, 147, 210–14 *passim*;
Americans and, 101, 110, 125, 128f,
269f; paranoia of, 214n
Rossetti, William Michael, 146
Rousseau, Jean-Jacques, 28
Rowe, John Carlos, 230
Ruskin, John, 1–3, 10, 30n, 34, 270;
Americans and, xxiii, 79–101, 105–
15 *passim*, 268–69; James and, xxvi,
62, 91–101 *passim*, 129, 131, 139, 202,
205, 224, 274; and social criticism,
12, 63f, 70f, 87–88, 99–101, 224–25,
266–67; and social position, 47–
63 *passim*; and commodity culture,
59–64 *passim*, 266–67; paranoia of,
214n
Ruskin Commonwealth, 91

Sacred Fount (James), 193, 203–4, 206,
214–15, 247
Sacred Wood (Eliot), 249
Sade, Marquis de, 57
Said, Edward, 266
St. George's Society, 91
Saltus, Edgar, xxiv, 79, 123, 130
Sandburg, Carl, 91
San Francisco, 112, 271–72
Santayana, George, 122, 124
Satire, xx–xxi, 104, 116–17, 146–53,
262; Du Maurier and, xx–xxi, 51,
104, 146–52 *passim*, 161–62, 241, 262,
277; *Portrait of a Lady* and, xxi, 146–
53, 157–62 *passim*; and Wilde, 51, 81,
102, 104, 116–17; *Tragic Muse* and,
185; *Ambassadors* and, 200; in *Wings of
the Dove*, 206–10, 217, 223, 227, 277;
Golden Bowl and, 241
Savile Club, 168
Schiller, F. von, xxvii–xxviii
Schopenhauer, Arnold, 65
Science, 66–67
Science: A Ruskin Anthology, 84
Scribner's, 112
Seeing, *see* Vision
Self, 71; -consciousness, 29, 42, 77, 153;
and otherness, 35–47; Pater and, 35–
46 *passim*, 66–69 *passim*; *Portrait of
a Lady* and, 153, 159f, 162; *Wings of*

the Dove and, 211–15 *passim. See also* Identification; Solipsism

Self-Portrait in a Convex Mirror (Ashbery), 24

Seltzer, Mark, xiv–xv, 224, 226, 278

Sense experience, xix–xx, 3, 81, 125–26; Pater and, 3, 14–15, 67, 69, 125, 134, 196–200 *passim*, 217, 261; Wilde and, 42–43, 194–200 *passim*; James and, 134, 136, 141, 142–43, 194–200 *passim*, 217, 261–62. *See also Aesthesis*; Intensity

Sexuality, 2, 35, 54f; James and, xvi, 168n, 169–73 *passim*, 194–95, 198, 234, 275–76, 279; Americans and, xxiv; Rossetti and, 2, 37; Wilde and, 2, 50n, 168n, 169–73 *passim*, 263, 270; "decadence" and, 202–3, 234

Shaw, George Bernard, 124, 181, 267

Shelley, P. B., 31, 34

Sherman, Stuart, xv

Sherwood, Mrs. M. E. W., 105, 108, 270–71

Siddal, Elizabeth, 210

Silent Noon (Rossetti), 16f, 19

"Sincerity," 105, 110

Six-Mark Teapot (Du Maurier), 149

Slave Ship (Turner), 97

Smith, Logan Piersall, 130

Snobbery, 148, 187–88

Social criticism, xxviii–xxix, 12, 58–78, 256, 265, 266–67; Ruskin and, 12, 63f, 70f, 87–88, 99–101, 224–25, 266–67; James and, 99–101, 224–27

Socialism, 12, 73, 74–75, 91, 172, 268

Social power, xxviii, xxix, 148–49, 169, 269; James and, xi, xiii, xiv–xv, 218, 222, 240–41; Wilde and, 48–58 *passim*, 71, 169, 173; Americans and Ruskin and, 87–88. *See also* Class; Professionalism, aesthetic

Society, 47–78, 255–56; and art, 1, 11–12, 255–56; transformation in, 8, 49, 91; climbing in, 50, 149, 151–52 (*see also* Professionalism, aesthetic); marginality in, 54–58 *passim* (*see also* Alienation); *Golden Bowl* and, 231–32. *See also* Bourgeois society; Culture; Politics; Social criticism; Social power

Society for the Advancement of Truth in Art, 84

Society of Authors, 178

Solipsism, 9, 35–36, 46, 127

Sonnets for Pictures (Rossetti), 19

Soul of Man Under Socialism (Wilde), 12, 36, 73, 176

Spatiality, 26–27

Sphinx (Wilde), 234–35

Spofford, Harriet Prescott, 105–10 *passim*

Spoils of Poynton (James), 106n, 130

Stead, C. K., 252

Stedman, Edmund Clarence, 270

Stein, Gertrude, 124n

Stein, Richard, 20, 205–6, 213

Stein, Roger, 117, 268–69

Stein, William Bysshe, 203, 277

Stevens, Wallace, 124–28 *passim*

Stickney, Trumbull, xxiv, 121–25 *passim*, 130

Stillman, William, 83–86 *passim*, 101

Stone, Herbert, 106n

Stone and Kimball, 79, 106n, 123, 177

Stones of Venice (Ruskin), 12, 85, 93–99 *passim*

Storm-Cloud of the Nineteenth Century (Ruskin), 63, 98

Stream's Secret (Rossetti), 14

Strether, Lambert, *see Ambassadors*

Studies in the History of the Renaissance (Pater), 5, 9, 19, 29, 58, 64–70 *passim*; and Morris, 5, 134; self in, 35–36, 42, 68–69; Americans and, 101, 114f, 125f; James and, 133–34, 142–43, 155, 163, 206, 211, 217, 273–74; modernists and, 251

Sturgis, Howard, 171

Sturgis, Russell, 84f, 171

Style (Pater), 5

"Stylism," xviii, 10, 130

Subjectivity, 43–47. *See also* Self

Sublime, 31–34 *passim*

Sunday Morning (Stevens), 125

Swinburne, A. C., 1–15 *passim*, 29–36 *passim*, 262; and history, 25; and social position, 48, 54, 57–58; James and, 141, 250; *belles dames* of, 235–36; modernists and, 250, 252; and Turner, 264; Americans and, 270

Symbolism, 27–28, 29, 36; Americans and, 117; *Wings of the Dove* and, 214, 215–16

Symonds, John Addington, 172, 276

Symons, Arthur, 8, 126, 128
Synchronicity, 25, 27
Synthesis, 8, 28, 77, 250–51f

Taste, xxix, xxx, 148–51 *passim*, 231n,
    256
Tea at the Palaz of Hoon (Stevens), 125
Temporality, 14–35; and historicism, xvi,
    25–30 *passim*, 64–65, 76, 128; Pater
    and, 9–10, 14–19 *passim*, 25–33 *passim*,
    64–65, 125, 127; and perfect mo-
    ments, 9–10, 15–20, 199; modernists
    and, 125–26, 251; *Ambassadors* and,
    197, 199–200. *See also* Historicism;
    Perfect moments
Tennessee, 91
Tennyson, Alfred, 4, 221
Theale, Milly, xvii
Theater, 167, 173, 174–75, 180–92
    passim
Theory of the Avant Garde (Bürger), 11–13
Theory of the Leisure Class (Veblen), 69,
    267
Thompson, E. P., 70, 267
Thompson, Vance, 271
Tiffany, Louis, 106
Time, *see* Temporality
Tobey Furniture Company, 61
Tolstoy, L., 90
Tomsich, John, 270
"Tradition," 251
"Tradition and the Individual Talent"
    (Eliot), 126, 273
Traffic (Ruskin), 94f, 98
Tragic Muse (James), xxv, 168, 170,
    182–92
Transcendence, xxiii, 59, 109, 154, 164,
    172
Transformation, social, 8, 49, 91
"Transgressive reinscription," 263
Travel, American, 84–85
Travelling Companions (James), 274
Trilby (Du Maurier), xxi, 145
"Trilby mania," 107
"Triumph of Time" (Swinburne), 15
True and the Beautiful in Nature, Art,
    Morals, and Religion (Ruskin), 83–84
Truth of Masks (Wilde), 72
Turner, J. M. W., 32, 97, 264
Turn of the Screw (James), 169n
Twain, Mark, 106n

Twyman, Joseph, 61
Tyndall, John, 92

United States, *see* America
Unity, 9, 19–20, 28, 41
Universities, American, 112
Upper class, 60, 106
Upward mobility, 50, 149, 151–52. *See*
    also Professionalism, aesthetic
Utopianism, 70, 75f, 91

Vanderbilt, Kermit, 119
Van Gogh, Vincent, 271
Veblen, Theodore, 69, 267
Venice, 95–99, 205
Vera, or the Nihilists (Wilde), 51
Verlaine, Paul, 123f, 204
Verver, Maggie, xvii
Vicariousness, 193–94
Violence, 45, 47, 58, 205
Vision, xviii, 142, 153–58 *passim*, 163–
    66 *passim*, 172, 230, 240–41. *See also*
    Contemplation

Warren, Austin, 254
Washington Square, 146
Weber, Max, 65
Weeks, Jeffrey, 172
Weiskel, Thomas, 32
Wells, H. G., 243
Wendell, Barrett, 88–89
Westminster Review, 4
Wharton, Edith, 82–83, 248
What Shall We Do with Our Walls? (Cook),
    105
Wheeler, Candace, 106
Where's the Cat? (Albery), 146
Whistler, J. A. M., 57, 93, 147
Wight, Peter, 84
Wilde, Oscar, 1–12 *passim*, 33, 146, 263,
    268; James and, xvii, xxv, xxvi, 47,
    131f, 143, 147, 150f, 167–202 *passim*,
    211, 214, 220–21, 242f, 250, 253; and
    commodity culture, xx, 42–43, 58–64
    passim; and "decadence," 2, 175–76,
    203, 226, 253; and contradiction, 7–8,
    22, 72; and social critique, 12, 71–
    76; and ekphrasis, 19, 214; and self,
    36, 41–47 *passim*; and otherness, 41–
    47 *passim*; and social position, 48–58
    passim, 71, 169, 173; Americans and,

51, 56, 80f, 102–5, 112f, 116, 123, 126, 129, 167, 270, 272; Du Maurier and, 51, 102, 104, 148; at Oxford, 53, 122; modernists and, 77, 249f, 252; and "House Beautiful," 106n; imprisonment, 168; and paranoia, 214n; Sphinx of, 234–35; and Eliot (George), 276
Wiley, John, 83, 269
William Morris (Thompson), 70
Williams, Raymond, 255–56, 267
Willowwood (Rossetti), 19
Wilson, Christopher, 108
Winckelmann, Johann, 27, 58, 64ff
Wings of the Dove (James), 82, 201, 245; and Ruskin, 94–100, 205, 224; "decadence" in, 132, 203–28 *passim*, 232; modernists and, 209, 248

Woman: Rossetti and, 22–24, 38, 219–23 *passim*; decadent *belle dame sans merci*, 205–6, 221–22, 232–40; Pre-Raphaelite, 210–13
Women's World, 51
Woodberry, George, 114, 116
Woodspurge (Rossetti), 33, 125
Wordsworth, William, 4, 28–34 *passim*, 68, 77, 198
Wright, Frank Lloyd, 107

Yale University Art Gallery, 83n
Yeazell, Ruth, 238
Yeats, W. B., 50, 123
Yellow Book, 1, 79, 81, 116–17, 123, 130, 176–77

Ziff, Larzer, 271–72

Library of Congress Cataloging-in-Publication Data

Freedman, Jonathan L.
  Professions of taste : Henry James, British aestheticism and
commodity culture / Jonathan Freedman.
     p.   cm.
  Includes bibliographical references.
  ISBN 0-8047-1784-2 (cl.):   ISBN 0-8047-2178-5 (pbk)
     1. James, Henry, 1843–1916—Aesthetics.   2. James, Henry,
1843–1916—Knowledge—Literature.   3. English literature—19th
century—History and criticism.   4. American literature—English
influences.   5. Aestheticism (Literature)   I. Title.
PS2127.A35F74   1990
813'.4—dc20   90-9773
                                                           CIP

⊗ This book is printed on acid-free paper